CRIMES AGAINST ART

INTERNATIONAL ART AND CULTURAL HERITAGE LAW

BONNIE CZEGLEDI, J.D.

To my dear sons
Andrew and Daniel
and
the memory of my father
Bill Czegledi

FOREWORD

You, dear reader, student, artist, art lover, collector, museum curator or registrar, gallery owner, auction house administrator or lawyer, will thoroughly enjoy reading *Crimes Against Art*. It reads well, is timely, practical, comprehensive and up to date.

As former General Counsel of the Smithsonian Institution for 13 years, I had occasion to address many of the issues discussed in this book, either through my practice at the Smithsonian; or through my participation in the International Bar Association's Committee on Art, Cultural Institutions & Heritage Law; the American Bar Association's (ABA) Committee on International Cultural Property; or the Smithsonian's Annual Program on Legal Issues in Museum Administration (now in its 38th year), co-sponsored with the American Law Institute and the ABA. About 10 years ago, I met Ms. Bonnie Czegledi, a Canadian lawyer with an international art practice, representing art museums, galleries, collectors and artists. I was impressed with her enthusiasm for, and intellectual pursuit of, all matters touching upon international art. This book represents the culmination of that intellectual drive. You, dear reader, will be the beneficiary of her diligent work!

I am familiar with most—if not all—the major treatises on international art law and, while each of them has their own strengths and weaknesses, Ms. Czegledi's work stands out for its ease of reading, its practical approach to the practice of art law, its up-to-date references to Internet resources and discussion of scientific advances in detecting fakes and forgeries and even for her advice in the last chapter on becoming an "International Art Lawyer." Reading this work has enhanced my knowledge of International Art Law. *Crimes Against Art* is definitely a "must-read" if you are intellectually curious about the laws and ethics surrounding the art trade.

John Huerta

PREFACE

I currently spend my time advising clients on such varied issues as the recovery of stolen art and cultural property; import and export of works of art; the rights of artists, galleries, museums and foundations; sales and loans of collections; issues of authenticity; and due diligence for collectors, museums and artists and their estates. In addition, I lecture throughout Canada, the United States, and Europe on these subjects. I am also a visual artist, and my paintings have been exhibited in both Canada and France and featured in international arts and architectural magazines.

The field of cultural property law is one that is growing internationally, in part as a result of increasing prices and a new awareness among nations of the real significance of their cultural heritage. The growth of the international art market since World War II paralleled developments in scientific evidentiary testing, such as DNA, methods of archaeological and anthropological study, and the recognition of a genuine need to comprehend our respective and collective pasts in a globalized world. These developments have produced a wide range of groundbreaking art law cases in a field in which six months do not go by without a new dispute, decision, or piece of legislation that alters the course of things to come.

These legal changes are also of psychological interest in that they reveal facets of human nature, such as the desire to right wrongs, demonstrated in such cases as Nazi-looted art disputes. As art crime gains more exposure, we become increasingly aware of the role that obsession can play in criminal behaviour, as illustrated in thefts of unsaleable art works to satisfy collectors' particular infatuations or fixations.

The practice of international art law is an ongoing learning experience. The interdisciplinary nature of the field brings to it people from all walks of life and all parts of the globe. It is their stories, and not just the law, that make the field such a dynamic one.

ACKNOWLEDGEMENT

I t is difficult to express sufficient gratitude to all those who have supported me in writing (and living!) this book. I am greatly indebted to many professional colleagues who generously shared their time and expertise with me. Many thanks to students and those who have attended my lectures whose enthusiasm has been greatly encouraging; to Catherine Morrow for her strength, friendship, high standards and brilliant editing abilities—words are not enough to convey my appreciation; to Emily Dippo, for her hard work and down-to-earth administrative assistance in the initial stages of writing this book; and to Christine Creighton, a superb research assistant, whose insight and rare and genuine desire to learn and understand kept me going and were essential to the success of the project.

I am also grateful to Carswell, a Thomson Reuters business, for their foresight in showing an interest in this developing field and for their support throughout the publishing process. As well, I am indebted to my editors and all those who worked diligently behind the scenes for their thoughtful input, time and effort.

To all those who work to make the art world a better place—artists, curators, museum directors, museum counsel, and other protectors of our cultural heritage—your dedication is truly inspirational.

TABLE OF CONTENTS

Why I Chose Art Law—Or Art Law Chose Me 1

Chapter 1: WHAT IS CULTURAL PROPERTY? A HISTORICAL OVERVIEW OF ITS MEANING

The Emergence of the Field of Art Andcultural Heritage Law 5
The Problem of Theft And Pillage and Attempts at Solutions 8
Contemporary Art Heists and Unsolved Mysteries 12
    1911: *The Mona Lisa* 13
    1946: O'Keeffe 14
    1949: The Fabiani Affair 14
    1961: The Duke of Wellington 15
    1960-1961: Art-Nappings in France 16
    1969: Caravaggio 17
    1972: Montreal Museum of Fine Arts 18
    1974: Systematic Looting in Cyprus 19
    1975: The Italian Heist 20
    1978: The Sevso Treasure 20
    1985: Marmatton Museum 22
    1985: Mexican Museum of Anthropology 22
    1987: Juan B. Castagnino Museum of Fine Art 23
    1988: Van Gogh Heists 23
    1988: Colnaghi Heist 24
    1988: Lucian Freud Cold Case 24
    1990: The Gardner Heist 25
    1990: Kuwait 33
    1991: The Netherlands 33
    1991: First Gulf War 33
    1990: Stephen Blumberg, the "Bibliokleptomaniac" 34
    1994 and 2004: *The Scream* 35
    1995: The Stradivarius 38
    1999: The Picasso on the Yacht 39
    1999-2000: Ashmolean 40

2000: Theft at the Fair 41
2000: Swedish Heist 41
2000: The Switch 42
2001: Lightning Strikes Twice 43
2002: Van Gogh Cold Case 44
2002: Paraguay Museum of Fine Arts 46
2003: Cellini Salt Cellar 47
2003: *The Madonna of the Yarnwinder* 47
2003: Manchester Heist 47
2005: The Bumbling Thief who Left a Calling Card 48
2006: Goya Stolen in Transit 49
2006: Rio de Janeiro Heist 49
2007: Beatty 51
2007: The Stolen *Cavalier* 51
2008: Buhrle 52
2009: Picasso's Sketchbook 54
2009-2010: Art Thefts Rock France 55
Conclusion 56

Chapter 2: INTERNATIONAL TREATIES, CONVENTIONS AND ENABLING DOMESTIC LAWS

The 1970 Unesco Convention 59
    Implementing UNESCO: The US Approach 61
    The Canadian Experience with the US Implementation Process 61
    Canadian Implementation of UNESCO 63
    Reforming the *Cultural Property Export and Import Act* 64
The 1954 Hague Convention 66
    The First Protocol to the 1954 Hague Convention 69
    The Second Protocol 70

Chapter 3: CRIMINAL SANCTIONS

Why Steal Art? 71
Best Practice Guidelines: What To Do If You Are Robbed 74
    BATA Shoe Museum Heist 75
Criminal Sanctions in the United States.. 76
    The National Stolen Property Act (NSPA) 77
    The Archeological Resources Protection Act (ARPA)....................... 78
    The Federal Anti-Smuggling Statute.. 79
    State Laws for Recovery of Stolen Property 79
    The Native American Grave Protection Repatriation Act
    (NAGPRA) 80
    Cultural Property Implementation Act (CPIA) 80
    Immigration and Customs Enforcement (ICE) 81
    The Importation of Pre-Columbian Monumental or Architectural
    Sculpture or Murals Act.. 81
    The Racketeer Influenced Corrupt Organization Act
    (RICO Dragnet) 82
    Criminal Sanctions Under NSPA... 83
Criminal Sanctions in Canada Under the *Cultural Property Export*
Import Act (CPEIA) 89
    Canada and Wilful Blindness.. 93
Summary of International Stolen Art Databases..................................... 95
    Jonathan Sazanoff's SAZTV.com: www.saztv.com............................. 95
    Royal Canadian Mounted Police: Sûreté du Québec Art
    Crime Unit 95
    London Metropolitan Police Department: The London Stolen
    Arts Database.. 96
    International Council of Museums: ICOM Red List........................ 96
    INTERPOL Stolen Works of Art.. 99
    US State Department 99
    FBI Art Crime Unit: National Stolen Art File............................... 100
    Art Loss Register and Trace 101
    The Lost Art Database.. 101
    Project for the Documentation of Wartime Cultural Losses 102

Holocaust-Era Assets 102
Holocaust Assets: US State Department 102
Presidential Commission on Holocaust Assets in the
United States 102
The Schloss Collection: Non-restituted Works Looted
1943-1998 102
Bruno Kreisky Archives Foundation 103
Enemy Property: The British Government Claims Scheme 103
Central Registry of Information on Looted Cultural Property
1933-1945 103
Origins Unknown.. 104
The Museum Provenance List Cleveland Museum of Art 104
Czech Republic Restitution... 104
Musées Nationaux Récupération (MNR) 104
Looted Art 105
Hungarian National Gallery of Budapest................................... 105
Italian Government.. 105
Wartime Losses: Polish Paintings 105
UK Museums' Provenance Research 106
The American Association of Museums Nazi-Era Provenance 106
Nazi-Era Provenance Internet Portal... 106
Find Stolen Art 107
Italian Carabinieri—Culture Police... 107
IFAR—Stolen Art Alert 107
Iraqi Cultural Property: United States Sanctions............................... 107

Chapter 4: DUE DILIGENCE

Due Diligence Checklist For Purchasers of Art 109
  Commentary... 112
  Purchasing On The Internet.. 112
Due Diligence: Donations and Loans... 113
  The Law Of Gifts 115
  Loans And The Law Of Bailment 116
Art as an Investment.. 118

Chapter 5: THE ART OF WAR

Holocaust Era Looted Art 121
International Legal Commitments.. 122
London Declaration (1943) 123
Bretton Woods Conference (1944)............................ 123
Washington Principles (1998)................................... 123
Terezin Declaration (2009) 125
Restitution and the Adversarial System 125
The Canadian Perspective: Recommendations for the Future....... 129
The Sacking Of Iraq 131
War—Opportunity for Wholesale Destruction of Cultural Heritage.... 134
Lessons Learned 137

Chapter 6: THE LOOTING OF ARCHAEOLOGICAL SITES

The Organized Crime Business Model 139
The Anatomy of Looting: Nigeria.. 143
Ethically Collecting Antiquities.. 145
Protecting Underwater Cultural Heritage... 146
Legal Framework: An International Perspective 148
Legal Framework: The American Perspective............................. 152
Legal Framework: The Canadian Perspective 155

Chapter 7: FAKES AND FORGERIES

Types of Fakes and Forgeries 160
Methods of Detecting Fakes and Forgeries... 161
The Expert Witness 161
Scientific Testing.. 164
Thermoluminescent (TL) Analysis 165
Radiocarbon Dating.. 165
Chemical Analysis... 166
Microscopic Techniques.. 166
Reconstructing Manufacturing Techniques.............. 167

Infrared Imaging.. 167
Ultraviolet Imaging.. 167
Conventional X-Ray.. 167
X-Ray Diffraction 168
X-Ray Fluorescence 168
Auto-Radiography... 168
Atomic Absorption Spectrophotometry (AAS) and Inductively
Coupled Plasma Mass Spectrometry (ICP-MS)....................... 169
Computerized Axial Tomography (CAT scans)...................... 169
Obsidian Hydration 169
Fission Tracks 170
Stable Isotope Analysis... 170
Dendochronology 170
Computer-Based Authentication Methods............................ 171
Cases of International Intrigue.. 172
Han van Meegeren (1889-1947) 173
Eric Hebborn (1934-1996)... 174
Elmyr de Hory (1906-1976) 177
Tom Keating (1917-1984) 178
David Stein (1935-1999) 179
John Drewe (1948-) and John Myatt (1945-)....................... 180
Ely Sakhai (1952-).. 181
The Greenhalgh Family 183
Authenticity Matters... 184

On Becoming an International Art Lawyer 185

Endnotes 195

Appendix A: INTERNATIONAL TREATIES, CONVENTIONS, AND AGREEMENTS

A1. 1970 UNESCO Convention 229

A2. Signatories to the 1970 UNESCO Convention 241

A3. The Hague Convention Of 1954 244

A4. First Protocol of the Hague Convention 262

A5. Second Protocol of the Hague Convention 266

A6. Agreement Between the Government Of Canada and the United States Regarding the Imposition of Import Restrictions on Certain Categories of Archaeological and Ethnological Material, E100789—CTS 1997 No. 8 289

A7. Emergency Actions and Bilateral Agreements 306

A8. UNESCO Convention on the Protection of Underwater Cultural Heritage (2001) 307

Appendix B: LEGISLATION AND RELATED ITEMS

B1. Canadian Cultural Property Export and Import Act, R.S.C. 1985, C. 51 333

B2. US Sentencing Guidelines: Cultural Heritage Resource Crimes, 18 U.S.C. APPX §2B1.5 336

B3. Letter from Judge Diana E. Murphy to the Honorable Patrick J. Leahy and the Honorable Orrin G. Hatch (3 April 2002) 343

B4. Native American Graves Protection and Repatriation Act, 1990, Public Law 101-601 349

B5. Convention on Cultural Property Implementation Act, 19 U.S.C. §§2601-13 (1983) 367

B6. Convention on International Trade In Endangered Species of Wild Flora and Fauna (Cites) 387

B7. American Endangered Species Legislation 410

B8. Canadian Endangered Species Legislation 416

B9. Foreign Cultural Objects Immunity from Seizure Act, R.S.O. 1990, C. F.23 420

Appendix C: MUSEUM AND GALLERY POLICIES AND CODES OF ETHICS

C1. UK Due Diligence Guidelines for Museums, Libraries and Archives on Collecting and Borrowing Cultural Material 421
C2. Report of the Aamd Task Force On The Acquisition Of Archaeological Materials And Ancient Art (Revised 2008)............ 444
C3. J. Paul Getty Museum Policy Statement... 449
C4. American Association of Museums, "Code of Ethics for Museums" (2000) 452
C5. Archaeological Institute of America Code of Ethics 461

Appendix D: OTHER

D1. Fabiani Affair—Archival Materials 463
   Annex "B" Pictures EX S.S. "Excalibur" 463
   Telegram from the French Government 467
   Art Looting Investigation Report on Fabiani and his Collaborators 469
D2. Sample Deeds of Gift 470
   Sample Deed of Gift (developed by an Art Museum) 470
   Sample Deed of Gift (developed by a History Museum).............. 471
D3. Sample Loan Agreements.. 472
   Agreement for Incoming Loan (developed by an Art Museum).... 472
   Sample Loan Agreement (developed by a History Museum) 474
D4. Films About Art and Law.. 478

Index 485

WHY I CHOSE ART LAW—OR ART LAW CHOSE ME

There was really nothing in my childhood that indicated that I would become an international art lawyer. I was not exposed to cultural exhibits, shown paintings in books nor did I know of the existence of galleries or museums where artistic exhibits could be found. I did not see many paintings, but what I did see sticks in my memory to this day.

On the walls of my grandparents' rambling house, I remember seeing English and Dutch watercolours of rural landscapes, tranquil vistas of forests and valleys, and views of ancient breeds of grazing cattle. These scenes looked not unlike both the southwest of France where I have a home and the region of Hungary my grandparents fled. I remember being shown an image of the *Mona Lisa* and my grandmother drawing my attention especially to the lady's hands, which she felt helped reveal the kind of person Mona Lisa was.

Another painting I remember seeing was a self-portrait by the violinist and composer Corelli (1653-1713) in whom I became very interested, perhaps in part because my father's family had a history in instrument building. My father introduced me to the work of Toulouse-Lautrec (1864-1901), born in the town of Albi in southwest France, whose family history became a source of fascination. The first-born of first cousins, Comte Alphonse and Comtesse Adele de Toulouse-Lautrec, Lautrec's form of escape from a stringent and constrained aristocratic upbringing was through his art, painting in the brothels of Paris' Montmartre and especially the Moulin Rouge.

Visually artistic by nature, I tended to see paintings in my imagination everywhere I looked, finding artistic potential in almost any everyday urban setting, something I shared with no one. When I produced drawings, I hid them safely under my bed; demonstrating artistic talent was not something my family encouraged. However, there was a great legacy of the arts in family heritage.

My maternal grandmother was an opera singer in Hungary and a couturier designer in Toronto. The dynamics of her marriage were such that she was forced to give up her career and she died quite young after a prolonged illness. The words of Martin Luther King Jr. ring true when I think of her: "You begin to die each day you are silent about the things that matter to you."

My paternal grandfather, John Czegledi, was a renowned stringed instrument-maker in Hungary. He made children's violins, cellos, double basses, harps, and cimbaloms, small piano-like instruments made in the shape of a trapezoidal box with steel strings played with a small hammer or by plucking. One of his is in the Royal Ontario Museum. When he came to Western Canada in the thirties he struggled in the evenings trying to make harpsichords in front of the fire in an unheated prairie house outside Regina. Not surprisingly, he discovered a very limited market for these instruments in Saskatchewan.

My grandparents and great-grandmother left Hungary in the twenties. As a result of the Trianon Treaty, the cradle of society and culture of Hungary was desecrated and divided up amongst the surrounding countries. The place my family came from is in the Carpathian Mountains and is called the Erdyi, which means "beyond the dark forest." Although a well-kept secret, my grandparents told me it is the most beautiful place on the earth. However, once fled, they never returned.

Ancient Hungarian families were targeted for a slow and torturous genocide by Romania. Land and names were taken away from the Hungarians and other minorities. In addition to starving them, the state made it impossible for their children, if they survived at all, to obtain an education, and they were stalked by the secret police.

Among other things, they were not allowed to sing their own music or practice their cultural traditions, which dated back thousands of years. Although this was not something that was spoken of in my family, I somehow sensed in my grandmother's eyes the loss and sadness caused by this cultural deprivation. Hungarian composer Béla Bartók toured villages of this area to collect melodies to put into his compositions, saving the intangible cultural heritage that was being destroyed. *Butzi, Buzti Tarka* (Little Red Apple), a song my grandmother sang to me as a baby, was illegal where she came from, something as incomprehensible to a child then as to adults today. With a better understanding later of the nature of genocide,

I came to learn that the most pernicious aspect of genocide, and the cycle of violence so pervasive on this planet, is perhaps not the violence itself, but the hatred that fuels it.

Pressured to find a practical career, I chose law school, as I have always had a keen desire for justice; it was to satisfy the more altruistic part of my personality. Although I have subsequently learned that law can, of course, be used to bring harm rather than good, I still hope that good intentions will, in the end, lead to positive change in this field.

With experience in legal research, defense litigation and commercial law, I kept abreast of issues in the art world. In the face of doubt from those around me who said it just could not be done, I was constantly thinking of how I could become an international art and cultural property lawyer. In addition to developing an international art law career, I always worked hard at my painting and, when they were very young, I raised my children using art as a successful method of conflict resolution. This too was unconventional and at first not accepted by many; however, it worked.

And that is how I was able to combine my love of art—my passion—with my legal practice—a sensible career—through an unusual but, for me, logical mingling. I also see a large part of my work as educating people on the importance of art in their cultural identity.

The path I have taken to be an international art lawyer is as individual-istic as the development of this relatively new field of law. This book will explore many early legislative tools and cases and the development of art and cultural heritage law.

1

WHAT IS CULTURAL PROPERTY? A HISTORICAL OVERVIEW OF ITS MEANING

THE EMERGENCE OF THE FIELD OF ART AND CULTURAL HERITAGE LAW

The purpose of this book is to explore the legal, ethical and practical issues concerning the sharing, mobility and protection of art and cultural heritage within the scope of international art law.

Institutions, galleries—both private and public—and collectors are currently faced with a balancing act amongst many competing interests. Ultimately these interests are not so much about ownership, misguided nationalism, perceived aesthetic value or decorative beauty, or legal disputes, but rather who is empowered with the right to control the historical evidence of our culture and the responsibility to protect our pieces of history. The following chapters will explore the latest developments in this complicated and fascinating field of international law in hopes of a greater collaboration and cooperation amongst participants. This is a field that combines a love of art, obsession, psychology, history, intrigue, criminal behaviour, law, spirituality, religion and the sacred, anthropology, archaeology, high-stakes money and the latest developments in science and technology.

It has become apparent in recent years, as demonstrated by the world's reaction to the looting and desecration of the Baghdad Museum in April

2003 and the subsequent theft and destruction of archeological sites in Iraq after the American invasion, that society cares when cultural property is damaged, destroyed, stolen or unavailable to the communities whose identity it defines.

Why does society care? We care because this material has an intangible, not just monetary, value and holds the key, in both form and spirit, to our human past and, from this source, to our future. How can we live a fulfilling and meaningful existence without having memory of our past? Humankind has always had an eternal yearning to understand information about our origins, where we came from and our creative process. Most of what we know from history, including the cultural and social development of humanity, technological advancements, religion and civilization, is obtained from archaeological excavation and scientific investigation conducted *in situ*, that is, on objects in the context of their found location. When material is exhibited without context or provenance, we learn little or nothing about the purpose of the material. Provenance should include the owner from whom it was acquired, its status as an archaeological artifact, and the time and place it was excavated. That way we can know the purpose and meaning of the material. Without provenance, we must assume the object is either looted or fake. Context is as important as the object itself. One example of this gap in knowledge brought about by lack of context is found in the case of the jade cong from the Chinese Neolithic Period where, despite 200 years of study, no one has ever provided an explanation of the meaning and purpose of the jade cong.[1]

There have been many recent developments in the field of protection of cultural property (perhaps more accurately described as cultural heritage), resulting in its becoming one of the fastest-growing areas of law today. The practice of art law includes advising and assisting clients on such varied issues as the recovery of stolen art; the import and export of art; artist, gallery, museum and foundation rights; sale and loan of collections; issues of authenticity; collectors' and artists' estates and due diligence for collectors and museums. This area of law is continually evolving, and it is up to the players involved to adapt accordingly.

In the field of Holocaust-looted art, in *Republic of Austria v. Altmann*,[2] we saw Austria, after an eight-year legal battle, return five Klimts looted by the Nazis to their rightful heirs. One of the paintings, the portrait of Adele Block-Bauer painted over a three-year period during which time she became Klimt's mistress, sold at Christie's Auction House for US$135 million in 2006.[3] This price tag shattered all records as the highest price ever paid for a painting. It was purchased by the Neue Gallery in New York on behalf of Ronald Lauder and remains part of that gallery's collection.

However, it is important to remember that only a tiny fraction of what the Nazis stole has been returned to its rightful owners. The restitution movement continues to face a lengthy, uphill battle that is only for those with determination to persevere.

There have been examples of restitutions of antiquities made without litigation—of the free volition of collectors and museums, as with the *Euphronios krater*. This vase is an ancient Greek terra cotta bowl used in its time for combining wine and water. It is dated circa 515 BC and is one of the most significant Greek artifacts ever discovered. It was created by the renowned artist Euphronios and is sometimes called the *Sarpedon krater*. The front side depicts the death of the warrior Sarpedon in a painting that rivals da Vinci. The Metropolitan Museum in New York acquired it in 1972 for US$1 million and, according to a recent agreement,[4] will return it to Italy. In 2008, Shelby White, a private collector, returned nine illegally excavated antiquities (and a tenth is on the way) to Italy and Greece.[5]

Theft of art in general has increased dramatically in recent years as a result of many factors, one of which is the economic recession, which has bred a higher crime rate. However, even before the economic downturn, theft of art had been steadily increasing, due in part to the speed at which cargo containers can now move across the planet. Art has become in many respects a commodity and an investment vehicle, the value of which has reached levels never seen before. The art market is also the largest unregulated worldwide economy, making it very attractive for investors. This demand in art, which has, for the most part, spiraled upward since World War II, has spawned looting and theft on an unprecedented scale. Unfortunately, neither art nor cultural property is a renewable resource.

After 65 years, the United States Senate has ratified the 1954 Hague Convention on the Protection of Cultural Property in the Event of Armed Conflict.[6] This was the first international treaty to deal with the protection of cultural property and was a direct response to the hideous lessons learned in the losses and destruction left by World War II. The protection of cultural heritage and its status has been significantly elevated as the military must take steps in their planning and conduct to protect cultural heritage in future military operations. Soldiers are now, ironically, among the protectors of our cultural future.

Also encouraging, in recent years many more nations have signed the 1970 UNESCO Convention on the Means of Prohibiting and Preventing the Illicit Import, Export and Transfer of Ownership of Cultural Property.[7] There are currently 118 States Parties to this Convention.[8] The growth of the illicit trafficking of cultural property and the realization that it has a value to society as a whole prompted the need for this Convention. It is significant that important market countries, such as Switzerland, the UK, Germany, Japan, and Belgium have recently become States Parties. These nations will be implementing their legal obligations under their own domestic laws, which will have an international impact.

A further interesting development in the field of cultural property law concerns terrorist activities. Hamas carried out bombings in Jerusalem in 1997 following which the American citizens who were victims sued in the United States for damages from Iran.[9] The grounds of this suit were that Iran was a sponsor to Hamas. Iran was unable to pay the judgment in this case and they are suing a number of museums in the United States who have antiquities on loan from Iran. The size of the claims is immense—US$423.5 million in damages and punitive damages of US$300 million. This matter was further complicated by amendments to the Foreign Sovereign Immunities Act in the United States in 2008.[10]

THE PROBLEM OF THEFT AND PILLAGE AND ATTEMPTS AT SOLUTIONS

Throughout history, society has witnessed aggressive military forces invade, plunder and destroy the heritage of culturally rich nations and peoples.

Do invading forces have the right to desecrate the cultural heritage of nations resulting in an irretrievable loss to society and future generations? Do individuals have a right to profit from such a community loss?

The resulting conflicts that arise from the theft and destruction of art and cultural property can have wide implications for generations to come. A historical overview of military plundering will reveal the nature of this problem and how the world community has tried to address it through international cultural heritage law.

The root of European civilization, the Minoans of the Early Bronze Age (2700-1400 BC), were invaded by the militarily aggressive Mycenaeans from the Peloponnesian Peninsula.[11] The Mycenaeans obliterated the highly sophisticated, matriarchal society that had traded with Egypt and throughout the eastern Mediterranean.

The Romans romanticized the notion of plundering as recounted in Homer's *Odyssey*: "to the victor go the spoils." However, the tables were turned when the Sacking of Rome took place in 410 AD and the Romans were attacked by the Barbarian tribe known as the Visigoths. Later that century, in 442 AD, for 14 days, the Vandals sacked, plundered and attacked whatever was left in Rome. Europe descended into the Dark Ages with the fall of Rome, leading up to the Crusades, one of the most horrific plunderings of all mankind, many centuries later. Marauding criminals thirsty for gold treasure and blood led a path of death and destruction in the name of religion, eventually destroying Constantinople in a wave a terror.[12]

The destruction and plundering of cultural heritage in times of war unfortunately was not confined to Europe in the Middle Ages but took place on a greater scale in the New World. This desecration of a people and civilization has been described aptly in the book **Guns, Germs and Steel**, written by Jared Diamond, recounting the conquest of the Incan Empire by the Spaniards.[13] Pizarro and a gang of about 180 Spanish soldiers captured the great Atahuallpa the King—a leader revered by the Incans. Pizarro held him prisoner for eight months and asked for the largest ransom in history as the price for his freedom—an amount of gold that would fill a room 222 feet long, 17 feet wide and 8 feet high. Upon receiving this gold ransom, Pizarro broke his promise to free Atahuallpa and murdered him after all, an act of treachery that was incomprehensible to the Incans.

These acts of barbarism were not without public condemnation. Society, through tradition and law, operates on the premise that artworks and cultural objects have a greater worth, distinct from other property. Legal scholarship has long reflected the opinion that artistic material deserves treatment distinct from other sorts of property. Once destroyed, a road can be rebuilt, which is not the case with such things as the first writings by humankind on cuneiform tablets. Once destroyed, their contents are lost forever and we will never know the words, laws and stories that were written for our communal benefit. In the eighteenth century, the Swiss jurist Vattel wrote about limitations on methods of conducting warfare as there are facets of society that should always be preserved and pro-tected.[14] His writings, however prophetic, were ignored until the devasta-tion brought about by Napoleon's plundering of Europe. In his conquests, Napoleon pillaged and ransacked the continent to fill his homeland with artistic masterpieces, where he felt they belonged. Hitler would later use similar excuses for his vast plunder, as he wished to make his homeland the centre of high culture.

In legal history, the view that the plundering and theft of art is more serious than other property crimes is documented as far back as Cice-ro's prosecution of Gaius Verres in Rome in 70 BC.[15] Verres was a Roman magistrate infamous for his corrupt and cruel misgovernment of Sicily and who was prosecuted by Cicero for extortion crimes. Verres' extortions were as notoriously ruthless as his heists of artworks. He abused his power as Praetor, pillaging sacred temples and private art collections in order to satisfy his own rapacious lust for art. Cicero's opening oration in prosecut-ing these heinous acts was so damning that Verres' lawyer, Hortensious, declined to respond and advised Verres to leave the country immediately. He subsequently fled to Massala, modern day Marseilles, to live in exile. It was there that Mark Antony demanded artworks from Verres that he had coveted. Verres refused to turn them over and was found murdered not long after.

This case was read and referred to throughout the Middle Ages and into the nineteenth century, when Lord Byron furiously campaigned against the purchase of the Elgin Marbles by the British Museum. He wrote of the destruction in his epic poem, *Childe Harold's Pilgrimage*, in 1812:

> Cold is the heart, fair Greece! that looks on thee,
> Nor feels as lover o'er the dust they loved;
> Dull is the eye that will not weep to see

Thy walls defaced, thy mouldering shrines removed
By British hands, which it had best behoved
To guard those relics ne'er to be restored.
Curst be the hour when from their isle they roved,
And once again thy hapless bosom gored,
And snatch'd thy shrinking Gods to northern climes abhorr'd![16]

One year later, in the fall-out of the War of 1812, the Vice-Admiralty Court of Halifax, Canada, ruled that the British had no right to keep the spoils of their seizure of Italian artworks en route to Philadelphia on an American ship.[17] The Court confirmed Cicero's premise that the art merited special treatment, and, unlike a market commodity, could not be seized during times of war. Cicero's prosecution and its legacy became the seeds of international cultural property law as we know it today.[18]

The creation of the Lieber Code of 1863 was America's attempt to incorporate army conduct in war times into a nation's legal obligations.[19] Signed by President Abraham Lincoln and named after German-American jurist Francis Lieber, the *Instructions for the Government of Armies of the United States in the Field* prescribed soldiers' behaviour in wartime. Although Section II, subsection 31 enunciates that

A victorious army appropriates all public money, seizes all public movable property until further direction by its government, and sequesters for its own benefit or of that of its government all the revenues of real property belonging to the hostile government or nation,

subsection 34 makes clear that certain categories of property, including works of art, are excluded from subsection 31's definition of private property, and merit special treatment. For example,

35.   Classical works of art, libraries, scientific collections, or precious instruments, such as astronomical telescopes, as well as hospitals, must be secured against all avoidable injury, even when they are contained in fortified places whilst besieged or bombarded.

36.   If such works of art, libraries, collections, or instruments belonging to a hostile nation or government, can be removed without injury, the ruler of the conquering state or nation may order them to be seized and removed *for the benefit of the said nation*. The ultimate ownership is to be settled by the ensuing treaty of peace. In no case shall they be sold or given away, if captured by the armies of the United States, *nor shall they ever be privately appropriated*, or wantonly destroyed or injured.

118.   The besieging belligerent has sometimes requested the besieged to designate the
       buildings containing collections of works of art, scientific museums, astronomi-
       cal observatories, or precious libraries, so that their destruction may be avoided
       as much as possible.[20]

The Lieber Code was a precursor to the Hague Conventions in recognizing the special status of cultural property and providing for post-war
ownership of works of art.

The Conference of Brussels in 1874[21] also recognized the importance
of an international effort to provide protection of art in times of war. This
declaration stated that institutions devoted to the arts, whether belonging to the State or not, should be treated as private property and that
seizure and destruction of these places should be prosecuted by competent
authorities under the law. The Conference confirmed that private property
should not be confiscated and pillage was prohibited. Europe followed
suit with the Hague Conventions of 1899, 1907, and 1954. Despite these
laws, up to the present day, conflict and warfare around the globe in Iraq,
Afghanistan, Pakistan, the Middle East, South-East Asia and elsewhere—
all provide golden opportunities to desecrate heritage, libraries, cultural
establishments, and archaeological sites to the detriment of all of society.
The protection of cultural heritage is an ongoing struggle, but is something
for which we must continue to fight if we hope to share the knowledge
that art imparts to humanity.

CONTEMPORARY ART HEISTS AND UNSOLVED MYSTERIES

An examination of the major art heists of the past century will shed
light on some of the motives and methods of art thieves. Art theft is so
prevalent in modern society that it would be impossible to compile a comprehensive list of heists—and that is not what this section intends to do.
The purpose of studying the past, naturally, is to learn for the future. An
examination of the most influential and bizarre art heists of our time can
educate collectors, museums and galleries on how to better protect their
art from future criminal activity.

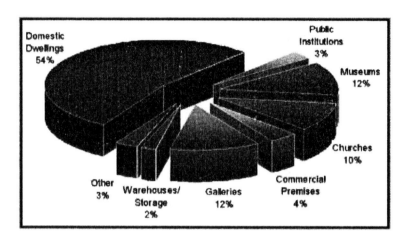

Art at Risk: Though museum and gallery heists tend to be better publicized, statistics indicate that private collections are more vulnerable.[22]

As the following cases will illustrate, modern art theft is no "gentleman's crime" as it is glamorized in popular culture.[23] Reality is seedier, uglier and often stranger than fiction.

1911: The Mona Lisa

The first major art theft of the twentieth century was that of the *Mona Lisa* on August 21, 1911.[24] The painting was missing for two years before the Uffizi Gallery in Florence notified the Louvre to tell them that a man named Vincenzo Peruggia had attempted to sell them the masterpiece. An employee at the Louvre, Peruggia had stolen the painting by hiding in a broom closet until closing time one evening, then walking out with it hidden under his coat. Possible motives were patriotism (he believed Leonardo's masterpiece should be returned to an Italian museum) and interest in his friend's business of making copies of the painting, which would increase in value with the theft of the original. Before the *Mona Lisa* was returned to the Louvre in 1914, it toured Italy. Italians treated

Peruggia as a patriotic hero, and he served just months in jail for the infamous crime.

1946: O'Keeffe

A notorious American art theft occurred in 1946, when three Georgia O'Keeffe paintings were stolen from her husband's gallery. O'Keeffe herself ultimately tracked down the paintings following their purchase by the Princeton Gallery of Fine Arts in 1975. Despite a six-year limitations period, a state appellate court ruled in O'Keefe's favour when she sued the museum for the paintings' return in 1979.

1949: The Fabiani Affair

By 1941 the Nazis had successfully drained Europe of many of its best treasures, mostly laundering them through neutral countries like Switzerland and Portugal, with destinations such as New York, Havana, Ottawa, and Buenos Aires.

Martin Fabiani was one of the most active dealers in Nazi-looted art of the Second World War. He was privy to some of the biggest deals in confiscated art and was chief art dealer to Hitler and other Nazi Party leaders.

He also brought into Canada the largest collection of Renoirs in existence in 1941 and disappeared with it in 1949. All other collections of the Impressionist Period pale in comparison: this collection contained 429 Renoirs, which consisted of 288 paintings, 49 water colours, 28 pastels and 64 drawings; 67 Cezannes; 7 Rouaults; and 13 Gaugins for a grand total of 635 works of art.[25] By comparison, the next largest collection of Renoirs is the Barnes exhibit, which has about 160 works.

The provenance of this collection is as interesting as it is complicated and raises questions concerning its legality.

Fabiani had befriended, and became executor to the estate of, the legendary art impresario Ambroise Vollard, who died mysteriously in a car crash on the weekend of 24 July 1939. Fabiani recounts in his memoirs the circumstances of Vollard's death. By his account, Vollard was riding in his black Talbot convertible when the steering wheel fell off and his chauffeur lost control of the car. The last words Vollard uttered: "a lawyer, a lawyer."[26] Fabiani benefited tremendously from Vollard's untimely death, inheriting some paintings, purchasing others from Vollard's brother, and allegedly taking some from other heirs.[27] There was a requirement that Vollard's collection be inventoried; Fabiani breached that condition. The massive list of paintings that journeyed on the SS *Excalibur* was unfortunately vague, preventing authorities from tracing them.[28]

While transporting Fabiani's massive stash of impressionistic paintings on 25 September 1940, the *Excalibur* ran into trouble in Bermuda. The British consul recognized the pictures' enemy origin, and, suspicious of Fabiani's Nazi sympathies, confiscated them and sent them to Ottawa, where they were stored in the charge of the Registrar of the Exchequer Court until the end of the War.[29] In 1949, the French government requested the assistance of the Canadian government in locating paintings from the Vollard estate.[30] The French Embassy estimated the collection's value at over $1 billion francs.[31] In June 1949, the Civil Court of the Seine in Paris appointed one Mr. Wiel as the judicial administrator charged with inventorying and conserving the paintings.[32] The restraining order was too late; a few days earlier, Fabiani had hastily removed the collection from Canada.[33] When asked, officials in Ottawa could not provide a full explanation. They stated that "Fabiani departed with paintings for Montreal in taxi, destination believed England."[34] How he could have fit hundreds of paintings in a taxi, no one knows.

Over 50 years later we are still stumped by the mystery of the Fabiani affair. In 2005, a Renoir came up for sale in a small Toronto auction house, with the owner listed as "Dr. Fabiani." Where did this painting come from, where has it been, and where will it show up next?

1961: The Duke of Wellington

In August of 1961, an American collector, Charles Wrightsman, purchased Goya's *Portrait of the Duke of Wellington*. His plan to take it back with him to the United States was enough to provoke both public outrage and the painting's theft. The reaction of the public prompted the government of the United Kingdom to raise money to prevent the American from buying the painting. After the government successfully purchased it and put it on display at the National Gallery, it was promptly stolen. There were no sightings of Goya's famed piece, unless one counts its appearance in the James Bond film, *Dr. No*, until 1965, when the thief sent a baggage claim ticket to the *London Daily Mirror*. Police collected the painting in a railway baggage office. Six weeks later, the thief, an unemployed bus driver named Kempton Bunton, surrendered to authorities. He claimed that he had only stolen the painting to get ransom money, which, he explained, he was going to use to buy television licenses for the poor. There are now suggestions, however, that he might have been innocent.[35]

Goya, Portrait of the Duke of Wellington

1960-1961: Art-Nappings in France

In a cautionary tale, there was a series of thefts for ransom in the south of France in 1960-61. First, 20 uninsured paintings that disappeared from a restaurant were returned amid speculation that the owners had paid the thieves a small reward. The following year, a small museum in Saint-Tropez was robbed of a shocking 57 paintings. The thieves threatened to destroy all of them unless the museum agreed to hand over US$100,000 for their safe return. The police suspected that French gangsters were behind the crime and discouraged the museum from paying any ransom because the paintings were unmarketable and the thieves would eventually have to return them in exchange for immunity. Shortly thereafter, another theft—eight Cezanne paintings—occurred and police believed that the same gang was behind it. This time, however, the paintings were well-insured, and the insurance company was willing to strike a bargain with the thieves. The gang ended up with US$60,000 plus immunity from prosecution in exchange for the return of the Cezannes. The other 57 paintings took 16 months to recover. This kind of reward for bad behaviour helps explain why art theft has become such an epidemic.

1969: Caravaggio

Two thieves entered the Oratory of San Lorenzo in Palermo, Italy, in October 1969 and stole Caravaggio's *Nativity* from its frame. Experts estimate its value at US$20 million.

Caravaggio, Nativity with San Lorenzo and San Francesco[36]

1972: Montreal Museum of Fine Arts

In September 1972, the largest art theft in Canadian history occurred when armed thieves entered the Montreal Museum of Fine Arts through a skylight and left with 18 paintings and 37 other artifacts. After binding and gagging three guards, the thieves fled in an armored truck when they set off the alarm. The paintings, by such esteemed artists as Delacroix and Gainsborough, included a Rembrandt landscape worth over CDN$1 million. Bill Bantey, a spokesperson for the museum, described the culprits as "discriminating thieves" who "had a fairly good idea of what they were looking for."[37] Only one of the 55 artworks has been recovered—a small piece by Flemish painter Jan Bruighel the Elder.[38]

1974: Systematic Looting in Cyprus

When Turkey invaded Cyprus in 1974, countless Christian monuments were destroyed or looted. The most notable pillaging incident was that of the mosaics of Panayia of Kanakaria from the sixth century. They were reported missing in 1979. Cyprus requested UNESCO's assistance in locating the pieces. The mosaics were some of the few surviving masterpieces of early Christianity. They depicted Jesus as a young boy and the Virgin Mary surrounded by two archangels and the twelve apostles. When an art dealer in New York tried to sell the fragments to the Getty Museum in 1988, the museum informed Cyprus. Peg Goldberg had purchased the fragments from a dubious Turkish antiquities dealer. The Greek Orthodox Church of Cyprus brought a replevin action for their recovery.[39] The Southern District Court of Indiana held in Cyprus's favour.[40] The court held that a buyer of stolen property could not acquire valid title or a right of possession. The court found that Goldberg was not a good-faith purchaser, because she knew or should have known that the mosaics were stolen. The United States Court of Appeals, seventh circuit, upheld the judgment.

One issue facing the court was whether the action was barred by the statute of limitations. In Indiana, a replevin action has a six-year limitation period. Goldberg argued that, since Cyprus had learned that the mosaics were missing in 1979, they were barred from bringing the action in 1989. The Court of Appeals rejected this argument on the basis of the "discovery rule," under which a replevin action accrues only when the plaintiff discovers (or should reasonably have discovered) the identity or location of the possessor of the stolen works. Applying this rule meant that Cyprus's cause of action accrued when the Getty informed them that Goldberg had the mosaics.[41]

The mosaics were returned to Cyprus on the 30th of August, 1991. They are just one example of looting as a result of conflict in Cyprus.[42]

1975: The Italian Heist

In February 1975, three famous artworks were cut from their frames in the Ducal Palace in Urbino, Italy. The inexperienced criminals had planned to sell Pierro della Francesco's *Flagellation of Christ* and *The Madonna of Singallia*, as well as Raphael's *The Mute*, on the international market. They eventually realized, however, that the masterpieces were highly unmarketable. All three paintings were recovered undamaged in Locarno, Switzerland a year later.[43]

1978: The Sevso Treasure

The story of the Sevso Treasure begins in Hungary in 1978. While digging in a quarry on Lake Balaton, not far from Budapest, a labourer hit a pot filled with silver that turned out to be one of the most splendid finds of silver from the Roman Empire. Jozsef Sumegh, the labourer, not realizing the value of the find, brought the pot back to his humble home. Piece by piece, he sold off the treasure to purchase himself small luxuries—such as Western denim jeans. One night, while arguing with his mother about the value of the treasure, his two brothers learned of its existence.

On an evening soon thereafter, two soldiers met Jozsef drinking in a bar. Three sets of footprints in the snow led into Jozsef's wine cellar, where he had buried the silver hoard, but only two sets left. The next morning, Jozsef was found hanging by a rope. The cause of death, however, was not asphyxiation. At first considered a suicide, the case was subsequently re-opened as a murder investigation.

After Jozsef's death, the treasure disappeared. Two of his co-workers, who had been with him on that fateful day when he found the treasure, turned up dead following the loot's disappearance. One had eaten poisoned cheese; the other was found hanging in a nearby forest. In the meantime, Jozsef's two brothers had landed themselves in jail for stealing a car. On the day of their release, their mother met them on the prison steps and told them to flee the country immediately because of their knowledge of the treasure. At great risk, she had them smuggled out of Hungary. Two weeks later, she was found dead on her front lawn. The official explanation was that she had fallen and suffered a head injury, but her husband denied these reports.

In 1990, the treasure showed up for sale at a Sotheby's auction in New York. Several countries made weak claims for the treasure. Although Hungary's claim was strong, its representatives argued ineffectively and failed to make full use of proofs, such as soil samples from Lake Balaton, a piece in the National Museum of Hungary from the same area matching the treasure, and the name on the coins that led to Lake Balaton. The New York Court of Appeals found that none of the countries had sufficiently proven title.[44]

Under the law, treasure belongs to the nation from whose soil it was taken. The goal for criminals, therefore, is to muddy the trail with moves and transfers, making a trace back to the original site as difficult as possible. Corrupt customs officials, forged or fraudulent export permits, and silenced witnesses make it difficult to prove the treasure's origins.

The purchaser of the Sevso Treasure from Sotheby's was one Marquess of Northampton, who sued his solicitors Allen and Overy for damages in relation to advice given during the purchase of the silver. They settled out of court, with newspapers reporting that Lord Northampton won as much as US$28 million in compensation.[45] In the fall of 2006, the items went on display at Bonham's for a private treaty sale. As Lord Northampton told the Sunday *Times of London*, "I do not want my wife or my son to inherit what has become a curse. I doubt it will be sold overnight, but eventually I hope somebody or some institution will buy it, and it will go on permanent display so that people can enjoy and appreciate its exquisite beauty."[46]

In October 2007 in Toronto, there was a lecture given on the Sevso Treasure based on the aesthetic qualities of this hoard, which is part of recent attempts to apply a patina of legitimacy on the loot. However, the only meaningful study on this hoard would be based on its context, where it was found and what that teaches us about history. As stated in the Archaeological Institute of America's Code of Ethics, archaeologists should not study unprovenanced material.[47] Cataloguing looted objects and subsequently making them part of a curriculum does not launder title. It is not ethically sound to study looted material. This practice is like looking at a stolen car, studying and publishing pictures about its design features. When a car is stolen, it is clearly understood that it must always be returned to the owner, and the persons perpetrating this crime are considered criminals, who, when caught, must suffer the consequences of their actions. Appreciating the stolen car's artistry and photographing it for a catalogue does not change its title. This activity of making academic study out of stolen property actually increases the demand for this material. This participation by academics in the looting cycle must cease in order to stem the tide of illicit trafficking in cultural property.

A Yugoslavian coin dealer and war criminal involved in dealing with this treasure, at least contributing to the muddying of its provenance, told a writer investigating this story: "I will be a barrier between you and the truth, a dam. It's the end of the story. If you keep coming after me, I'm going to fuck your soul."[48]

1985: Marmatton Museum

Toward the end of 1985, two major art heists occurred. First, the Marmatton Museum in Paris was robbed of nine paintings. The police initially believed that the radical group "Action Direct" had stolen the works, which included Renoir's *Bathers* and Monet's era-defining *Impression, Soleil Levant*. As it turned out, Japanese gangster Suinichi Fujikuma was the culprit. He had hired Philippe Jamin and Youssef Khimoun, members of an art theft syndicate with whom he became acquainted while serving a five-year jail sentence for heroin possession, to pull off the job for him. The paintings were recovered in Corsica in 1991.[49] The short statute of limitations in Japan presented a potential issue.

1985: Mexican Museum of Anthropology

In Mexico, meanwhile, the National Museum of Anthropology was targeted by thieves on Christmas Eve. It was the single largest theft of precious objects from any museum and a sad example of the risks of poor security. Lack of vigilance by guards as well as an alarm system that had been broken for more than three years allowed the thieves to remove the glass and items from seven showcases and make off easily with 124 pre-

Columbian treasures, including jade and gold pieces from the Mayan, Aztec, Zapotec and Miztec cultures. Since most of the pieces were less than an inch in height, it is conceivable that the culprits simply carried them away in a couple of suitcases. In June 1989, police recovered 111 of the artifacts in a home outside Mexico City. Eight more have since been recovered, and five remain missing.

1987: Juan B. Castagnino Museum of Fine Art

On March 24, 1987, armed robbers stole six major European works from the Juan B. Castagnino Museum in Rosario, Argentina. One of the six paintings, Goya's *Dove and Hen*, was recovered. El Greco's *Evangelist*, Goya's *War Scene,* Titian's *Portrait of Philip II*, Magnasco's *Landscape*, and Veronese's *Portrait of a Gentleman* remain missing.[50]

1988: Van Gogh Heists

Sometimes, art theft can be used as a form of kidnapping. In December 1988, thieves took three Van Gogh paintings from the Kroller-Muller Museum in Otterlo, Holland. They then held *Dried Sunflowers*, *Weaver's Interior* and an early version of *The Potato Eaters* for ransom. Police recovered the paintings in a raid without paying.

The thieves were apparently knowledgeable about the art market; a week before they carried out the heist, a list had been published of the top prices paid for art at Sotheby's and Christie's. Five Van Goghs had been listed in the top ten. Prices for Van Goghs were reaching new highs. In 1987, *Irises* sold for US$53.9 million, and *Sunflowers* for US$20.3 million. The thieves followed in the footsteps of others before them: a year earlier, the Noordbrabants Museum in Den Bosch was robbed of three early Van Goghs, and in May 1988, *Carnations* was stolen from the Stedelijk Museum in Amsterdam but recovered in an undercover operation.[51]

1988: Colnaghi Heist

The break-in and robbery of the New York Colnaghi Gallery revealed the increasing potential of great hauls from private galleries as compared to those from museums and public galleries. It involved an entry, worthy of the opening scene in a heist film, in which the thieves scaled down ropes hung through a sky-light. Once inside the gallery, however, the thieves proved less sophisticated than their Hollywood counterparts: not only did they damage numerous canvases, but they also overlooked the most valuable art in the building. Nevertheless, they managed to make off with eighteen paintings and ten drawings, including two by Fra Angelico insured at US$4 million and Chardin's *Rayfish with Basket of Onions*. The thieves were likely not knowledgeable about art, as choosing works by Old Masters of the fifteenth and sixteenth centuries would make the booty difficult to sell.

The Colnaghi theft was New York's biggest art heist up until that point, with the stolen works valued at US$6-10 million at the time. The International Foundation for Art Research (IFAR) put out a worldwide alert, complete with photographs of the missing pieces. The publicity surrounding the heist made it even more difficult for the thieves to dispose of the goods. All they could have hoped for was to unload them at a steep discount to a crooked dealer, or to an insurance company.[52] All but four works were recovered.[53]

1988: Lucian Freud Cold Case

Lucian Freud's 1952 portrait of the late artist Francis Bacon was stolen from the Neue Nationalgalerie in Berlin during a British Council exhibition in broad daylight in 1988. In 2001 at age 78, Freud designed and distributed 2500 campaign posters across Berlin offering a reward of £100,000 by an anonymous donor. The British Council commissioned the posters because the government hoped to recover the painting for a Freud retrospective at London's Tate Gallery in 2002. The Tate's curator said the painting was the most important small portrait of the twentieth century, and one of the three crucial paintings of Freud's early career. Freud made a public statement requesting that the person holding the painting "kindly consider allowing me to show it in my exhibition."[54] Despite the Council's promise that whoever returned the painting could claim the money without fear of prosecution, it remains missing to this day.[55]

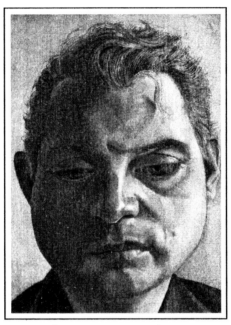

Lucian Freud, Portrait of Francis Bacon, oil on copper, 1951, 5" x 7"

1990: The Gardner Heist

In the early morning hours of St. Patrick's Day in 1990, two armed men, disguised as police officers, broke into the Isabella Gardner Museum in Boston and made off with 13 of the most famous paintings in the world. The Gardner heist is the most significant and provocative example of art theft in modern history and it remains unsolved. Although the thieves overlooked the museum's entire Renaissance collection, they made off with loot valued at US$300 million.

The theft was nearly identical to one that had occurred four years earlier at the Russborough House outside Dublin, where the millionaire Sir Alfred

Beit housed his family's art collection. The similarity of the cases has led to speculation that they may be connected. In both cases, smaller, independent museums lacking sophisticated security systems were the targets. The thieves took Vermeers in both situations. The 1986 robbery of Russborough House was the second theft the museum suffered, the first having occurred in 1974 at the hands of IRA terrorists for political purposes with the culprits being caught and imprisoned soon thereafter.[56] In the 1986 heist, 18 paintings were taken. Although 16 were recovered, 2 eighteenth-century landscapes by Francesco Guardi are still missing. The collection was robbed twice more—mere days apart—in 2001.

The Gardner heist is still an active case, with the investigation continuing 20 years later. Despite a tantalizing US$5 million reward for information, there are still no solid leads. Boston antiques dealer William Youngworth III told Tom Mashberg of the *Boston Herald* that he and one Myles Connor could procure the art's safe return in exchange for immunity and Connor's release from prison—in addition, of course, to the hefty reward. Connor could not have robbed the Gardner in person, as he was in jail for a different art heist at the time, but he claimed that, if released, he could locate the art. The United States Attorney demanded that one of the paintings be returned as proof that the works were in fact available to Connor. When he refused, negotiations ended. Connor is now out of jail, but none of the paintings has turned up.

The thieves managed to leave the museum with Jan Vermeer's *The Concert*, which is the most valuable stolen painting in the world. In addition, they made off with three Rembrandts: a self-portrait etching, *A Lady and Gentleman in Black*, and his only known seascape, *The Storm on the Sea of Galilee*. Making up the rest of their loot were Manet's *Chez Tortoni*, five drawings by Edgar Degas, Govaert Flinck's *Landscape with an Obelisk*, an ancient Chinese Qu, and a filial that once stood atop a flag from Napoleon's Army. In 2005, the Gardner Museum dramatically improved its security in an attempt to avoid repetition of the 1990 theft. Until the case is solved, the empty frames will remain on the wall.

*Rembrandt, The Storm on the Sea of Galilee, oil on canvas,
161.7 x 129.8. cm; inscribed on the rudder, REMBRANDT. FT: 1633*

Rembrandt, A Lady and Gentleman in Black, oil on canvas,
131.6 x 109 cm; inscribed at the foot, REMBRANDT. FT: 1633

Vermeer, The Concert, oil on canvas, 72.5 x 64.7 cm

Rembrandt, Self Portrait, etching, 1 3/4" x 2" (postage stamp size)

Govaert Flinck, Landscape with an Obelisk, oil on an oak panel, 54.5 x 71 cm; inscribed faintly at the foot on the right; R. 16.8 (until recently this was attributed to Rembrandt)

Degas, La Sortie du Pelage, pencil and water color on paper, 10 x 16 cm

*Degas, Three Mounted Jockeys, black ink, white, flesh and rose washes,
probably oil pigments, applied with a brush on medium brown paper,
30.5 x 24 cm*

Manet, Chez Tortoni, oil on canvas, 26 x 34 cm

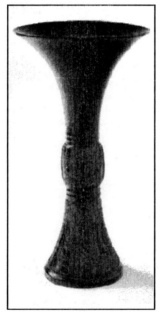

Bronze Beaker or "Qu," SHANG DYNASTY, 1200-1100 BC;
height: 10", diameter: 6 1/8", weight: 2 lb., 7 oz

1990: Kuwait

During Iraq's seven-month occupation of Kuwait, the Iraqis looted the Kuwait National Museum and the House of Islamic Antiquities before torching both buildings. More than 20,000 items were packed into crates and taken to the Iraq National Museum in Baghdad in the state-sponsored theft. This type of art theft recalls conquering empires and facilitates the rape of a culture. Like Hitler's plundering methods in World War II, Saddam Hussein tried to erase Kuwait's cultural identity. Armour, ceramics, earthenware, seals, and decorative arts from ancient Persia, Egypt, India, and Kuwait were stolen. Although curators facilitated the return of 16,000 pieces between September and October 1991, after the ceasefire, the rest remain in Iraq.[57]

1991: The Netherlands

An astonishing 20 paintings by Van Gogh were stolen from Amsterdam's Stedelijk Museum in April 1991. Despite a hasty recovery—police managed to retrieve the art within an hour—significant damage occurred to three of the canvasses, including *Wheatfield with Crows*, one of Van Gogh's later and most imaginative paintings. The police did not believe that the thieves planned to demand any ransom. Instead, they hypothesized that, had the heist succeeded, the canvasses would have become financial instruments on the black market economy. This brief and thwarted heist illustrates the fragility of art and shows that recovery, no matter how swift, does not always ensure a stolen artwork's protection.[58]

1991: First Gulf War

Toward the end of the Gulf War in 1991, nine of Iraq's thirteen national museums were ransacked.[59] The Gulf War has an especially dismal record of returning stolen artifacts. Of the 4,000 stolen archeological items, those recovered can be counted on one hand.[60] Most are presumed to have been traded on the international antiquities market or sold to private collectors overseas.[61] Market demand for illicit goods is high despite reputable dealers' insistence that their pieces were ethically obtained. Collectors, dealers, and law enforcement officials claim that Saddam Hussein's son, Uday, had a role in the organized smuggling system. [62]

1990: Stephen Blumberg, the "Bibliokleptomaniac"

Over a period of 16 years, a wealthy college drop-out named Stephen Blumberg travelled Canada and the United States, visiting every major library along the way. In that time, he stole more than 24,000 rare books and manuscripts, each valued between US$5 and $20 million. William Moffett, director of the Huntington Library, called Blumberg "the number one thief of books in American history." Blumberg managed to steal 684 books from the Claremont Colleges' Honnold Library alone.

Before burglarizing a library, Blumberg would carefully study its layout and security system. He found creative ways of reaching secret collections, earning the nickname of "Spiderman." In May of 1990, FBI agents entered his house on an informant's tip to find an immaculately preserved collection. It took the FBI two days to confiscate Blumberg's 867 boxes full of books, most of which were stolen. They found entire collections of diaries written by American explorers, as well as oversized, gold-inlaid volumes from the fifteenth century.

With each of the hundreds of books he stole, Bloomberg carefully removed all evidence of previous ownership. He would soak and iron the pages on which libraries had embossed identification stamps. Therefore, when the FBI confiscated them, it was difficult (and, in many cases, impossible) to trace their provenance.[63]

This notable book bandit proved how easy it was—and is—to steal books, especially when many libraries are unwilling to admit to being robbed. Improving security and reporting thefts will only go part-way toward stopping book thieves. There must also be stiffer sentencing and better monitoring. Like art theft, book theft is a crime against cultural heritage. Blumberg served 71 months in prison but went right back to his old habits when he was released in 1995.

1994 and 2004: *The Scream*

Multiple versions of Edvard Munch's *The Scream* have been the target of art theft. In February 1994, during the Lillehammer Olympic Games, four men broke into Oslo's National Gallery to steal their version of the painting. The note they left was telling: "Thanks for the poor security." The Norwegian police, with assistance from the Getty Museum and British Police, ran a sting operation to recover the painting. The four men were convicted but later released on appeal because the British agents had used false identities when entering Norway.

Another version of *The Scream* fell victim to art thieves in August 2004. The theft exhibited the hallmarks of an organized crime hit: brazen, violent, rapid, well-timed and well-coordinated. Masked gunmen armed with .357 Magnums entered Oslo's Munch Museum in broad daylight on a busy Sunday afternoon amid crowds of onlookers, some of whom even snapped photos of the burglars as they transported the paintings to their getaway cars. Realizing that Oslo's police headquarters were mere minutes from the museum, the thieves chose to operate on Sunday, when the station would be relatively empty. They simply ripped the paintings off the walls while spectators lay on the ground in fear. They fled in a black Audi, which they abandoned ten minutes away from the museum and sprayed with a fire extinguisher to erase fingerprints and obscure any traces of DNA. From there, the paintings made their way to the home of a famous Norwegian racecar driver, Thomas Nataas. In 2006 Nataas was acquitted for his role in the heist when the court accepted the defence that he was involved against his will. After a month, the paintings were moved to an unknown location.

The timing of the heist troubled police. Four months before *The Scream* was taken, there had been an armed robbery at the Norwegian Cash Service offices in which Arne Sigve Klungland, a senior police officer, was fatally gunned down. Theories circulated that the same perpetrators had carried out the Munch Museum heist in an attempt to divert police resources from the murder investigation. *The Scream*'s status as a national treasure would heighten public pressure to retrieve the masterpiece and distract investigators and the public from the Klungland murder case.[64]

In 2006, six men went on trial for the Munch Museum robbery. Three were convicted, their sentences ranging from four to eight years' imprisonment. (A fourth conviction came on July 8, 2009, in which an accomplice received two-and-a-half years in prison.[65]) One of the suspects was killed while awaiting trial. Still, nobody would speak of the paintings' whereabouts.

Norwegian police recovered *The Scream* and *Madonna* on August 31, 2006. The details of how this happened are hazy. When David Toska was sentenced to 19 years in jail for his role as the mastermind of the Norwegian Cash Services robbery, newspapers reported that it was his lawyer who tipped off police about the location of the paintings. Upon recovery, it became increasingly clear that the thieves had no artistic interest in the paintings. The careless and unsophisticated criminals had kept the paintings wrapped in a damp blanket and never once looked at them. Some of the water damage that *The Scream* suffered was irreparable, and *The Madonna* had several tears in it.

Sobered by the experience, the Munch Museum closed for nine months to undertake a US$6.4 million security upgrade.[66] *The Scream* and *The Madonna* are on display again—this time behind bulletproof glass—but the physical damage to the canvasses serves as a constant reminder of their vulnerability.

Munch, The Scream

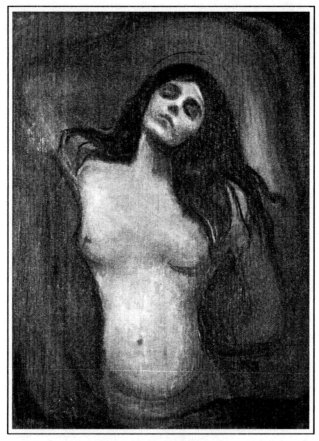

Munch, The Madonna

1995: The Stradivarius

Musical instruments are works of art in themselves, and are sought-after targets for theft. Smaller instruments such as violins are easily portable. In 1995, the noted concert violinist Erica Morini reported her US$3 million Stradivarius violin missing. The instrument, made in 1727 by Antonio Stradivari, had been stolen from her New York City apartment. It has yet to be recovered.

Davidoff-Morini Stradivarius

1999: The Picasso on the Yacht

While a yacht called *Coral Island* was stationed at the French port of Antibes, *Portrait of Dora Maar*, an abstract oil painting by Picasso of his muse and mistress, was stolen from it. The yacht's owner, a Saudi Arabian multi-millionaire, had moved the painting at the request of subcontractors hired to refurbish the yacht's salon. It is worth noting that the lavish yacht, worth £60 million, housed artworks with a whopping value of £151 million. The stolen portrait was one of two Picasso works on the yacht, and it was particularly vulnerable when the thieves struck because it was not in its usual location. When the owner moved it to facilitate renovations, the painting was placed under lock and key, but was no longer protected by its sophisticated alarm system, and the video surveillance system had not been functioning for three months. The last person to see it was the English packing expert who the owner had hired to pack up his goods and arrange for their safekeeping in a bank vault while *Coral Island* underwent mechanical repairs. When the packing expert returned to collect the painting for storage the next week, it was gone. Strangely, the Matisse in the same room had been left untouched.

Police have two theories. On the one hand, they suspect that the perpetrators might have been a well organized criminal gang of art experts. On the other, perhaps it was a "theft to order" for a private collector. The owner claimed that, even though he employed a permanent staff of 25, only two other people knew about the existence and location of the portrait, which, if true, leads to the conclusion that there must have been an inside leak of information.

Although the FBI has photographs of the painting on its website, it has yet to be recovered. The painting, which came from Picasso's own private collection, has never been publicly exhibited by any museum or art gallery.[67]

1999-2000: Ashmolean

On the eve of millennium celebrations from December 31, 1999 to January 1, 2000, thieves broke through the glass roof of Oxford's Ashmolean Museum and stole Cezanne's *View of Auvres-sur-Oise*. The painting, valued at £3 million, exemplifies the artist's important transitional phase and has yet to be recovered.[68] Like many other cases, this one demonstrates that art collections are particularly vulnerable during holiday periods.

Cezanne, View of Auvers-sur-Oise

2000: Theft at the Fair

Antique and art fairs are vulnerable to theft because of their combination of great selection and minimal security. On March 25, 2000, a floral still life by Jan van Kessel disappeared from an antiques fair in the Netherlands. The painting is still missing.

Jan van Kessel, Untitled, 20.7 x 14 cm

2000: Swedish Heist

In late December 2000, an unarmed guard at Stockholm's National Museum was accosted by a man with a submachine gun while his two accomplices inside stole three masterpieces. Their exit was as dramatic as the entry of Manhattan's Colnaghi Gallery. They delayed their pursuers by scattering their trail with spikes, distracted them with exploding cars, and raced away in a motorboat. Their next step was to approach a lawyer, who relayed to the police their US$10 million ransom demand. The police asked for photographic proof of the loot and, when convinced of their authenticity, demanded that the lawyer surrender his clients' identities. The lawyer refused to do so.[69] However, eight men were arrested in connection with the case before Renoir's *Conversation* was recovered in Sweden in 2001. In 2005, the other two missing paintings resurfaced in different parts of the world through a carefully-coordinated undercover operation. Renoir's *Young Parisienne*, valued at US$13 million, was recovered in Los Angeles. Police kept the news quiet in order not to disrupt the search for the last masterpiece, Rembrandt's 1630 *Self-Portrait*. Months later, Danish police arrested four men in a sting operation as they presented the painting to potential buyers at a Copenhagen hotel.[70] The paintings were in excellent condition.

2000: The Switch

In September 2000, staff at the Museum Naradowe w Poznaniu in Poland noticed that Claude Monet's *Beach at Pourville* had been replaced with a forgery of the same painting. The original has not yet been found.

Monet, Beach at Pourville, 60 x 73 cm

2001: Lightning Strikes Twice

The Gardner Heist of 1990 mirrored the 1986 theft of the Beit Collection at Russborough House in County Wicklow, Ireland. History repeated itself in 2001 when the same two paintings by Thomas Gainsborough and Bernardo Bellotto were once again stolen by a gang of armed robbers.

Bernardo Bellotto, View of Florence, oil on canvas

Thomas Gainsborough, Portrait of Madame Bacelli Dancing,
oil on canvas, 55.5 x 39.4 cm

2002: Van Gogh Cold Case

In yet another example of poor security, on the morning of December 7, 2002, two thieves managed to break into the Vincent Van Gogh Museum in Amsterdam using a ladder that workmen had left behind. The thieves worked quickly, breaking the window with towels on their elbows. They immediately set off the alarms, but left before museum security or police could respond. They made their way down a rope with two Van Gogh paintings: *View of the Sea at Scheveningen* and *Congregation Leaving the Reformed Church in Nuenen*, valued at US$30 million. The thieves were caught on the security cameras and convicted two years later using

DNA evidence from hats found at the scene. One of the culprits, Octave Durham, had earned the nickname "The Monkey" in his many years as a crafty and elusive art thief. He received four-and-a-half years in prison, and his accomplice, Henk B., received four years. Despite the conviction of both men, the paintings remain missing. Authorities believe that the thieves might have hidden the goods, since an outdated Dutch law allows thieves to become the owners of stolen private art after 20 years and publicly-owned art after 30 years, as long as they can prove that they were indeed the thieves.[71]

Van Gogh, View of the Sea at Scheveningen, oil on canvas, 1882, 34.5 x 51 cm

Van Gogh, Congregation Leaving the Reformed Church in Nuenen,
oil on canvas, 1884, 41.5 x 32 cm

2002: Paraguay Museum of Fine Arts

The Paraguay Museum of Fine Arts fell victim to a creative group of criminals when it held the most valuable art exhibition in its history in July 2002. At least one thief rented a store about 25 metres away from the museum in Asuncion. Authorities believe that he recruited people to help him dig a 10-foot-deep tunnel, running from the shop to the museum. After closing time on July 30, 2002, he burrowed through the tunnel and stole 12 paintings—more than a million American dollars worth of art.[72] The stolen works include Murillo's *Self Portrait*, Coubert's *The Virgin Mary and Jesus*, and Piot's *Landscape*. One witness came forward claiming she was asked by the heist's mastermind to be part of the operation. Although there are three suspects, all of the paintings remain missing.[73]

2003: Cellini Salt Cellar

In May 2003, a thief stole a gold, ivory, and enamel salt cellar by the Renaissance master Benvenuto Cellini, valued at $55 million. It is the only surviving work of Cellini's goldsmithing. The thief entered the Kunsthistorisches Museum in Vienna through a first-floor window, simply smashing the glass display case to take the salt cellar.[74] When he set off an alarm, the guard assumed there was a glitch and simply reset the system.[75] Since it is the only item of its kind, the Cellini salt cellar is extremely unmarketable. It was recovered three years later, undamaged.

2003: The Madonna of the Yarnwinder

Like Edvard Munch, Van Gogh, and Picasso, Leonardo da Vinci is a repeat victim of art theft. Unlike *The Scream*, which was stolen from public galleries, da Vinci's *The Madonna of the Yarnwinder* was stolen from the Duke of Buccleuch's home in Scotland in 2003. Two men posing as tourists overpowered the student guide at Drumlanrig Castle and escaped out a window with the painting, worth between US$50-$105 million. As they fled with the painting, they reportedly told two tourists: "Don't worry love, we're the police. This is just practice."[76] The painting was recovered in October 2007 and four men were charged. Unfortunately, the heartbroken Duke of Buccleuch had died in September.[77]

2003: Manchester Heist

Overnight between April 26 and 27, 2003, thieves broke into Manchester's Whitworth Gallery and stole three paintings valued over US$1.5 million: Gauguin's *Tahitian Landscape*, Van Gogh's *Fortification of Paris with*

Houses and Picasso's *Poverty*. The thieves evaded CCTV cameras, alarms, and 24-hour guards. A day later, an anonymous phone call to the police informed them that the paintings were in a public toilet near the museum. The tip turned out to be correct: all three works had been crammed into a cardboard tube and left behind a toilet just 200 yards away from where they had been taken. The culprits had left a handwritten note with the art, explaining that they did not intend to steal the paintings, but rather, to highlight a breach in security. Investigators were not convinced; they thought it was more likely that the thieves panicked when they realized that they had no idea how to dispose of such a hot commodity. The paintings had suffered some water damage and tearing, but were repaired and returned to their places within weeks of the heist. The museum took the thieves' advice and improved its security measures.[78]

2005: The Bumbling Thief who Left a Calling Card

On May 4, 2005, a down-on-his-luck trucker named Anthony Porcelli decided on a whim to swipe a cargo container from the JFK airport. Little did he know, the 6-by-7-foot box contained a 1982 painting by Jean-Michel Basquiat, valued at US$1.5 million. It had been on its way to a buyer in Rome. Two days later, warehouse security reported it missing. They immediately watched the surveillance tapes, where they saw a man who looked like Porcelli loading the crate into the back of his truck. They checked the warehouse records; sure enough, Porcelli had provided them with a copy of his driver's licence. The painting was recovered from the trucking company unharmed. The crate had not even been opened. According to his landlord, "Vinnie," Porcelli had stolen the box to spite the loading dock workers who had kept him waiting.[79] Porcelli was charged with first-degree larceny and criminal possession of stolen property. He pleaded guilty to grand larceny and was sentenced to one to three years in prison.[80]

2006: Goya Stolen in Transit

While on transit from Ohio's Toledo Museum of Art to the Guggenheim in Manhattan, *Children with a Cart*, a 1778 work by Francisco de Goya insured at just over US$1 million, disappeared. The picture was in the care of a professional art transporter when the theft occurred near Scranton, Pennsylvania, on 14 November. Authorities suspected that it was a theft-to-order, because the painting would not be marketable. The painting's insurers offered a US$50,000 reward for information. The painting remained missing for only a week. On 21 November, New Jersey FBI agents recovered the painting unharmed. The FBI did not reveal any details about how they recovered the painting.[81]

2006: Rio de Janeiro Heist

During the Carnival celebrations of February 24, 2006, four armed men overpowered the guards at the Museo Chacara do Ceu in Rio de Janeiro. The thieves forced the guards to turn off the security cameras while they stole four extremely valuable paintings by Salvador Dali, Henri Matisse, Pablo Picasso, and Claude Monet. They exited the museum and were lost amidst the Carnival's crowds.

Salvador Dali, 1929, Two Balconies, 23.5 cm x 34.5 cm

Henri Matisse, 1905, Luxembourg Garden, 40.5 cm x 32 cm

Pablo Picasso, 1956, Dance, 100 cm x 81 cm

Claude Monet, 1880-1890, Marine, 65 cm x 91 cm

2007: Beatty

A landscape by J. W. Beatty, a contemporary of the Group of Seven, was stolen from a private office in the Ontario College of Art and Design on January 8, 2007. Police cannot fathom how the thief managed to remove the ornately-framed *Winter Sunshine, Belfountain (Cabin at Rover's Edge in Winter)*, worth $25,000, from the school in broad daylight. It has not been recovered.[82]

2007: The Stolen Cavalier

On June 10, 2007, during public viewing hours at the Art Gallery of New South Wales in Sydney, Australia, a relatively small portrait by Dutch Master Frans Van Mieris disappeared. *A Cavalier* is valued at over US$1 million.

Van Mieris, A Cavalier, oil on wood panel, 20 x 16 cm

2008: Buhrle

In February 2008, the Foundation E. G. Buhrle Collection in Zurich fell victim to art thieves who took four impressionist works: Monet's *Poppy Field at Vetheuil*, Degas' *Count Lepic and his Daughter*, Van Gogh's *Blooming Chestnut Branches*, and Cezanne's *Boy in the Red Vest*. The booty had a value of 180 million Swiss francs, making it the largest art robbery in Switzerland's history. The masked men were armed and violently forced museum personnel to the floor while they collected the paintings from the exhibition hall. The theft was not sleek and sophisticated; it was simple, brute violence. The thieves had little time to act, so they simply pulled the paintings off the wall with their heavy glass cases and ignored the alarms. Officials speculated that the motive was most likely an insurance ransom, a reward or leverage for someone that could be facing prosecution for larger crimes.[83] As in other cases, the thieves stole the most accessible, rather than most valuable, paintings. Police recovered the Van Gogh and Monet paintings from a nearby car—the thieves probably ditched them because they were too heavy to carry—but the Degas and Cezanne remain missing.[84]

Paul Cezanne, Boy in the Red Vest, 1894/95, oil on canvas, 80 cm x 64.5 cm

Edgar Degas, Count Lepic and His Daughters, c. 1871,
oil on canvas, 65.5 cm x 81 cm

2009: Picasso's Sketchbook

On June 9, 2009, a sketchbook of 33 Picasso drawings made between 1917 and 1924 was stolen from a display case at the Picasso Museum in Paris. The item is valued at CDN$11 million.[85] There was no sign of a break-in and no alarms went off. A museum employee explained that the lock on the case was not broken, so it had simply been left unlocked. It is difficult to determine whether the theft was planned or spontaneous. Authorities believe that it took place overnight, but since nobody even noticed that the notebook was missing until lunchtime, there is some speculation that a visitor could have walked off with it. Without an alarm, or even a lock, the theft would be easy to execute. The notebook disappeared while the museum was holding a special temporary exhibit with vast installations, which obscured visibility.[86] The sketchbook can be added to a long list of over 500 stolen Picassos.[87]

Whether looking at the increasing problem of theft from archaeological sites, or from museums or galleries, in order to have a healthier art market, focus must shift from the thieves themselves to those who are creating a market for this illicit material. The simple equation of supply and demand is at play. When there are finally negative consequences for those creating the demand for these illegal objects, and some shame attached to this activity, demand will lessen and there will be no motivation to steal it.

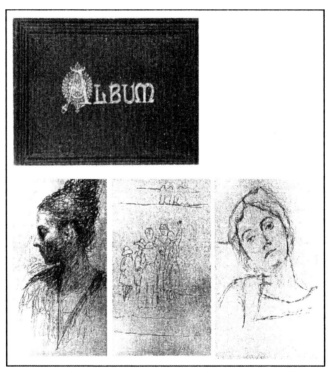

Cover and selected sketches from Picasso's Sketchbook

2009-2010: Art Thefts Rock France

A rash of high-profile art thefts in France over the 2009 Christmas holidays brought to the forefront the loss caused by the illegal trafficking of the world's cultural treasures, which, once disappeared into the black market, may never be seen again.

Some 30 paintings were stolen from a private collector's home in La Cadière d'Azur on the French Riviera, including pieces by post-Impressionist painters Rousseau and Picasso. This haul was worth somewhere in the neighbourhood of $1 million and occurred just days after the Impressionist painter Edgar Degas' *The Choir Singers* was stolen from The Cantini Museum in Marseilles. The delicate pastel, on loan from the Musée d'Orsay in Paris, with an estimated value of £800,000 (US$1.14 million), had simply been unscrewed from the wall and taken away on New Years Eve.

These thefts took place against the backdrop of hundreds of French churches and scores of historical châteaux being targeted for their art by relentless looters and organized thieves for highly prized cultural treasures. In addition, an auctioneer and eight agents from the well-known and respected Paris auction house, Drouot, were charged with "organized theft" following the discovery of a stolen Gustave Courbet painting in the Drouot warehouse.

CONCLUSION

Art theft is a pervasive cultural phenomenon that victimizes all. The examples above serve as a warning to private collectors and institutions of the factors that make a particular victim an attractive target to criminals.

Of course, theft is not the only risk to collections. Art can fall prey to man-made or natural disasters. Unruly patrons might damage art, as occurred in January 2010 when an overly eager woman tripped and slashed a Picasso at the Metropolitan Museum of Art.[88] Arson is another threat to cultural property. Museums and collectors must take steps to protect art from accidental fires or water damage. The International Foundation for Cultural Property Protection offers risk-prevention courses and professional certification for persons working in, or responsible for, cultural property protection.[89] Recognizing that art collecting can be a high-risk endeavour, what can collectors do to protect themselves? Recent studies suggest that, in art theft and other burglaries, repeat victimization is a significant factor. The first robbery will usually occur because of what Ken Pease has dubbed the "flag effect." Certain property is attractive to thieves because it is a marked target: it has no visible security, the entry point is obscured from sight, it has small windows or an unsophisticated lock system. To prevent the first incident, one should screen very carefully those who have access to the collection, since most crimes are perpetrated by an acquaintance of the victim. It is also advisable to bolster visible security measures to deter criminals.

Unlike proverbial lightening striking, once a collector has already experienced a theft, the risk of subsequent victimization increases significantly. According to one criminologist, 4% of people suffer 44% of all crime. Prior victimization is one of the best predictors of future victimization. Pease attributes this in part to the "known quantity" effect.[90] Burglars will return to the same crime scene for psychological or practical reasons. They feel more comfortable navigating property they already know, rather than uncharted territory that might contain unidentified risks.

INTERNATIONAL TREATIES, CONVENTIONS AND ENABLING DOMESTIC LAWS

Conventions and treaties have evolved globally over the last 75 years as a way of dealing with the increasing scope of the international movement of art and problems that have ensued concerning questionable provenance, theft, looting, legality and ethical issues in the international art market. The two most significant conventions in this field are the 1970 UNESCO Convention on the Means of Prohibiting and Preventing the Illicit Import, Export and Transfer of Ownership of Cultural Property and the 1954 Hague Convention on the Protection of Cultural Property in the Event of Armed Conflict and First Protocol, and in 1999 the Second Protocol. The 1970 UNESCO Convention came into force mainly to deal with the worldwide problem of the looting and destruction of cultural property from archeological sites. The 1954 Hague Convention and Protocols evolved in an attempt to protect cultural heritage in times of war. Each nation that becomes a States Party to the 1970 Convention and High Contracting Party to the 1954 Hague Convention develops its own enabling domestic legislation to enforce its respective obligations to these treaties, which is what this chapter begins to explore.

THE 1970 UNESCO CONVENTION

Clients often ask why many dealers and auction houses often tell purchasers of antiquities that the provenance of objects is "acquired from a private seller in 1969." Was there a flurry of antiquities-buying that year? The explanation, in fact, is that the United States signed the UNESCO Convention on the Means of Prohibiting and Preventing the Illicit Import, Export and Transfer of Ownership of Cultural Property in 1970.[1] So, 1970 marks the date that the United Statese, one of the most significant markets in the world, made a commitment not to participate in this illicit trade. Therefore, one way that those selling illegal cultural objects can appear not guilty of doing so is to claim, regarding the object's provenance, that the object was acquired in 1969. Buyer, beware.

The growth of the illicit trafficking of cultural property since World War II and the realization that cultural property has an intangible value prompted the need for this international convention. There are currently 118 States Party to the Convention,[2] which has proved to be one of the most important treaties for curbing the illicit trafficking of cultural property. In 1969, archaeologist Clemency Coggins wrote an article that documented and exposed the ongoing assault on archaeological sites by looters taking place in Central America of the monumental stelae of the ancient Maya civilization. The plunder was taking place, Coggins explained, "in order to feed the international art market."[3] The highly evolved Classic Mayan civilization is one about which little is known, ignorance that is a result of looting and mutilation of Mayan monuments, tombs and sites. The reporting of this information helped to raise public awareness and, as a result, legislation was passed in the United States to help halt the tide of illegal imports of this material with the enactment of the Importation of Pre-Columbian Monumental Stone Sculptures or Mural Act in 1972.[4] In order to try to halt the illicit trafficking if antiquities, works of art and ethnographic material, UNESCO drafted the Convention on the Means of Prohibiting and Preventing the Illicit, Export and Transfer of Ownership of Cultural Property. This convention went through many drafts in order to placate those in the art market objecting to the regulation and wishing to continue to profit from this activity.

Implementing UNESCO: The US Approach

The Convention on Cultural Property Implementation Act[5] is the enabling American legislation to the 1970 UNESCO Convention. Pursuant to this legislation, States Party to the 1970 Convention may make a request for an agreement with the United States for controls on imports in certain categories of archaeological or ethnographic material. The US State Department has the authority to administer this process in terms of making a decision as to whether a source country may have such an agreement. Before a decision is made, under the auspices of the US State Department, the Cultural Property Advisory Committee hears evidence from the source country concerning the location and extent of pillaging, looting and theft.[6] The process for requesting an agreement is lengthy, complex and arduous for the requesting country. All the while, the looting and illegal trade in the requesting country's cultural material continues unimpeded. China, for instance, made its request to the US State Department in 2003, which accepted it in 2009.[7] Currently, bilateral agreements that the United States has with requesting countries are: Bolivia, Cambodia, Columbia, Cyprus, El Salvador, Guatemala, Honduras, Italy, Mali, Nicaragua and Peru.[8]

The Canadian Experience with the US Implementation Process

In 1985, the Government of Canada made a request to the Government of the United States to enter into a bilateral agreement, pursuant to the Cultural Property Implementation Act. This request became a target of vociferous attack from those trading in the material that the agreement was seeking to protect. Twelve years later, in 1997, Canada finally entered into an agreement with the United States which, unfortunately, expired five years later[9] and as yet has failed to be renewed. Even during the brief period that the agreement was in force, it was under constant attack, including by the Moynihan legislation, introduced in 1999.

Sadly, the First Nations of Canada, whose cultural heritage continues to be lost to theft and illegal trafficking, were not even invited to the hearings to renew the bilateral agreement, which took place in Washington, D.C.

First Nations representatives would have been a crucial source of information that was needed by the governments of Canada and the United States to make an informed decision. The press was silent on this issue. The Agreement Concerning the Imposition of Import Restrictions on Certain Categories of Archaeological and Ethnographic Material sought to protect Canada's cultural patrimony. As the treaty expired on April 9, 2002, there is currently no such filter.

The continued theft and looting of works of art and archaeological material does not take place only in times of armed conflict and its aftermath, as the world has witnessed recently in Iraq. This type of theft is also a major concern in other areas of the world, such as Canada where archaeologists have been held at gunpoint by professional looters of material for the lucrative international trade in First Nations artifacts. Enormous losses and thefts regularly take place from Canadian university laboratories and storage rooms, as First Nations property is highly prized by international dealers. The very poor will often take material from archaeological sites in Canada's far north in return for foreign or Canadian currency, often for sums that are a mere fraction of an item's true value.

When looting occurs, valuable scientific and even botanical material is destroyed in the process. Amber beads, traded in historical times with inhabitants of Siberia, are easily shattered; fragile flowers planted 2000 years ago are recklessly destroyed in search for arrowheads and other artifacts that bring cash.

For many First Nations peoples, Inuit and other indigenous people around the world, items with cultural and religious significance have more than a monetary value. The theft of a medicine bag essential to religious and spiritual community practices, which the art market might value at $100,000, for First Nations people amounts to the loss of the right to properly practice their religion. These stolen pieces are not merely objects; for their creators and those of their culture, the objects have a life in and of themselves, and their return is akin to the return of a kidnapped child.

It is time for this issue to be addressed in Canada. Canadians are not helpless. Canada did have an imperfect, but nonetheless useful, agreement for the return of some materials entering the United States illegally. Because the agreement expired, Canada's cultural heritage continues to leak unabated across its borders. Part of the solution would be for Canada to re-establish a treaty with the United States, although this time it should not be subject to a five-year renewal condition. Moreover, such a treaty should be fully reciprocal, allowing the United States to request restitution of material that has entered Canada illegally, hence respecting and recognizing the cultural heritage of both countries. Both Canada and the United States are market as well as source countries. Moreover, while the old bilateral agreement covered material 250 years or older, a new treaty should protect material that is 100 years old as there is a thriving market in colonial and underwater cultural heritage from the lakes, rivers, bays and oceans from the last 100 years.

Why does the illegal trade of cultural property still thrive today? Before there can be any change, there must be a shift in focus by legislators and law enforcement from supply to demand. To date, the focus has been primarily on the thief, not the receiver of stolen goods. This illegal art economy, however, is a business based on the simple economic principle of supply and demand. As long as there is a demand, looters will go to the trouble of stealing and receive cash for their efforts. There must be shame attached to those willing to participate in the illegal trade of cultural material and deterrent negative consequences for those who are purchasing and dealing in it. Until now the negative consequences have fallen only to the relatively few thieves who are caught. Little attention is paid to those marketing these objects and to the buyers lining up to purchase illegal material. And little sympathy is felt for the communities who have suffered the loss of their history and humanity. Culpability for stolen art lies as much in the hands of the buyer and dealer as it does the thief's. This vital shift in the public perspective regarding the sharing of criminal responsibility is necessary in order to meaningfully curtail the illegal trade of stolen art.

Canadian Implementation of UNESCO

The *Cultural Property Export and Import Act* (CPEIA), which came into force in 1977, is the enabling legislation to the 1970 UNESCO Convention to which Canada became the 35th signatory.[10] The CPEIA allows for foreign nations to restitute from Canada cultural property that was illegally exported. There are three conditions to be met in order to make a claim for restitution:

1. The object must have originated from a country that is a signatory to the 1970 UNESCO Convention.
2. The object must have been exported illegally from that country.
3. The material must have been exported after 1977, when Canada became a signatory to the 1970 UNESCO Convention.

When these three conditions are met, an application by a foreign nation may be made for restitution from Canada to that state.[11] There are criminal sanctions under the CPEIA, which will be discussed in Chapter 3.

Reforming the *Cultural Property Export and Import Act*

As Canada is a signatory to the 1970 UNESCO Convention on the Means of Prohibiting and Preventing the Illicit Import, Export and Transfer of Ownership of Cultural Property, brought into force in 1977, it seems almost unfathomable that our government should certify unprovenanced material for the purposes of tax deductions. Indeed, the citizens of Canada have an obligation under this Convention to refuse to participate in such illicit activities. There is nothing particularly progressive or pioneering about this position; it is simply a question of keeping in step with many other nations whose values and position as ethical world leaders are similar to Canada's.

The time has now come for Canada to join the ranks of other Western nations in taking a stance on acquisition of unprovenanced material in public institutions and the relating tax practices in terms of deductions to donors of unprovenanced material.

There are examples we can look to of ethical conduct for collecting and exhibiting art in the Western world. In the United Kingdom, national museums refuse to lend to exhibitions material that may have been looted or illegally exported.[12] In addition, the UK *Due Diligence Guidelines for Museums, Libraries and Archives on Collecting and Borrowing Cultural*

Material published by the Department for Culture, Media and Sport, Cultural Property Unit states:

> Museums should acquire and borrow items only if they are legally and ethically sound. They should reject an item if there is any suspicion about it, or about the circumstances surrounding it, after undertaking due diligence. Documentary evidence, or if that is unavailable an affidavit, is necessary to prove the ethical status of a major item. Museums should acquire or borrow items only if they are certain they have not been illegally excavated or illegally exported....[13]

In California, the Acquisition Policy of the J. Paul Getty Museum provides an example of ethical art purchasing. Some of the Conditions of Acquisition include:

> 1. No object will be acquired without assurance that valid and legal title can be transferred.
> 2. The Museum will undertake due diligence to establish the legal status of an object under consideration for acquisitions, making every reasonable effort to investigate, substantiate, or clarify the provenance of the object.
> 3. No object will be acquired that, to the knowledge of the Museum, has been stolen, removed in contravention of treaties and international conventions of which the United States is a signatory, illegally exported from its country of origin or the country where it was last legally owned, or illegally imported into the United States.[14]

In 1999, the Canadian Museums Association (CMA) updated its ethical guidelines, which had been in existence since 1979, to reflect the ICOM Code of Professional Ethics and its emphasis on serving society. The CMA incorporated elements from the ethical guidelines of other Canadian and foreign institutions to meet the needs of modern Canadian society. The CMA guidelines serve as a framework upon which individual museums can build their own ethical policies.[15]

In 2000, the American Association of Museums (AAM) established its Code of Ethics,[16] and in 2008, the American Association of Museum Directors (AAMD) formulated a new set of guidelines for the purchase of antiquities.[17] Although these guidelines are not binding on member museums, several museums have indicated that they will follow the AAMD's recommendations.

We are beginning to see the tide of change. Following the lead of admirable collections in the United States and Europe, reputable collectors in

Canada are, for the first time, seeking to protect the integrity of their collections by doing careful due diligence both in acquiring works of art and in donating and loaning them. The Canadian government must be seen as being part of the movement forward.

After reviewing the practices of other nations, the question arises: how could Canada, under any circumstances, consider certifying material that in other nations would be deemed illicit until proven otherwise? The current system, which allows acceptance and certification of unprovenanced material, in fact contributes to the criminal cycle of illicit trafficking of cultural property. Illicit traffickers who donate stolen property receive financial reward in the form of tax deductions, whereas they would face criminal sanctions in many other countries.

THE 1954 HAGUE CONVENTION

Long before UNESCO, the only cultural property laws in existence applied to wartime scenarios. The 1899 Hague Convention was the first establishment of guidelines for the protection of cultural property in the event of armed conflict. The Convention of 1907 stated:

> Art 46. Family honor and rights, the lives of persons and private property as well as religious connections and practice, must be protected. Private property cannot be confiscated.

These guidelines set forth the basic principles that all interested parties would govern situations involving the destruction of world treasures and heritage. Both the 1899 and 1907 conventions laid down principles against the destruction of cultural property. Although their provisions would be inadequate and inapplicable for modern warfare, their principles were later developed in the 1954 Hague Convention. Unfortunately, the earlier conventions were ineffective at protecting cultural heritage. Those who initiated World War I ignored these treaties. Many cultural treasures were destroyed as the hideous war spread throughout Europe. Numerous libraries were victim of this destruction and, notably, the Cathedral of Rheims, which suffered destruction when German troops bombed it and pillaged Rheims for ten days.

The Treaty of Versailles allowed for war claims. Under the terms of the Treaty, Germany accepted full responsibility for loss and damage that had occurred as a result of the War; however their resources were so depleted that they could not afford to compensate for losses.

During World War II, Hitler ignored all rules of international law. The Hague Conventions were meaningless to him. However, following the Allies' victory, many countries prepared catalogues of lost or stolen art and circulated them amongst dealers in the hope of stopping trade and locating these pieces. As documented in the National Archives in Washington, the State Department declared after the war, "It is an undeniable fact that works of art lost through the Nazi depredation of European countries which shocked the civilized world, will never be saleable."[18]

The 1954 Hague Convention for the Protection of Cultural Property in the Event of Armed Conflict was at long last signed by the United States Senate on 25 September 2008. This was the first international treaty to focus specifically on the protection of cultural property.

The 1954 Hague Convention is useful in part because it provides a definition of cultural property.

Article 1. Definition of Cultural Property
(a)   movable or immovable property of great importance to the cultural heritage of every people, such as monuments of architecture, art history, whether religious or secular; archaeological sites; groups of buildings which, as a whole are historical or artistic interest; works of art; manuscripts, books and other objects of artistic, historical or archaeological interest; as well as scientific collections and important collections of books or archives or reproductions of property defined above;
(b)   buildings whose main and effective purpose is to preserve or exhibit the movable cultural property defined in sub-paragraph (a) such as museums, large libraries and depositories of archives and refuges intended as shelter, in the event of armed conflict defines in subparagraph (a).

Article 3 deals with the safeguarding of cultural property in times of peace within the High Contracting Parties' territory "against foreseeable effects of armed conflict, by taking such measures as they consider appropriate."

Article 4 contains the foundation and nucleus of obligations during times of war of this Convention, including the waiver of obligations "only in cases where military necessity imperatively requires such waiver."

Article 4. Respect for Cultural Property

1. The High Contracting parties undertake to respect cultural property situated within their own territory as well as within the territory of other High Contracting Parties by refraining from any use of the property and its immediate surroundings or of the appliances in use for its protection for purposes which are likely to expose it to destruction or damage in the event of armed conflict; and by refraining from any act of hostility directed against such property.

2. The obligations mentioned in Paragraph 1 of the present Article may be waived only in cases were military necessity imperatively requires such waiver;

3. The High Contracting parties further undertake to prohibit, prevent and, if necessary, put a stop to any forms of theft, pillage or misappropriation of, and any acts of vandalism directed against, cultural property. They shall refrain from requisitioning movable cultural property situated in the territory of other High Contracting Parties.

4. They shall refrain from any act directed by way of reprisals against cultural property.

5. No High Contracting Party may evade the obligations incumbent upon it under the present Article, in respect of anther High Contracting party by reason of the fact that the latter has not applied the measures of safeguard referred to in Article 3.

Article 5 provides for the duties of occupiers.

Article 5. Occupation

1. Any High Contracting Party in Occupation of the whole or part of the territory of another High Contracting Party shall as far as possible support the competent national authorities of the occupied country in safeguarding and preserving its cultural property.

2. Should it prove necessary to take measures to preserve cultural property situated in occupied territory and damaged by military operations, and should the competent national authorities be unable to take such measures, Occupying Power shall as far as possible, and in close co-operation with such authorities, take the most necessary measures of preservation.

3. Any High Contracting party whose government is considered their legitimate government by members of a resistance movement, shall, if possible, draw their attention to the obligation to comply with those provisions of the Convention dealing with respect for cultural property.

In summary, Article 6 sets out the requirement of the Blue Shield, which is a special marking for cultural property. Importantly, Article 7 requires

High Contracting Parties to educate its armed forces. Articles 8 through 11 grant special protection to centres containing monuments and immovable cultural property in addition to refuges intended to shelter movable cultural property.[19]

The First Protocol to the 1954 Hague Convention[20]

Canada became a High Contracting Party to the 1954 Hague Convention in 1999. In 2005, Canada acceded to the first and second Protocols.

The First Protocol is significant in that it governs the movement of movable cultural property during war and occupation. Those forces occupying must "undertake to prevent the exportation, from the territory occupied by it during an armed conflict, of cultural property," and it must be "returned at the end of occupation."

Section 1.

(1)   Each High Contracting party undertakes to prevent the exportation, from a territory occupied by it during an armed conflict, or cultural property as defined in Article 1.

(2)   Each High Contracting Party undertakes to take into its custody cultural property imported into its territory either directly or indirectly from any occupied territory. This shall either be effected automatically upon the importation of the property or failing this, at the request of the authorities of that territory.

(3)   Each High Contracting party undertakes to return, at close of hostilities to competent authorities of the territory previously occupied, cultural property which is in its territory, if such property has been exported in contravention of the principle laid down in the first paragraph. Such property shall never be retained s war reparations.

(4)   The high contracting Party whose obligation it was to prevent the exportation of the cultural property from the territory occupied by it shall pay an indemnity to the holders in good faith of any cultural property which has to be returned to in accordance with the preceding paragraph.

Section 2.

(1)   Cultural property coming from the territory of a high contracting party and deposited by it in the territory of another High Contracting Party for the purpose of protecting such property against dangers of an armed conflict, shall be returned by the latter, at the end of hostilities, to the competent authorities from which it came.

The Second Protocol[21]

The Second Protocol to the Convention came about for the most part as a response to the destruction of cultural property during the Balkan War in the 1990s. It fortifies and enhances the effectiveness of the Convention. The Second Protocol is significant in that it attaches criminal responsibility to those who are in contravention of its sections. This Protocol also narrows the definition of when there may be a waiver. Article 6(a) states that troops can only attack cultural property if "there is no feasible alternative available to obtain a similar military advantage to that offered by directing an act of hostility against that objective."

Canada acceded to the 1954 Hague Convention and First Protocol in December 1998. Canada acceded to the Second Protocol in November 2005. On 25 November 2005, Bill S-27, *An Act to amend the Criminal Code and the Cultural Property Export and Import Act*, received Royal Assent and came into force. Before acceding, Canada had already followed the principles of the 1954 Hague Convention and Protocols in accordance with customary international law. However, by acceding, Canada demonstrated its commitment to the protection of cultural property and enhanced the importance of the status of cultural property under domestic law.

The amendments in Bill S-37 allow for the return of cultural property that has been illegally exported from occupied territories or states that are High Parties to either of the Protocols of the 1954 Hague Convention. Bill S-37 also amends the *Criminal Code*, extending jurisdiction for numerous offences that are already a crime if committed against cultural property in Canada: theft, vandalism ("mischief" is used in the *Criminal Code*), robbery, arson, fraud and fraudulent concealment. If these acts are now committed outside Canada by a Canadian citizen (permanent residents of Canada, stateless persons residing in Canada) against cultural property as defined by the 1954 Hague Convention, they may be prosecuted in Canada under the *Criminal Code*.

As more and more market countries, such as the UK, Japan and Switzerland, sign on to the 1970 UNESCO Convention and the 1954 Hague Convention, there is hope that the illicit trafficking of cultural property can be halted in coming years.

CRIMINAL SANCTIONS

WHY STEAL ART?

O
ften, the art thief's motive is purely monetary. When a thief steals for money, what happens to the art depends on a number of factors. If the stolen piece is too famous, it is unmarketable. Even a crooked dealer will have no business with it. Works like this that are "too hot to handle" often end up on the black market, bartered for weapons and drugs. Alternatively, they can be held for ransom. The thief might even try to sell the art back to the owner's insurance company, which would rather buy back the art at a discounted rate than pay out the high insurance claim.[1]

Sometimes art is stolen on a lark by those who do not know that fencing these creations is, in fact, a specialized skill and, without the requisite knowledge of the players in the chain of offenders, the ignorant thieves end up dumping the stolen pieces and walking away. With luck, the pieces are recovered without too much damage. Other categories include insurance fraud or organized crime, the latter forming one of the reasons for which the FBI Art Crime Unit was established in the United States in 2005. Art theft is also intertwined and competes with other multi-billion dollar organized criminal activities such as drug trafficking.

Art thieves tend to think of their work as a bloodless hunt, a victimless crime, a convenient untruth. Many are victimized by art theft—not only the artist and the owner. The public also becomes a victim, both in their taxpayer dollars, when museums, by accepting illicit donations, allow donors to evade taxes, and in the loss of cultural experience and national identity. Art theft also results in higher insurance premiums that are now sufficiently prohibitive for both collectors and galleries, as much as 50% of art is uninsured.[2]

Experience demonstrates, moreover, that art theft is closely interlinked with violent crime. In fact, most art heists cannot be carried out without some degree of violence. Art thieves typically subdue museum guards using weapons and brute force. Other cases involve disturbing patterns of violence and domination of the weak, such as the recent case of Suzanne de Canson, whose caregiver imprisoned, restrained, and starved her to gain access to her valuable art collection.[3] Joelle Pesnel, who was a bar owner before becoming Suzanne de Canson's nurse, treated her so poorly that neighbours claimed to have heard cries for help. When her physical and mental health had sufficiently deteriorated, Pesnel tried to sell a painting by Bartolome Esteban Murillo entitled *The Gentleman of Seville* at Christie's in London for US$1.2 million. However, her attempt failed as a result of issues of title and complaints from French customs that the painting was illegally exported from France. The caregiver served ten years in France after being convicted of the murder of the heiress, and the painting now hangs in the Louvre.

Not only are many art crimes violent, but they are also linked to more nefarious activities, including terrorism. The Nazis relied on stolen artwork to fund their regime in the 1930s-40s; in the 1970s-80s, the IRA hit Alfred Beit's collection twice, stealing a total of 37 paintings, including ones by Rubens, Vermeer, and Goya. Now, with interest in Afghan antiquities on the rise, Germany's secret service has tied suspected 9/11 hijacker Mohamed Atta to the illicit trade of cultural property. According to Giuseppe Proietti, Secretary General of Italy's Ministry of Culture, the German secret service was informed of Atta's attempt to sell looted Afghan antiquities to a German archaeologist. Atta allegedly told the prospective buyer that he needed the money to enroll in flying lessons. The archaeologist declined and contacted German authorities.[4] Terrorists are using the art market to finance their illegal activities. A recent investigative report by *Spotlight* revealed how Afghanistan's cultural heritage is being exploited to finance terrorism and support the Taliban.[5] While many dealers in stolen cultural property are in it for the money, the most chilling art thief is the obsessed psychopath. Much like a stalker, this type of art thief has a sense of entitlement toward the art and is indifferent to the impact of his behaviour on the victim. The desire to possess a particular work of art that cannot be sold or shared comes from deep within the criminal psyche. The psychopathic art thief desires something that makes him feel sophisticated and refined, and replenishes some personal deficiency. Perhaps the thief feels the art is fragile and needs his protection; perhaps he steals to express his hatred of the snobby cultural establishment; maybe he craves the adrenaline high of the steal; or perhaps he simply wants to complete his collection and impress his wealthy friends. On the other hand, perhaps the thief's motive is far simpler—he steals the art because he loves it. Such was the case with Stephane Breitwieser.

Between 1995 and 2001, Breitwieser, a waiter who lived with his mother, stole US$1.4 billion worth of art. This means that, on average, he carried out one art heist every 15 days. His method was to cut paintings from their frames and walk out with them under his coat while his girlfriend caused a distraction. Like most psychopaths, Breitwieser was described as being an "outwardly ordinary person."[6] He was caught and arrested at the Richard Wagner Museum in Switzerland in November 2001. His mother destroyed the evidence, smashing, slashing, and throwing many of the works down the garbage disposal unit or into a nearby river. In the ensuing trial, Breitwieser explained that when he was not stealing, he had a feeling of emptiness that made him ill. In their desperate yearning for control and possession, art criminals like Breitwieser deprive the rest of the world of the enjoyment of art. Rare art fulfils the criminal's desire for power and control by giving him something that no one else has.

BEST PRACTICE GUIDELINES: WHAT TO DO IF YOU ARE ROBBED

The following are best practice guidelines for law enforcement, art galleries and collectors when dealing with theft or loss of art and antiquities. Taking the five steps outlined below will facilitate recovery and help to curb the illicit trafficking of cultural property.

1. File a police report, including a description of the stolen work that is as detailed and specific as possible
2. Register the theft with the FBI,[7] the Art Loss Register,[8] and Interpol[9]
3. Report the theft to Customs
4. Use the *Criminal Code*[10] wherever possible. (The American equivalent is the National Stolen Property Act (NSPA)[11])
5. Publicize the theft in every way possible, as one would do in the event of other thefts and losses. Undertake a PR campaign. Do not be embarrassed to speak to the press. Get photographs posted wherever possible. Secrecy only benefits the offender

Buyers of art must likewise take precautions in order not to be victimized by the acquisition of stolen art (see Due Diligence Checklist in Chapter 5). If you suspect something is amiss, ask questions. The relevant section of the Canadian *Criminal Code* is s. 354, which reads as follows:

> 354. (1) Every one commits an offence who has in his possession any property or thing or any proceeds of any property or thing knowing that all or part of the property or thing or of the proceeds was obtained by or derived directly or indirectly from
> (a) the commission in Canada of an offence punishable by indictment; or
> (b) an act or omission anywhere that, if it had occurred in Canada, would have constituted an offence punishable by indictment[12]

If the offence took place in another country, for example France or Germany, and it was not considered an offence under that jurisdiction but was considered so under Canadian law, then it is actionable under Canadian law. Furthermore, there is no statute of limitations under this section. It could therefore be used in cases of Nazi-looted art.

There are also criminal sanctions under the Canadian *Cultural Property Export and Import Act* (CPEIA).[13] Sections 45 and 46 read as follows:

> 45. (1) Every person who contravenes any of the provisions of subsection 36.1(2) and sections 40 to 44 is guilty of an offence and liable
>
> (a)   on summary conviction to a fine not exceeding five thousand dollars or imprisonment for a term not exceeding twelve months or to both; or
>
> (b)   on conviction on indictment to a fine not exceeding twenty-five thousand dollars or to imprisonment for a term not exceeding five years or to both.
>
> (2) A prosecution under paragraph (1)(*a*) may be instituted at any time within but not later than three years after the time when the subject-matter of the complaint arose.
>
> 46. Where a corporation commits and offence under this Act, any officer director or agent of the corporation who directed, authorized, assented to, acquiesced in or participated in the commission of the offence is a party to and guilty of the offence and is liable on summary conviction or on conviction on indictment to the punishment provided for the offence whether or not the corporation has been prosecuted or convicted.

If cultural property is illegally imported into Canada from another jurisdiction, there are criminal penalties under the CPEIA:

> 43. No person shall import or attempt to import into Canada any property that is illegal to import into Canada under subsection 37(2).

The definition of an illegal import is provided in s.37(2), which states,

> 37. (2) From and after the coming into force of a cultural property agreement in Canada and a reciprocating State, it is illegal to import into Canada any foreign cultural property that has been illegally exported from that reciprocating State.

BATA Shoe Museum Heist

A model example of what should be done when one's gallery or collection is robbed occurred in 2006, when a pair of precious eighteenth-century gem-encrusted slippers, which had once belonged to the first Prince of India, disappeared from the Bata Shoe Museum in Toronto, Ontario. The thief also made off with a gold toe ring and anklet. This case demonstrates the positive role public awareness can play in recovering stolen art. When the objects disappeared on January 22, 2006, the Museum publicized the theft with photos of the valuable shoes on the cover of national newspapers. The owner of a local photography shop recognized the stolen goods on a roll of film that the thief had dropped off for processing. The film also contained a picture of two women, which the shopkeeper sent to the *Globe and Mail,* which then published the photograph on the front page. The subjects of the photo soon came forward and revealed the identity of their photographer. The police contacted Miko Petric of Montenegro, who agreed to return the stolen goods by leaving them behind the doors of St. Paul's Church on Bloor Street. Petric was charged with theft over CDN$5000 and possession of property obtained by crime over CDN$5000. The prosecution sought jail time, but Provincial Court Judge Bonnie Croll sentenced Petric to 18 months of community service, 6 months of conditional house arrest and curfew, and ordered him to stay away from the Bata Shoe Museum.[14]

This case is instructive for a number of reasons: it demonstrates the importance of photographing art and antiquities; and it shows the importance of publicizing art theft—the more information given to the public, the greater the possibility of recovery. The media was a crucial factor leading to Petric's arrest, as the museum launched a nation-wide public relations campaign and offered a reward of $25,000 to spark the public's interest in the case. However, in the end, the lenient sentencing revealed the need for judges and lawyers to be properly briefed on the serious nature of the illicit art trade.

CRIMINAL SANCTIONS IN THE UNITED STATES

The looting of archeological material and works of art is theft. The United States Sentencing Commission has separate guidelines for cultural heritage resources that recognize the intangible value and irreplaceable nature of such resources and enhance the gravity of cultural property crimes.[15] The loss or destruction of cultural items is a community loss; the criminal, not society, should have to pay the penalty.

Liability in the United States can be divided into the following categories:

- The National Stolen Property Act
- The Archeological Resources Protection Act

- The Federal Anti-Smuggling Statute
- State laws for recovery of stolen property
- The Native American Grave Protection Repatriation Act
- Cultural Property Implementation Act
- Immigration and Customs Enforcement
- The Importation of Pre-Columbian Monumental or Architectural Sculpture or Murals Act
- The RICO Dragnet (Racketeer Influenced Corrupt Organization Act)

The National Stolen Property Act (NSPA)[16]

NSPA is the American federal law that governs dealings in stolen property. The relevant section states:

> Whoever receives, possesses, conceals, stores, barters, sells or disposes of any goods, wares, or merchandise… of the value of $5000 or more… which have crossed a State or United States boundary after being stolen, unlawfully converted, or taken, knowing the same to have been stolen, unlawfully converted, or taken… [s]hall be fined under this title or imprisoned not more than ten years, or both.[17]

Thus NSPA broadens the law's ability to prevent stolen goods from moving across the United States, as it makes it illegal to transport stolen items. Transporting stolen goods—not just theft itself—becomes illegal. By making it a criminal offence to receive stolen antiquities, NSPA not only stops crime in the United States but also deters looters of archaeological sites abroad.[18]

It is challenging to secure a conviction under NSPA as a result of its high burden of proof—because NSPA is under the criminal law, the prosecutor must prove all elements of the statute beyond a reasonable doubt to a unanimous 12-person jury. This might require testimony from expert witnesses regarding the value of the antiquity. Another challenge is to prove that the object in question was, in fact, stolen. To do this, prosecutors might rely on foreign patrimony laws that vest ownership of an antiquity with a particular nation. Alternatively, they might carry out a sting operation; an object is considered stolen when undercover police represent that it is stolen during a staged business deal.[19] Since NSPA is a criminal law, the defendant must satisfy the *mens rea* requirement of knowledge. Persuading the jury that the defendant *knew* the property was stolen is another challenge faced by the prosecutor.

Under NSPA, almost a quarter of the states contain provisions that make it easier to prosecute dealers. The New York City penal law, for example, holds dealers to a higher standard in section 165.55(2), which states:

> A ... person in the business of buying, selling, or otherwise dealing in property who possesses stolen property is *presumed to know* that such property was stolen if he obtained it without having ascertained by *reasonable inquiry* that the person from whom he obtained it had a legal right to possess it.[20]

A dealer or trader of art or antiquities thus has a greater duty of due diligence because of his heightened knowledge of the field.

NSPA is the statute most frequently used to prosecute art criminals. The next section in this chapter, heading (i) "Criminal Sanctions Under NSPA," outlines some of the major NSPA cases.

The Archeological Resources Protection Act (ARPA)[21]

ARPA has sections that allocate criminal responsibility for looting in antiquities and archeological material. ARPA was used in a 2008 raid of four American museums: the Los Angeles Museum of Art, the Pacific Asia Museum, the Bowers Museum, and the Mingei International Museum. The Southern California museums were raided after a five-year investigation into smuggled antiquities from Thailand, Myanmar (Burma), China, and Native American sites.[22] The IRS also became involved because appraisals for the donation values were discovered to be greatly inflated. The investigation began when a park ranger found people digging up Native American archeological and ethnographic material from national parks. This led him to discover that the same network of people was smuggling Taiwanese and Cambodian artifacts into the United States. This triggered the raid under ARPA.

The Federal Anti-Smuggling Statute[23]

This statute, first adopted in 1948, makes it a crime of strict liability to import, receive, conceal, buy, or sell any merchandise that is "contrary to law."[24] Items recovered under this statute are subject to forfeiture. Laws for dealing in forged documents and false statements (such as the Customs Act) also apply to art and archeological finds.[25]

State Laws for Recovery of Stolen Property

Transporting a stolen item from one state into another triggers federal laws. There are administrative laws governing non-profit organizations in the United States that stipulate that non-profit organizations must not deal in stolen property. The Attorney General's office in each state governs the conduct of non-profits. Museums can be subpoenaed and their conduct of practice reviewed. This is a powerful enforcement tool, which sometimes uncovers evidence that results in corollary allegations that non-profit organizations have used their funding improperly.

In 2006, Bill Lockyer, as Attorney General of California, investigated the Getty Museum for this reason. Among other improprieties, Lockyer discovered that the Getty Trust had paid for Trustee Barbara Fleischman's legal fees when she gave testimony and documents to Italian authorities in a related smuggling case. Lockyer explained his sentiments about the discovery, saying, "Charitable trusts such as the Getty are subsidized by taxpayers. They provide substantial benefits to society and add great value to our communities, but they must at all times spend money lawfully and to further their charitable purposes. Board members and executives have a legal duty to make sure that happens." He assured the public that "we are taking extraordinary measures to ensure that the board's recently adopted reforms take root."[26]

The Native American Grave Protection Repatriation Act (NAGPRA)[27]

NAGPRA is a federal law legislating the return of American Indian cultural property to the tribe from which it originated. It provides a process through which federally funded museums and other federal agencies can return certain Native American cultural items to their lineal descendents, culturally affiliated tribes, or Native Hawaiian organizations. The Act divides cultural property into human remains, funerary objects, sacred objects, and objects of cultural patrimony. Despite frequent theft of First Nations' cultural property, Canada has no such legislation.

Cultural Property Implementation Act (CPIA)[28]

Whereas NSPA is a criminal statute, CPIA is a civil remedy that authorizes the American government to seize illegally imported items. CPIA was enacted in 1983 to give force to the UNESCO Convention. CPIA "neither preempts State law in any way nor modifies any Federal or State remedies that may pertain to articles to which the provisions of this bill apply."[29] Lawmakers ensured, therefore, that CPIA would leave existing federal and state laws accessible to authorities to act against antiquities trafficking. Prosecutions under American law thus remained an option after CPIA was enacted in 1983. The FBI enforces CPIA through customs laws, and it applies when material is smuggled into the United States from foreign countries. CPIA's civil remedy is forfeiture of the unlawfully imported object. There has yet to be a prosecution that involved both CPIA and the criminal penalty of the smuggling statute, although the court in *Schultz*[30] pointed out the possibility of overlapping the two.[31]

Under CPIA, the President can enter into a bilateral agreement with a country that requests protection of its cultural heritage. The President can authorize the imposition of import restrictions and, if the importer of cultural material cannot show that the item was lawfully taken, it may be subject to seizure or forfeiture. Seizure of contraband has mostly been used for drugs, but it can also be used for stolen artifacts. In civil forfeiture cases, the state owning the item sues the receiving state for the confiscated item, which is repatriated.The owner state can seize anything the contraband touched (e.g., the helicopter, truck, house used for transport).

Antiquities collector/dealer Michael Steinhardt experienced seizure when he attempted to bring a gold phiale into the United States, falsely stating on his customs form that it was from Switzerland and worth $700,000, when in fact it was Italian and he paid over $1.2 million for it.[32] The Phiale was unlawful because it came into the United States by use of false statements. Forfeiture and repatriation is a civil remedy, driven by criminal law. In this case, the state used a criminal statute to recover the material (it is a crime to lie on a customs form). Although there was no criminal prosecution as such, the material was restituted to Italy following which the Italians prosecuted criminally. There was therefore a civil remedy for restitution of material, followed by criminal prosecution in another country. The Italian prosecution of Steinhardt failed on evidentiary grounds.

Immigration and Customs Enforcement (ICE)

ICE is responsible for conducting smuggling investigations for all forms of contraband. While narcotics comprise the most publicized aspect of ICE's work, it is also within the scope of ICE's duty to intercept contraband cultural property. If suspicious materials, such as cylinder seals, come through an airport, an ICE agent would govern the investigation. ICE tracks and seizes the illegal proceeds derived from smugglers' illegal activities, the goal being to dismantle the criminal organizations doing the smuggling.[33]

The Importation of Pre-Columbian Monumental or Architectural Sculpture or Murals Act[34]

This Act was enacted as a direct result of articles written by Clemency Coggins that exposed the extent of looting and destruction of Central American archeological material and the trafficking thereof into the United States. The Act protects stone carvings and wall art from pre-Columbian

Indian cultures of Mexico, Central America, South America, or the Caribbean Islands. Unless the American importer can prove that the item was exported lawfully, it will be confiscated and returned to its country of origin.

The Racketeer Influenced Corrupt Organization Act (RICO Dragnet)[35]

RICO is a federal law, enacted in 1970, that was originally intended to prosecute organized crime. It provides for extended criminal penalties and a civil cause of action for acts performed as part of an ongoing criminal organization. It has not yet been applied to cultural property crimes but could theoretically be used for any crime involving a network of criminals trading in illegal material. Under RICO, everybody in a given criminal network can be charged under conspiracy and accomplice laws.

For a full definition of racketeering crimes, see Appendix 17 of the statute. Notable racketeering activities include robbery, bribery, extortion, theft from interstate shipment, engaging in transactions in property derived from illegal activity, and interstate transportation of stolen property.[36] Mail fraud and wire fraud are also included, which can be relevant in some art crimes.

The *Antiques Roadshow* case combined wire and mail fraud with art crime.[37] Russ Pritchard III, an appraiser on the popular PBS television show, informed several elderly guests that their Civil War memorabilia— including swords, firearms, and uniforms—were worth far less than their real value. He then would convince the guests to sell the items to him at the low price at which he had appraised them. His next step would be to re-sell the items to museums at their higher actual market value. He and his two accomplices perpetrated historical memorabilia fraud at a value of US$1.2 million. In December 2001, Russ Pritchard III pleaded guilty to more than 20 counts, including mail fraud, wire fraud, and interstate transportation of stolen property.[38]

One of the reasons prosecutors are not inclined to prosecute in cultural property cases is because of how the laws are codified. When lawyers deal with a specific statute every day, they become familiar with that legislation.

But when a lawyer works in cultural property law, it is necessary to go to numerous statutes and codes. Tackling art crime is complicated mainly for reasons of technical legal issues, which partly explains why there have not been many prosecutions in the field.

Another reason it is difficult to punish art criminals in both Canada and the United States is the lack of public knowledge concerning the issue. It is not possible to achieve successful prosecutions in art and cultural heritage crimes without public support, which will not come about without education as a foundation. Sometimes prosecutors can play a role in educating the public. For example, in both the United States and Canada (and elsewhere), prosecutors, police, legislators, and others affiliated with the justice system have successfully educated the public concerning menaces, such as drunk driving or domestic violence, which were once considered essentially non-criminal activities. Canada has further to go than many jurisdictions in the United States regarding education concerning violence against women, or other instances of domestic violence, through the trial process; however, as with driving under the influence of alcohol, both domestic violence and crimes related to the abuse of cultural heritage will, with consistent and coordinated messaging and education, become part of what the public understands to be criminal behaviours. This process will be significantly enhanced in both cases when the prosecution works in cooperation with other education and outreach programs.

Criminal Sanctions Under NSPA

In addition to seizing and repatriating stolen cultural property, authorities can send a strong message to criminals and reduce the trafficking of illicit art and antiquities by using the criminal law. The United States has had only three successful prosecutions under the NSPA, a number that can hardly provide any meaningful deterrent.[39]

The first cultural property theft conviction under NSPA arose in 1974 in *United States v. Hollinshead*.[40] Clive Hollinshead, a dealer in pre-Columbian artifacts, conspired with a man named Alamilla to procure a rare item known as Machaquila Stele 2 from Central America. Funded by Hollinshead, Alamilla found the Stele in a Mayan ruin in the jungle of Guatemala.

He then cut it into pieces and sent it to the fish packing plant of the co-accused, Johnnie Brown Fell, in Belize. Fell packed the pieces in boxes labelled "personal effects" and shipped them to Miami. He and another co-conspirator, a person called Dwyer, picked up the artifacts in Miami and attempted unsuccessfully to sell them to various collectors and museums. They crossed a number of state lines in the process, travelling with the Stele to Georgia, New York, Wisconsin, and South Carolina. It eventually landed in Hollinshead's hands in California, where he attempted to sell it. After their conviction, Hollinshead and Fell appealed. One point that the court considered on appeal was whether the judge had erred in instructing the jury that every person is presumed to know the law. The defendants asserted that the instruction was overly broad; since the theft occurred in Guatemala, they argued, the judge should have added the caveat that there is no presumption that everyone has knowledge of *foreign* laws.

Although Judge Duniway conceded that the trial judge's failure to clarify the issue of knowledge of foreign laws "may have been an error," he held that it was not prejudicial given the overwhelming evidence that Hollinshead and Fell were aware that their actions were contrary to Guatemalan law. The case's important conclusion is that it is not necessary for the prosecutor to prove under NSPA that the culprits knew the law of the place where the theft occurred. As Judge Duniway concluded, such knowledge "is relevant only to the extent that it bears upon the issue of their [the defendants'] knowledge that the stele was stolen."[41]

Three years later, NSPA was used again to prosecute as criminal traffickers in stolen property American citizens who brought pre-Columbian objects into the United States from Latin America. In *United States v. McClain*,[42] several dealers were convicted for conspiring to deal in stolen Mexican antiquities. At issue in the case was whether Mexican legislation from 1972 that nationalized pre-Columbian artifacts within the country's borders created government ownership rights that would come under NSPA's auspices.

In 1974, an FBI informant approached American art dealer Patty McClain and her four co-defendants in San Antonio, Texas. He purported to represent an international combine with Mafia connections seeking to purchase pre-Columbian artifacts in the United States, which they could re-sell abroad. McClain and her co-defendants told the informant (who was later joined by an FBI Agent on the case) that they did indeed deal in pre-Columbian objects and explained that they were expecting a shipment of artifacts through Mexico at the California border in the coming days. Before the shipment even arrived, McClain and her colleagues offered to sell the FBI Agent a number of pre-Columbian objects she had on hand in Texas. They were arrested the next day and charged under NSPA for receiving, concealing, and selling stolen goods that had been transported in interstate or foreign commerce. On top of this, they were charged with conspiracy to violate NSPA. Because the case contained two separate charges, and because of evidential problems, it made its way through the courts slowly.

In *McClain I*, the Fifth Circuit reversed the convictions and sent the case back for a new trial on account of conflicting expert testimony. The issue on appeal was whether the artifacts that the FBI Agent had "purchased" from McClain were stolen merchandise within the meaning of NSPA. It was uncertain at what date Mexico vested ownership of all pre-Columbian artifacts in its government, bringing cultural patrimony laws into effect. The prosecution contended that Mexico's government owned all pre-Columbian artifacts within the country because of a series of five statutes enacted between 1897 and 1972. The defendants, on the other hand, claimed to have purchased the items legally from the private Mexican citizens who owned them. In *McClain I*, the court held that the Mexican government did not definitively vest ownership of pre-Columbian antiquities in the government until 1972. This meant that only artifacts imported after June 5, 1972, the date of the most recent statute, could be considered to have been stolen from the government for the purposes of the NSPA.

At the second trial there was, once again, conflicting evidence concerning Mexico's cultural property laws. The Court in *McClain II* reversed the conviction for the substantive count of violating NSPA on the grounds that the jury had not been instructed to ignore the pre-1972 statutes, but upheld the conviction for conspiracy, since the defendants had attempted to bring in a new load of illicit artifacts.

Although the prosecution in *McClain* failed to secure a conviction for violation of NSPA, it is instructive in its shortcomings. Looking at the court's reasons for reversing the original convictions, the lesson to be drawn from *McClain* is that nations must take steps to protect their cultural heritage. Foreign nations need to adopt unambiguous laws declaring national ownership of cultural property within their borders. Moreover, they need to enact laws prohibiting the export of such property so that American authorities can prosecute violators of the export ban as transporters of stolen property under NSPA.

After *McClain*, NSPA lay dormant in the cultural property world for nearly 30 years. It would not be used again until the landmark case of *United States v. Frederick Schultz*.[43] In 2002, Frederick Schultz was convicted for his role in illegally importing and selling stolen Egyptian antiquities. Schultz' conviction of one count of conspiracy to receive stolen property that had been transported in interstate and foreign commerce, in violation of 18 U.S.C., s 371. The underlying substantive offence was a violation of 18 U.S.C., s. 2315 of the National Stolen Property Act.

During the 1990s, Schultz was at the peak of his career as a preeminent antiquities art dealer based in New York City, president of the National Association of Dealers in Ancient, Oriental, and Primitive Art (NADAOPA), advisor to the Cultural Property Advisory Committee in Washington (under the Clinton Administration), and owner of the Frederick Schultz Ancient Art Gallery in Manhattan, a district at the centre of a robust and lucrative illicit antiquities trade.

Schultz was providing funding to the operations of Jonathan Tokeley-Parry, who was a conservator-restorer by training, and a UK smuggler who served three years in prison from 1997 to 2000. Schultz bought stolen antiquities from him and sold them at a profit. With the assistance of Egyptian smugglers Ali and Toutori Farag, Tokeley-Parry illegally removed more than 2000 Egyptian antiquities from Egypt, most of which he sold to Frederick Schultz. He painted antiquities with gaudy colours in an effort to trick officials into thinking that ancient antiquities, such as the magnificent marble sculpted head of the pharaoh Amenhotep III, were actually chintzy tourist souvenirs. He also tried to fool authorities by manufacturing fictional provenances for these stolen antiquities, claiming the pieces derived from the "Thomas Alcock" collection, named after Tokeley-Parry's great uncle.[44] He also produced forged documentation and labels to back this false information in order to make the antiquities look as though they had departed Egypt before the key date of 1983, when that nation passed vesting ownership laws.[45]

Despite an abundance of incriminating evidence, such as the impeccable written records kept by Tokeley-Parry, including diaries and explanations related to the fictional provenances, Schultz managed to mount an effective defence. The prosecution put up a difficult fight to obtain a conviction. Substantial support in the Unites States for these activities became apparent when the National Association of Dealers in Ancient, Oriental and Primitive Art (NADAOPA) and Christie's Auction House filed amicus briefs showing their support of Shultz's activities.

In 1994, Tokeley-Parry had been exposed when a British Museum employee alerted Scotland Yard to the fact that they had been asked to authenticate a papyrus that had been stolen from an Egyptian storage unit. Investigators searched the estate of Andrew May, who had delivered the stolen goods. The search led them to Tokeley-Parry's workshop, where they discovered photos of his smuggling activities and more stolen antiquities. In addition to all of this, Tokeley-Parry arrived during the search with another antiquity in his suitcase, which he tried to explain away as a chance find in the desert.

The prosecution was successful in proving that Schultz received stolen property and resold it. He purchased the head of eighteenth Dynasty Pharaoh Amenhotep III for US$900,000 and then sold it for US$1.2 million, knowing that the object was looted. This action resulted in his conviction in 2002, which he appealed in 2003.[46] The conviction was subsequently upheld the same year. He claimed that he did not conduct this business knowingly, that is, that he was not aware that the objects were illicit. This brings to the forefront the concept of "wilful blindness" as it is known in Canada, or "conscious avoidance" as it is known in the United States, with respect to the notion of criminal intent.

At the trial, Judge Rakoff presented the jury with the following instructions:

> A defendant may not purposefully remain ignorant of either the facts or law in order to escape the consequences of the law. Therefore, if you [the jury] find that the defendant, not by mere negligence or imprudence but as a matter of choice, consciously avoided

learning what Egyptian law provided as to ownership of Egyptian antiquities, you may [infer], if you wish, that he did so because he implicitly knew that there was a high probability that the law of Egypt vested ownership of these antiquities in the Egyptian government. You may treat such deliberate avoidance of positive knowledge as the equivalent of such knowledge, unless you find that the defendant actually believed that the antiquities were not the property of the Egyptian government.[47]

In *United States v. Draves*,[48] Judge Eschbach articulated the so-called "ostrich doctrine," describing that:

...knowledge may be inferred from a combination of suspicion and indifference to the truth. If you [the jury] find that the defendant had a strong suspicion that things were not what they seemed or that someone had withheld some important facts, yet shut his eyes for fear of what he would learn, you may conclude that he acted "knowingly" [...] This type of ostrich instruction is appropriately given when the defendant claims he had no guilty knowledge of the illegal activity yet the evidence supports an inference that defendant had a strong suspicion of wrongdoing, yet made a deliberate effort to avoid guilty knowledge by "burying his head in the sand."

Therefore, by deliberately maintaining ignorance of the illegality, the defendant is implicitly realizing that what he is doing is illegal. In Schultz's case this holds especially true, given the antiquities trade was his area of expertise and his livelihood. The defendant was an extremely experienced art dealer specializing in antiquities and could not therefore credibly claim that he was unaware of the law. His livelihood depended on his knowledge in the field. As well, his written correspondence with Tokeley-Parry demonstrated that they were conniving to violate Egyptian law by illegally removing and concealing these objects complete with fictional provenances.

CRIMINAL SANCTIONS IN CANADA UNDER THE CULTURAL PROPERTY EXPORT IMPORT ACT (CPEIA)

Canada does not have such numerous means for punishing art criminals as the United States; only CPEIA has ever been used in Canadian art crime cases.[49] One shortcoming that demands swift remedy is the fact that Canada has no equivalent to the United States' NAGPRA. This leaves First Nations material particularly vulnerable to thieves, as it is in high demand on the international market and retrieval is nearly impossible. One example of the First Nations' inability to recover their artistic heritage is the case involving Blackfoot Crossing Historical Park. President Jack Royal describes the struggle to recover sacred items taken, legally or otherwise, from the tribe years ago: "You almost feel helpless. Because if there's no policy or legislation or funds to support bringing it home, the Nation can't afford to buy everything back." The museum built up a catalogue of missing Blackfoot artifacts and prioritized the items they hoped to retrieve as quickly as possible. Royal acknowledges that, with Blackfoot artifacts having made their way across the globe, retrieval will be challenging and costly. "It's a big task," he admits. "We're talking about artifacts in London and Germany and France and the United States and Canada."[50]

Sometimes, First Nations artifacts seem to mysteriously disappear. In 2003, boxes containing stone tools, pots, and animal bones dating back to the fifteenth century went missing from a tunnel where they were being stored at the University of Toronto's Scarborough campus.[51] The native peoples had trusted the university to preserve their heritage. There was little media coverage of the incident, and nothing was ever recovered from these mysterious disappearances. Police and government made little effort to recover the materials, which they claimed had ended up in an American garbage dump. Where the artifacts really ended up is an unsolved question. There is no repository for native archaeological items.

One possible remedy yet to be attempted would be the victimized First Nations group to bring a civil action of conversion against the entity in possession of its cultural property. As explained by Iacobucci J., the tort of conversion "involves a wrongful interference with the goods of another, such as taking, using or destroying these goods in a manner inconsistent with the owner's right of possession."[52] Conversion is a common law tort of strict liability; thus, although the dispossession must arise through the defendant's intentional actions, "it is no defence that the wrongful act was committed in all innocence."[53] As the civil counterpart to the crime of theft, conversion does not require an element of dishonesty or *mens rea.*

Though it has yet to be done in an art law case, it would also be potentially possible to charge an art or antiquities smuggler under s. 340 of the *Criminal Code*, which prohibits the destruction of documents of title for fraudulent purposes.

Criminal prosecutions in the field of stolen art and antiquities are even more rare and difficult in Canada than in the United States; however, as public awareness of the value of cultural heritage increases, there is greater interest in such prosecutions. A successful prosecution requires an understanding of the nuances of white-collar crime in the art world and the means by which business is conducted. It also requires perseverance and dogged determination on the part of the Crown and investigators, who seem to be fighting against all odds.

CPEIA contains provisions that make it a criminal offence to import cultural property into Canada from another country that is a signatory to the UNESCO Convention. The penalty is a fine of up to CDN$25,000, imprisonment, or both. The major notable criminal conviction under the CPEIA was *R. v. Yorke.*[54] Yorke was (and still is) a dealer of antique textiles who was charged with illegally importing into Canada cultural property from another signatory nation of the 1970 UNESCO Convention.

An examination of this case is instructive for prosecutions in this field. In July 1988, the Canadian Customs Agency seized a parcel mailed to Roger Yorke from Bolivia to Canada. It contained a textile that was declared as a gift with a value of US$100. Yorke had been under surveillance by Canadian Customs for many months. After the arrival of this fragment, customs began to monitor his activities closely. Customs learned that Yorke was a collector of and dealer in pre-Columbian, Bolivian, and Peruvian artifacts. It was also learned that the shawl fragment in the parcel was a ceremonial cloth that had been an exhibit in an American grand jury investigation for Stephen Berger, a former business partner of Yorke's. In August 1988, customs officials and members of the RCMP searched Yorke's residence and seized more than 6000 items, of both Bolivian and Peruvian origins. These were seized as items in contravention of both the *Customs Act* (for false declarations and under-evaluation) and CPEIA (illegal import of foreign cultural property). Of the 6000 items seized, five categories were identified:

1. woven textile clothing from northern Bolivia, representing the Aymara weaving tradition,
2. material from the nineteenth century,
3. material produced in the first half of the twentieth century,
4. recently produced textiles for tourists, and
5. several metal objects and stone carvings, believed to be Pre-Columbian.

An archaeologist from the University of Calgary and a textile conservator from the Canadian Conservation Institute in Ottawa examined the collection in the temporary holding cell at RCMP headquarters. They advised authorities that the collection should be moved to storage facilities with museum standard environmental conditions to ensure the preservation of these objects. A warehouse with appropriate temperature and humidity controls was found to which the items were transferred. The next step was to have the objects identified and dated by an expert in Bolivian and Peruvian cultural property. This was done for two reasons: to determine exactly what had been seized so accurate descriptions could be provided to Bolivian and Peruvian governments; and to determine if the objects were subject to export restrictions in Bolivia and Peru. Bolivia defines cultural property as objects made before 1900 and Peru prohibits the export of objects made before 1929. Finding someone with sufficient expertise to examine the collection proved difficult. An expert was finally found in the United States who had conducted similar work for United States Customs who agreed to examine all 6000 items. In her evaluation, 625 of the objects were "cultural property" as defined by Bolivia and Peru. The other roughly 5400 objects were of more recent manufacture and not considered to be of cultural significance. As in *Schultz*, the importer mixed antiquities with less valuable modern products in an attempt to avoid suspicion. Antiquities are making their way through Dubai from Syria and Iraq in a similar fashion.

In July 1989, it was discovered that the textile collection seized from Yorke was infested with moths. The senior textile conservator and conservationist from the Canadian Conservation Institute examined the collection and advised that only one woven bag was contaminated with moth larvae. The non-cultural property contained both moth larvae and adult moths, and it was necessary therefore to vacuum by hand all 6000 objects. They were then placed individually in plastic bags and returned to storage. In July 1990, further evidence of moth presence was discovered. This time, the collection was sprayed with Vapona 20%, a powerful insecticide. Moth larvae again were discovered and sprayed in October 1990, at which point it was decided that the only way to ensure that there would be no further infestations would be to freeze the entire collection.

The preliminary inquiry was held from September to December 1990. In October, the government of Peru advised that it did not wish to proceed with the case and would not be sending expert witnesses, a decision probably based on the expense of sending an expert witness. Yorke was committed to stand trial for illegal import of Bolivian cultural property, though the judge ruled that Peruvian law was not specific enough in its definition of cultural property to meet the requirements of Canadian law. Although Yorke was not committed to trial for the Peruvian material, it was not returned to him; instead, it was seized under the *Customs Act* for alleged under-evaluation.

The trial for the illegal importation of Bolivian cultural property was scheduled to begin in September 1991. However, in August, Yorke succeeded with a motion to have the trial order quashed. In overturning the lower court's decision, the Supreme Court of Nova Scotia ruled that Yorke had been prohibited from asking certain questions in preparing his defence during the preliminary inquiry. The Crown successfully appealed this ruling to the Supreme Court of Nova Scotia Appeal Division, and the trial was scheduled to begin October 1991. Yorke then obtained an adjournment so he could seek leave to appeal to the Supreme Court of Canada, which dismissed his application. The trial was rescheduled for April 1992. Before it could begin, Yorke's counsel filed a motion to challenge the search and seizure as a violation of the *Canadian Charter of Rights and Freedoms*. The motion contended that the search warrant was illegal because it had been obtained using a section of the *Customs Act* that had since been declared unconstitutional, and that the warrant did not specify what the police were looking for nor that the goods would be found at Yorke's residence. The court agreed to dismiss all charges against Yorke. The Crown appealed to the Supreme Court of Nova Scotia and a new trial was again ordered. Yorke then sought leave to appeal this decision to the Supreme Court of Canada to pursue the argument that the search and seizure violated the *Charter of Rights*. This time he was granted right to appeal and in October 1993 the Court ruled that the search and seizure did not violate the *Charter*.[55] Further arguments were brought in June 1994 but were dismissed by the Supreme Court of Nova Scotia. The trial took place from September-December 1994. In June 1996, the Honourable Justice N. Robert Anderson found Roger Yorke guilty as charged. On August 29, 1996, he was fined $10,000 and sentenced to 2 years' probation. This was the first conviction for illegal import of foreign cultural property under CPEIA, and it remains the only one as of March 2010.

Since *Yorke*, there have been numerous restitutions of stolen cultural property back to their countries of origin but no further criminal prosecutions. In fact, there are sometimes positive consequences for thieves instead of the negative ones they deserve. In 2008, when several gold pieces by the late Haida native artist Bill Reid disappeared from the University of British Columbia's Museum of Anthropology, the RCMP did not lay charges and also paid the criminal to retrieve the stolen goods. Actions like this propagate the illicit trafficking trade by rewarding criminal behaviour. White-collar criminals respond to fear of incarceration. Until the negative consequences of stealing antiquities become more severe, the illegal trade will continue to thrive.

Canada and Wilful Blindness

While the "ostrich doctrine" of wilful blindness was applied by the court in *Schultz*, it has yet to be used in a Canadian art law case. The Canadian criminal law requires *mens rea*, or a guilty mind, as an element of any criminal offence. Having said this, can a person hide behind the excuse of being an innocent buyer? Under s. 354 of the *Criminal Code*,

> everyone commits an offence who has in his possession any property or thing… knowing that all or part of the property… was derived directly or indirectly from an act or omission anywhere that, if it had occurred in Canada, would have constituted an offence punishable by indictment.

The question is: What is "knowingly" for the purposes of the *Criminal Code*? What if a person has a suspicion of questionable provenance of a painting but asks no questions? Is he safe from criminal prosecution?

The answer was articulated in 1995 in *R. v. Jorgensen*,[56] which outlines the conduct that constituted wilful blindness.

> Deliberately choosing not to know something when given reason to believe further inquiry is necessary can satisfy the mental element of the offence [...] A finding of wilful blindness involves an affirmative answer to the question: Did the accused shut his eyes because he knew or strongly suspected that looking would fix him with knowledge?

Judge Doherty for the Ontario Court of Appeal reasserted this principle in *R v. Duong*, explaining that "actual suspicion, combined with a conscious decision not to make inquiries which could confirm that suspicion, is equated in the eyes of the criminal law with actual knowledge."[57] As a concept of *mens rea*, wilful blindness applies to all criminal offences, including those involving theft of art.

In another situation, it is possible that the alleged thief held an honest belief that he owned the artifact in question. In such a case, colour of right might afford a defence against theft. An example of such a case would be a Holocaust survivor "stealing back" art that was stolen from him by Nazi looters. Though such a case has yet to be tried, the *Criminal Code*'s definition of theft ostensibly allows for such a defence. Section 322 incorporates a lack of colour of right as an element of the offence of theft.

> 322. (1) Every one commits theft who fraudulently and without colour of right takes, or fraudulently and without colour of right converts to his use or to the use of another person, anything, whether animate or inanimate, with intent…

Colour of right is similar to the defence of mistake of fact, as opposed to mistake of law which, under s. 19, does not excuse criminal behaviour. In *R. v. Wright*, the Alberta Court of Queen's Bench held that "where an accused has an honest belief in a state of fact which, if actually existing, would justify the act done, the acts are done under colour of right which is a complete defence to the charges."[58] To return to the earlier example, if the Holocaust survivor honestly believed that he was the owner of the art in question, he would lack the *mens rea* for theft, as one cannot steal what one owns.

SUMMARY OF INTERNATIONAL STOLEN ART DATABASES

Many jurisdictions and organizations are attempting to track stolen art. Undoubtedly these databases will assist in the recovery and return of a great many treasures.

Jonathan Sazanoff's SAZTV.com: www.saztv.com

One of the most comprehensive sites in the field of stolen art covers art recovery and how to report stolen art, recent updates in the field, and links to stolen art research websites. Additionally it contains an index of art crime listed by country and artist, lists of record sale prices for artists and summarizes major art thefts and recoveries.

Royal Canadian Mounted Police: Sûreté du Québec Art Crime Unit

The Sûreté du Québec, in conjunction with the RCMP, has a new Art Crime Unit as of January 2009. They send data on stolen works of art regularly to a list server. This much-welcomed unit works in Montreal, Quebec. It is hoped that other units will also include the rest of the country, especially Vancouver, Calgary, Toronto, and Halifax.

London Metropolitan Police Department: The London Stolen Arts Database

The London Stolen Arts Database (LSAD) (www.met.police.uk/artandantiques/index.htm) contains images and details of 54,000 items of stolen art and antiquities. Searches of the database may be requested by contacting the Art and Antiques Unit. Certificates are issued proving that a check was completed for due diligence purposes. The database includes the following categories: paintings, furniture, books, maps, manuscripts, carpets, rugs, clocks, watches, coins, medals, glass, ivory, jade, musical instruments, postage stamps, pottery, porcelain, silver, gold, textiles, and toys and games.

International Council of Museums: ICOM Red List

The Red List (icom.museum/redlist/) includes categories of archaeological items particularly prone to looting.

African Archaeological Objects
- Nok terracotta from the Bauchi Plateau and the Katsina and Sokoto regions (Nigeria)
- Terracotta and bronzes from Ife (Nigeria)
- Esie stone statues (Nigeria)
- Terracotta, bronzes and pottery from the Niger Valley (Mali)
- Terracotta statuettes, bronzes, potteries, and stone statues from the Bura System (Niger, Burkina Faso)
- Stone statues from the North of Burkina Faso and neighbouring regions
- Terracotta from the North of Ghana (Komaland) and Côte d'Ivoire
- Terracotta and bronzes so-called Sao (Cameroon, Chad, Nigeria)

Latin-American Cultural Objects

1. Pre-Columbian Objects
    ◾ Ceramics: Maya Polychrome Vessels, Urns from the Amazon River Region, Moche Vessels from Peru, Nayarit Figures from Mexico, Jama Coaque Figures and Vessels from Ecuador
    ◾ Lithics: Openwork Grindstones, Maya Stelae, Teotihuacan Masks from Mexico, San Agustin Statues from Colombia
    ◾ Jade: Hacha [axe] Pendants, Olmec Figurines from México, Maya Pendants
    ◾ Metals: Tumaco-Tolita Masks, Eagle Pendants
    ◾ Wood: Inca Keros, Snuff Trays, Carved Oars from Peru
    ◾ Textiles: Nasca, Chimu and Wari Feather Weavings from Peru, Paracas, Wari, Chimu and Chancay Textiles from Peru

2. Colonial Objects
    ◾ Sculpture: Colonial Religious Sculptures, Ivory Christ from Mexico, Corn-Stem Paste Figures from Mexico
    ◾ Painting: Mexican and Guatemalan Paintings, Cuzco and Quito Paintings
    ◾ Silver Crafts: Liturgical Silver Objects

Iraqi Antiquities

◾ Tablets of clay or stone with cuneiform writing
◾ Cones and any other objects with cuneiform writing
◾ Cylinder seals of stone, shell, frit, etc.
◾ Stamp seals of stone, shell, etc., and their impressions
◾ Ivory, bone plaques and sculptures
◾ Sculpture, 3-dimensional and relief
◾ Vessels/Containers (large or small)
◾ Jewellery, carved gems and personal adornments
◾ Manuscripts, calligraphy, books and archival documents
◾ Architectural and furniture fragments
◾ Coins

Afghanistan Antiquities

1. Pre-Islamic Period
- Ancient pottery/ceramics
- Early metal artifacts
- Cosmetic jars of metal
- Bactrian statuettes
- Reliquaries
- Stone batons (scepters)
- Stone weights
- Seals
- Ivories
- Coins
- Manuscripts
- Fragments of wall paintings
- Buddhist sculpture
2. Islamic Period
- Manuscripts
- Metalwork
- Tiles
- Pottery/Ceramics
- Architectural elements

Peruvian Antiquities

1. Pre-Columbian Period
- Textiles
- Metals
- Ceramics
- Semi-precious stones
- Stone
- Wood
- Fossils
- Human remain

2. Colonial and Republican Period
- Ethnographic objects
- Paintings
- Sculpture
- Silvercraft
- Numismatics
- Furniture
- Drawings and engravings
- Textiles
- Documents
- Ceramics

INTERPOL Stolen Works of Art

This is a DVD series consisting of six discs and an up-to-date website detailing materials stolen from around the world. It is available in English, French or Spanish at (www.interpol.int/Public/WorkOfArt/Default.asp).

US State Department

This site (culturalheritage.state.gov/) covers issues such as the problem of pillage. It provides: commentary on the purpose of the United States law that implements the 1970 UNESCO Convention (Excerpt from Senate Report No. 97-564); news stories and press releases on discoveries, repatriations, and prosecutions; documents relating to United States customs import restrictions by country; charts of current and expired import restrictions with image databases; and links to United States and international law enforcement agencies and non-governmental organizations.

Detailed databases are available for the following materials:

1. Mali: List of archaeological artifacts from the Niger River Valley Region, Mali, and the Bandiagara Escarpment (Cliff), Mali;
2. Nicaragua: Pre-Columbian archaeological materials from Nicaragua representing Prehispanic Cultures ranging in date approximately from 8000 BC to 1500 AD;

3. Honduras: Designated list of Pre-Colombian archaeological material from Honduras;
4. Guatemala: Designated list of materials including ceramic/terracotta/fired clay, stone, metal, shell, and animal bone;
5. El Salvador: Illustrative list of categories of Prehispanic archaeological objects from the Cara Sucia Archaeological Region;
6. Columbia: Categories of objects from Colombia designated for protection from importation into the United States including: Archaeological materials (c.1500 BC-1530 AD) and ecclesiastical ethnological materials (1530-1830 AD);
7. Bolivia: List of archaeological and ethnological materials from Bolivia;
8. Cyprus: List of archaeological objects from Cyprus representing pre-classical and classical periods ranging in date from approximately the eighth millennium BC to approximately 330 AD; and
9. Italy: Import restrictions imposed on archaeological material originating in Italy and representing the Pre-Classical, Classical, and Imperial Roman Periods.

FBI Art Crime Unit: National Stolen Art File

The website (www.fbi.gov/hq/cid/arttheft/arttheft.htm) introduces the Art Crime Team. It provides links to the National Stolen Art File, summarizes jurisdiction and legislation, and posts theft notices and recoveries by geographic region. It provides resources, famous cases and stories, Top Ten Art Crimes List, and information on recent thefts. The National Stolen Art File (NSAF) indexes stolen art and cultural property as reported by law enforcement agencies throughout the world. It consists of images and physical descriptions of stolen and recovered objects, and includes investigative case information. The NSAF aids law enforcement officials with investigations concerning art and cultural artifact crime.

To be eligible for entry into the NSAF, an object must fit the following criteria: the object must be uniquely identifiable and have historical or artistic significance; and be valued at at least US$2,000 (or less if associated with a major crime). The request for entry on the file must come through a law enforcement agency accompanied by a physical description of the object, a photograph of the object if available, and a copy of any police reports or other information relevant to the investigation. All requests for searches of the National Stolen Art File must be made through a law enforcement agency in support of a criminal investigation. Individuals or organizations in the United States wanting to access the NSAF should contact their local FBI office. Foreign organizations should contact an FBI Legal Attaché office.

Art Loss Register and Trace

The recent merger of these formerly separate databases has consolidated the two at <www.artloss.com> in order to form a new international centre for due diligence searching and for registration by insurers and victims of theft. The ALR's services are provided by trained art experts. Some of the services the ALR offers include: registration of the legitimate ownership of works of art and other valuable possessions; registration of the loss of works of art and other valuable possessions; registration of fake and forged works of art and other valuable possessions; due diligence services; expert provenance research of works of art and other valuable possessions; specialist World War II provenance research; and investigative and recovery work.

The ALR can be used by collectors, auction houses, art dealers, art fairs, museums, financial institutions, law enforcement agencies, government authorities, or private individuals.

The Lost Art Database

The Lost Art Database (www.lostart.de) is run by the Koordinierungsstelle für Kulturgutverluste. It is Germany's central office for the documentation of lost cultural property. It was set up jointly by the government and the Länder of the Federal Republic of Germany, and registers cultural objects that, as a result of persecution under the Nazi dictatorship and the Second World War, were relocated, moved, or seized, especially from Jewish owners.

Project for the Documentation of Wartime Cultural Losses

This site (docproj.loyola.edu/) contains official reports on the Nazis' seizure of cultural property in France, Russia, Europe, Occupied Territories, Neutral countries, and Latin America.

Holocaust-Era Assets

This site (www.ushmm.org/assets/index.html) contains an international list of current activities regarding Holocaust-era assets. This is a project of the United States Holocaust Memorial Museum in conjunction with the Washington Conference on Holocaust-Era Assets.

Holocaust Assets: US State Department

This site (www.state.gov/www/regions/eur/holocausthp.html) contains links to American government documents relating to Holocaust-era assets, including looted art.

Presidential Commission on Holocaust Assets in the United States

This site (www.holocaustassets.gov/) presents a historical record of the collection and disposition of the assets of Holocaust victims that came into the possession or control of the government of the United States.

The Schloss Collection: Non-restituted Works Looted 1943-1998

The French Ministry of Foreign Affairs has published on its website (www.france.diplomatie.fr/archives/dossiers/schloss/index_ang.html) the catalogue of Dutch and Flemish art stolen from Adolphe Schloss' collection during World War II. Adolphe Schloss was an internationally renowned art collector with one of the last great collections of Dutch art in nineteenth-century France. The online catalogue only lists the works not restituted by July 1, 1997. The research may be made on the whole collection and by the name of painters.

Bruno Kreisky Archives Foundation

This is a database (www.kreisky.org/) of art looted by the Nazi regime in Austria. It includes an article by Oliver Rathkolb on restitution policies and a list of privately owned artworks still missing.

Enemy Property: The British Government Claims Scheme

This is a site (www.enemyproperty.gov.uk/) based in the United Kingdom that contains details of the claims scheme and how to apply. It also has summary details of records held at the Public Record Office relating to United Kingdom property seized during World War II from organizations and individuals resident in countries with which the United Kingdom was at war.

Central Registry of Information on Looted Cultural Property 1933-1945

This site (www.lootedart.com/) provides a range of resources to advance knowledge of the cultural spoliation of Europe by the Nazi regime and the fate of the families, objects, and institutions which were its target. The Central Registry is designed to be of use to anyone interested in this subject and will be continually expanded.

Origins Unknown

After the war, the Stichting Nederlandsch Kunstbezit (SNK) returned many of the recovered works of Nazi looted art to their rightful owners on behalf of the Dutch State. Nevertheless, there is still a large number of works of art in the state's custody. These constitute the Nederlands Kunstbezit-collectie (NK collection). This website (www.herkomstgezocht.nl/) allows one to search the database for art objects or family names.

The Museum Provenance List Cleveland Museum of Art

This is a compilation of information from museums that have listed works of art in their collections of uncertain or dubious provenance (between 1933 and 1945). This website (www.clemusart.com/provenance/index.html) attempts to list the artworks in one place so that claimants do not have to search through several different websites. A subscription is necessary to access the information.

Czech Republic Restitution

This is a database (www.claimscon.org/index.asp?url=czech) created by the Czech Ministry of Culture and the Moravian Museum containing works of art from the victims of the Holocaust. It does not provide photographs of the works. Searches are carried out by title, artist, or the name of the current owner, which can be the museum housing the work.

Musées Nationaux Récupération (MNR)

The Direction des Musées de France has created a database (www.culture.gouv.fr/documentation/mnr/pres.htm) of the 2000 art works classified as MNR (National Museums Recovery programme), which have been stored in national or provincial museums and the Mobilier National (national furniture collection) since 1949. A catalogue of these works, consisting of descriptions of each art work accompanied by illustrations, has been accessible online since November 1996.

Looted Art

This site (www.beutekunst.de/service.html) has a catalogue that lists the works looted from the museums, archives, and libraries of the region of Saxony-Anhalt.

Hungarian National Gallery of Budapest

This is a database of World War II losses that was set up at the Hungarian National Gallery of Budapest following the decision of the Hungarian Restitution Committee in 1992. The objectives are to describe artworks lost between 1938 and 1945 as well as artworks smuggled from Hungary between 1945 and 1949. The estimated number of references to lost artworks is about three million, of which 170,000 have already been entered into the database. The data is stored on CDs. (Contact: Laszlo Mrávol, Art Historian—Magyar Nemzeti Galéria—Budavári Palota, P.O. Box 31, 1250 Budapest, Hungary. Tel. (36 1) 375 7533. Fax (36 1) 375 8898.)

Italian Government

In October 1995, the Italian Government supervised the publication of a catalogue entitled *Treasures Untraced—An Inventory of the Italian Treasures Lost during the Second World War*, available in Italian, English and German. This catalogue lists over 2,500 objects and has been put online on the website of the International Commission for Art Works. It includes two sections: Treasures Untraced and Treasures Retraced.

Wartime Losses: Polish Paintings

The electronic version of this first of a planned series of catalogues (www. polamcon.org/lostart/index.html) has been made possible through the generosity of the Polish American Congress. It comprises 440 oil and pastel paintings, watercolours from the seventeenth to the twentieth centuries and provides an index of painters and of owners.

UK Museums' Provenance Research

This site (www.nationalmuseums.org.uk/spoliation.html) provides a list of works with incomplete provenance in national and non-national museums and galleries in the United Kingdom.

The American Association of Museums Nazi-Era Provenance

The American Association of Museums lists on this site (www.aam-us.org/ museumresources/prov/index.cfm) the museums that are in compliance with AAM's guidelines and makes available to the public a list of works of art in their collections that have gaps in provenance for the period 1933-1945.

Nazi-Era Provenance Internet Portal

Designed and managed by AAM on behalf of the American museum community, the Nazi-Era Provenance Internet Portal (www.nepip.org) provides a searchable registry of objects in American museum collections that were created before 1946 and changed hands in Continental Europe during the Nazi era (1933-1945). People seeking objects can use the Portal to refine their search. For each registered object, the Portal provides basic descriptive information along with links to additional information provided by the participating museum. Museums with objects in their collections that changed hands in Continental Europe during the Nazi era can participate in the Portal. By participating in the Portal, museums fulfill their responsibility under the Guidelines and Recommended Procedures adopted by the museum field to make Nazi-era provenance information accessible.

Find Stolen Art

This website (www.findstolenart.com/) has been developed to assist police forces across the United Kingdom in the recovery and return of stolen antiques and to enable auction houses, collectors, and dealers to comply with the code of due diligence.

Italian Carabinieri—Culture Police

In 1969 the Carabinieri formed a special unit for the protection of cultural heritage. The art theft squad works in cooperation with academics and other police forces to identify stolen cultural goods and arrest the culprits. The Carabinieri maintain a database (www.carabinieri.it (Italian)) of more than 240,000 stolen Italian artifacts and artworks, as well as working with foreign law enforcement to track down smugglers outside the country.

IFAR—Stolen Art Alert

IFAR is a New York-based non-profit organization (www.ifar.org/) dedicated to integrity in the visual arts. Selected items are published in the Stolen Art Alert section of the IFAR Journal. Owners, insurance companies, police, the FBI, Interpol, and the Art Loss Register, amongst others, provide the theft information.

IRAQI CULTURAL PROPERTY: UNITED STATES SANCTIONS

The UN Security Council 661 in August 1990 was the international prohibition on material from Iraq that imposed sanctions on trade with Iraq in preparation for the first Gulf War. There was fear even before the war began that there would be illicit trafficking in cultural property. The International Emergency Economic Power Act[59] gave the President power to return material to Iraq. As a result of this, two executive orders were passed by the President preventing contraband from coming into the United States from Iraq (orders #12722, 12744). This was governed under the authority of the Office of Foreign Assets Control, which is under the auspices of the Department of the Treasury.

There was a further UN Security Council resolution passed (#1483) on May 22, 2003, which called for the lifting of sanctions and was binding on all UN members. The day after trade sanctions were lifted, there was an exemption on Iraqi cultural property. All UN members were prohibited from dealing in Iraqi cultural property.

On the administrative level, there is also a Code of Federal Regulations.[60] The Treasury Office enforces these sanctions. The lifting of the ban on Iraqi goods except for cultural property was extended on May 3, 2004, and again in 2005. A state of emergency with respect to Iraqi cultural property was passed in 2004 with executive order #13350, *The Emergency Protection for Iraqi Cultural Antiquities Act*.[61] This allowed the President of the United States to use the CPIA to prevent contraband Iraqi cultural property from coming into the United States. This put import restrictions on Iraqi cultural property. It was like a bilateral treaty, though done through an executive order.

The illicit trafficking of cultural property is composed of an organized chain of offenders starting with looters and thieves, moving to middlemen and, ultimately, to those who provide the demand for these objects. Until there are sufficiently negative consequences, including prosecutions, prison sentences, and public shaming for those creating this demand, and consequently dealing in stolen property, the criminal chain will continue unabated. For successful prosecutions to occur, there must be education of the public, lawyers (including specific courses in law school), and of judges, arbitrators and law enforcement. As well, understanding the significance of cultural heritage should be a mandatory part of school curricula to help children to understand their own cultural identities, to respect the heritage of others, and, as adults, to contribute to protecting cultural heritage for future generations.

DUE DILIGENCE

T he purchase of art is fraught with risks particularly from unknown sellers in other countries against whom it may be very difficult to obtain an effective legal remedy. Art can be stolen, in which case good title may not be aired. Art may be a forgery or counterfeit, in which case it is not what it is presented to be. Art can be illicit in that export may be prohibited or otherwise restricted by laws of one or more jurisdictions, including: where the painting originates, where the vendor resides, and where the purchaser resides. So whether buying, selling, collecting, loaning, or donating art, due diligence is a mandatory step.

DUE DILIGENCE CHECKLIST FOR PURCHASERS OF ART

A basic Due Diligence Checklist has been provided, which purchasers of art may find instructive to use prior to completing an acquisition. This checklist is not a complete solution to ensuring that a purchaser does not become the victim of stolen, forged, or otherwise illicit art. Even if the purchaser has no reason to believe something is amiss, ask the necessary questions. The questions rising from this checklist need to be further investigated, answered and professionally verified.

Due Diligence Checklist

You need to perform due diligence on the seller as well as the item itself.

I Seller

❑ Bill of Sale and Warranty

The bill of sale is a record of the agreement between the seller and buyer of a piece of art. It lays out the rights and duties of both parties in the transaction. It specifies what has been sold, when, to whom, and for what price. Ideally, a bill of sale should contain a warranty of good title—in other words, the seller must promise that he or she is the lawful owner of the art and is passing clean title to the new owner. Both parties should keep copies of the bill of sale for future reference.

❑ Who is the Seller?

Name: _____

Address: _____

❑ What is the seller's reputation?

_____
_____
_____
_____
_____

❑ References:

_____
_____
_____
_____
_____

❑ Internet search:

_____
_____
_____
_____
_____

❑ How long has the seller been in business?

_____

❏ Bankruptcy searches:

_____
_____
_____
_____
_____

❏ Executions:

_____
_____
_____
_____
_____

❏ Independent Legal Opinion good and marketable title or ensure it was not otherwise illegally obtained

_____
_____
_____
_____

II Item

❏ Determine that it is not stolen
    ❏ Be suspicious if an object of art, book or antique is priced well below market value
    ❏ Be very cautious if asked to pay cash for item
    ❏ Check art loss registers
    ❏ Investigate provenance of piece
    ❏ Seek professional advice regarding gaps in provenance
    ❏ Determine provenance is not a fiction
    ❏ If piece has no provenance, assume that it is stolen and take appropriate steps to satisfy yourself that it is not stolen

❏ Determine that it is a genuine article
    1. Rely on warranty
    2. Rely on experts

❏ Determine that it is not war loot, undermining good and marketable title, or otherwise criminally obtained

❏ Country of origin
Determine that the object is not cultural patrimony or otherwise subject to export restrictions

Commentary

It is best to consult a lawyer before attempting to import or export a piece, as different countries have their own restrictions and permit requirements. The concerns extend beyond what the cultural property of the nation in question is to encompass, such as environmental issues. In 2004, Lawrence M. Small, secretary of the Smithsonian museum, was convicted on a misdemeanor charge of violating the Migratory Bird Treaty Act[1] and the Endangered Species Act.[2] Several pieces in his private Amazonian art collection were discovered to contain feathers from protected birds. He surrendered the impugned collection to the government but stubbornly maintained that the legislation was outmoded.[3] The Canadian counterparts to such legislation are the *Species at Risk Act*[4] and the *Migratory Birds Convention Act*.[5]

In accordance with the Convention on International Trade in Endangered Species of Wild Flora and Fauna (CITES),[6] both Canada and the United States are cooperating to protect animal and plant materials being traded across international borders. Under CITES, which came into force in 1975, 30,000 species and their derived products are subject to strict trade regulation. The protected species are listed in the Appendices to the Convention. Import and export restrictions depend on the level of protection offered by CITES. If you suspect that an item you are interested in purchasing might contain contraband material, refer to the Canadian CITES Control List.[7] Canada's domestic implementing legislation for CITES is the Wild Animal and Plant Protection and Regulation of International and Interprovincial Trade Act (WAPPRIITA).[8] The Act and its Regulations cement Canada's commitment to CITES, as well as expanding the CITES list to encompass additional species of particular concern to Canada.

Purchasing on the Internet

When purchasing on the Internet, there are several factors to consider, including potential loss or damage in shipping, and a higher risk of fraud and misrepresentation. This method of acquisition may be the way of the future; however, it will always be a case of "buyer beware."

In 2005, a man in Ohio was charged with 20 counts of criminal attempt to receive stolen property. The investigation began when a genealogical researcher discovered rare old county documents for sale on eBay. State Trooper Robert Erdley of the computer crimes task force discovered a total of 20 documents, dated between 1811 and 1826, that had been stolen from the county records.[9] Among other potentially looted items on the Internet are Sumerian cylinder seals and Peruvian masks.

Some countries, recognizing the threat that online shopping sites pose to cultural property, have taken steps to restrict the selling of particular goods on the Internet. In July 2008, eBay Germany propagated a new policy restricting the sale of "archaeological finds," which it defined as "an object of historical, artistic or scientific importance, which laid for a time in the ground or under water." The policy covers items such as coins, weapons, grave goods, ceramics, jewellery, tools, sacral objects, and fossilized animal and plant remnants. Under eBay Germany's new rules, sellers of antiquities must provide adequate documentation for their auction items. Moreover, items originating from other countries can no longer be sold through the eBay Germany without proof of a valid export license.[10]

The Federal Culture Office of Switzerland recently followed Germany's example when it reached an agreement with eBay to limit the sale of cultural artifacts. The memorandum of understanding states that eBay "will only permit the sale of archaeological artifacts in Switzerland with proof of legality issued by the competent authorities in Switzerland or abroad." Since Switzerland has been a central hub of the illicit trafficking of cultural property, this is a significant step toward curbing the illegal trade of art and heritage objects.[11]

Those collecting art through eBay should conduct thorough provenance research before purchasing an item, lest they inadvertently contribute to the trade of looted cultural property.

DUE DILIGENCE: DONATIONS AND LOANS

It is my considered opinion, and the prevailing opinion of many respected experts in museum law, that effort and investment should be made by every donor in verifying for themselves the provenance of all pieces in a collection loaned or gifted. This is in order to protect the collector's good name and to prevent damage to the philanthropic gift. The reputational damage that can be done without such a precaution is not one that money could reverse.

It is imperative that donors of works of art undertake their own legal audit before completing a donation to a public institution. It is not prudent to rely on the provenance research (either volunteer or professional) provided by the public gallery. I would go so far as to extend this legal audit checklist on the part of the donor to long-term and other loans to public art institutions as well.

When making a donation or loan, the collector has very little control in terms of how potential future claims or allegations are handled or who performs provenance research on behalf of the interests of the public institution. Even with a non-disclosure agreement from the institution, the donor is vulnerable as those documents can be overturned by a judge. While public institutions are eager to accept donations, they are much less motivated to do full and proper due diligence, which leaves the donor vulnerable to future claims, legitimate or not, or to being cast as the scapegoat should provenance issues arise in the future. These sorts of disputes are, unfortunately, becoming all too common in the art world today.

As many collectors amassed collections over the last 60 years or so, the legal problems arising in international art law today were simply not on the radar screen for purchasers in the past. Until recently it was even considered rude to ask questions; deals were often made on a handshake, which, although civilized between trustworthy parties, can also create a perfect breeding ground for unscrupulous dealings involving objects with serious problems with authenticity and provenance.

The vetting and verification of each piece should be done by someone independent of the public institution, a qualified person who can provide privilege, confidentiality and expertise to deal with these issues. If an issue arose with one or more piece and the research was undertaken by such a qualified third party, the issue could be dealt with ethically.

In the event that a private collector or institution came under media scrutiny—for instance, if there is a title dispute or allegations of unethical practices—it is prudent to have developed beforehand a crisis management team and strategic communication plan.[12] It should be clear, before any crisis arises, who will respond to criticisms and how. It is harder to combat negative publicity with a slow or ill-considered response.

The Law of Gifts

A gift as legally defined is a voluntary transfer of property without compensation.[13] If the gift is made during the donor's lifetime, it is an *inter vivos* gift; if it is made through a will, it is a *testamentary gift* or *bequest*. Upon hearing the offer, a museum has no obligation to accept it, but the museum should promptly inform the donor of its decision. To be a gift, the item must be offered freely by the donor, accepted by the institution, and title transferred. Upon accepting a gift, the institution incurs obligations: it must ensure that the gift is properly stored, maintained, conserved, documented, and made available for the benefit of the public in perpetuity or until the work is de-accessioned.

Completion of the gift requires a transfer of ownership. Direct property transfer is the most straightforward means of indicating that the object has been gifted. If outright transfer is not a viable option, it is best to seek professional advice, especially for tax purposes, before entering into the arrangement. Once the offer, acceptance, and transfer of ownership have occurred, the gift is complete and cannot be revoked unless the donor has expressly reserved the right to do so. Donor relinquishment of control is a requirement for a tax deduction.[14]

In the gray area between gift and loan is the "promised gift." Sometimes a collector will offer an institution an object for safekeeping and express an intention to donate it in the future. However, promised gifts are not enforceable in Canada, so the owner might simply decide not to honour the promise and will be able to claim the object back. It is also possible for a donor to make a gift fractional, conditional, or restricted. In any of these situations, the institution should carefully consider the implications of such an arrangement before accepting it. The institution should be willing to discuss alternatives with the donor to observe the donor's wishes in an appropriate manner.

It is good practice for any cultural institution to have an acquisition policy. When an object is being donated, the use of a formal deed of gift is essential to avoid future legal disputes. The deed of gift must accurately document the passage of title from owner to institution and clearly state any restrictions that might be attached. For sample deeds of gift for art galleries and museums, see Appendix D2.

Loans and the Law of Bailment

In legal terms, a loan constitutes a "bailment," that is, a delivery of personal property by one person (the *bailor*) to another (the *bailee*) who holds the property for a certain purpose under an express or implied contract.[15] Bailment involves only a change in possession, not in title. A loan imposes on the bailee (in this case, the receiving institution) a legal duty to treat the borrowed property with care. The standard of care to which the law will hold the bailee depends on the nature of the bailment relationship.[16] An institution should never accept a loan without a written contract that clearly states the rights and duties of both parties, including detailed insurance arrangements.

Acceptance of a loan opens the bailee up to substantial liability. As with donations, the recipient of a loan needs to examine closely all issues of provenance. If a loaned article is discovered to be stolen or otherwise illegal, the party in possession of the object might become involved in a legal battle. Thus, the bailee, like the recipient of a gift, should know that the bailor in fact has authority to loan the object in question.

A problem that frequently arises in cases of loans to museums is that of the indefinite loan period. By definition, a loan is a temporary legal arrangement. In practice, however, museums can end up possessing a loaned object indefinitely. In formulating a loan agreement, the bailee should specify the duration of the loan and provide for renewals of the loan arrangement if desired. Some items devolve into long-term loans simply because the owner neglects to retrieve the object. To avoid becoming custodians of unclaimed loans, museums should specify in loan agreements what will happen if the property is not claimed in a reasonable time. Keeping a work in a reputable institution relieves the collector of the cost of care, security, and insurance, while also enhancing the work's value. To prevent collectors from taking advantage of loan situations, every museum should develop and implement a long-term loan policy.

Another long-term loan problem can arise when the bailor dies or cannot be located. The law does not view an indefinite loan as a testamentary instrument; it will not infer that a loan was meant to outlive the owner. The loaned property accrues to the lender's estate upon death. It is then up to the museum either to return the loaned property to the estate or heirs, or to enter a new loan agreement with the current owner. An unclaimed loan can cause a museum difficulties because it is left with the duty to care for the object without the corresponding right to use it. After the expiration of the loan agreement, the benefits accrue only to the bailor.

On the other hand, sometimes a museum will refuse to return a loaned work when the owner requests it back. In this case, the owner's only remedy is litigation, which is costly. Where a museum is withholding a lender's work against the owner's request, the owner will have to act quickly if civil litigation is the preferred recourse; otherwise the action will be statute-barred. Limitations periods are problematic in these situations. Sometimes the owner does not have the time or resources to battle the museum in court and risks being left without remedy when the museum denies the request for the piece's return. There is no statute of limitations on a criminal action. Although it has not yet, to my knowledge been done, a criminal proceeding for theft might be an option worth pursuing if the owner is unable to reclaim the piece in a civil action.

Special considerations arise when the bailor and bailee are both institutions. When lending or borrowing a work of art from another jurisdiction, it is recommended that the lender ensure that the receiving jurisdiction has an "immunity from seizure" order as a term of the loan agreement. This way, even if someone files a claim for ownership while the object is on loan, the institution's ability to return the piece to its lender will not be compromised. Without an immunity from seizure order, there is the risk that a loaned work could be retained indefinitely during litigation.

In Canada, immunity from seizure orders come under provincial jurisdiction; four Canadian provinces—Ontario,[17] British Columbia,[18] Alberta,[19] and Manitoba[20]—have immunity from seizure legislation.[21] Under Ontario's *Foreign Cultural Objects Immunity from Seizure Act*, there are three prerequisites to obtaining an order: the object must be of cultural significance; it must be brought in from a foreign country pursuant to an agreement; and importation must be for the purpose of a temporary non-profit exhibition.

The current authority on art loans is Norman Palmer, whose book examines in detail the practice of lending art worldwide.[22] For sample loan agreements for art galleries and museums, see Appendix D3.

ART AS AN INVESTMENT

The legal trade of art and antiquities is quickly becoming part of the mainstream financial market. In times of financial and political upheaval, art does not bottom out to the same extent as stocks and bonds. After the 9/11 terrorist attacks, while the markets suffered over the longer term, art sales quickly bounced back. Studies comparing the price fluctuations of securities listed on the Dow Jones and S&P 500 Index reveal that art has consistently outperformed stocks and bonds.[23] In this day and age, art is generally accepted as a respectable investment vehicle.

In some ways, investing in art is similar to making any other investments. One would not purchase stocks on a whim; likewise, art collectors should know what factors make for a wise investment. A diligent investor will inquire as to the details of a potential investment, examining its operations and management and verifying material facts; this pertains equally to art as an investment. Common mistakes made by imprudent art investors include buying solely based on the artist's name, buying on impulse without sufficient research, and buying a heavily-restored piece. Unlike common stocks, art is not a highly liquid investment. It also incurs increased security and insurance costs, which are factors that prospective buyers should consider. Investing in art does entail risk—it is difficult to predict what an artist's level of popularity will be like in the future.

This is why prospective buyers should conduct as much research as possible before investing in a piece of art. It is worth noting as well that art, unlike traditional investments, does not have a specific market regulation scheme. Some experts suggest that the securities laws in place are broad enough to encompass art but, in practice, this is not being done.

Another principle that holds true for art as well as other investments is the wisdom of keeping a diverse portfolio. If art collectors stay in one particular area, they risk losing money if it should go out of style. Art collectors have the additional worry of verifying title and authenticity before buying a piece. When buying abroad, one must also be sure that nothing illegal (for example, ivory, whalebone, or feathers from an endangered bird) is contained in the artifact. The collector should be certain, before investing, that the item can be brought back across the border.

If one considers art as an investment, what is the dividend? Unlike stocks, there are no periodic returns in art investments. On the one hand, it can be said that, for art to produce an investment gain, it must sell at a profit greater than the total capital gain for other investments. On the other hand, it is possible to analogize aesthetic enjoyment as the visual reward or esthetic satisfaction of an art investment. The return on a piece of art is the collector's enjoyment of it. If this enjoyment declines, the investor might consider selling the piece and reinvesting in one that brings in a better aesthetic dividend. Similarly, if the monetary value of the work appreciates, the investor should consider whether it is worth keeping for the aesthetic dividend, or if it should be sold.[24]

THE ART OF WAR

HOLOCAUST ERA LOOTED ART

During World War II, art was a key policy tool of the Nazi state. Hitler firmly believed that Germany was the centre of high culture and that it "rightfully" deserved to house the world's finest art. In the lead-up to World War II, the Nazi Party launched its political attack against the Left with its campaign against modernist "degenerate art." Seizures of such works began in 1937 and led to the removal of more than 17,000 works from state collections and private individuals' collections. Many of these works are believed to have been burned, others sent abroad; none of these works has been subject to a legal claim since the end of the War.[1] The Nazis also used art as a weapon against the Jews, both to propagate antisemitism (such as through the Degenerate Art Exhibition of 1937), to strip the Jews of their heritage (for instance, through the systematic destruction of religious objects), and to further "Aryanization." Expropriation of art was one of many methods of dehumanizing the Jews; the takeover of Jewish businesses included Jewish art galleries. Seizing art from foreign lands was also a way of fulfilling Germany's geopolitical ambitions.

In history's greatest art plunder, the Nazis stole more than 600,000 pieces from museums and private collections valued in today's currency at US$20.5 billion.[2]

The Nazis authorized, coordinated, and systematized the looting of art and cultural heritage. In July 1940, Hitler established the *Einsatzstab*

Reichsleiter Rosenberg (ERR), a special unit that would work alongside the *Wehrmacht* and Security Police to appropriate any cultural materials that would be useful for the ideological tasks of the Nazi Party. The ERR began its task by raiding synagogues and libraries to collect writings related to the "Jewish question." Some of the books were sold for pulp to paper mills while others were kept for the purpose of enemy study. Ironically, because of their interest in examining "enemy materials," the Nazis inadvertently protected a significant amount of looted Jewish cultural material from destruction.

By 1941 the Nazis had, through outright confiscation or divestiture under distress, emptied Europe of its cultural treasures. The Nazis "laundered" stolen art through neutral countries like Switzerland and Portugal. Much of it ended up in western market countries including Canada and the United States. Records were deliberately vague, creating evidentiary problems for future claimants. The Nazis covered their tracks so effectively that little of what was stolen will ever be recovered.

More than 60 years after the end of World War II, the movement for repatriation of Nazi-looted art and cultural property continues full force. The atrocities committed during World War II were so grave, their trauma and aftermath so immense, that we still feel their impact two generations later. Recovering Nazi-looted art after it has made its way into a legitimate collection is a fight against the odds. Considering the loss of documentation that took place during the war, victims' heirs are faced with the daunting task of tracking down and adequately identifying the piece in question. Even if they manage to do this, they are likely to encounter resistance from the museum or gallery currently housing the disputed piece. For Holocaust survivors and their heirs, the fight for restitution comes at great expense, not just of money, but of time and emotional turmoil. The legal barriers to restitution mean that most cases remain unresolved—and, until they are resolved, they will haunt generations to come.

International Legal Commitments

There have been a number of international declarations, conferences, and agreements, some before the end of the war and others as recent as this decale. While many jurisdictions have signed these documents, there have been varying degrees of action.

London Declaration (1943)[3]

The allied powers did not wait until after the War to condemn the confiscation and pillaging of cultural property. Seventeen nations, including Canada, signed the London Declaration of 1943 stating their intention to "do their utmost to defeat the methods of dispossession practiced by the Governments with which they are at war against the countries and peoples who have been so wantonly assaulted and despoiled." The signatories to the declaration reserved the right to declare any property transfers during enemy occupation invalid. The declaration specified that this included not only plundered property, but also "transactions apparently legal in form," recognizing that forced purchase was a common Nazi method of operation.

Bretton Woods Conference (1944)[4]

All 44 Allied nations met in Bretton Woods, New Hampshire, in July 1944 for the United Nations Monetary and Financial Conference. The UN was not officially founded until 1945, but this Conference realized its inception and established the International Monetary Fund (IMF). Although the major focus of the Agreement to come out of that Conference concerned the international economy, Section VI addressed enemy assets and looted property. With the end of World War II in sight, the allies realized that the axis powers were transferring their assets (including works of art) through neutral countries. The participating governments declared their goal of preventing looted property from making its way into their market countries. At the Bretton Woods Conference, the allied nations pledged that they would take all appropriate measures to return looted goods to their lawful owners.

Washington Principles (1998)

In 1998, Canada was one of 44 parties to the Washington Conference on Holocaust-Era Assets. One of the key issues addressed at the Conference was art and cultural property confiscated by the Nazis. The participating nations undertook the task of uncovering stolen art and promising to seek fair resolutions to conflicting claims. The Washington Principles built on the American Association of Museum Directors (AAMD) guidelines for provenance research, making them a key priority.[5]

The first four principles call for heightened efforts to identify and locate Nazi-looted art, allowing for some flexibility in evidential standards. The next three principles articulate the goal of publicizing any discoveries to notify rightful heirs. Principle eight calls for swift and fair resolutions to ownership disputes. If a piece is found to have been plundered but no rightful heir comes forth to claim it, principle nine recognizes the power of acknowledgment. Even if the rightful heirs cannot be found, the museum should recognize the origins of the painting and attempt to reach a just solution for the public education, interest, and benefit. The two final principles encourage member nations to appropriately implement the principles.

The 11 Art Principles of the Washington Conference were non-binding. Some nations have followed them more faithfully than others. In November 1999, the Parliamentary Assembly of the Council of Europe, representing 41 nations, passed Resolution 1205 facilitating the restitution of looted Jewish cultural property within Europe. The Resolution cemented their commitment to the Washington Principles but did not lead to the international claims process that is truly necessary to fulfill the goals of the Washington Principles. Likewise, at the Vilnius Forum in 2000, the Council of Europe reaffirmed its obligations and encouraged cultural institutions to improve the accessibility of information.[6] In 2003, the Legal Affairs Committee of the European Parliament addressed the need for a more uniform approach to ownership claims amongst member nations. Since Holocaust-related claims span decades and cross national borders, not only within Europe but also in North America, parties to the Washington Principles need to work cooperatively to facilitate restitution on a larger scale.

Terezin Declaration (2009)

By June 2009, it had become painfully clear that the international community was failing to fulfill adequately its obligations under the Washington Principles, despite numerous reaffirmations of their goals. It was clear that the lack of uniformity between member countries was making it impossible to restitute Holocaust-looted cultural property effectively.

The Terezin Declaration, whose 46 members included Canada and the United States, established the European Shoah Legacy Institute to promote education and awareness of the issues addressed in the Declaration. This was a commendable step in the right direction. However, like the Washington Principles, the Terezin Declaration was non-binding. It reads like a plea for cooperation:

> We *reaffirm* our support of the Washington Conference Principles [...] we *encourage* all parties including public and private institutions and individuals to apply them as well [...] we *stress* the importance for all stakeholders to continue and support intensified systematic provenance research [...] we also *recommend* the establishment of mechanisms to assist claimants and others in their efforts [...] we *urge* all stakeholders to ensure that their legal systems or alternative processes, while taking into account the different legal traditions, facilitate just and fair solutions with regard to Nazi-confiscated and looted art...[7]

Like other efforts following the Washington Principles, the Terezin Declaration essentially re-affirmed previous obligations, which still have not been fulfilled, without establishing any legal incentives for enforcement or accountability.

Restitution and the Adversarial System

Since the end of World War II, European and North American leaders have repeatedly affirmed their commitment to returning Nazi-looted art works to their rightful owners. However, these leaders have failed to reach a consensus on how such restitutions should be administered. There are fewer Holocaust survivors as the years go on. Lengthy litigation is not a feasible option and does not serve the interests of justice—not only because of its financial and emotional toll, but also because survivors should not have to spend the last years of their life in court. The great relief associated with discovering artwork once thought lost forever quickly changes to despair when it leads to adversarial fighting. Based on the Washington Principles, rightful heirs should not have to *fight* for restitution. Unfortunately, if they refuse to do so, they might be left empty-handed if a museum does not honor its ethical obligation to return the art and see that justice is done.

Restitution of Nazi-looted art has been recognized internationally as an important step to begin to rectify the injustices of the Holocaust. As one commentator noted, "The objects are symbols of a terrible crime; recovering them is an equally symbolic form of justice."[8] For practical purposes, most disputes are litigated under American law; in many European civil law jurisdictions, there are laws protecting "good faith" purchasers against the claims of rightful owners after a given number of years of innocent possession.[9] In the United States and Canada, it is impossible to obtain good title to stolen property, regardless of how long one possesses it. This rule is based on the Latin maxim *nemo dat quot non habeat* (you cannot give what you do not have). This fundamental tenet of property law favours the original title-holder, not the good-faith purchaser.

There is no statute of limitations on the criminal act of theft.[10] Criminal law is the preferable route to recover a stolen painting; any civil actions for recovery will be more expensive and potentially statute-barred. Moreover, the success of a civil action will depend largely on the jurisdiction in which it is litigated. In New York, for example, the earliest Holocaust-looted art case of *Menzel v. List*[11] determined that the "Demand and Refusal" rule applied to the claim, which meant that the statute of limitations did not begin to run until the true owner discovered the whereabouts of the stolen property and the possessor refused the owner's demand for its return. Other courts, however, apply the vague notion that the statute will run from the time when the discovery "ought to have been made."[12]

After the Washington Principles were acclaimed in 1998, a number of disputes between private individuals were litigated in American courts. Most of them resulted in out-of-court settlements.[13] Some have dragged on for years, at great cost to all participants. The Egon Schiele case is a striking example of the type of aggressive litigation that only exacerbates the suffering of plaintiffs. Following the annexation of Austria in 1938, the Nazis seized Jewish businesses as part of their Aryanization campaign. Lea Bondi Jaray, an Austrian Jew, was forced to sell her art gallery to Nazi art dealer Friedrich Welz. Upon a visit to Bondi's apartment, Welz was intrigued by an Egon Schiele painting, *Portrait of Wally*. He insisted that he was entitled to the ownership, despite Bondi's objections that it was part of her private collection. Bondi's husband, hopeful that the two of them would flee Austria together, pressured her into giving the painting to Welz to avoid any trouble. Welz also acquired works from a Viennese art collector by the name of Dr. Heinrich Rieger, who died shortly thereafter in Theresienstadt concentration camp. At the end of World War II, Welz was forced to surrender his paintings to American authorities in Austria when he was interned as a war criminal. American records indicate that *Wally* was somehow separated from Bondi's other pieces and misplaced into Rieger's collection. By law, the seized works ended up in the hands of the Austrian government.

When the Gallery Belvedere purchased Rieger's collection, they recognized the mistake but did nothing. When Bondi discovered the painting was in the Belvedere, she asked a knowledgeable acquaintance, Dr. Rudolf Leopold, if he would help her recover it. Instead, Leopold betrayed her and, in 1954, acquired the work for himself. With the Belvedere insisting that Rieger was the original owner, Bondi thought it would be futile to fight Leopold in an Austrian court. She died in 1969 without having recovered the painting.

In 1994, Leopold placed *Wally* in his own museum, altering the provenance records to show that Rieger had purchased the work from Bondi. In 1997, he loaned the Rieger Collection to New York's Museum of Modern Art (MoMA). When Bondi's heirs heard the news, they asked the MoMA to refuse to return the painting to Leopold. The MoMA was uncooperative, explaining that they were contractually obligated to return the work when the exhibition was over. The Bondi heirs turned to the American government for assistance. The District Attorney issued a subpoena, but it was quashed because of a New York statute preventing seizure of loaned cultural property.[14] Not to be deterred, the United States Magistrate Judge issued a warrant of seizure for the painting and initiated civil forfeiture proceedings under the National Stolen Property Act. The American government argued that the Nazis had stolen *Wally* from its lawful owner, Leopold had converted it, and it was therefore stolen property when it entered the United States.

In 2000, the Court granted Leopold's motion to dismiss the complaint on the grounds that the work could not have been considered stolen, since the American forces that recovered it were acting as "agents" for the true owner (even if they did not know that the work had been stolen).[15] The government amended its complaint, and the District Court denied another motion to dismiss by the Leopold Foundation and the MoMA. The Court revised its finding about the American Armed Forces. It held that, in order to be agents of the true owners, the soldiers would have needed to have knowledge that the property was stolen and knowledge that they were under a legal duty to return it. Since the American forces responsible for confiscating Nazi property at the end of World War II had neither, they could not be deemed to have been acting as the true owner's agents. The Leopold and MoMA brought numerous other motions to dismiss, all of which the court rejected. The District Court allowed the forfeiture action to proceed.[16]

After ten years of vicious litigation, a motion for summary judgment was heard on 21 September 2009 in the South District New York Court. The judge denied summary judgment, holding that "trial is warranted on the issue of whether Dr. Leopold knew *Wally* was stolen when the Museum imported it into the United States for exhibition at the MoMA."[17] The decade-long conflict still awaits resolution.

In contrast to this drawn out litigation, the North Carolina Museum of Art returned Lucas Cranach the Elder's *Madonna and Child in a Landscape* to two Austrian sisters, the heirs of the rightful owner from whom the Nazis had seized it. Marianne and Cornelia Hainisch were the heirs of Dr. Philipp Gomperz; the Gestapo confiscated the painting from his collection in 1940. This case illustrates that issues are resolved more quickly and effectively without litigation, to the benefit of both parties. The sisters were so pleased with the Museum's willingness to cooperate that they ended up selling it back to the museum at a reduced rate, US$600,000, as a partial gift from the family. The sisters stated that "in our opinion the public should know that the heirs of Philipp Gomperz appreciate the sense of justice shown by the [Museum's] decision to restitute the painting."[18]

This handling of a restitution of Nazi-looted art exemplifies a fair, expeditious resolution of a title dispute. When there is mutual respect and cooperation between the parties, everyone benefits. As the Chair of the Museum's Curatorial Department described, the painting "teaches about our own times. The dramatic story—the painting's theft by the Nazis, the subsequent succession of 'owners' (both guilty and innocent) and the search for, discovery, and return of the painting to its rightful owners— endows this object with extraordinary fascination." This case shows how claims for title do not have to be turned into spiteful, expensive, winner-takes-all ownership disputes, but rather, can be resolved in the best interest of both parties. Acknowledgment is empowering.

The Canadian Perspective: Recommendations for the Future

Since signing the Washington Principles more than ten years ago, Canada has largely ignored its obligations. Canada's gravest failings relate to sections II, IX, X, and XI.

> II. *Relevant records and archives should be open and accessible to researchers, in accordance with the guidelines of the International Council on Archives.*
> IX. *If the pre-War owners of art that is found to have been confiscated by the Nazis, or their heirs, can not be identified, steps should be taken expeditiously to achieve a just and fair solution.*
> X. *Commissions or other bodies established to identify art that was confiscated by the Nazis and to assist in addressing ownership issues should have a balanced membership.*
> XI. *Nations are encouraged to develop national processes to implement these principles, particularly as they relate to alternative dispute resolution mechanisms for resolving ownership issues.*

The following is a list of suggested remedies, in order of urgency, which Canada should consider if it wishes to respect its commitment to the Washington Principles and the fair resolution of Holocaust-looted art claims.

1. The Canadian *Criminal Code* should be the primary tool for stolen cultural property cases. Section 354, "Possession of Property Obtained by Crime," applies to corporations as well as private

individuals.[19] Actual knowledge or wilful blindness will fulfill the *mens rea* requirement of s.354 (see Chapter 4 for a discussion of wilful blindness). If there is any reason for suspicion that an artwork might have been obtained through crime, a museum has no excuse to avoid making appropriate inquiries.

2. There should be a readily accessible venue of dispute resolution for legal disputes concerning Nazi-looted art. Litigation is prohibitively expensive in both time and money. It is in the interest of museums, private individuals, and the public that the claims are resolved swiftly and fairly. Canada should establish some form of mediation tribunal to determine legitimate claims. It is crucial that such a tribunal was devoid of any conflicts of interest.

3. Canada should establish a third-party review mechanism or commission to address Nazi-era property claims. Canada can look to other signatory countries of the Washington Principles who have more effectively implemented their obligations: the United Kingdom, for example, has a Spoliation Advisory Panel to help resolve claims for cultural objects lost in the Nazi era. The panel provides advice to claimants, possessors, and the government.[20] The United States is also a step ahead of Canada, as Congress created the Presidential Advisory Commission for the purpose of finding Holocaust-looted assets in the United States. Europe also has the Commission for Looted Art in Europe, an expert representative body to deal with all matters related to Nazi-looted cultural property. Canada can learn from these international examples.

4. Provenance research should not be conducted by parties with a financial interest in the outcome. Appraisals of art should be conducted by independent third parties, not the institutions or individuals who own the piece. Again, the United States gives Canada a model to follow.

Canada needs to take initiative and responsibility in returning Holocaust-looted art to its rightful heirs.

THE SACKING OF IRAQ

So much of what we are was born in Mesopotamia. The first libraries and archives, the first poems and songs (*The Epic of Gilgamesh*), the earliest mathematical system, the first wheel, the first written laws (Hammurabi's Code), the first monotheistic religions (Christianity, Judaism and Islam). Abraham, the father of all fathers, hailed from Ur, in southern Iraq. The influence of ancient Mesopotamia spanned Babylonia, Sumer, Assyria, Persia, Asia, Anatolia, Levant and Arabia. This region of ancient Mesopotamia is known as modern-day Iraq and has been victimized by war, loss of life, pillage and sacking for at least the last two decades.

It is futile to differentiate between the 1991 Gulf War and the 2003 War in terms of looting, ransacking, and theft, as there has been a long continuum of stealing and destruction, including a heist of archaeological material, which continues to this day. What was not ransacked or looted in the 1991 War was taken care of in the War of 2003. In addition, archaeological sites all over Iraq are currently being looted at a rapid rate, as evidenced by data provided by high-resolution satellite imagery.[21] This vital historical record has been desecrated and the loss to the archaeological record is permanent.

When American forces invaded Iraq in April 2003, the looting of the Baghdad Museum occurred in three waves. The first round of looting must have been perpetrated by knowledgeable dealers, since they skipped over all reproductions and went straight for the valuable originals. In a second round of looting, local opportunists took copies. Finally, the basement was looted. This must have been an inside job, since it was perpetrated in complete darkness, the thieves had keys, and they knew how to find small objects—such as coins and jewels—in the maze-like basement. All this took place over approximately a three-day period. It took the American military eight days to arrive and, by then, it was too late. This ransacking was completely preventable, it transpired after cultural property experts had cautioned the US State Department and the Pentagon about potential looting, and requested protection of numerous sought-after items that had survived the looting of the Gulf War. Ironically, under Saddam Hussein's regime, the looting of archaeological sites was an offence punishable by death. Now it is a widespread occurrence in Iraq, whose two main exports are oil and antiquities.[22] For a discussion of the criminal sanctions for Iraqi looting, see Chapter 3. Included here is a sampling of what is still missing.

Ivory plaque of lion killing a Nubian, Assyrian from Nimrud, 1cm x 10.5cm base, 9.8 cm high

White marble head of Eros-Cherub, from Hatra, almost life-size

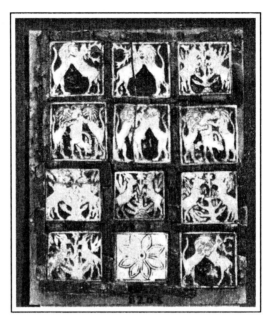

Sumerian Plate, inlaid with shell, 13.5cm x 27cm

Chair back, white ivory relief, from Nimrud, Assyrian period,
1cm x 50cm x 91cm

WAR—OPPORTUNITY FOR WHOLESALE DESTRUCTION OF CULTURAL HERITAGE

The ransacking and theft that took place in Iraq was not an isolated incident. This crime has taken place many times over globally and seems to be a rampant occurrence when invading forces descend upon a nation and during the time after when chaos reigns. The victims of this crime are too numerous to list, but some egregious examples of this conduct include the following:

- The National Museum of Afghanistan (Kabul) which in 1988 was emptied and desecrated with many of the stolen goods illegally exported. This museum housed an astonishing collection of antiquities of the Hellenistic Period as well as sculptures from the school of Gandhara and Bimiyan and medieval Islamic decorative arts.[23]
- In the surrounding areas of Afghanistan and Pakistan archaeological and historical sites have been continually harvested since 1988 for material that would be profitable and marketable in the trade.
- In Cambodia, in the 1970s, the contents of the Depot for the Conservation of Antiquities of Angkor disappeared. This was probably the home of the greatest Khmer antiquities in existence.[24]
- In Somalia in 1991, the Museum in Mogadishu was the first casualty of war when its treasures were emptied.[25]

This problem has become epidemic. What are our hopes for solutions to this problem?

On 9 March 2009 the United States ratified the 1954 Hague Convention for the Protection of Cultural Property in the Event of Armed Conflict. Prospects for change in the future lie partly in what positive and concrete actions the United States military will take to ensure compliance with this Convention to alleviate and prevent damage to cultural property in times of armed conflict. What are the possibilities for the United States ratifying the First and Second Protocol to the Convention to better protect cultural heritage?

Tales of wartime looting provide a grim picture of humanity, but it is important to remember that there are also unsung heroes who risked their lives to protect cultural heritage. One such example is Rose Valland.

During France's Nazi occupation, the ERR recruited Valland, a curator for the Louvre, to oversee the Jeu de Paume Museum in Paris, which they used as the hub of their looting practices. As the ERR confiscated works from museums and individuals in France, they would be temporarily stored in the Jeu de Paume until the Nazis decided where in Germany to send them. Valland presented herself as naively compliant, all the while secretly compiling lists of paintings that the Nazis had confiscated. Unbeknownst to the Germans, Valland understood everything they said. When the Nazis took photographs of their stolen goods, Valland made copies of them by night. When the Nazis, aware of their impending defeat, tried to remove as many artworks as possible before the Allies arrived, Valland got in touch with members of the French Resistance. They managed to delay the train until the Allies liberated Paris—an act of heroism later dramatized in *The Train*, starring Burt Lancaster. Valland's contribution to the preservation and restitution of cultural heritage was recognized with numerous national and international awards.[26]

Valland's list of Nazi-looted art, *Répertoire des biens spoliés en France Durant la guerre 1930-1945*, is available at the Frick Museum Library in New York. This is one source that museums can consult when they come across a gap in provenance. Although museums have agreed to make every effort to return Nazi-looted art, in practice, they are often reluctant to let it go. It is important to continue to evaluate efforts to restitute works of art, including the findings of the recent Prague Holocaust Era Assets Conference, Terezin Declaration in June 2009, as well as leveraging current laws to recover artworks stolen by the Nazis.

A more recent example of courageous protection of cultural heritage in the face of violence and destruction is the story of director Omara Khan Massoudi and his trusted officials at the National Museum of Kabul. In an astounding act of bravery and sacrifice, Massoudi and other museum employees buried many of Afghanistan's cultural treasures in the vaults of the Presidential Palace to protect them from looters. Throughout a quarter-century of strife, seven people held the keys to the nation's history. The "key-holders" kept their promise of secrecy until the safes were opened in 2003 after American-led forces defeated the Taliban regime. Many of the treasures had been thought lost forever, but there in the vaults were more than 33,000 artifacts, including 22 kilograms of Bactrian Gold, hundreds of ancient coins, and thousands of ivory carvings. Had they not been hidden, the valuable artifacts would almost certainly have been used to purchase weapons or destroyed in the Taliban's anti-idolatry campaign.

The travelling exhibition, *Afghanistan: Hidden Treasures*, contains artifacts that span two millennia and reveal a rich and diverse culture. The pieces are a fascinating amalgam of the artistic achievements of history—including Chinese, Indian, Greco-Roman, and nomadic influences. They derive from four archaeological sites: the ancient city of Fullol; the Greek city of Ai Khanum; a French dig in Begram in the 1930s; and the precious Bactrian Hoard discovered in the nomadic graves in Tillya Tepe in the 1970s. One particularly breathtaking piece is the *Collapsible Crown*, circa 100 BC, found in the tomb of a high-ranking nomadic woman. Another is the *Statuette of a Woman Standing on a Makara*, dated at 1-200 AD, thought to represent the Indian river goddess Ganga upon a "makara," a part-elephant, part-crocodile, part-fish creature. It shows an unusual mixture of Greek and Indian deities. The delicate glass pieces in the exhibit, such as the painted goblets made in Roman Egypt, are rare, fragile, and beautiful pieces that have amazingly survived since the time they were traded along the Silk Road around 30 BC. A hair ornament of gold, turquoise, garnet, lapis lazuli, carnelian, and pearl, from roughly 100 BC, combines Persian, Siberian, Central Asian, and Indian influences. These artifacts, shown below, are just a few of the two hundred artifacts in the travelling collection.[27] The National Museum of Kabul was rebuilt with UNESCO's assistance. Since then, a repatriation movement has occurred. More than 5,000 artifacts from Switzerland and Denmark have been confiscated by border agents and returned to Afghanistan.[28] The rebuilding of a nation's cultural heritage cannot occur overnight but, despite the continuing war, the process is well underway. The exhibit is an eloquent homage to Massoudi's raison d'etre: "A nation stays alive when its culture stays alive."

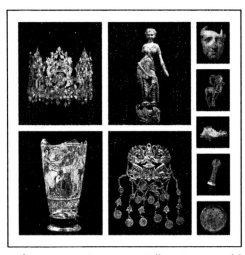

Left-hand column, from top: 1) Crown, Tillya Tepe, gold, 100 B.C.–100 C.E.; 2) Goblet, Begram, painted glass, 1–200 C.E. Middle column, from top: 1) Statuette of a Woman Standing on Makara, Begram, ivory, 1–200 C.E.; 2) Pendant depcting the "Dragon Master", Tillya Tepe, gold, turquoise, garnet, lapis, lazuli, carnelian and pearl, 100 B.C.–100 C.E. Right-hand column, from top: 1) Sculpture Fragment, Aï Khanum, Unfired Clay, about 150 B.C.E.; 2) Ram-shaped Headdress Ornament, Tillya Tepe, gold, 100 B.C.E.–100 C.E.; 3) Fish-Shaped Vessel, Begram, glass, 1–200 C.E.; 4) Chieftain's Dagger, Tillya Tepe, iron, gold and turquoise, 100 B.C.E.–100 C.E; 5) Aquarium Lid, Begram, bronze, 1–200 C.E.

LESSONS LEARNED

Man-made disaster is not the only threat to a country's cultural heritage. As the recent earthquake in Haiti has shown, natural disasters also provide the opportunity for the illegal trade in cultural treasures. In the aftermath of Haiti's devastating earthquake, on 27 January 2010, UNESCO took the positive step of issuing a ban on the export, import, and trade of Haitian artifacts in order to prevent pillaging of that country's rich cultural treasures.[29]

UNESCO's rapid response comes as a result of the ugly lessons learned from Iraq and Afghanistan, just two examples of nations that fell victim to devastation, unfortunately providing opportunity to thieves and looters waiting to profit from such loss to a community. In the case of Iraq, the Bagdad Museum was robbed in the first days of the American-led invasion, and it is now widely known that this was a preventable crime, following repeated, clear warnings that the material in the museum was hotly sought after and was certainly at risk of being looted.

Some of the cultural heritage at risk in quake-hit Haiti is contained in numerous sites that are on the UNESCO World Heritage List, including the former Presidential Palace and the Port-au-Prince Cathedral, in addition to many art collections, libraries, museums, and archives.

The United States Committee of the Blue Shield issued a statement on 14 January 2010 expressing its sorrow and solidarity with the population of Haiti for the loss of lives and the destruction caused by the earthquake. The Blue Shield's Mission is "to work to protect the world's cultural heritage threatened by armed conflict, man made and natural disasters." Their statement continued:

> Culture is a basic need and cultural heritage is a symbolic necessity that gives meaning to human lives connecting past, present and future. Cultural Heritage is a reference full of values helping to restore a sense of normality and enabling people to move forward. Cultural Heritage is fundamental in rebuilding the identity, the dignity and the hope of the communities after a catastrophe.

Protecting Haiti's heritage will play an integral part in rebuilding that nation's infrastructure and hopes for normalcy in the future.

Surprisingly, Canada does not have a Committee of the Blue Shield, and it is time that we did. As Canada is a High Contracting Party to the 1954 Hague Convention and has acceded to the First and Second Protocols, in addition to playing a significant and active role in military action and other similar missions, there is certainly a pressing need for such a committee's presence in this country.

6

THE LOOTING OF ARCHAEOLOGICAL SITES

he looting of antiquities robs society of its ability to make any kind of meaningful or accurate historical study of ancient artifacts. There is irrefutable evidence that the looting of antiquities has evolved into a well organized criminal business driven by profit that employs looters and petty thieves at the bottom of the food chain, fencers of illegal objects in the middle, and those purchasing the material at the top. The antiquities trade has proven relatively recession-proof: even in late 2008, at the height of the worst economic crisis since the Great Depression, auction houses like Christie's and Sotheby's made millions of dollars in antiquities sales.[1] Still, they did not break the record previously set in 2007, when a 3.25-inch-tall unprovenanced artifact sold for US$57.2 million at Sotheby's.[2] At the time, there were 115 signatories to the 1970 UNESCO Convention. One wonders what effect international laws are having when unprovenanced antiquities continue to sell at such staggering prices.

THE ORGANIZED CRIME BUSINESS MODEL

The illegal antiquities market is comparable to criminal enterprises such as drug trafficking and arms smuggling. Illicit cultural property undergoes a lengthy and complex journey to reach the ultimate consumer. There is a diverse collection of players in the antiquities trade whose relationships are interdependent, each feeding into the next one's hunger for profit (see Figure 6.1).[3] On the ground level, an overseer with knowledge of archaeology will employ petty thieves for hire to do the dirty excavations work. The grave-robbers themselves usually have no motivation beyond quick money. The overseer will provide his goons with the necessary equipment for looting and send them to the chosen site. The activity will usually take place at night, with watchmen patrolling the area for law enforcement while gangs do the manual labour. Any artifacts found are given to the overseer, who pays the workers either by the piece or by the job.

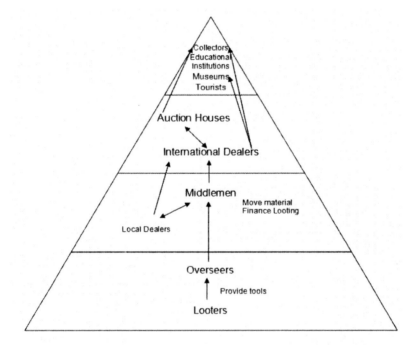

Figure 6.1: A Pyramid Market: The Archaeological Looting Process

The overseer, in turn, sells any discovered goods to the middleman who bankrolled the operation. The middleman has a better understanding of the antiquities market than the overseer; it is the middleman's task to inform the overseer about consumer demand. The middleman, who usually has a legitimate profession outside of the antiquities trade, then contacts local dealers interested in purchasing the goods. These dealers then sell the material to larger international dealers with connections to auction houses, museums, educational institutions, and collectors. As the price of the artifact increases for each transaction, there are rewards at every level (see Figure 6.2, "Cycle of Looting").

Figure 6.2: Cycle of Looted Cultural Property

Dealers who manufacture a marketplace to sell to museums and collectors play a pivotal role in the illicit trafficking of cultural property. Collectors, personal or institutional, can participate knowingly or unknowingly in the illicit aspects of the antiquities trade. As Mackenzie explains, many dealers, collectors, and museums are victims of circumstance who get drawn into the illegal aspects of the trade because the mechanisms to commit wrongdoing are intrinsic to the current market for antiquities.[4] One way that museums can avoid becoming complicit in this cycle is to implement and adhere to a code of ethics (see, for example, the J. Paul Getty Museum Policy Statement on acquisitions, Appendix C3).

The collectors at the top of the pyramid are the driving force behind the illicit trade of antiquities; they are the demand end of the criminal economic equation of looting. Those collecting antiquities determine what to purchase based on their particular cultural and historical interests; ownership of cultural property has emotional as well as financial value. Once removed from their original context and placed in a consumer's hands, artifacts acquire new meaning. Psychologists who study the act of collecting note that collectors tend to see objects as extensions of themselves. For the most obsessive consumer, no price is too high to pay for self-fulfillment. For many, acknowledgement of their impressive collection is crucial. They display their purchases in the hope of impressing their peers not only with their wealth, but also with their culture. Collecting is as much about status as it is about connecting to the past or preserving antiquities for posterity. Owning a rare antiquity will gain the purchaser membership into an exclusive group, instilling a feeling of accomplishment, belonging, and self-worth.

It should be noted, of course, that this is only a general description of the illicit market, which is a complex web that varies depending on the characteristics of source countries rich in archaeological material and mechanisms of market countries acquiring the material. For example, museums can be on the victim end of the equation, as occurred in 1990 when the Corinth Museum (an archaeological museum located on the ancient archaeological site of Corinth) was desecrated by violent thieves who brutally assaulted a night guard to steal approximately 286 items. Six items from that theft showed up in Christie's Auction House in 1997.[5] Some 265 more of the stolen pieces were discovered in crates of fresh fish in a Miami warehouse in 1999.

The problem of the illicit trafficking of cultural property is further compounded by the secrecy of auction houses that provide vague provenances. For instance, in December 2009, an "Eastern Mediterranean or Italian Core-Formed Glass Oinochoe" (a 61/4-inch tall wine jug, circa mid-to-late fourth century BC) sold for US$374,500. Christie estimated its value at US$120-180,000. The only provenance listed for this pristine piece read, "Swiss Private Collection, acquired prior to 1974."

Many collectors want to know where an object originally came from, not necessarily how the current seller acquired it. Provenance is desirable, but it does not always determine whether the collector will purchase an artifact. This makes looters' jobs easier: they supply "a market which is not demanding of credentials, provenance or documentation."[6] The looting process moves from production to distribution to consumption and back again in a cyclical manner as in Figure 6.2.

The Anatomy of Looting: Nigeria

An examination of recent events in Nigeria provides a clearer picture of the looting process. In the early 1990s the soil of the middle belt and Northern parts of Nigeria was discovered to be rife with archaeological material. Terracotta figurines of the Nok and Kwatakwashi (Sokoto) cultures (500 BC-200 AD) are currently being harvested from this region at a rapid rate. The illicit trafficking of cultural property occurs in a specific pattern.

- *Step One:* Archaeological permits are required to legally excavate the terrain. Businesspeople can by-pass this legal requirement by applying to become Accredited Agents in mining instead. While "mining" they unearth antiquities at an average rate of 3000 per year.[7] Only a few of these items will fetch big prices.
- *Step Two:* Traders thoroughly clean the artifacts to remove any traces of soil in order to disguise as much as possible. The cleansing of the artifact can also skew the accuracy of dating tests.
- *Step Three:* Dealers have the terracotta pieces dated by thermoluminescent testing, which involves drilling a small hole in the back to obtain a pottery fragment. These tests are conducted only under looters' watchful eyes, rather than the scientific supervision of independent third parties. This conflict of interest means the test results are of questionable accuracy.
- *Step Four:* Dealers send the results of the dating tests along with a Polaroid of the object to interested buyers. This Polaroid is the only record of the terracotta's existence, and it ends up in the private collector's hands.

- *Step Five:* The looted objects make their way into Europe through forged export permits and bribery of customs agents. Smuggling the illegal material across borders is relatively easy in a state where there is economic despair and rampant poverty. The artifacts travel through a number of countries before reaching their final destination. This makes it difficult to trace the object back to its place of origin and prepares the ground for conflicting and fraudulent claims.

- *Step Six:* Collectors find archaeologists who are willing to catalogue unprovenanced material. This completes the "laundering" of the looted goods. The presence of the terracotta figurine in a glossy catalogue gives it the appearance of legitimacy.[8]

As a result of this looting process, Nigeria has no record of what it has lost. Moreover, the loss has no corresponding gain, aside from the corrupt financial one on the other end of the deal. According to Mallam Yusuf Abdallah Usman, the Director-General of Nigeria's National Commission for Museums and Monuments (NCMM), illicit trafficking is harmful to the country's tourism industry and has diminished the growth of the country's arts and culture sector.[9]

Little is learned from objects without provenance. There is no educational value to the figurines when they have no records of associated artifacts, no mapping of past settlement distribution, and no stylistic comparisons. As the result of looting, nothing is learned about the ancient societies that produced the terracotta figurines.

The increased presence of unprovenanced antiquities on the market provides a perfect environment for fakes and forgeries. An estimated 80% of terracottas leaving Africa are counterfeit.[10] Crime breeds crime.

When the original contexts of archaeological artifacts are destroyed, people are unable to reconstruct and understand the past. A whole period of history is compromised, and all of humankind loses information about its scientific, social, educational, and spiritual development. This is a dear price for society to pay for theft, but little will change until the law shifts the cost to all those participating in the illicit trafficking of antiquities.

Ethically Collecting Antiquities

The rampant looting of antiquities extends, of course, well beyond Nigeria. Archaeological theft is currently being perpetrated in, among many other places, Afghanistan, Cambodia, Cameroon, Chad, Ecuador, Ethiopia, Ghana, Guatemala, Greece, Iraq, Italy, Indonesia, Mali, Mexico, and Peru.[11] Meanwhile, in Australia, Canada and the United States, looters target indigenous cultural property, including human remains and sacred items.[12] Those at the top of the looting pyramid, including academic institutions and collectors, hold the power to halt this cycle of desecration; however, looting will not stop until collectors refuse to purchase undocumented artifacts and academics refuse to study them.[13]

Collecting antiquities is a high-risk endeavor given the percentage of fakes, forgeries, and stolen material on the market. Ethical collection of antiquities requires that the purchaser ask questions. Nobody enjoys the awkward conversations about a piece's origins, but by staying silent on the matter and turning a blind eye to possible issues, legitimate collectors end up colluding with looters.

The importance of provenance cannot be underestimated. For the purpose of illustration, compare the two following descriptions. The first is from the British Museum's exhibit of the Elgin Marbles. A card beside the haphazard row of stone carvings reads:

> Probably Dionysus or Hercules. Probably had a hand, possibly holding a glass of wine, probably had feet.

The marbles were looted by the infamous Lord Elgin, who sold them to the British Museum when they did not fit in his dining room. They were created to look out over the highly-developed cultural centre of Athens; instead, they are now housed in a dingy museum chamber. This kind of nebulous, incomplete scholarship does not lead to cultural education. Compare the Elgin descriptor to the following description accompanying a weapon from China's terracotta army, which the British Museum also houses:

> This dagger axe-blade was hafted onto a wooden pole. The inscription on the blade, 'Made in the 26th Year [of Ying Zheng]', shows that the manufacturing of weapons was

strictly controlled and accounted for during the period when Lu Buwei was Chancellor of the Qin state from 249-246 BC.[14]

Provenance for the terracotta army includes information about find spots, dates of discovery, measurements, composition, and cultural significance. Each object has its context amongst the others.

There are countless examples of antiquities with bad provenance, or none at all. It is the ethical collector's duty to avoid these items, even if finding antiquities with legitimate provenance can be a challenging task. Before purchasing an item, buyers should ask to see an export permit. They must also be wary about the authenticity of these documents. Well-informed, ethical collectors of antiquities can use their position at the top of the market to stem the illicit trafficking of cultural property for the good of all society.

PROTECTING UNDERWATER CULTURAL HERITAGE

The exploration of underwater archeological sites including shipwrecks and other evidence of human existence presents a variety of fascinating and complicated ethical and legal issues. This is particularly true in light of technological advancements in this field that have taken place over recent years. The purpose of this section is to bring to light and address, from various perspectives, some of these issues concerning the protection and conservation of underwater cultural heritage (UCH).

From the perspective of marine archeologists, shipwrecks are time capsules that can tell us about a slice of time in a particular culture. They are self-contained, miniature, condensed societies. Unfortunately, underwater archaeological sites are as vulnerable to pillage as those on land. In addition to robbing countries of their cultural property, underwater looting often damages the archaeological site, for instance by the use of explosives to blow open ships to locate gold and other treasures.[15] Regardless of the risks involved, underwater archaeological sites have been pillaged since antiquity for their monetary value. Some of the greatest examples of bronze sculpture have come from the depths, particularly the Mediterranean and Aegean Seas. The Italian government has recently made claims against the Getty Museum for the return of a bronze statue, Victorious

Youth. Accusations that the statue was unlawfully exported from Italy came during the trial of the Museum's former curator, Marion True, on criminal charges relating to trafficking in stolen antiquities. Italian fishermen discovered the statue, encrusted with layers of shells and barnacles, in 1964. After it was smuggled into the United States, the Getty purchased it in 1977 for US$3.98 million.[16] Victorious Youth was one of the 52 pieces that the Italian government requested for return, though it was not amongst the 26 pieces for which the court ordered restitution.[17]

In addition to the cultural harm caused by looting, the pillaging of UCH sites has an environmental cost.[18] With the growth of public awareness on environmental damage in recent years, there has been greater understanding and acceptance of the fact that UCH is a non-renewable resource worthy of protection. The law must take more stringent measures to ensure that this cultural resource and the natural environment in which it is found are not damaged or destroyed in the name of profit.[19] Likewise, institutions and collectors interested in UCH have responded to environmental and ethical concerns about marine looting. Museum practices are sensitive to these issues.[20] Since the 2001 UNESCO Convention on the Protection of Underwater Cultural Heritage,[21] awareness has only increased.

The purpose of this Convention is to try to ensure more effective safeguarding of submerged shipwrecks and underwater ruins. It is founded upon four major principles:

1. the obligation to preserve underwater cultural heritage;
2. *in situ* preservation, i.e., underwater, as a preferred option;
3. no commercial exploitation of this heritage; and
4. cooperation among states to protect the precious legacy to promote training in underwater archaeology, and to raise public awareness of the importance of sunken cultural property.

Countries party to the Convention (in chronological order of acceptance/ratification) are: Panama, Bulgaria, Croatia, Spain, Libyan Arab Jamahiriya, Nigeria, Lithuania, Mexico, Paraguay, Portugal, Lebanon, Saint Lucia, Romania, Cambodia, Ecuador, Ukraine, Cuba, Montenegro, Slovenia, Barbados.[22] On 2 January 2009, after Barbados deposited its instrument of acceptance as the 20th member, the UNESCO Convention on the Protection of Underwater Cultural Heritage entered into force. The convention directs signatory nations to impose legal sanctions on anyone who violates its measures.

Legal Framework: An International Perspective

International laws regulating behaviour at sea were developed before those for behaviour on land. When naval navigation was the principal method of international travel, rights and obligations developed as between nations. The law of the sea is an old body of law that is rapidly changing. At play in the legal field of UCH protection are the disparate competing interests of salvage rights, rights of cultural patrimony, national claims, and private ownership claims. There is a myriad of treaties, bilateral and multilateral agreements, international and domestic laws, customary practices, conventions, and other legal mechanisms that tackle the subject. Listing them would be of little practical value.[23] Instead, the famed case of the *RMS Titanic*, which sank in international waters after striking an iceberg the evening of April 14, 1912, will illustrate some of the legal and practical issues involved in salvaging submerged cultural property.

After the "unsinkable" ship met its doom, its owners were faced with claims for personal injury, loss of life, and loss of property from both the United States and United Kingdom, from the 700 survivors as well as families of the 1523 deceased passengers and crew members. In 1916, the Ocean Steam Navigation Company settled all the claims at the cost of US$664,000.[24] When the White Star Line was sold to Cunard Shipping Lines in 1934, there was no mention of the *Titanic* in the agreement, presumably because it was considered unrecoverable.[25] Ownership of the *Titanic* was therefore unclear; it would ultimately be up to the American courts to apply the general maritime law of nations in determining who had rights to the ship and its contents.

The *Titanic* lay at the bottom of the sea undisturbed for 73 years until, in 1985, a joint French-American expedition located the wreck. Initially, the Woods Hole Oceanic Institution, at the urging of co-leader Dr. Robert

Ballard, decided not to salvage artifacts from the wreck. Instead, Dr. Ballard placed a plaque on the ship and argued that it should be left undisturbed as a memorial. In 1986, Congress followed Dr. Ballard's advice when it passed the *RMS Titanic Maritime Memorial Act*, which directed the United States and other nations to negotiate with one another to formulate a set of guidelines for the protection of the *Titanic*.[26] The *Titanic Act* stipulated that no one should physically disturb the wreck until the establishment of such an agreement, and promoted the management of historical and archaeological underwater material for the benefit of all humankind. Congress encouraged "research and limited exploration activities" on the *Titanic* while also noting that such activities should be carried out "for the purpose of enhancing public knowledge of its scientific, cultural, and historical significance."

The French half of the expedition, however, did not share Dr. Ballard's passion for preserving the ship in its sunken state; nor did they have the patience to wait while countries took their time in the formation of the international agreement mandated by the *Titanic Act*. In 1987, The Institute of France for the Research and Exploration of the Sea (IFREMER) entered a salvage agreement with a private company called Titanic Ventures, which recovered approximately 1800 artifacts in the course of its 32 dives. The French government took possession of the artifacts, giving potential owners three months to file claims for recovery. When three months passed, Titanic Ventures retained the unclaimed artifacts. The operation garnered much publicity, both positive and negative. Eva Hart, a *Titanic* survivor, fumed that the salvage team members were "fortune hunters, vultures, pirates." Others felt more curious than outraged.

It was not until 1992 that the legal battle over the *Titanic* exploded. At this point in the story it is important to situate the *Titanic* within the international legal framework. Laws of the sea consist both of common law principles and statutes. UCH resources are subject to the law of admiralty, which consists both of the law of finds and the law of salvage. The law of finds applies if a ship has been legally "abandoned"—meaning that the court has determined that its owner has relinquished title to and possession of the ship. The law of salvage, on the other hand, encourages rescue of people and goods when a ship is in peril by promising the salvor a reward without requiring a contractual relationship with the ship's owner. The goal of salvage law is to deter looting by providing commercial incentives for recovery of property. Courts in admiralty favour the law of salvage over the law of finds, although it admittedly strains the principle to call a ship that has been lying at the bottom of the sea for decades "in peril."[27] Nonetheless, courts are usually willing to find that a shipwreck is in peril in that it is at risk of deterioration, loss, or destruction.

If the court deems a shipwreck legally abandoned, the next question is one of jurisdiction. It is a murky question: who owns the water? A country's ability to enforce its laws concerning UCH off its coast depends on the maritime zone in which the shipwreck is located. Under customary international law, a nation has sovereign authority within 12 nautical miles of its baseline (the "territorial zone").[28] The *Titanic*, at roughly 400-460 nautical miles from Newfoundland's shores, was far outside of this range.

In 1992, Marex Titanic Inc., a rival company to Titanic Ventures, claimed that it had discovered the shipwreck and sued in the Eastern District of Virginia for ownership of the 1800 recovered artifacts. The court asserted its jurisdiction over a non-US ship in international waters, apparently because it hoped to restore international order.[29] The Court issued an injunction preventing Marex from conducting salvage operations and declared Titanic Ventures to be salvagers of the wreck as long as they did not sell any of the artifacts for commercial profit. The decision was reversed on appeal because of a procedural technicality. In 1993, Titanic Ventures became R.M.S. Titanic Inc. (RMST) and recovered 800 artifacts. It filed an action in the Eastern District Court of Virginia for exclusive salvage rights. Liverpool and London Steamship Protection and Indemnity Association (LLSP), one of the *Titanic*'s original insurers, came forward as an interested party. RMST settled outside of court with LLSP, and the court named RMST salvor-in-possession of the wreck and sole owner of all items recovered from it.

After recovering and exhibiting more than 1000 artifacts in 1994, RMST attracted enough public attention that the United States, United Kingdom, France, and Canada finally initiated negotiations under the 1986 *Titanic Act*. The RMST's salvage efforts also inspired third-party salvagers to try to enter the wreckage and retrieve artifacts, which instigated more litigation.[30] RMST further increased public awareness when it joined forces with The Discovery Channel to create educational programs about its expeditions. Museums world-wide staged exhibitions about the ship and its contents. James Cameron's massively successful blockbuster movie, released by Paramount Pictures in late 1997, raised public interest in the *Titanic* to a level of frenzy. Anything associated with the *Titanic* was a marketable commodity. For wealthy *Titanic* enthusiasts, Deep Ocean Expeditions advertised an underwater tourism program. For US$32,500, the participants of "Operation *Titanic*" could dive into and take pictures of the famed shipwreck from a Russian deep-sea submersible. RMST sought a preliminary injunction and, in response, one of the private individuals who had planned to participate in the tourist expedition filed an action for a declaratory judgment that he had the right to visit and photograph the wreck.[31] Balancing the interests of both parties, the Court found in RMST's favour and granted a preliminary injunction. On appeal, however, the Fourth Circuit Court partially overturned this ruling. The Court affirmed the injunction preventing private tourists from interfering with RMST's salvage operations but ruled that salvage rights did not encompass the right to exclusive photographing of the wreck. After all, the Court reasoned, "salvors would be less inclined to save property because they might be able to obtain more compensation by leaving the property in place and selling photographic images or charging the public admission to go view it." The ruling was financially detrimental to RMST and led to sweeping management changes. Under its new management, RMST's policy shifted from lending of artifacts to cultural institutions to maximizing revenue through the sale of artifacts.[32]

In 2000, the District Court issued an order prohibiting RMST from selling or disposing of any of the wreck's artifacts. The Court reminded RMST that it was named salvor-in-possession on the basis that it would use its role to further public education. In response, RMST argued that the 1994 decision had affirmed the company as absolute owner of the artifacts and that they were therefore entitled to dispose of them howsoever they wished. In rejecting this contention, the Court of Appeal had to remind RMST that it was operating under the law of salvage, not the law of finds. Salvors have a lien on the property salvaged, not absolute title.[33]

While RMST was engaged in its ownership dispute, the United Kingdom, United States, Canada, and France drafted an agreement in 2000, naming *in situ* preservation as their preferred policy for the wreck site. RMST filed a motion against the US Secretary of State, Secretary of Commerce, and Administrator of the National Oceanic and Atmospheric Administration (NOAA) seeking a declaration that their efforts to implement the agreement constituted an unlawful interference with RMST's exclusive salvage rights. The District Court dismissed the motion as premature.

RMST then filed a motion asking the court to award it the entire *Titanic* and its contents under the law of finds. In the alternative, it argued that it should be rewarded US$225 million for its salvage efforts. The District Court rejected RMST's request to change its status from salvor to finder.[34] The Court of Appeal judge clarified in strong terms admiralty law's preference for the law of salvage over the law of finds, noting that "a free finders-keepers policy is but a short step from active piracy and pillaging."[35] As for the matter of the salvage award, the Court of Appeal remanded the case to the District Court. As of September 2009, the fate of 5900 artifacts, RMST's ownership status, and the establishment of a monitoring system for future activity on the wreck site lie in the hands of a District Court judge.[36]

The complicated saga of lawsuits and legislation surrounding the *Titanic* demonstrates the clash of interests and jurisdictional issues involved in recovering UCH from ancient wreck sites. The parties to international conventions have different policy goals for UCH than legislators and courts.

Legal Framework: The American Perspective

The turf war among international law principles, American Federal laws and the state's interests in the protection and management of UCH is exemplified in the case of *Sea Hunt Inc. v. The Unidentified Shipwrecked Vessel or Vessels*. Of the numerous laws that can potentially be applied to activities involving UCH, the Abandoned Shipwreck Act arises most often in American cases.[37] The Act itself poses jurisdictional problems, a fact that played out in the *Sea Hunt* case.

The facts of the *Sea Hunt* case are as outlined here: *La Galga*, a 50-gun military frigate, was escorting Spanish merchant ships from Havana to Spain in 1750 when it was hit by a hurricane near Bermuda. Although most of the crew survived the wreck, the *La Galga* floundered near the eastern shore of Virginia. A second storm caused the ship and its contents to sink entirely. In 1802, another Spanish frigate fell to the same fate. The *Juno* was transporting troops to Cadiz from Puerto Rico when a storm swept her toward American waters. Despite a rescue attempt from an American schooner, the ship sank near Asseteague Island. In the mid-1990s, a private salvage company, Sea Hunt Inc., located the ships 1500 feet off the Virginia shoreline. The State of Virginia asserted ownership over the ships pursuant to the Abandoned Shipwrecks Act of 1987 (ASA).[38] The ASA overwrites the common law of finds by vesting title in "abandoned" shipwrecks located in territorial waters to the federal government. The federal government in turn transfers title to the appropriate State, which is presumably in a better position to regulate the excavation and retrieval of cultural property contained in the wrecks. The definition of "abandonment" and standards of proof for finding that it has occurred are recurring issues in litigation involving the ASA, which vaguely describes "abandoned" shipwrecks as those that "have been deserted and to which the owner has relinquished ownership rights with no retention."[39] The case of *La Galga* and *Juno* helped to clarify the legal status of UCH by delineating what steps a nation must take or not take in order for the courts to deem its sunken cultural property legally abandoned.

Having been promised 25% of the value of the salvaged goods, the State of Virginia gave Sea Hunt permission to conduct commercial salvage operations. The Virginia Marine Resources Commission granted Sea Hunt a license of commercial salvage that did not require any scientific or archaeological standards for the company's work. In 1998, to secure its position as salvager of *La Galga* and *Juno*, Sea Hunt sought a declaratory judgment from the Federal District Court that Spain had abandoned its title to the two ships and that the Commonwealth of Virginia was their rightful owner. In an unorthodox move, the American government intervened on Spain's behalf. There was good cause for this action. The United States set out to establish that a country that loses a warship maintains ownership of it regardless of when and where it sank. A successful ruling for Spain would set a legal precedent, meaning that American ships found in non-American waters would be granted the same protection. The court ultimately decided that the United States did not have standing to intervene; nonetheless, the United States sided with Spain rather than the State of Virginia.

In district court, Virginia and Sea Hunt attempted to demonstrate that the ships were abandoned based on treaties from 1763 and 1819 in which Spain ceded its interest in property on the continent to Britain and then the United States. Moreover, Sea Hunt argued, the court should infer abandonment because Spain had made no effort to recover the ships over the course of two centuries. On the other hand, Spain argued that sovereign warships cannot be deemed abandoned unless their flag nation demonstrates clear and affirmative intention to abandon them. The 1763 and 1819 treaties did not contain sufficiently strong language to effect abandonment, Spain contended. The district court held that the 1763 treaty contained language that indicated express abandonment of all property interests, but that the 1819 one did not. Both parties appealed.

At the Court of Appeals, Fourth Circuit, Sea Hunt argued that the ASA allows a court to infer abandonment if the sovereign fails to declare ownership in a timely fashion.[40] The court rejected this contention, and instead called upon standards of traditional maritime salvage law to read in a higher standard of abandonment. Spain brought up the fact that it did not want commercial salvagers with no knowledge of scientific or archaeological standards of exploration to desecrate the burial place of its sailors. On appeal, the Court upheld the District Court's ruling that Spain still had ownership of the *Juno*, and overturned the ruling that it had abandoned its right to *La Galga*. This was a landmark case in which a foreign nation successfully claimed ownership of an ancient shipwreck in American waters. Significantly, the Court of Appeals showed that it was sensitive to the issue of marine looting, and that the advancement of technology could in some cases become a threat to cultural patrimony. As it becomes easier for looters to prey on shipwrecks for profit, protection for UCH becomes increasingly important. The passage of time is meaningless; the sovereign does not lose ownership of a vessel when it sinks.[41]

The major issue in the case of *Juno* and *La Galga* was for the court to decide which laws apply. The ASA exempts shipwrecks within its jurisdiction from admiralty law, but traditional notions of ownership and abandonment continue to inform the court's understanding of the issues. Critics of the ASA feel that it disrupts the uniformity of admiralty law and raises issues of how to protect foreign wrecks.[42] There is ongoing debate about whether the ASA is the appropriate method of protecting UCH sites, or whether the traditional law of finds and salvage can better accomplish the task. These debates illustrate the tensions between the commercial interests of salvors and the societal interest of retrieving scientific, cultural and historical information contained in the wrecks. Which interests should the law protect, and what is in the interest of public policy?

Legal Framework: The Canadian Perspective

Canada has the world's longest coastline and borders on three oceans.[43] Moreover, there are 3000 sunken ships on the Ontario side of the Great Lakes alone.[44] Combining these facts with the improvement of technology, rising demand for colonial collectibles, and the increasing price of gold, UCH disputes will be an expanding field of Canadian law.

The case of the *Atlantic* steamship demonstrates the interests at play with sunken ships in the Great Lakes. The *Atlantic* sank to the bottom of Lake Erie on a late August evening in 1852 carrying hundreds of immigrants and a hoard of gold coins. The boat left Buffalo with 150 cabins full of passengers and an additional 250 immigrants on the deck. When the owner of the ship heard that there were more immigrants waiting at Erie, he stopped to pick up another 100 passengers, leaving 70 angry ones behind. In fact, they were the lucky ones.

Fog developed as a result of the cool, late summer air hitting the warm lake water. At 2:00 am, another ship, the *Ogdensburgh*, pierced the *Atlantic*'s baggage room with its oar. All passengers could have fit onto the *Ogdensburgh* but, instead of moving them, the captains argued over who was to blame for the collision. The *Ogdensburgh* removed its oar from the *Atlantic* and continued on its trek as water poured into the boat. The *Atlantic's* captain tried to run the ship aground on the Canadian shore at Long Point; meanwhile, the crew did nothing to inform the passengers of the situation. As time passed, the engine room flooded with water, dousing the boiler's flames and causing the steamship to halt in its tracks. Pandemonium and horror broke out amongst the passengers. One immigrant wrote that the screams were indescribable and he would never forget them as long as he lived.[45] Three hundred passengers drowned before the *Ogdensburgh* returned to rescue surviving passengers from the sinking *Atlantic*, which was soon at the bottom of Lake Erie.

The location of the shipwreck in Lake Erie became well known. Divers vied to find the American Express safe containing the passengers' cash fares, which had gone down with the ship. One diver, John Green, got so close that he could touch the safe; unfortunately, at that moment he was afflicted with the bends and left permanently crippled.[46] Following that, Elliot Harrington managed to retrieve the safe with US$36,700 worth of gold. American Express sued, ultimately settling for half of the safe's contents.

The owners of the *Ogdensburgh* and the *Atlantic* continued the argument that the ships' captains had begun on that fateful night. The case went up to the United States Supreme Court in 1858, which held that both crews were equally at fault. More than a century later, an Ontario court would find that, by treating the ship as a write-off, the owners of the *Atlantic* had implicitly abandoned the wreckage.

In 1872, an American company was established in order to salvage the ship. It was not clear if ownership transferred from the owner to the salvagers. In 1914, Western Wrecking Company's articles of incorporation were revoked when they deserted the salvage project.

The ship remained untouched in its watery grave until 1984 when Michael Lynn Fletcher of Port Dover, Ontario, rediscovered the wreckage, made video recordings of it, and marked it with a buoy. Two years later, an American diver named Borsse used the buoy to locate and identify the wreck. Borsse joined with Joe Morgan, a treasure hunter, to form Mar-Dive Corporation and Atlantic Western Ltd. The court of Ohio allowed them to resurrect Western Wrecking Company and salvage the *Atlantic*, which was believed to have 25,000 ounces of gold coin preserved in the baggage compartment. Coin collectors would pay handsomely for nineteenth-century gold coins, especially in such prime condition.

In March 1992, Mar-Dive brought an *in rem* action in the District Court of California to affirm Western's ownership of the *Atlantic*. No federal or provincial representatives attended, nor did Fletcher, the original finder, appear to argue against Mar-Dive's application for certification of ownership of the shipwreck. Borsse claimed that he had discovered the ship, and labelled Fletcher an interloping embezzler. In May, the court issued an order granting a motion for summary judgment and an injunction against Fletcher. Significantly, it was never brought to the court's attention that the Government of Ontario or the Canadian Federal Government had claims to the ship under the *Canadian Shipping Act* or the royal prerogative that shipwrecks and their booty belong to the Crown. In May 1992, the court issued an order stating that Atlantic Western was the undisputed owner of the *Atlantic*, even though there were no other parties in attendance. The Government of Ontario issued warrants of arrest for Mar-Dive's principals for removing objects from the wreckage.

Mar-Dive requested that the Federal Court of Canada, as the country's court of admiralty, enforce the California court order. The Federal Court referred the case to the Ontario Court (General Division).[47] Mar-Dive argued that the judge should either uphold the California order or, alternatively, certify Mar-Dive's ownership based on the uninterrupted line of ownership from the Western company that was dissolved in 1914. Mar-Dive argued that there was a real and substantial connection between the United States District Court and the *Atlantic*: she was a United States flag vessel passing through Canadian territorial waters on a voyage between two American ports when another United States flagship caused her to sink. The modern-day litigation surrounding the 1852 incident was all conducted in American courts—the only connection with Canada was that the *Atlantic* happened to sink in its territorial waters and was discovered by a Canadian in 1984. With both parties present, allegations that Fletcher was an interloper were no longer credible. Ontario argued that the California Court had no real and substantial connection to the wreck, and that the *Atlantic* became the property of the Crown when it was embedded in Lake Erie's muddy floor. Even if embedment had not occurred, the royal prerogative would have meant that the Crown, which is immune from any salvage claims, owned the wreckage. The Ontario court did not enforce the Californian court order, explaining that the only connection between the shipwreck and the state was that California was where Mar-Dive's directors lived. Furthermore, the Ontario court held that Borsse had misled the California court by claiming that he had been the original discoverer of the wreck, and that the rulings had been "artificial." Mar-Dive did not have the financial capacity to appeal the decision. Today, the *Atlantic* belongs to the Crown, and its treasures still lie at the bottom of Lake Erie.

Cases like this are only a small sample of the complex issues raised in UCH disputes. Cultural heritage resources discovered in the world's waterways bring to the forefront the same issues as cultural property found on dry land: who owns history and who is entitled to attribute meaning to it? What sets underwater cultural heritage apart is the long history of international "laws of the sea." Principles of admiralty law, such as the laws of salvage and finds, support the individual interest in private profit over the societal interest in public education. Such principles conflict with international policies that recognize the non-monetary value of cultural property to all of humanity and are designed to protect and preserve cultural heritage in an age where technology and greed threaten it. Eventually the law will have to evolve to meet the demands of public policy in the interest of society.

FAKES AND FORGERIES

I t is not illegal to reproduce or imitate an artist's work, but it becomes a crime when the act is coupled with the intent to deceive. Passing off an imitation as a famous artist's work is fraud. The Canadian *Criminal Code* contains offences both for forgery and fraud. Under s. 366:

(1)   Every one commits forgery who makes a false document, knowing it to be false, with intent
        a)   that it should in any way be used or acted on as genuine, to the prejudice of any one whether within Canada or not;
        b)   that a person should be induced, by the belief that it is genuine, to do or to refrain from doing anything, whether within Canada or not.

(2)   Making a false document includes
        (a)   altering a genuine document in any material part;
        (b)   making a material addition to a genuine document or adding to it a false date, attestation, seal or other thing that is material; or
        (c)   making a material alteration in a genuine document by erasure, obliteration, removal or in any other way.[1]

When fakers and forgers sell their works as the real thing, they commit fraud, which is defined in s. 380:

(1)   Every one who, by deceit, falsehood or other fraudulent means, whether or not it is a false pretence within the meaning of this Act, defrauds the public or any person, whether ascertained or not, of any property, money or valuable security or any service,
        (a)   is guilty of an indictable offence and liable to a term of imprisonment not exceeding fourteen years, where the subject-matter of the offence is a testamentary instrument or the value of the subject-matter of the offence exceeds five thousand dollars; or
        (b)   is guilty

(i)   of an indictable offence and liable to imprisonment for a term not exceeding two years, or

(ii)   of an offence punishable on summary conviction,

where the value of the subject-matter of the offence does not exceed five thousand dollars.

(2)   Every one who, by deceit, falsehood or other fraudulent means, whether or not it is a false pretence within the meaning of the Act, with any intent to defraud, affects the public market price of stocks, shares, merchandise or anything that is offered for sale to the public is guilty of an indictable offence and liable to imprisonment for a term not exceeding fourteen years.[2]

Fakes and forgeries are both unapproved copies of original works, but there is a fine distinction between the two. A fake is an object in the style of another artist, whereas a forgery is an exact replica of another work. Both are illegal when represented as authentic.

TYPES OF FAKES AND FORGERIES

While fakes and forgeries fall under two sections of the *Criminal Code* only, there are many categories or methods to create fakes and forgeries.

1. *Intentional Fabrication.* This is a straightforward case of fraud. The criminal purposely creates a piece of art, copying another artist, and then claims that it is the real thing. This often involves falsification of provenance records as well.

2. *Innocent Reproductions.* Many copies of famous works are initially created without any intent to deceive. It is only when someone passes it off as an original that it becomes a forgery. These might include copies that were made during the artist's lifetime and never intended to be passed off as the original. Making copies of masters' works has long been a method of artistic teaching.[3]

3. *Reworking of Genuine Objects.* This type of forgery refers to art that is altered by an individual other than the artist. During the Renaissance, it was thought necessary that all art reflect contemporary ideologies and religious beliefs, so works were altered

accordingly. This is no longer common practice, but it does occasionally occur.

4. *Pastiche*. This method of forgery combines smaller elements of different works to create one "complete" piece of art. The works used in creating a pastiche might not even be from the same artist; the famous forger Eric Hebborn combined unrelated profile portraits of two women by Botticelli and Pollaiuolo to create a rare double-portrait of the fifteenth century.[4]

5. *Fragmentation*. One method of forgery, rather the opposite of pastiche, is to subdivide one large piece of art into a number of smaller works. They are attributed to the appropriate artist, but do not fully represent the original creation. This was a common practice in the eighteenth and nineteenth centuries.

6. *Apprentice Work Attributed to Master*. Unintentional misattribution can occur when a student's work is mistaken for a master's. Even if it was an honest mistake, purchasers will suffer. Unintentional misattribution occurred with several Rembrandts. During the seventeenth and eighteenth centuries, works "from the studio of" or "the school of" Rembrandt were attributed to Rembrandt himself. Many of these paintings were hanging in the Metropolitan Museum, and there was a heated debate over whether these newly reattributed works should be considered as less worthy fakes or forgeries.[5]

METHODS OF DETECTING FAKES AND FORGERIES

Of course, identifying these imitations requires much research and many scientific processes. In most cases we must rely on both subjective and objective information.

The Expert Witness

This section raises issues involved in authenticating works of art and cultural property when an expert is asked to make an examination in terms of its stylistic qualities. Scientific testing alone is not always sufficient to determine whether a piece of art is authentic. For example, many works by the artist Vincent Van Gogh were copied and forged around the same period that the artist was painting and might therefore pass paint analyses. It would be necessary to get the opinion of an expert on Van Gogh, based on comprehensive knowledge about the artist, examining aspects such as style of brush stroke, how paint was applied, the catalog of Van Gogh's works, and historic documentation. Experts can also employ their intuition based on experience in their field of expertise, research based on the life of the artist, and from archival records. Hence, both subjective and objective tests are required to determine whether a work is authentic.

The Rembrandt Research Project[6] was established to deal with the problem of misattribution concerning the authenticity of Rembrandt paintings. About a century ago it was believed that there were approximately 700 paintings in the body of Rembrandt's work. Now it is believed that there are in fact only about 350, a reduction that occurred as a result of the discovery that some paintings were signed "by the master" when they were in fact found to be "in the style of the master." It is necessary to use scientific testing as well as the subjective test and the chain of documentation available on the paintings in question in order to determine whether they are really by Rembrandt.

Yet another complication that can arise when relying on the subjective test occurs when an expert changes his or her mind. This happened to an Iranian businessman who purchased a Faberge egg from Christie's in 1977. The price of the egg increased when an expert identified it as having belonged to the Russian Imperial Family. After bidding, however, the purchaser questioned the egg's authenticity and refused to pay for it. Christie's found another expert to testify to the origins of the egg. When the egg was again consigned to Christie's in 1985, the same expert who had verified its provenance in the 1977 auction changed his mind about its authenticity.[7] Just as one must be wary of evolutions in science and technology, opinions are susceptible to change. It is therefore difficult to verify with 100% certainty the authenticity of any piece of art.

Experts can also be reluctant to give their opinions because of the liability that can be incurred. A painting potentially worth millions of dollars becomes virtually worthless if deemed inauthentic. Holding oneself out as an expert on art opens one up to causes of action for disparagement, defamation, fraud, misrepresentation, and interference with contractual relations, among others. Experts caught in an outright lie on the stand will of course be charged with perjury, but an expert's liability extends beyond courtroom testimony. In a famous 1929 case, an art dealer's off-the-cuff statement to a reporter from the *New York Word* caused the owner of a Leonardo da Vinci painting to sue for slander of title.[8] The painting, La Belle Ferroniere, was a wedding gift to Harry and Andree Hahn from the bride's wealthy aunt. Problematically, a copy of the same painting hung on the wall of the Louvre. The Hahns had the painting authenticated by an expert and brought it with them when they moved to Kansas City, where it caught the attention of the Kansas City Art Institute. Before the Hahns could complete their sale of the painting to the museum, a reporter asked for art expert Joseph Duveen's remarks on it. Although he had not seen the work in question, he commented that it must be a fake, since Leonardo did not make replicas and the original was at the Louvre. After that statement was splashed over the news, the Hahns had an un-sellable painting on their hands. They sued Duveen for slander of title, claiming that his statements had lost them US$500,000. At the trial, "experts" for both sides merely confused the jury of laymen, splitting opinion 9-3. As the *Herald Tribune* commented, "an artist, an accountant, and a bank worker said Mme. Hahn's picture was not original, while two salesmen, two brokers, a man without a vocation, a shirtmaker, a dressmaker, a clerk and a barber said it was."[9] The parties settled out of court with Duveen paying US$60,000 plus the Hahns' legal fees.[10]

Probably the most insidious problem in authentication disputes occurs when expert opinions are diametrically opposed to one another. The defense produces an expert who claims the object is real and the prosecution produces a witness who claims it is fake. This strategy usually leads cases to be thrown out of courts. In the St. James Ossuary trial, which is taking place in Israel, the head of the Israeli Antiquities Authority (IAA) states that some famous authorities in the field are conspiring with the forgers.[11] Inconclusive scientific testing makes expert opinion all the more relevant in determining the authenticity of the ossuary. It is a high-stakes case given the religious and cultural significance of the box, not to mention the money involved for its owner, Tel Aviv collector Oded Golan, who is being charged for forging a number of items in addition to the ossuary. The prosecution and defence have both recruited leading archaeological experts to their cause. Judge Aharon Farkash, before whom the case stands, has a degree in archaeology himself. The predicament in this case is not a lack of expertise, but a lack of experts who can agree with one another.

One final note of caution when dealing with the experts: as cynical as it sounds, anyone can be bought. There is a serious issue surrounding who is authorized to appraise a work of art.

Canadian law lacks conflict of interest guidelines for providing appraisals for donations. An accredited expert independent of the transaction should appraise an artwork's value to prevent conflicts of interest and protect buyers against fraud. The United States Internal Revenue Services (IRS) has an Art Advisory Panel to evaluate appraisals, which is an important step toward cleaning up the art trade. The Panel was set up in 2001 when the IRS became aware of collusion between art collectors and appraisers. A collector might approach an unscrupulous authenticator to evaluate various pieces at an inflated value. The collector will then donate those pieces to a museum and receive a sizable income tax write-off, a portion of which is given to the appraiser. The Panel reviews applications to prevent this conduct from occurring. The Panel consists of 25 renowned experts who serve without compensation. Any tax audit claiming art purporting a value over US\$20,000 will be referred to the Art Advisory Panel for review.[12] These efforts at accountability, transparency, and protection against fraud are commendable.

Scientific Testing

Modern science enables experts to verify the authenticity of a piece of art with some degree of objective certainty. Depending on the composition of the artifact in question, different methods will yield the most reliable results. Multiple authentication procedures are usually necessary for the sake of accuracy. These procedures currently consist of the following:

- thermoluminescent (TL) analysis,
- radiocarbon dating,
- chemical analysis,
- microscopic techniques,
- reconstructing manufacturing techniques,
- infrared imaging,
- ultraviolet imaging,
- conventional x-ray,
- x-ray diffraction,
- x-ray fluorescence,
- auto-radiography,
- atomic absorption spectrophotometry (AAS) and inductively coupled plasma mass spectrometry (ICP-MS),
- computerized axial tomography (CAT scans),
- obsidian hydration,
- fission tracks,
- stable isotope analysis
- dendochronology, and
- computer-based authentication techniques

This section will outline in straightforward terms the role of modern science in detecting artistic fakes and forgeries.

Thermoluminescent (TL) Analysis

TL refers to the light produced by heating. Some materials, when heated, emit a faint but visible light. TL is commonly used to date pottery, since the concentration of charge-carrying particles in clay builds over time but is released whenever the clay is fired. When a sample is heated and the particles are freed, they emit a TL that can be measured to reveal the time elapsed since the clay was last fired.

Radiocarbon Dating

Every living organism contains a fixed amount of radiation, Carbon-14. When an organism dies, the level of radiocarbon deteriorates at a steady rate. By measuring the amount of radiocarbon left in an organic object, its age can be estimated fairly accurately. This method works best on objects less than 10,000 years old, though with special procedures it can be used to date objects up to 50,000 years old.[13] Radiocarbon dating is a popular technique of detecting fakes and forgeries for art that contains materials such as charcoal, wood, paper, parchment, hair, textiles, seeds, pollen, plants, flesh, dung, peat, organic muds and soils, bones, or shells.

Chemical Analysis

Chemical analysis is mainly used for dating fossils of bones or teeth in a single area under comparable conditions. While buried in the soil, the hydroxy-apatite in bone irreversibly changes its composition. Bones buried in the same place at the same date will accumulate the same amount of fluorine through the groundwater. Bones that have been buried more recently on an older site might appear outwardly identical to the older fossils, but they will have lower fluorine levels. The relative ages of bones from the same burial site can also be determined through a comparison of their organic contents, as nitrogen levels decrease over time. High nitrogen plus low fluorine and uranium indicates more recent material.

Microscopic Techniques

Some fakes and forgeries are blatant enough as to be detectable to the naked eye. In most cases, however, it is necessary to take a much closer look. Microscopic examination is a common method of detecting fakes and forgeries of various materials. With a painting, the expert can inspect whether cracks in the paint are real or simulated by pencil lines. A powerful microscope makes it possible to study the uniformity of pigment particles, which can indicate if a modern mechanical mill was used to mix and grind the paints. For stone sculptures, microscopic examination reveals erosion patterns and mineral accretions. With a strong enough microscope, a metallurgist can determine the processes used in the creation of a metal artifact. Electron microscopes, which magnify the sample over 20 times, make it possible to identify elements, compounds, particles and fibres smaller than a human blood cell.

Reconstructing Manufacturing Techniques

Careful recreation of ancient processes is one way of testing the authenticity of antiquities. Method and outcome are inseparable, which makes reconstruction of manufacturing techniques a useful way to detect fakes. Studies of the metallurgical and glassmaking procedures of ancient times make it possible for experts to recreate the objects the way they would have been produced in the past. The experts can then compare the composition of their creations with that of the alleged antiquities.

Infrared Imaging

Infrared light penetrates the surface of a painting to reveal the drawing beneath it. Infrared light reflects off of dense black pigments. If an artist used charcoal or other carbon-based black pigments on a lighter-coloured canvas, infrared imaging makes it possible to view the original drawing, concealed or altered signatures, and compositional changes that the artist made before applying the final layers of paint. Infrared imaging is useful for Northern European works of the fifteenth to sixteenth century, when it was common to use black underdrawings on contrasting white backdrops.[14]

Ultraviolet Imaging

Ultraviolet light reflects off of a painting's surface elements. Colours and varnishes fluoresce differently depending on their chemical composition. UV imaging is a useful method of detecting where a painting has been cleaned or retouched, because the more recently the paint was applied, the more UV light it will absorb.[15]

Conventional X-Ray

A conventional X-ray will expose what lies beneath the surface of a painting. Artists often re-use canvasses or paint over their own works, so the presence of another layer does not necessarily indicate a forgery. There have been cases, however, in which paintings supposedly from the seventeenth century have been X-rayed to reveal people in nineteenth-century garb underneath. A basic X-ray can also reveal brushstroke patterns, which can then be compared with known authentic works by the same artist. The copycat will make slow, careful, deliberate strokes in an attempt to imitate the original artist as precisely as possible. The true artist's brushstrokes, on the other hand, tend to have a more natural flow.[16] In some cases, X-rays can even reveal the artist (or forger's) fingerprints.

X-Ray Diffraction

Knowing what materials were used in an object is crucial in identifying whether it is a fake or forgery. Every material has its own unique diffraction pattern. X-ray diffraction, a technique which identifies crystalline inorganic materials, is most commonly used to analyze paint samples and determine what pigments are present. It can be applied to a variety of other substances, including glass, jewellery, metal, pottery, glazes, and jades.[17]

X-Ray Fluorescence

When blasted with enough energy, an object will emit X-rays. The secondary X-rays released by excitation of a given material have energies specific to the element that produced them. X-ray fluorescence is a non-destructive method of analyzing art and cultural property. The results of an X-ray fluorescence examination appear in a graph that shows the presence and amounts of the chemical elements within the tested artifact. This method was used to detect a Raphael forgery in 1994. The Getty Conservation Institute examined the suspicious drawing using X-ray fluorescence spectroscopy and discovered "a considerable amount of titanium" on the surface. Titanium oxides were not manufactured until after World War II over 400 years after Raphael lived.[18]

Auto-Radiography

Auto-radiography is different from conventional X-radiography in that it produces a series of different radiographs of a painting, rather than a single one. Analysis of the series of images uncovers information about how pigments were originally applied by the artist and how they are distributed throughout the piece of art. The technique requires that the entire painting be irradiated in a nuclear reactor until its thermal temperature reaches 30 degrees Celsius, at which point it will be covered with sheets of X-ray film. The exposed film creates a "map" of pigments.[19]

Atomic Absorption Spectrophotometry (AAS) and Inductively Coupled Plasma Mass Spectrometry (ICP-MS)

A piece of art can be authenticated through comparative analysis to a known sample from the same artist or period. Differences between the elements or composition patterns can indicate a fake or forgery. With a painting, it is useful to test for the presence of certain pigments. Some common elements used in contemporary paintings have a known date of discovery, and, were they to appear in an earlier work, would indicate that it was inauthentic. Simply put, AAS and ICP-MS determine what elements are present in an object. If tests reveal the presence of an element that does not typically appear in objects from that artist or era, it could very well be a fake. In the seventeenth century, for instance, artists like Vermeer used ultramarine blue paint derived from lapis lazuli. Presence of cobalt blue pigment, which was discovered in the eighteenth century, would reveal the painting to be a forgery. Similar tests could be applied to the composition patterns of varnishes, either on paintings or pottery.

Computerized Axial Tomography (CAT scans)

Conducting a CAT scan of a sculpture or ceramic artifact can reveal if it has been assembled using segments of ancient material.[20] It is a useful method for detecting a "pastiche" fake. A CAT scan has greater power of penetration because it uses high energy X-rays, and is therefore useful in the study of three-dimensional objects. Due to the expense and commercial unavailability of the equipment, CAT scans are not a widely used method of detecting artistic forgeries.[21]

Obsidian Hydration

Obsidian, or volcanic crystal, absorbs water from its surroundings to form a hydration layer that can be measured under a microscope. The thickness of the hydration layer depends on time, temperature, and volcanic composition. Since 1960, obsidian hydration has been used as a method of dating volcanic crystal artifacts, such as knives, drills, sickles, hooks, and carvings, as the test reveals how much time has elapsed since a fresh surface was exposed or shaped.

Fission Tracks

For glassy or crystalline substances containing uranium, measuring the fission tracks caused by radiation damage will provide an estimate of the time that has passed since the creation of the material. Dating an object through fission tracks is only possible if the object contains sufficient uranium and has not been overheated (heat causes fission tracks to fade). Measuring fission tracks is most valuable for dating objects between 70,000 and 1 million years old. Radiocarbon dating is ineffective on materials this old, because the amount of Carbon-14 left would be immeasurably small. The fission tracking technique is appropriate for glass, glazes, minerals in pottery, and slags. However, it is important to note that fission tracking determines the age of the formation of the material, not the time elapsed since it was shaped into an artifact. The test is therefore of limited applicability for man-made objects, with the exception of man-made glass artifacts.

Stable Isotope Analysis

An isotope is stable when it is not radioactive and therefore does not decay. The ratio of stable isotopes in some elements vary depending on their geological source. Until the nineteenth century, the lead in paint came from European ores. Modern lead sources, on the other hand, are typically from the United States, Canada, and Australia.[22] Stable isotope analysis of an object containing lead can reveal when it was made. Stable isotope analysis can also reveal where the marble in a statue was quarried.[23]

Dendochronology

The age of a wooden artifact can be determined by studying its tree rings. It will determine the date at which the wood used in the artifact was sawn, and is a useful method of dating wooden panels, sculptures, and musical instruments. The accuracy of dendochronology depends on the condition of the artifact and the availability of comparative data.[24] It is limited to trees from temperate regions, such as oak, beech, fir, pine and spruce.[25]

Computer-Based Authentication Methods

Most of the above-mentioned scientific methods reveal fakes and forgeries by determining the age of the piece in question. Knowing when a piece was created is less helpful when it comes to fakes and forgeries of contemporary art. Similarly, chemical testing often overlooks the possibility of copycats painting in the same time period as the artist. The expert eye is one way of detecting such frauds, but accuracy cannot be guaranteed. Another method that is gaining popularity is computer-based authentication.

Novel methods of computer testing have made it possible to detect fakes and forgeries in a non-invasive fashion. While computer analysis of art is a complex and highly technical area of study, it is the wave of the future in authentication of cultural property.

Put in its simplest terms, computer analysis involves scanning the surface of an artwork and comparing it against a database of verified works of the true artist. The computer gathers information and matches the "fractals"—the patterns, colours, lines, negative space, and other compositional elements of the piece—against those in the artist's known works. The pioneering study was that of University of Oregon physicist Richard Taylor, who catalogued a database of Jackson Pollock's work. When 32 "new" Pollock paintings turned up in a warehouse, Taylor's information revealed that six of the works did not have the same fractal patterns as those in the authenticated database. The new collection even contained inconsistencies amongst its own pieces, suggesting that they were not all painted by the same hand.[26]

As technology becomes more sophisticated, so do art criminals. For example, computer technology has made it possible to scan the dimensions of an authentic classical Greek marble frieze and then use computer controlled lathes to cut fresh marble, creating a near-identical fake. Some forging laboratories have the technology to chemically reproduce original paints, which makes it harder to detect fakes and forgeries in a chemical pigment analysis.[27] Whenever scientific advancements improve detection methods, forging methods equally improve.

CASES OF INTERNATIONAL INTRIGUE

The practice of making fakes and forgeries goes back to the time of the Romans and Byzantines, who reproduced Greek compositions and sold them as originals. Fakes became prevalent in China during the Sung Dynasty, 960-1280 AD, when the upper class became interested in art collecting. Art counterfeiting became a twentieth-century epidemic, especially with the growth of the art market after World War II. It was common practice for students to imitate their masters and sell them as his work. Today, experts estimate that as much as 40% of the art market involves trade in fakes and forgeries.[28] The most commonly forged works claim to be by Giorgio de Chirico, Jean-Baptise-Camille Corot, Salvador Dali, Honore Daumier, Vincent van Gogh, Kazimir Malevich, Amedeo Modigliani, Frederic Remington, Auguste Rodin, and Maurice Utrillo. One joke goes that "Carot painted 800 pictures in his lifetime, of which 4000 ended up in American collections."[29]

A look back at some of history's most scandalous forgery cases will flesh out the profile of the art criminal and reveal that fakers and forgers often have the same motives and fixations as looters and thieves. Similarly, they tend to fall for the same reasons: overconfidence and carelessness. One forger of a Rubens was recently snared when an interested purchaser noticed that the artist's name was spelled incorrectly. Illicit trafficking of stolen art generally corresponds with high trade in fakes and forgeries; both crimes rely on market forces.

Counterfeiting art is no simple crime. Not only does it require the talent to paint like the masters, but also a deep knowledge of science and an understanding of the marketplace. Only the most determined criminal would take to art forgery. Despite the riches involved, forgery is often a highly personal crime. Those who forge art waste their energy being vindictive rather than focusing their abilities on developing as artists in their own right. Collectors, museums, and galleries must exercise extreme caution when it comes to fakes and forgeries, because, with a few exceptions, purchasers of illegitimate cultural property usually end up as victims without a legal remedy or compensation for their losses.

Han van Meegeren (1889-1947)

In 1937, a man named Boon travelled to Monaco to meet with the noted Vermeer expert, Dr. Abraham Bredius. He was visiting Dr. Bredius on behalf of his friend, Han Van Meegeren, who was interested in Dr. Bredius's opinion on a piece he had recently acquired. The painting, entitled *The Supper at Emmaus*, depicted the Disciples staring in awe at the risen Christ, who, with a poignant and serene air about Him, breaks His bread. Upon inspection, Dr. Bredius could hardly contain his excitement:

> It is a wonderful moment in the life of a lover of art when he finds himself suddenly confronted with a hitherto unknown painting by a great master, untouched, on the original canvas, and without any restoration, just as it left the painter's studio! And what a picture! Neither the beautiful signature "I. V. Meer" (I.V.M. in monogram) nor the pointille on the bread which Christ is blessing, is necessary to convince us that we have here a—I am inclined to say—the masterpiece of Johannes Vermeer of Delft, and, moreover, one of his largest works (1.29m by 1.17m), quite different from all his other paintings and yet every inch a Vermeer.[30]

Little did Dr. Bredius know, it was not Vermeer but Van Meegeren himself who had created the exquisite piece. The Rembrandt society purchased the painting for 520,000 guilders—about US$4 million in today's currency. Between 1932 and 1945, Van Meegeren lived luxuriously off of the proceeds of his illicit trade.

Van Meegeren had gained a moderate degree of esteem in the Netherlands as an artist in his own right throughout the 1920s. However, as interest in Cubism and Surrealism grew, appreciation for Van Meegeren faded. Derided by critics as banal and out of date, Van Meegeren became embittered against the art world. He set out to prove to his critics that he was no mere imitator, but rather, could create a piece of such genius that he would outshine even the greatest of master painters. *The Supper at Emmaus* was this piece.

Encouraged by the financial success and emotional rush of selling his forgery, Van Meegeren continued churning out fake Vermeers. During

World War II, one of them ended up in Hermann Goering's hands. When Allied forces discovered Goering's hidden art collection in an Austrian salt mine, they traced the mysterious new "Vermeer" back to Van Meegeren. He was charged as a Nazi collaborator for plundering Dutch cultural property to the Germans. The stigma and penalty for Nazi collaboration being as extreme as it was, Van Meegeren had no realistic choice but to confess to his true crime of fraud. In his confession, he explained that fooling the experts had been the sweetest revenge, and that no feeling could compare to that of humiliating the condescending critics who had scorned his work.[31]

Van Meegeren's Nazi collaboration charges were dropped when expert testimony confirmed that the work was indeed a forgery and therefore not cultural property of the Netherlands. Nonetheless, he was prosecuted on charges of forgery and fraud. The Regional Court in Amsterdam sentenced him to one year in prison; one month later, he died a national hero.[32]

Eric Hebborn (1934-1996)

On January 8, 1996, a man was discovered in a park in Rome suffering from severe head trauma. The back of his head had been bludgeoned repeatedly with a hammer. It was smashed beyond recognition.

Later, he was identified as Eric Hebborn—a master forger who had infuriated dealers by writing *The Art Forger's Handbook*, a how-to guide on forging simply and subversively. He had completed the book two weeks earlier and it was published posthumously.

The case was closed with the Italian police calling it "an accident."

The art world was understandably abuzz after Hebborn's death. Speculations began circulating about the culprit: was it a dealer? An agent? A curator who had been tricked by Hebborn? Or, was it someone who he had revealed in his book as having purchased a forgery? Over a decade later, we still do not have all the answers.

Hebborn's posthumous publication was a "cookbook on art": an eraser was a potato; a stain remover, olive oil; for stain, eggs. Like painting, the book explained, forgery is not just an art but a craft. The best place to create one was in the kitchen. Hebborn's best advice for would-be forgers was to use period paper: if the paper is good, an expert can forge many flaws, which would be typical in an original work. He instructs the reader on how to create watermarks, explains how tea and coffee can create a "period" look, and outlines tips for creating "smoked" effects. Another ingenious trick revealed in Hebborn's book was how to put a fake over a fake. Hebborn's techniques were frighteningly powerful, and the art world had been fooled by them in the past. The British Museum, London's Colnaghi Gallery, New York's Metropolitan Museum of Art, and the Washington National Gallery are but a few who have had Hebborn's handiwork in their direct possession.

Hebborn felt there was a moral justification for his actions, which he never considered illegal. His 1991 autobiography, *Drawn to Trouble*, painted a portrait of a troubled man. Born in Essex, England, to a poor Cockney family, Hebborn had a violent childhood. He claimed to have been beaten constantly at school and home alike. His first foray into art came when he was locked in his room for hours; he passed the time making sculptures out of his excrement. Not surprisingly, his mother was unimpressed by this early display of talent.

After burning down his boarding school at the age of eight, Hebborn made his way through a series of foster homes, in which he was repeatedly raped. As a teenager, Hebborn's artistic talents garnered him attention at London's Royal Academy. He began copying other artists' works as a young man, and quickly realized the possibilities for profit. However, his incentives were more political and personal than financial; Hebborn's real goal was to outsmart and humiliate the elitist establishment. Working as an assistant to George Aczel, an art restorer, Hebborn honed his forging skills: "under Mr. Aczel's guidance I began, little by little, to develop my abilities and improve my knowledge of the materials and methods of the Old Masters until I would one day be able to 'restore' a whole painting—from nothing at all."[33]

His techniques refined, Hebborn began forging prolifically. He moved to Italy, where he became close friends (or perhaps lovers, some sources speculate) with Sir Anthony Blunt. Blunt, an art connoisseur who would later be revealed as a Soviet spy, provided Hebborn with an understanding of the marketplace. Blunt's reputation for being an expert on Nicholas

Poussin meant he had connections with dealers and auction houses. It also meant he could credibly vouch for the authenticity of Hebborn's work —though eventually Hebborn's forging skills were good enough to deceive even Blunt.[34]

Hebborn was well aware of the criminal implications of selling forged art works. He believed, however, that he could evade the law by simply presenting a work to a potential buyer and feigning ignorance. Hebborn did not walk up to a dealer and say, "I have a Poussin that might interest you." Instead, he would show up with one of his forgeries and let the prospective buyer reach his own mistaken conclusions about what exactly it was and how much it was worth.[35] Hebborn treated his criminal endeavors as if it were all a game:

> To make delightful duality worth playing one must choose worthy opponents. Just as there could be little satisfaction in scoring a goal in the absence of a goalkeeper, so it is that to sell a master drawing to someone lacking the necessary expertise to make a proper appraisal of it is at best a hollow victory. In other words, only the experts are worth fooling, and the greater the expert, the greater the satisfaction of deceiving him.[36]

Hebborn continued to play his forbidden game even after Konrad Oberhuber, a curator at Washington's National Gallery of Art, exposed him as a forger in 1978. None of Hebborn's victims filed charges against him. Hebborn confessed to being an art forger in 1984, and used the publicity to heap scorn on every one of the game's players—the highly-educated yet surprisingly naïve experts, the avaricious dealers, the pretentious collectors, and the pompous critics.

By the time Hebborn was dealt the losing blow in his devious game, hundreds—maybe even thousands of his works had found their way into the art world. By Hebborn's own account, he had created roughly one thousand pieces that passed for Castiglione, Mantegna, Rubens, Breughel, Van Dyck, Boucher, Poussin, Ghisi, Tiepolo, Piranesi, Corot, and Boldini, among others.[37] It is impossible to say with any accuracy just how many works Hebborn forged and where they are now.

Elmyr de Hory (1906-1976)

After surviving stints in a Transylvanian prison and a German concentration camp in the 1940s, Hungarian artist Elmyr de Hory began a lengthy career selling imitations of Picasso, Vlaminck, Chagall, Toulouse-Lautrec, Duf, Derain, Matisse, Degas, Bonnard, Laurencin, Cezanne, Braque, Derain, Renoir and Modigliani in 1946. It all began in post-war Paris when de Hory befriended Lady Malcolm Campbell. One afternoon she expressed interest in buying a wonderful piece that she saw hanging in his humble apartment. De Hory, short on funds, could not refuse her US$750 offer for what she believed to be a "Greek-period Picasso." Afterwards, de Hory felt terrible that his dear friend had paid him so much for a mere ten minutes of work. Racked with guilt, de Hory was about to confess when she confessed to him: "I sold your Picasso to a dealer in London. I got US$1400 for it. Can I make it up to you with lunch at the Ritz?"[38]

De Hory was a faker, not a forger—he sold works in the style of famous artists rather than direct copies. He repeatedly tried to make an honest living selling his own work, but would return to making lucrative fakes when he failed to find interested purchasers for genuine de Hory works.

In 1952, de Hory attended a meeting with art dealer Frank Perls at a Beverly Hills gallery. De Hory had been hoping to unload a number of his paintings on Perls, but Perls quickly recognized them as fakes. He threw de Hory out of his gallery and threatened to call the police if he ever saw him again. Fearful that Perls would blow his cover with other purchasers, de Hory began using aliases and selling his work by mail-order.[39] He would write to museums and galleries to offer them "the remnants of his family's art collection" from World War II. He set up shop in Florida under the name Louis Raynal. Things were going smoothly until he received a telephone call from one of his best customers, Chicago art dealer Joseph Faulkner. Faulkner asked if Mr. Raynal could provide papers to help in the further authentication of a small Matisse oil painting he had sold him. De Hory said he would have a look around and call Faulkner back. He hung up the phone and immediately cleared out his apartment. Two days later, the FBI showed up and interrogated de Hory's boyfriend about his whereabouts. De Hory fled to Mexico, then to Montreal, all the while continuing his illegal business. In 1966, two of his agents/co-conspirators were arrested in Ibiza on charges of cheque fraud. De Hory fled and lived in exile for two years, but grew tired of his secretive life and eventually returned to Ibiza, where he was arrested and convicted to two years in prison for the crimes of homosexuality and consorting with criminals.

After his release, de Hory returned to Ibiza as a celebrity. He told his story to Clifford Irving, who later became notorious for his own faked autobiography of Howard Hughes. Orson Welles turned Irving's book about de Hory into a film, *F For Fake*. De Hory used his new-found fame to market his own original works. In the meantime, French authorities sought to have him extradited to stand trial on charges of fraud. In 1976, the Spanish government agreed to hand de Hory over to French authorities. Before this could happen, de Hory committed suicide by overdosing on sleeping pills.

In his decades-long career as an art criminal, de Hory produced thousands of fake paintings, watercolours, and drawings that generated over US$2 billion.[40] He was celebrated in posterity as one of history's greatest and most prolific forgers. His "real fakes" are now valuable collector's items.[41]

Tom Keating (1917-1984)

Born into a poor Cockney family in Lewisham, Tom Keating shocked the art world in the early 1970s by admitting that he had created and sold over 2000 forgeries that claimed to be painted by over 100 artists, including Rembrandt, Palmer, Goya, Constable, Renoir, Gainsborough and Degas.

John Brandler, a friend of Keating, described him as having "all the technical skills, but he was missing the one thing that kept him out of the list of the great painters he copied. He didn't have an original vision."[42] Keating began forging works as a method of revenge against the artistic establishment that rejected his personal creative style. Every work Keating forged contained a not-so-secret message of utter disdain and disgust for the art world: beneath the surface, he would write obscene comments in lead white paint that was sure to show up when the painting was x-rayed. He was more concerned with insulting and humiliating the pompous network of arrogant so-called authorities than getting caught. He also planted in each forgery obvious flaws and used anachronistic materials, tempting the "experts" to catch him.[43] The purpose of him crimes was to give the art world its come-uppance and expose those at the top for the frauds he felt they were.

When the London *Times* expressed suspicions about Keating's work, he published a confession in which he voiced his contempt and disgust at the art world. He downplayed his own talent to embarrass the so-called experts, describing himself as "a terrible faker. Anyone who sees my work and thinks it genuine, must be around the bend."[44] He went on to announce, "I have so much contempt for the dealers who prostitute the art of genuine painters that I was willing to sell them any old rubbish." The amazing part was that they bought his rubbish—and at a high price. Keating was tried for conspiracy to defraud, but the case was dropped due to his poor health. He went on to star in his own television program on Channel 4, teaching his viewers how to paint like the masters.[45]

David Stein (1935-1999)

Working out of New York and France, Stein made 41 known copies of Chagall, Matisse, Braque, Klee, Miro, Cocteau, and Rouault.[46] He was uncovered as a forger in 1967 when Chagall himself noticed one of "his" works—which he had never made—hanging in a New York gallery. Stein pled guilty to six counts of art forgery and grand larceny and was sentenced to two and a half years in prison,[47] during which time he continued to paint "in the style of famous artists." He exhibited these works at the Wright Hepburn Webster Gallery, where it turned out many collectors were interested in paying top dollar for Stein's famous forgeries. There was some concern that Stein's works were so similar to those of famous artists that crooked dealers could easily doctor his signature and replace it with that of the imitated artist, then flood the market with the forgeries. In response, New York's Attorney General sought an injunction to prevent the gallery's sales. In *State v. Wright Hepburn Webster Gallery Ltd.*,[48] the court found that there was insufficient basis to issue the injunction and his works continued to sell.[49] At the time of his conviction, Stein was thought to have cost collectors a modest $168,000.[50] Realistically, to collectors and to the public, the cost of Stein's forgeries was much higher.

John Drewe (1948-) and John Myatt (1945-)

Between 1986 and 1995, two men combined their unusual talents to forge and sell over 200 works of art, 140 of which remain on the market.[51] Drewe, whose shady past contains decade-long gaps in records, met Myatt through a magazine advertisement in 1985. Myatt, an impoverished former art teacher, was advertising his high-quality replicas of famous nineteenth and twentieth century masterpieces for low prices. He had an uncanny ability to mimic a range of artistic styles there are at least 30 artists he has been known to copy.[52] Drewe became a regular customer, and began using his own talent at forging provenance documents to sell Myatt's work as authentic. To do this, Drewe infiltrated museum and gallery archives and altered the provenance of real paintings to establish a paper trail for Myatt's forgeries. He would insert pages into old art catalogues so they would include Myatt's forgeries. Archivists will never know how much history was compromised by these actions.

When Drewe admitted to Myatt that he had sold some of his paintings as the original, Myatt was flattered. Recognizing the lucrative possibilities, he became Drewe's willing accomplice. Myatt's paintings raked in an average of £1 million apiece when Drewe sold them through auction houses. Myatt was happy to receive his relatively small share of the profit (about £50,000 per painting) when Drewe managed to sell off his work. As Myatt later explained, "I was flattered into thinking I was a man of importance." Myatt was acutely aware that his works would not withstand scientific scrutiny—"the moment they started to restore them they would know what they were faced with"—and he told Drewe so. His use of modern paints and K-Y Jelly (to speed up drying time and give the appearance of smoother brushstrokes) was shockingly careless. "I took no trouble technically," he later admitted. "There was a negligence to everything I did."

Even so, Drewe managed to sell over 200 of Myatt's forgeries for profits over £1.8 million. It was Drewe's personal life, not Myatt's slipshod techniques, that led to both men's demise. In 1995, Drewe left the mother of his two children, Bat-Sheva Goudsmid, to marry another woman. His jilted ex-girlfriend went through the documents he had left behind. Not surprisingly, many were incriminating. She began blackmailing him; Drewe allegedly told Myatt he was going to burn down her house. Days later, Goudsmid's tenant found a man fitting Drewe's description hiding in the basement. The house burned to the ground hours later. The 25-year-old woman renting the top floor died from her injuries when she jumped out the window to escape the flames. Drewe drastically altered his appearance after the incident, shaving off his moustache, changing his hairdo, and removing his glasses. The tenant failed to identify him in the police lineup as the man seen in the basement that tragic evening. Police had no choice but to release him.

By this point, it became clear to Myatt that Drewe was insanely dangerous. His fear of Drewe and his desire to return to his own painting style made Myatt desperate to end their partnership. Watching his fraudulent works sell in major auction houses for vast sums eventually made Myatt feel bitter and depressed; he knew a "real Myatt" would never be worth much. Feeling hopeless and trapped, Myatt turned himself into police and told them everything. His confession, along with Goudsmid's decision to turn over the surviving documents, led to Drewe's arrest. Drewe mounted an outrageous defence alleging that he was being framed as part of an international conspiracy. When his lawyer refused to conduct this defence, Drewe fired him. The jury returned a guilty verdict in only six hours.

For perpetrating the largest con in art history, Myatt served four months of a one-year prison sentence for conspiracy to defraud. Upon his release, he returned to painting and selling "genuine fakes" under his own name. Drewe served two of his six years in prison for conspiracy. The man who the British prosecution office declared "a menace to Britain's cultural patrimony" maintains his innocence.

Ely Sakhai (1952-)

Until his arrest in 2001, New York antiquities dealer Ely Sakhai ran a successful gallery on Broadway. An Iranian immigrant, Sakhai was known for his reserved demeanor and eccentric fashion sense. He was an avid collector of well-known artists, but not well-known art. He was smart enough to know that famous paintings would attract attention, so he avoided recognizable works. Instead, Sakhai would purchase millions of dollars worth of relatively unknown pieces by big-name artists, pay poor Chinese artists to replicate them, then sell off both the original and the forgeries to make a massive profit. Part of his method was to buy worthless, but very old, paintings; he would then paint his forgeries on these canvasses to give them the appearance of age. A key element of his scheme was to attach the genuine certificate of authenticity to the forged work rather than the original, making it easier to pass off. Throughout the 1990s, Sakhai's elaborate scheme raked in an estimated US$3.5 million.[53]

Things did not always go smoothly for Sakhai; in fact, it is astounding that he evaded authorities for as long as he did. The problem with his method was that multiple versions of the same painting would make their way into the art market, and he was always traceable as the source of each version. Sakhai would usually sell the fakes in Asia and originals in the United States, but in an increasingly global community, this was not as effective as he might have thought. Inevitably, word began to spread in the art world and cautious buyers avoided Sakhai.

Sakhai's downfall is a true testament to human hubris. The jig was up when, in May 2000, the same Gauguin appeared on the covers of the spring catalogues for both Christie's and Sotheby's. One version of *Vase de Fleurs* had to be a fake, but which one? The auction houses sent both paintings to the Wildenstein Institute for testing, where art expert Sylvie Crussard determined that Sotheby's had the original, Christie's the forgery. Sotheby's successfully sold the authentic Gauguin on behalf of its owner, Sakhai. However, when the FBI was called in to track down the forger, they made an alarming discovery: Tokyo's Gallery Muse had acquired the forgery from one Ely Sakhai. As the investigation progressed, the FBI learned that Sakhai's web of deception was more tangled than anticipated. After arresting him on charges of mail and wire fraud in 2004, the FBI traced numerous impressionistic and post-impressionistic forgeries back to Sakhai. He pleaded guilty in his 2005 trial and received a 41-month jail sentence; the judge also ordered him to pay US$12.5 million in restitution to the victims of his forgeries and to give up 11 of his authentic works.[54]

The Greenhalgh Family

Between 1989 and 2006, a high-school dropout and his octogenarian parents managed to fool the art world with hundreds of fakes and forgeries. Working out of their garden shed in Bolton, England, the Greenhalghs experimented with a diverse range of styles. They claimed that the numerous watercolours, pastels, sketches, modern and ancient sculptures, busts, statues, jewellery, plates, Assyrian reliefs and other works in their collection that spanned 4000 years had been inherited from their grandparents or purchased long ago. Shaun, 46, was a self-taught artist skilled in forging art and authentication documents who boasted that he made the Amarna statue, purchased by the Bolton Museum for £440,000, in three weeks. His father George, 84, was a partially-deaf, wheelchair-bound World War II veteran who acted as the family's naïve salesman. Mom, Olive, 83, contacted potential buyers because her shy son did not like to use the telephone.[55] Working as a criminal team, the family raked in approximately £850,000 per year. Nevertheless, they continued to live modestly with battered furniture, an old TV, no computer, and a used Ford Focus in the driveway. The "Artful Codgers," as one London newspaper dubbed them, were caught when Shaun accidentally misspelled a few words on a cuneiform tablet that he sold to the British Museum.[56] Shaun was sentenced to four years and eight months in prison, but the court was unsure how to handle his elderly parents. George, who showed up to his trial in slippers and a shawl, was sentenced to two years' imprisonment but had his punishment delayed because the judge could not find him a wheelchair-accessible jail. Olive got one year's suspended sentence.

The bizarre story raises questions about why people forge art. Here it seems that money was not necessarily the motive. Investigators of the Metropolitan Police's Art and Antiquities Unit speculated that perhaps Shaun had failed in his own career as an artist because he simply did not know the right people, and that he felt jilted and wanted to show up the snobbish elite. This seems to be a recurring theme amongst art criminals.

AUTHENTICITY MATTERS

Why does it matter to the public if a work of art is authentic or not? Authenticity has a significance that goes to our core. A piece of artwork is not just aesthetically attractive material for the viewer or connoisseur. What also is important is where the piece stood in the passage of time, the creative process involved in making it, who really created it and why, what it meant to those around it and what it meant to the artist.

One of the greatest jobs that a museum has is to educate the public. How do you repay the public when they have been lied to about history with fake and forged information? How do we regain the trust of students who learn that they have been lied to about history? Do we return their admission fee?

Hans Van Meegeren, the master forger who sold his fake Vermeers to Goering during WWII, stated it perhaps most eloquently, "Yesterday this picture was worth millions of guilders, and experts and art lovers would come from all over the world and pay money to see it. Today it is worth nothing and nobody would cross the street to see it for free. But the picture has not changed. What has?"[57]

ON BECOMING AN INTERNATIONAL ART LAWYER

One of the most common questions students and lawyers ask me is how I came to practice cultural property law, and what steps they should take to do the same. There is no simple answer.

The field of Canadian art law is still small, at least relative to its international counterparts. When I decided I wanted to combine my passion for art with my legal training, no Canadian law schools offered any courses on the subject. Universities in the United States had a more open-minded attitude toward my goals. By the mid-1990s, I had taken international law courses at Harvard and Yale. I began representing visual artists either *pro bono* or accepting artwork in lieu of payment for my legal services.

In 1999 I made a conscious decision to practice international art law to the exclusion of other legal pursuits. In 2000 I attended the business meeting of the International Cultural Property Committee held by the American Bar Association Section of International Law and Practice, in Washington, D.C. There I met Patty Gerstenblith, Lawrence M. Kaye, Howard N. Spiegler, and Willi Korte, all pioneers of the field of international art law. It is the people whom I have met working in this area of law who are the real treasures. It has been a privilege to have a collegial and professional working relationship with them based on mutual respect. Also at this conference I learned that European and American museums had published gaps in provenance for works of art between 1933 and 1945, which Canadian museums had not done. In an article for The *National Post*, I expressed the need for Canadian galleries both to come clean on what was acquired and to make amends for this period of acquisition.[1]

In September 2000, I attended the International Bar Association's annual meeting in Amsterdam and spoke on the topic of "Legal, Practical, and Business Issues for Exhibitors of Art in Canada."[2] Later that month, I delivered a speech to the International Trade Club of Toronto about fakes and forgeries.[3]

My entry into the field coincided with a significant development in the world of art law: in October 1999, United States Senator Daniel Patrick

Moynihan proposed an amendment to the Convention on Cultural Property Implementation Act of 1983 (CCPIA) that would change the impact of import restrictions between the United States and a number of countries.[4] The Archaeological Institute of America (AIA) immediately cautioned the Senate that the proposed change would nullify restraints on the trade of illicitly exported antiquities and would increase archeological pillage. The Moynihan Legislation, critics warned, would render CCPIA ineffective.[5] The CCPIA had been enacted by Congress in 1983 as part of the UNESCO Convention on the Means of Prohibiting and Preventing the Illegal Import, Export, and Transfer of Ownership of Cultural Property.

The UNESCO Convention's 91 signatories, including Canada, could enter into bilateral agreements with the United States to legally curb the tide of certain archaeological and ethnographic materials. Under these bilateral agreements, countries who demonstrated that looting and pillaging was putting their cultural heritage in jeopardy could notify US Customs to prohibit their import into the United States. The United States' Cultural Property Advisory Committee advised the President about requests from foreign governments for import restrictions. The Committee had eleven members, from four categories: museums, archaeology/anthropology, dealers, and the public. Senator Moynihan proposed a procedural amendment by which a quorum of one representative from each category would be required to make a recommendation to the President. This meant that if one person failed to attend, there would be no recommendation and hence no import restriction. Some dealers, for example, who would benefit from a free and open trade in cultural heritage, could simply refuse to attend the meetings and prevent the imposition of import restrictions. Passage of the Moynihan Legislation would essentially reverse attempts to enable obligations under the UNESCO Convention.

My experience in raising awareness about the problems with the Moynihan Legislation was my first foray into the diplomatic realm of international art law. Upon learning about the procedural proposal, I worked with a group of dedicated people in my field, contacting those whose rights might be affected by the change, warning them that Canada's bilateral agreement with the United States was at risk of being nullified by a procedural amendment. If the Moynihan Legislation passed, its procedures could prevent the restitution of cultural heritage that had illicitly entered the United States from Canada.

In October 2000, the amendment was not passed. The ultimate failure of the Moynihan Legislation confirmed my commitment to the full-time practice of international art and cultural heritage law.

The whirlwind continued. Shortly after the Moynihan issue was, from my viewpoint, successfully resolved, I returned to the controversial issue of Nazi-looted art in Canada and suggested an inquiry in Canada akin to the Presidential Advisory Commission for the purpose of finding Holocaust-looted assets located in the United States.[6] Several writers, including award-winning investigative journalist Isabel Vincent,[7] urged Canadian museums to make their provenance records public. Four Canadian museums fulfilled the public's need for the information by publishing provenance lists in December 2000. It should be noted, however, that the National Gallery in Ottawa omitted from its list of 106 paintings with "questionable provenance" the many paintings acquired by Sir Anthony Blunt, who acted as the chief adviser to the Gallery on European acquisitions after World War II. The Gallery's most significant purchases were made under Blunt's guidance, despite his well-documented connections with disreputable art dealers. Blunt was later stripped of his knighthood following his exposure as a Soviet spy in 1979.[8] For many Cold War-era acquisitions, the National Gallery provides only the date of purchase.[9]

In March 2001, I attended the International Bar Association's "World Women Lawyers Conference" in London, England, where I met Marilyn E. Phelan, who invited me to be the Vice Chair of the Art and Cultural Heritage Law Committee of the American Bar Association Section of International Law and Practice. Meanwhile, public awareness of the significance of cultural property increased as news spread of the Taliban's wanton destruction of Afghanistan's historic and irreplaceable Buddhas. Responding to public interest in art and cultural heritage law, in May 2001, I delivered an address to the Mystery Writers of America in Chicago. Art crime in all its salacious reality is popular amongst both authors and fans of detective fiction.

In September 2001, I attended the International Bar Association meeting in Amsterdam and spoke on "Restitution of Art and Collecting in Canada."

While at the conference, I met more key players in the field of international art law, including John Huerta, then General Counsel of the Smithsonian Institution in Washington, D.C.

A month later, I spoke at the conference for the International Cultural Property Committee, American Bar Association Section of International Law and Practice, in Monterrey, Mexico.[10] From there, I went on to speak at the International Bar Association Annual Meeting in Cancun, Mexico.[11] Next, I flew to Ottawa to give a lecture at the Canadian Symposium on Holocaust-era Cultural Property at the National Gallery.[12] Museum and gallery directors from across Canada attended. There was no media in attendance, but the who's who of the art world was there. I met Anne Webber, who headed the European Commission on Looted Art; Sarah Jackson, provenance researcher for London's Art Loss Register Office; Lucian Simmons, provenance researcher at Sotheby's Europe; Van Kirk Reeves, an American attorney and noted restitution expert working out of Paris and New York; Wojciecj Kowalski, the Polish Special Ambassador on restitution issues; Nancy Yeide, author and curator of records at the United States National Gallery of Art; Robert Morgenthau, the Manhattan District Attorney who seized the Egon Schiele paintings in a famous American case; and Ian Christie Clark, Chair of the Cultural Property Review Board of Canada. I then returned to Toronto to participate in the International Art Law Lecture Series at the Royal Ontario Museum.[13]

Also in November 2001, I testified in a hearing headed by Martin Sullivan for the renewal of a bilateral treaty between the United States and Canada. Sullivan was Chair of the Cultural Property Advisory Committee for the US Department of State. I provided information based on my knowledge of looting and illicit trafficking of cultural heritage in Canada. There were no representatives at the hearing of the First Nations, the people whose heritage was being robbed and whose interests were most at stake. When the State Department decided in April 2002 not to renew the treaty, no public reason was provided. With the treaty expired, there was no longer a filter in place concerning illegal import and export of cultural property. A few years later, Sullivan resigned in protest from his position as Chair of the Cultural Property Advisory Committee of the US Department of State after the looting of the Baghdad Museum in April 2002, explaining to the President that, although the looting was "foreseeable and preventable… the tragedy was not prevented, due to our nation's inaction."[14]

In 2002, the issue of Nazi-looted art became a subject of interest to the media. I was asked to speak on the topic at a meeting for Toronto's Hadassah WIZO in April, at a meeting of the American Bar Association in New York in May, and at the UJA Federation of Greater Toronto's Holocaust Education Week in November.[15]

In the autumn of 2002 I became a faculty member and lecturer in Law and Taxation in the Art Market (LL.M) at the University of Jean Moulin 3, in Lyon, France,[16] where I made the acquaintance of Gerard Sousi, Director of the LL.M. program in Lyon, and Jean François Canat, General Counsel to the Louvre in Paris. That same year, Frederick Schultz, a preeminent Manhattan dealer in antiquities, was convicted for smuggling ancient Egyptian artifacts into the United States.

On April 8, 2003, on the eve of the looting of the Baghdad Museum, I was contacted by Joshua Knelman, an investigative journalist based in Toronto, to discuss his interest in the recent robberies of art galleries in Toronto. Initially, he hoped simply to speak with a lawyer who advocated for victims of art robbery to go public. As time went on, however, he became fascinated by the topic of cultural property law and ended up interviewing many in the field. Knelman and I ended up meeting regularly over a period of more than two years as he wrote a feature article about art theft and its legal ramifications. "Artful Crimes" appeared in the November 2005 issue of *The Walrus*, and won Knelman a Gold Medal at the Canadian National Magazine Awards.[17]

Days after my first interview with Knelman, the looting of the Baghdad Museum became a major news story. The extent of the theft was unclear at the start, and Donald Rumsfeld only deepened confusion by trying to downplay the significance of the event. "The images you are seeing on television you are seeing over and over," he assured the public at his Department of Defence news briefing on April 11, 2003. "It's the same picture of some person walking out of some building with a vase. And you see it twenty times, and you think, 'My goodness! Were there that many vases? Is it possible that there were that many vases in the whole country?'" While this misinformation spread, I met with Interpol's General Secretariat Karl-

Heinz Kind and his art crime team in Lyon, to discuss the issues of recovering Iraqi materials. We also discussed Nazi-looted art, private property and churches, and the role that education plays in stemming the illicit trade of cultural heritage.

With public awareness on the rise, 2003 was another busy year. I co-chaired a program panel on "The Protection of Underwater Cultural Heritage" for the American Bar Association, Section of International Law and Practice, in Washington, D.C., on May 9. In October, I spoke in Brussels at the fall meeting of the American Bar Association on "The Cultural Heritage of Iraq: An Assessment." In Belgium I met Professor Norman Palmer, the United Kingdom's preeminent expert on art and cultural heritage law, and the author of a seminal book on art loans. Dr. Patty Gerstenblith attended, as did Neil Brodie, head of the Archaeological Institute of Cambridge and an expert on Iraq. I also met Richard Aydon at the conference, who is legal counsel to Christie's London. That autumn, I began my independent Art Law Practice sharing space with an art gallery I opened in Toronto.

The Baghdad Museum incident continued to fascinate the legal community. In the April 2004 American Bar Associtaion (ABA) meeting, I gave a follow-up lecture to my fall piece called "The Cultural Heritage of Iraq: an Assessment a Year After." While in New York, I met some more of the field's major figures, such as archaeologist Zainab Bahrani, a specialist in Iraqi archaeological material and authentications. I also made the acquaintance of Matthew Bogdanos, the author of *Thieves of Baghdad*, a marine trained in Classical History who investigated looting in Iraq. With all the buzz surrounding Iraqi issues, the press was in attendance this time.

After the ABA meeting, I returned to Toronto to lecture at the ROM with Lucille Roussin, a New York art lawyer who specializes in the restitution of Holocaust-looted art, which was the topic of our discussion. Later that year, in the fall, I found myself speaking at the ROM again, this time as part of the International Art Law Lecture series. I gave a four-part lecture entitled "From Collector to Criminal: When Collectors Cross the Line."[18]

Some dealers and collectors were indeed crossing the line into criminality and some frequently so. The public and law enforcement officials became increasingly aware of the issue when Edvard Munch's *The Scream* and *Madonna* fell victim to brazen art thieves in 2004. That same year, the

FBI established its Art Crime Unit to deal with the expansive economy of stolen art. Thirteen Special Agents were assigned to different regions in which they would address cultural property crime cases. With specialized training in the field, the Special Agents would be able to get involved with foreign law enforcement officials and help with art crime investigations worldwide. The Department of Justice assigned three Special Trial Attorneys to give prosecutive support to the Art Crime Team which, to date, has recovered more than 1000 cultural property items worth over US$135 million.[19] I was invited to attend the International Foundation for Art Research's conference in New York in June 2005 to learn more about the FBI's new unit.[20] This gave me the opportunity to talk to Special Agent Robert Wittman, who had worked undercover for the FBI on art crimes. It was also there that I met Thomas Galbraith of the New York Art Loss Register and Jane Levine, the New York District Attorney with experience prosecuting art crimes. Both have moved to new positions in the art world but remain valued colleagues.

In January 2006, an Austrian court ruled in favour of plaintiff Maria Altmann at an arbitration, which meant that her five Klimt paintings stolen by Nazis were to be restituted to her. This decision shocked and upset many Austrians who regarded the paintings as national treasures. Months after their return to her, Altmann consigned the Klimts to Christie's to be sold on her behalf, where they brought in a record of US$327 million.[21]

While Nazi-looted art and Iraqi antiquities occupied the international stage, First Nations' cultural heritage became an increasingly contentious legal issue in North America. At the eighth Annual Conference for the Association for the Study of Law, Culture and the Humanities in March 2005, I spoke to the audience in Austin, Texas, from a Canadian lawyer's viewpoint on native issues.[22] Once again, I provided a Canadian perspective at the ABA's International Cultural Property Committee in October 2005.[23] The larger discussion at the conference was what Europe had been doing with illegal cultural property and how different countries were implementing the UNESCO convention. I had the privilege of speaking on the topic with renowned members of the art law community, including international art lawyer Kevin Chamberlain, Swiss cultural specialist Yves

Fisher, and Cristian DeFrancia, head of the War Crimes Tribunal in The Hague International Court of Justice.

It was also at this Conference that I met a senior representative of the crime unit of the Brussels Police Department, who asked me to go incognito with her to observe first-hand the art crime world. The experience was eye-opening, to say the least. I learned that some wealthy dealers' tastes determine which nations' cultural artifacts are available: in Brussels, for instance, illicit cylinder seals tend not to be for sale because dealers there are uninterested in Iraqi culture, whereas, in New York, cylinder seals are easy to find.

Our first stop was a Chinese boutique. As I posed as a collector, the dealer there assured me I would have no trouble shipping two carved wooden heads to the United States or Canada and I could buy them both for 3000 Euros, or just one for 1500. Needless to say, I made no purchase, but the notion of splitting them up seemed a particularly sad fate for them, since they were depictions of a married couple whose likenesses had already been torn out of the entrance of their fourteenth-century home in southwest China. Our next stop was a chic little gallery of African antiquities. The proprietor proudly showed us religious ceremonial objects from the Republic of Congo, Angola, Zambia, Cameroon, Benin, the delta of the River Niger, and elsewhere in east and central Africa. Another proprietor in the same upscale district asked if we were interested in buying lovely ivory African bracelets. I asked if there would be any trouble getting the ivory pieces into the United States or Canada, and he assured me it would not be a problem. Next, we checked out hot Egyptian artifacts in an antique gallery that sold everything from mosaics, ripped out of floors somewhere in Turkey, to restrung ancient Egyptian beaded necklaces. The proprietor had a wooden bull from a tomb on sale for 350 Euros. He admitted he had no idea from which tomb it was extracted or what era it represented. He also had Roman figurines for 450 Euros although, again, he could tell us nothing about their historical context or artistic provenance. His website let us browse through dozens of other unprovenanced items for sale. The lesson brought home to me first-hand was that the world's cultural heritage was and is available anywhere, with very inadequate regulatory filters to catch it before it disappears.

Fakes, forgeries, and stolen art—the more sensationalist aspects of my art law practice—made for exciting discussions at a number of events in 2006.[24] The legal community also took notice of my work, with *Law Times* and *The Lawyers Weekly* featuring articles that year.[25]

In January 2006, I attended the conference of the Archaeological Institute of America in Montreal to speak about law enforcement and archaeology. This was where I met Rick St. Hilaire, a well-known New Hampshire prosecutor who was counsel to SAFE (Saving Antiquities For Everyone). Others in attendance included Roger Atwood, the investigative journalist and author of *Stealing History*; Bonnie Magness-Gardiner, who was at the time Senior Cultural Property Analyst for the Department of State and is currently Head of the FBI Art Crime Unit; and Lina Theberge, an RCMP officer from Montreal specializing in art-related crimes.

Although art law is a particular niche of the legal profession, its cross-disciplinary nature means it draws a rich variety of characters to its conferences. At the ABA's spring 2006 event I met Oscar Muscarella, a curator for the Metropolitan Museum who fervently opposed the purchasing of the *Euphronius Krater*, and Jim Wynne, the FBI agent from New York whose eight-year investigation led to Eli Sakai's conviction for art forgeries. Fittingly, "Fakes and Forgeries in the Art Market" was the topic of my lecture that day.[26] After speaking at the ABA I returned to Toronto for the launch of The Institute of Art and Cultural Heritage at the Gallery Contempra, when it was based in Toronto's Yorkville area.

Practicing in an international field such as art law has taken me all over the globe. In just over a year, I attended conferences and gave lectures in Toronto, Budapest, Cairo, Washington, D.C., Milan, Singapore, and New Delhi, all the while continuing my visits to teach in Lyon.[27] My efforts were paying off; publications featured articles about art and cultural heritage,[28] and CBC interviewed me twice regarding topics of the day.[29]

Throughout the development of my career as an art lawyer, I continued my growth as an artist and remained as involved as possible in the contemporary visual art world. I showed my support to various cutting-edge, first-of-a-kind exhibitions. Some of these included "Walk the Talk", an exhibit representing women and children who lost their lives to domestic violence; Canada's first paint-by-number exhibition; shows about the influence of war on fashion design and the combination of sculpture and couturier; and exhibits of contemporary First Nations paintings and sculptures. The art of today is the cultural heritage of the future. The existence of a dark side to the world of art was unfathomable to me when I first began combining my love of art and desire to work for art and artists through the law. Despite this, all artists continue to go out into the world and try to create work that shows the power of the human spirit, which is truly indomitable, and I can say they are supported by a small but fierce cadre of legal and law enforcement experts who want to protect their work today and for the future.

Although an artist first and foremost, what continually keeps me fascinated by my work, both on canvas and in law, is that both provide me with an opportunity to see and learn something new. It is my love of art that keeps me hopeful that there will be a healthier art trade one day, which is the goal toward which most in this field work as best we can.

ENDNOTES

Chapter 1

1   Anne Underhill, "The Chinese Antiquities Trade: Why it is a Problem and What Should be Done" Paper presented at the American Bar Association Symposium on Collecting Chinese Art and Antiquities, Washington, D.C., 4 May 2007 [unpublished].

2   *Republic of Austria v. Altmann*, 541 U.S. 677, 124 S. Ct. 2240 (2006).

3   Carol Vogel, "Lauder Pays $135 Million, a Record, for a Klimt Portrait" *New York Times* (19 June 2006), E1.

4   Elisabetta Povoleto, "Ancient Vase Comes Home to a Hero's Welcome" *New York Times* (19 January 2008), online: <http://www.nytimes.com/2008/01/19/arts/design/19bowl.html?_r=1&ref=world>.

5   Elisabetta Povoledo, "Collector Returns Art Italy Says Was Looted" *New York Times* (18 January 2008), online: <http://www.nytimes.com/2008/01/18/arts/18collect.html>.

6   Convention for the Protection of Cultural Property in the Event of Armed Conflict, 14 May 1954 (entered into force 7 August 1956).

7   See Convention on the Means of Prohibiting and Preventing the Illicit Import, Export and Transfer of Ownership of Cultural Property, adopted by the General Conference, UNESCO, at its Sixteenth Session, Paris, 14 November 1970. For full text, see <http://portal.unesco.org/en/ev.php-URL_ID=13039&URL_DO=DO_TOPIC&URL_SECTION=201.html>.

8   See Appendix A2.

9   See *Ruben v. Islamic Republic of Iran*, 2006 U.S. Dist. LEXIS 73383.

10   Foreign Sovereign Immunities Act, 28 U.S.C. §1602.

11   Polemos: Le Contexte Guerrier en Egée à L'Âge du Bronze: Actes de 7e Rencontre Égéanne Internationale, Université de Liège, 14-17 avril 1998, Robert Laffineur, ed. (Austin, Texas: University of Texas at Austin, Program in Aegean Scripts and Prehistory, 1999).

12 For more on this topic see Helen J. Nicholson, *The Crusades* (West-port, Connecticut and London: Greenwood, 2004).

13 Jared Diamond, *Guns, Germs and Steel* (New York: W.W. Norton & Co., 1999).

14 See Emmerich de Vattel, *Le Droit de Gens* (Londres, 1758).

15 For more on this topic, see Margaret M. Miles, *Art as Plunder: The Ancient Origins of Debate about Cultural Property* (Cambridge: Cambridge University Press, 2008), or Margaret M. Miles, "Cicero's Prosecution of Gaius Verres: A Roman View of the Ethics of Acquisition of Art" (2002) 11 Int'l J. Cult. Prop. 28.

16 George Gordon Lord Byron, "Childe Harold's Pilgrimage," 1812.

17 *The Marquis de Somerueles* (1813), 482 Nova Scotia Stewart's Vice-Admiralty Reports.

18 Margaret M. Miles, "Cicero's Prosecution of Gaius Verres", *supra*, note 15.

19 See Lieber Code, also known as Instructions for the Government of Armies of the Unites States in the Field By Order of the Secretary of War, 1863, online: Shotgun's Home of the American Civil War, <http://www.civilwarhome.com/liebercode.htm>.

20 See Lieber Code, *ibid.*

21 Project of an International Declaration Concerning the Laws and Customs of War, Brussels, 27 August 1874.

22 Katherine Dugdale, "Art Theft: An Overview" International Art Law Lecture Series delivered at the ROM, 12 November 2006 [unpublished].

23 See Simon Mackenzie, "Criminal and Victim Profiles in Art Theft: Motive, Opportunity and Repeat Victimization" (2005) 10 Art Antiquity and Law 353.

24 "Top 25 Crimes of the Century" *TIME* Magazine, online: <http://www.time.com/time/2007/crimes/2.html>.

25 Lynn Nicholas, *The Rape of Europa: The Fate of Europe's Treasures in the Third Reich and the Second World War* (New York: Vintage, 1995), at 92.

26 Martin Fabiani, *Quand j'etais marchand de tableaux* (Paris: 1976), at 83.

27 National Archives, Washington, D.C., Record Group 59/10, Ardelia Hall Records, MF/JF No. 202. In a telegram from the Embassy of France in the United States to the US Department of State in Washington, D.C., on 23 June 1949, the French Government wrote that there had been "an arbitrary division of the [Vollard] estate which took place illegally with respect to registration and prejudiced the interest of the State and of certain heirs, of which the City of Paris is one."

28 See Appendix D1 for three pages of the list of works on the *SS Excalibur* (the list was 6 pages in total).

29 National Archives, Record Group 239/82, British Economic Advisory Board Report, 2 July 1945.

30 National Archives, supra, note 27, Dispatch 9E135341, 13 July 1949.

31 National Archives, supra, note 27, MF/JF No. 202. In a telegram from the Embassy of France in the United States to the US Department of State in Washington, D.C., on 23 June 1949, the French government cautioned the American government that "the paintings belonging to the Vollard estate constitute national property temporarily subject to the regulation governing assets in foreign countries, and their sale in the United States would defraud the French Treasury of a large sum in foreign exchange."

32 National Archives, *supra*, note 27, MF/JF No. 202. The order, made 2 June 1949, is attached to the French Embassy's telegram to the US Department of State, sent 23 June 1949.

33 National Archives, *supra*, note 27, Dispatch 9E135341, 13 July 1949. According to the French government, Fabiani and his business partner, Edouard Jonas, had taken possession of the paintings on 30 May 1949. See Appendix D1.

34 National Archives, *supra*, note 27, Control 6858. Telegram from Ottawa to Secretary of State, 19 July 1949.

35 "Greatest Heists in Art History." BBC News (23 August 2004), online: <http://news.bbc.co.uk/2/hi/entertainment/3590106.stm>.

36 All photos courtesy of FBI Art Theft Program, online: <http://www.fbi.gov/hq/cid/arttheft/arttheft.htm>.

37 "Art Heist at the Montreal Museum of Fine Arts" CBC News (4 September 1972), online: <http://archives.cbc.ca/on_this_day/09/04/>.

38 "Crime World Bargains with Stolen Art" Canwest News Service (26 May 2008), online: <http://www.canada.com/topics/news/national/story.html?id=afc30bb6-5ce4-4778-a48f-19cfbc1f3520>.

39 Definition of "replevin" from *Black's Law Dictionary*: An action for the repossession of personal property wrongfully taken or detained by the defendant, whereby the plaintiff gives security for and holds the property until the court decides who owns it.

40 *Autocephalous Greek-Orthodox Church of Cyprus v. Goldberg & Feldman Fine Arts, Inc.*, 717 F. Supp. 1374, 1377 n.1 (S.D. Ind. 1989).

41 M. Christiane Bourloyannis and Virginia Morris, "Autocephalous Greek-Orthodox Church of Cyprus v. Goldberg & Feldman Fine Arts, Inc." (1992) American Journal of International Law, 86:1 128.

42 See website for Republic of Cyprus, Department of Antiquities: <http://www.mcw.gov.cy/mcw/DA/DA.nsf/All/5C63072411078AB9C22572750055D67D?OpenDocument>.

43 "Greatest Art Thefts of the Twentieth Century" *Forbes* (28 February 2001), online: <http://www.forbes.com/2001/02/28/0228connguide_print.html>.

44 Peter Landesman, "The Curse of the Sevso Treasure" *The Atlantic Monthly* 288:4 (November 2001) 66.

45 Alan Riding, "14 Roman Treasures, On View and Debated" *New York Times* (25 October 2006), online: <http://query.nytimes.com/gst/fullpage.html?res=9C00E0D8173FF936A15753C1A9609C8B63&sec=&spon=&pagewanted=all>.

46 Alan Riding, *ibid.*

47 See Appendix C5.

48 Peter Landesman, *supra*, note 44.

49 "Greatest Art Thefts of the Twentieth Century", *supra*, note 43.

50 Jonathan Sazonoff, "Search for the World's Most Wanted Art," online: <http://www.saztv.com/page102.html>.

51 Paul L. Montgomery, "Lost and Found: Huge Van Gogh Theft Fails" *New York Times* (15 April 1991), online: <http://www.nytimes.

com/1991/04/15/arts/lost-and-found-huge-van-gogh-theft-fails.
html>.

52   Mitchell Landsberg, "Stolen Art May Not Net Thieves Much" *The
Free-Lance Star* (21 March 1988), online: <http://news.google.com/n
ewspapers?nid=1298&dat=19880321&id=Yg8QAAAAIBAJ&sjid=C4
wDAAAAIBAJ&pg=4780,4032238>.

53   "Greatest Art Thefts of the Twentieth Century", *supra*, note 43.

54   Louise Jury, "Lucian Freud Appeals for Return of his Stolen Portrait
of Francis Bacon" *The Independent* (22 June 2001), online: <http://
www.independent.co.uk/news/uk/this-britain/lucian-freud-appeals-
for-return-of-his-stolen-portrait-of-francis-bacon-675068.html>.

55   "Greatest Heists in Art History", *supra*, note 35.

56   John E. Conklin, *Art Crime* (Westport, Connecticut: Praeger, 1994),
at 150.

57   "Greatest Art Thefts of the Twentieth Century", *supra*, note 43.

58   "Greatest Art Thefts of the Twentieth Century", *supra*, note 43.

59   Alan Riding, "Loss Estimates are Cut on Iraqi Artifacts, but Questions Remain" (1 May 2003), online: <http://www.museum-security.
org/03/067.html>.

60   Interview of Donny George by Bonnie Czegledi (27 May 2009).

61   Alan Riding, *supra*, note 59.

62   Alan Riding, *supra*, note 59.

63   Laurie Becklund, "Man Writes Novel Chapter in Annals of Library
Theft" *L.A. Times* (28 April 1991), online: <http://articles.latimes.
com/1991-04-28/news/mn-1571_1_book-theft?pg=3>.

64   Jonathan Jones, "The Bigger Picture: was the theft of Munch's The
Scream really about art?" *The Guardian* (17 February 2007), online:
<http://www.guardian.co.uk/artanddesign/2007/feb/17/art.arttheft>.

65   "Man Sentenced in 'Scream' Heist" *New York Times* (29 June 2009),
online: <http://www.nytimes.com/2009/06/30/arts/design/30arts-
MANSENTENCED_BRF.html?_r=2>.

66   Associated Press, "Munch Masterpieces Damaged, but Repairable"
MSNBC (1 September 2006), online: <http://www.msnbc.msn.com/
id/14625906/>.

67 Deirdre Mooney and Colin Blackstock, "Art Pirates Steal a Picasso from Wealthy Arab's Yacht" *The Independent* (2 May 1999), online: <http://www.independent.co.uk/news/art-pirates-steal-a-picasso-from-wealthy-arabs-yacht-1090944.html>.

68 Sarah Lyall, "Art World Nightmare: Made-to-Order Theft; Stolen Works Like Oxford's Cezanne Can Vanish for Decades" *New York Times* (3 February 2000), online: <http://www.nytimes.com/2000/02/03/arts/art-world-nightmare-made-order-theft-stolen-works-like-oxford-s-cezanne-can.html?pagewanted=all>.

69 "Greatest Art Thefts of the Twentieth Century", *supra*, note 43.

70 Laura Vinha and Steve Gorman, "Missing Rembrandt, Renoir Masterpieces Recovered" redOrbit (16 September 2005), online: <http://www.redorbit.com/news/entertainment/242117/missing_rembrandt_renoir_masterpieces_recovered/>.

71 Rachael Bell, "Sensational Art Heists" TruTV (2004), online: <http://www.trutv.com/library/crime/gangsters_outlaws/outlaws/major_art_thefts/index.html>.

72 Jessica Wong, "Art thefts: Timeline." CBC News Online (23 August 2004), online: <http://www.cbc.ca/arts/features/artthefts/>.

73 "Paraguay Theft." Museum Security Network (30 July 2002), online: <http://www.museum-security.org/02/095.html#3>.

74 Jessica Wong, *supra*, note 72.

75 Jim Lewis, "Cellini's Stellar Cellar" *Slate* (23 May 2003), online: <http://slate.msn.com/id/2083452/>.

76 Jessica Wong, *supra*, note 72.

77 "Arrests after da Vinci work found." *BBC News* (4 October 2007), online: <http://news.bbc.co.uk/2/hi/uk_news/scotland/south_of_scotland/7028557.stm>.

78 Rachael Bell, *supra*, note 71.

79 Anahad O'Connor and Ann Farmer, "When Taking a Painting, Don't Leave Your Picture" *New York Times* (17 May 2005), online: <http://query.nytimes.com/gst/fullpage.html?res=9502E2D81F30F934A25756C0A9639C8B63>.

80   "New York: Queens: Sentence in Basquiat Theft" *New York Times* (4
     November 2005), online: <http://query.nytimes.com/gst/fullpage.htm
     l?res=9A03E0D9173EF937A35752C1A9639C8B63>.

81   "Stolen Goya Painting Recovered by the FBI" *The Guardian* (22
     November 2006), online: <http://www.guardian.co.uk/world/2006/
     nov/22/arts.artsnews>.

82   "Theft of Painting by Group of Seven Contemporary has Investi-
     gators Flabbergasted" Canwest News Service (11 January 2007),
     online: <http://www.canada.com/topics/news/national/story.
     html?id=2abe7cc4-9f26-4f32-899f-a12de51863e7&k=48051>.

83   Associated Press, "163 Million Art Heist in Zurich" *CBS News*
     (11 February 2008), online: <http://www.cbsnews.com/
     stories/2008/02/11/world/main3815033.shtml>.

84   Henry Samuel, "Paintings worth £85 Million Stolen in Zurich" *The
     Telegraph* (11 February 2008), online: <http://www.telegraph.co.uk/
     news/worldnews/1578325/Paintings-worth-85-million-stolen-in-
     Zurich.html>.

85   "Valuable Sketchbook Stolen from Picasso Museum in Paris" *CBC
     News* (9 June 2009), online: <http://www.cbc.ca/arts/artdesign/
     story/2009/06/09/picasso-museum-theft-sketchbook.html>.

86   Angelique Chrisafis, "£6.9m Picasso sketchbook stolen in Paris"
     The Guardian (9 June 2009), online: <http://www.guardian.co.uk/
     artanddesign/2009/jun/09/picasso-sketchbook-stolen-paris>.

87   As listed by the Art Loss Register.

88   "Picasso Painting Ripped by New York Woman's Fall" *BBC News* (25
     January 2010), online: <http://news.bbc.co.uk/2/hi/8478347.stm>.

89   One can become a Certified Institutional Protection Specialist (CIPS),
     Certified Institutional Protection Technician (CIPT), or Certified
     Institutional Protection Manager (CIPM), depending on one's role
     in the protection of cultural property. For more information, see the
     International Foundation for Cultural Property Protection, online:
     <http://ifcpp.org/articles/certification>.

90   Simon Mackenzie, "Criminal and Victim Profiles in Art Theft: Motive,
     Opportunity and Repeat Victimization" (2005) 10 Art Antiquity and
     Law 353.

Chapter 2

1   United Nations Educational, Scientific Cultural Organization, Convention on the Means of Prohibiting and Preventing the Illicit Import, Export, and Transfer of Ownership of Cultural Property 1970.

2   See Appendices A1 and A2.

3   Clemency Coggins, "Illicit Traffic of Pre-Columbian Antiquities" (1969) 29 Art Journal 94.

4   Importation of Pre-Columbian Monumental or Architectural Sculpture or Murals Act, 19 U.S.C. 209 (1972).

5   Convention on Cultural Property Implementation Act, 19 U.S.C. §§2101-2106 (1983).

6   For an overview of CPAC, see Marina Papa Sokel, "The US Legal Response to the Protection of the World Culture Heritage" in Neil Brodie, Morag M. Kersel, Christina Luke, and Katherine Walker, eds. *Archaeology, Cultural Heritage, and the Antiquities Trade* (Gainesville: University Press of Florida, 2006) 36 at 44.

7   See Saving Antiquities for Everyone, online: <www.savingantiquities. org>.

8   See Appendix A7.

9   See Appendix A6.

10   *Canadian Cultural Property Export and Import Act*, R.S.C. 1985, c. C-51. See Appendix B1.

11   *Canadian Cultural Property Export and Import Act, ibid.*

12   See "British Museums adopt tougher stance on unprovenanced antiquities" *The Art Newspaper*, No.183, September 2007.

13   See Department for Culture, Media and Sport, News Release, "Combating Illicit Trade: Due Diligence Guidelines for Museums, Libraries and Archives on Collecting and Borrowing Cultural Material" (October 2005), online: <http://www.culture.gov.uk/images/publications/CombatingIllicitTrade_v5.pdf>.

14   See Appendix C3.

15   *CMA Ethical Guidelines 1999*, online: Canadian Museums Association <http://www.museums.ca/media/Pdf/ethicsguidelines.pdf>.

16 See Appendix C4.

17 See Appendix C2.

18 Ardelia Hall, "The Recovery of Cultural Objects Dispersed During WWII," Department of State Bulletin (27 August 1951) at 337.

19 See Appendix A3.

20 See Appendix A4.

21 See Appendix A5.

Chapter 3

1   Bernhard Schulz, "Art-Napping" *The Atlantic Times* (March 2008), online: <http://www.atlantic-times.com/archive_detail.php?recordID=1233>.

2   Leonard D. DuBoff, Christy O. King, and Michael D. Murray, eds. "Booklet C: Theft" in *The Deskbook of Art Law,* 2nd ed. (Dobbs Ferry, NY: Oceana Publications, 2005) at C-5.

3   See Steve Greenhouse, "Scandal Over Heiress' Art Entangles a Louvre Curator" *New York Times* (28 December 1988) and Steve Greenhouse, "Louvre Curator Cleared in Stolen Painting Case" *New York Times* (30 May 1990).

4   Cristina Ruiz, "9/11 Hijacker Attempted to Sell Afghan Loot: Mohammed Atta Offered Artifacts to German Archaeologist" 210 *The Art Newspaper* (February 2010), online: <http://theartnewspaper.com/articles/9-11-hijacker-attempted-to-sell-Afghan-loot%20/20188>.

5   The film, "Blood Antiques," is available online: <http://www.linktv.org/programs/blood-antiques>.

6   Ian Thompson, "The Artful Dodgers" *The New York Times* (20 October 2002), online: <http://www.timesonline.co.uk/tol/life_and_style/article1171265.ece?token=null&offset=24&page=3>.

7   See Federal Bureau of Investigation, online: <http://www.fbi.gov/hq/cid/arttheft/artcrimeteam.htm>.

8   See Art Loss Register, online: <http://www.artloss.com/>.

9   See Interpol, online: <http://www.interpol.int/Public/WorkOfArt/Default.asp>.

10   See *Criminal Code*, R.S.C. 1985, c. C-46.

11   National Stolen Property Act, (1934) 18 U.S.C. §2315.

12   *Criminal Code, supra*, note 10, s. 354.

13   *See Canadian Cultural Property Export and Import Act,* R.S.C. 1985, C.-51. See Appendix B1.

14   "Man who Stole Nizam's Slippers is Spared" *Rediff India Abroad* (6 June 2008), online: <http://www.rediff.com/news/2008/jun/06nizam.htm>. See also Emily Mathieu, "No Jail Sentence for Shoe Museum

Theft" *Toronto Star* (4 June 2008), online: <http://www.thestar.com/Sports/Hockey/article/436548>.

15 See Appendices B2 and B3.

16 National Stolen Property Act, *supra*, note 11.

17 National Stolen Property Act, *supra*, note 11.

18 Rick St. Hilaire, "International Antiquities Trafficking: Theft by Another Name" in Vasilike Argyropoulos, Anno Hein, and Mohamed Abdel Hareth, eds., *Strategies for Saving our Cultural Heritage* (Athens: TEI of Athens, 2008).

19 Rick St. Hilaire, *ibid.* St. Hilaire points out that foreign patrimony laws were used in the Schultz case: Egypt's Law 117 infused a stolen character to the antiquity at issue.

20 N. Y. Penal Law §165.55(2), Title 7, Title 13 (emphasis added).

21 Archaeological Resources Protection Act, 16 U.S.C. 470AA-470MM.

22 Edward Wyatt, "Four California Museums are Raided" *New York Times* (25 January 2008), online: <http://www.nytimes.com/2008/01/25/us/25raid.html>.

23 18 USCS §545.

24 Rick St. Hilaire, *supra*, note 18.

25 Interview of Rick St. Hilaire (10 July 2009).

26 California Office of the Attorney General, News Release, "Attorney General Lockyer Issues Report Criticizing Getty Trustees, Former President Munitz for Improper Spending and Legal Violations" (2 October 2006), online: <http://ag.ca.gov/newsalerts/release.php?id=1376>.

27 Native American Graves Protection and Repatriation Act, 25 U.S.C. §3001-13. See Appendix B4.

28 Public Law 97-446 [H.R. 4566], 96 Stat. 2329, approved January 12, 1983; as amended by Public Law 100-204 [H.R. 1777], 101 Stat. 1331, approved December 22, 1987.

29 United States Senate Report 22.

30 *United States v. Schultz*, 178 F. Supp. 2d 445 (S.D.N.Y. 2002).

31 Rick St. Hilaire, *supra*, note 18.

32 *United States v. An Antique Platter of Gold, Known as a Gold Phiale Mesomphalos, c. 400 B.C.*, 991 F. Supp. 222; 1997 US Dist LEXIS 18899.

33 U.S. Immigration and Customs Enforcement, online: <http://www.ice.gov/pi/investigations/publicsafety/contraband.htm>.

34 The Importation of Pre-Columbian Monumental or Architectural Sculpture or Murals Act, 19 U.S.C. §§2091-95 (1972).

35 The Racketeer Influenced and Corrupt Organizations ("RICO") Act, 18 U.S.C. §§ 1961-68 (1994).

36 *Ibid.*, at 1961(1).

37 *U.S. v. Pritchard*, 346 F.3d 469, C.A.3 (Pa.), 2003.

38 Federal Bureau of Investigation, News Release, "Recoveries — Civil War Militaria Fraud", online: FBI <http://www.fbi.gov/hq/cid/arttheft/northamerica/us/militaria/militaria.htm>.

39 Rick St. Hilaire, *supra*, note 18.

40 *United States v. Hollinshead*, 495 F.2d 1154 (9th Cir. 1974).

41 *Ibid.*, at para. 5.

42 545 F.2d 988 (5th Cir. 1977).

43 *United States v. Schultz, supra,* note 30.

44 Alexi Shannon Baker, "Selling the Past: *United States v. Frederick Schultz*" *Archaeology* (22 April 2002), online: <http://www.archaeology.org/online/features/schultz/details.html>.

45 Egypt, The Public Law 117/1983.

46 *United States v. Schultz*, 333 F.2d 393 (2d Cir. 2003).

47 *United States v. Schultz, supra,* note 30.

48 *United States v. Draves*, 103 F.3d 1328 (7th Cir. 1997).

49 It is interesting to note that there is a Canada-US treaty from 1924 that deals with smuggling of stolen goods between the two countries. Though primarily enacted to curb narcotics smuggling, Article III explicitly states that all stolen property flowing between Canada and the United States should be seized by customs authorities and returned to its rightful owners. This suggests that the treaty would be applicable to stolen art and antiquities, though it has never been so employed. Entitled "Convention between Canada and the United States of America to aid in suppressing Smuggling Operations along

the Border between the Dominion of Canada and the United States and in the Arrest and Prosecution of Persons violating the Narcotic Laws of either Government," the treaty can be viewed online at <http://www.lexum.umontreal.ca/ca_us/en/cus.1924.511.en.html>.

50 Jamie Komarnicki, "More than 18 months after a sprawling Black-foot cultural centre opened on the Siksika reserve, museum officials say scores of displaced artifacts potentially worth millions of dollars remain out of reach" Canwest News Service (9 February 2009).

51 Caroline Alphonso, "280 Boxes of Artifacts at U of T Carted Off to Dump" *Globe and Mail* (6 June 2003) A9.

52 *Boma Manufacturing Ltd. v. Canadian Imperial Bank of Commerce*, [1996] 3 S.C.R. 727, at para. 31.

53 *Ibid.*, at para. 31.

54 *R. v. Yorke*, 1996 CanLII 5380 (N.S. S.C.).

55 *R. v. Yorke*, [1993] 3 S.C.R. 647, 84 C.C.C. (3d) 286.

56 *R v. Jorgensen* (1995), 102 C.C.C. (3d) 97 (S.C.C.) at 135.

57 *R. v. Duong* (1998), 124 C.C.C. (3d) 392 (O.C.A.) at 22.

58 *R v. Wright* (1985), 41 Alta. L.R. (2d) 361.

59 International Emergency Economic Power Act, 50 U.S.C. §1701-1707 (1977).

60 Fed Reg 31 CFR 575.53 s. b(4).

61 H.R. 1047, TITLE III.

Chapter 4

1   Migratory Bird Treaty Act, 16 U.S.C. §703-712; see relevant segment in Appendix B7.

2   Endangered Species Act, 7 U.S.C. §136, 16 U.S.C. §1531; see relevant segment in Appendix B7.

3   See Jacqueline Trescott, "U.S. Charges Smithsonian Secretary" *The Washington Post* (21 January 2004), online: <http://www.washingtonpost.com/wp-dyn/content/article/2004/01/21/AR2005040308766.html> and Eric Rosenberg, "Convicted Museum Boss Still Quibbling" *San Francisco Chronicle* (17 February 2005) A2.

4   *Species at Risk Act*, S.C. 2002, c. 29; see relevant segment in Appendix B8.

5   *Migratory Birds Convention Act*, S.C. 1994, c. 22; see relevant segment in Appendix B8.

6   See Appendix B7.

7   Available on Environment Canada website: <http://www.cws-scf.ec.gc.ca/enforce/cites/pages_e/cites_e.htm>.

8   *Wild Animal and Plant Protection and Regulation of International and Interprovincial Trade Act*, S.C. 1992, c. 52; see relevant segment in Appendix B8.

9   Sam Kusic, *Tribune Review* (1 June 2005), online: <http://www.pittsburghlive.com/x/pittsburghtrib/s_339685.html>.

10 "Ebay.de (Germany): New Rules on the Selling of Archaeological Materials" in *Saving Antiquities for Everyone* (14 July 2008), online: <http://safecorner.savingantiquities.org/2008/07/ebayde-germany-new-rules-on-selling-of.html>. Official policy available online: <http://pages.ebay.de/help/policies/artifacts.html> (German).

11 "eBay to Limit Sale of Cultural Artifacts" in *Museum Security Network* (21 October 2009), online: <http://groups.google.com/group/museum_security_network/browse_thread/thread/02bd6f9ef81dfeb5/0728e350795d7b28?#0728e350795d7b28>.

12 John E. Huerta, "The Lawyer's Role in Crisis Management" (Paper presented to ALI-ABA, Philadelphia, Pennsylvania, 14 May 2007), in *Legal Issues in Museum Administration* (American Law Institute and American Bar Associations, 2007), at 177.

13 *Black's Law Dictionary*, 8th ed., "gift".

14 Marie C. Malaro, *A Legal Primer on Managing Museum Collections*, 2d ed. (Washington and London: Smithsonian Institution Press, 1998), at 208.

15 *Black's Law Dictionary, supra*, note 13, "bailment".

16 For example, in the case of a loan or gift via a trust arrangement, the trustees are under a fiduciary duty to follow the donor's expressed intentions. See *In re Charles M. Bair Family Trust*, 343 Mont. 138, 183 P.3d 61. In this case, the testator established a charitable trust for the purpose of establishing a museum. The board of directors, as appointed by the trustees, was to "use whatever principal and income of the [Trust] that is necessary to establish, improve and maintain the museum," and included detailed directions of how the museum was to be administered. In failing to spend enough money on the museum's upkeep, the board had breached its fiduciary obligation. See Stephanie Strom and Jim Robbins, "Montana Museum Board Breached Duty, Court Says" *New York Times* (30 April 2008), online: <http://www.nytimes.com/2008/04/30/us/30museum.html>.

17 See Appendix B9. To view immunity from seizure orders granted in Ontario, see the *Ontario Gazette*, online at <http://www.ontario.ca/en/ontgazette/STEL01_033657>.

18 *Law and Equity Act*, R.S.B.C. 1996, c. 253, s. 55.

19 *Foreign Cultural Property Immunity Act*, R.S.A. 2000, c. F-17.

20 *The Foreign Cultural Objects Immunity from Seizure Act*, R.S.M. 1987, c. F-140, s.1.

21 For Quebec's position under civil law, see *Code of Civil Procedure*, Book IV, Execution of Judgments, Title II, Compulsory Execution, Chapter I Preliminary Provisions, Division III, Exemption from Seizure, RSQ, c. 25. In loaning or donating within Quebec, foreign parties must be aware of the difference between Quebec's civil law and the common law in other Canadian jurisdictions.

22 Norman Palmer, *Art Loans* (London: Kluwer Law International, 1997).

23 Leonard DuBoff, Michael Murray, and Christy King, eds. *The Deskbook of Art Law*, 2d ed. (New York: Oceana Publications, 2006), at J-9.

24 *Ibid.*, at J-9.

Chapter 5

1   Jonathan Petropoulos, "Art Looting During the Third Reich: An Overview with Recommendations for Further Research" (Paper presented at the Plenary Session on Nazi-Confiscated Art Issues, December 3, 1998), US State Department, *Proceedings of the Washington Conference on Holocaust-Era Assets* (Washington, D.C.: Office of the Coordinator for the Washington Conference on Holocaust-Era Assets, April 1999). Full-text of Conference Proceedings is available on the US State Department website: <http://www.state.gov/www/regions/eur/holocaust/heac.html>.

2   Michael J. Bazyler, *Holocaust Justice: The Battle for Restitution in America's Courts* (New York: New York University Press, 2003).

3   *Inter-Allied Declaration against Acts of Dispossession committed in Territories under Enemy Occupation of Control* (London, 5 January 1943), online: <http://www.lootedartcommission.com/inter-allied-declaration>.

4   *United Nations Monetary and Financial Conference* (Bretton Woods, New Hampshire, 22 July 1944), online: <http://www.lootedartcommission.com/bretton-woods>.

5   J. D. Bindenagel, "Washington Principles on Nazi-Confiscated Art: Ten Years and Promises of the Washington Principles" (Address at Holocaust Era Assets Conference, Prague and Terezin, 26-30 June 2009), online: <http://www.commartrecovery.org/docs/bindenagel.pdf>.

6   Vilnius International Conference on Holocaust-Era Looted Cultural Assets, 3-5 October 2000, Vilnius, Lithuania, online: <http://www.lootedartcommission.com/vilnius-forum>.

7   Terezin Declaration, 30 June 2009, online: <http://www.lootedartcommission.com/NPNMG484641>.

8   Eric Gibson, "De Gustibus: The Delicate Art of Deciding Whose Art It Is" *Wall Street Journal* (16 July 1999) W11.

9   See Robert Paterson, "Resolving Material Culture Disputes: Human Rights, Property Rights and Crimes Against Humanity" (2006) 14 Willamette J. of Int'l L. & Disp. Resol. 155, at 158. Paterson

advocates a principle-based solution, arguing that Nazi-looted art should be viewed as the proceeds of a crime against humanity. The rationale for statutes of limitations (closure) does not apply to crimes against humanity—hence the International Criminal Court's War Crimes Act contains no limitation period.

10 For more detailed analysis of statutes of limitations, see Patty Gerstenblith, *Art, Cultural Heritage, and the Law: Cases and Materials* (Durham: Carolina Academic Press, 2008), Chapter 8.

11 *Menzel v. List*, 253 N.Y.S.2d 43 (1st Dept. 1964) and 267 N.Y.S.2d 804 (Sup. Ct. N.Y. 1966), modified on other grounds, 279 N.Y.S.2d 608 (1st Dept. 1967), modification rev'd, 298 N.Y.S.2d 976 (1969).

12 *Autocephalous Greek-Orthodox Church of Cyprus v. Goldberg & Feldman Fine Arts Inc.*, 917 F.2d 278 (7th Cir. 1990) cert. denied, 112 U.S. 377 (1991).

13 See for example *Goodman v. Searle*, 96 Civ. 5310 (S.D.N.Y. 1996); *Rosenberg v. Seattle Art Museum*, 70 F Supp 2d 1163 (WD Wash, 1999); *Warin v. Wildenstein & Co.*, No. 115143/99 (N.Y. Sup. Ct. 2001), aff'd, 740 N.Y.S.2d 331 (N.Y. App. Div. 2002), vacated, M-3035, 2002 N.Y. App. Div. LEXIS 7897 (N.Y. App. Div. 2002), substituted opinion at 746 N.Y.S.2d 282 (N.Y. App. Div. 2002) (affirming trial court judgment); see also *Warin v. Wildenstein & Co.*, 824 N.Y.S.2d 759 (N.Y. Sup. Ct. 2006) (dismissing complaint with prejudice), time to perfect appeal extended, M-2069,2007 N.Y. App. Div. LEXIS 6118 (N.Y. App Div. 2007), 45 A.D. 3d 459, 846 N.Y.S. 2d 153 (N.Y. App. Div. 1st Dep't. 2007). For discussions of restitution cases, see Michael Bazyler and Roger P. Alford, eds. *Holocaust Restitution: Perspectives on the Litigation and its Legacy* (New York and London: New York University Press, 2006), or Michael J. Bazyler, *Holocaust Justice: The Battle for Restitution in America's Courts, supra*, note 2.

14 *People v. Museum of Modern Art: In the Matterof the Application to Quash Grand Jury Subpoena Duces Tecum Served on the Museum of Modern Art*, 677 N.Y.S.2d 872 (Sup. Ct. 1998), rev'd 253 A.D.2d 211, 688 N.Y.S.2d 3 (App. Div. 1999), rev'd and trial court affirmed 719 N.E.2d 897, 93 N.Y.2d 729 (N.Y. 1999).

15 *United States of America v. Portrait of Wally, a Painting by Egon Schiele*, 105 Fed. Supp. 2d 288 (S.D.N.Y. 2000).

16 *United States v. Portrait of Wally, A Painting by Egon Schiele*, 2002 U.S. Dist. LEXIS (S.D.N.Y. 2002).

17 *United States v. Portrait of Wally, A Painting by Egon Schiele*, 2009 663 F. Supp. 2d 232 (S.D.N.Y. 2009).

18 "Madonna and Child Painting to Return to North Carolina" *Museum Security Network*, online: <http://www.museum-security.org/00/120. html>.

19 354. (1) Every one commits an offence who has in his possession any property or thing or any proceeds of any property or thing knowing that all or part of the property or thing or of the proceeds was obtained by or derived directly or indirectly from

(a) the commission in Canada of an offence punishable by indictment; or

(b) an act or omission anywhere that, if it had occurred in Canada, would have constituted an offence punishable by indictment (*Criminal Code*, R.S.C. 1985, c. C-46, s. 354.)

20 On a related note, it is also worth looking to the United Kingdom's example of the Human Remains Working Group under the auspices of the Department of Culture, Media and Sports. The Group's chair, Norman Palmer, explains that "there is a compelling case for an open, public, objective resolution mechanism by which claims can be heard." See *BBC News*, "Aborigines Back UK Bones Panel" 5 November 2003, online: <http://news.bbc.co.uk/2/hi/science/nature/3241369.stm>.

21 Elizabeth C. Stone, "Patterns of Looting in Southern Iraq" Antiquity 82:315 (2008) 125.

22 Neil Brodie, "The Market in Antiquities and Iraq" (Paper presented at the ABA Fall Meeting, Brussels, Belgium, 14 October 2003).

23 For more on this topic, see Noriaki Tsuchimoto's documentary, *Traces: the Kabul Museum 1988*, available through UNESCO.

24 Neil Brodie, "Focus on Iraq: Spoils of War" *Archaeology* 56:4 (July/ August 2003), online: <http://www.archaeology.org/0307/etc/war. html>.

25 *Ibid.*

26 William R. Ferris, "On the Trail of Lost Art: A Conversation with Lynn H. Nicholas" *Humanities* 22:3 (September/October 2000), online: <http://www.neh.gov/news/humanities/2001-05/conversation.html>.

27 All images courtesy of the Canadian Museum of Civilization. Online exhibition of "Afghanistan: Hidden Treasures" available at <http://www.civilization.ca/cmc/exhibitions/cmc/afghanistan/afghanistan05_e.shtml>.

28 Roger Atwood, "Afghanistan's Hidden Treasures" (June 2008) 213 *National Geographic* 131.

29 UNESCO Media Services, "UNESCO calls for ban on trade in Haitian artifacts to prevent pillaging of the country's cultural heritage" (29 January 2010), online: <http://www.unesco.org/new/en/media-services/single-view/news/unesco_calls_for_ban_on_trade_in_haitian_artefacts_to_prevent_pillaging_of_the_countrys_cultural/back/18256/>.

Chapter 6

1   Christie's Auction reports its results for antiquities sales on October 13, 2008, in London as £755,550. The antiquities auction on December 9, 2008, in New York brought in US$4,735,100. For these and other auction results, see official Christie's website at <www. christies.com>.

2   Elizabeth Gilgan, "Selling Our Past to the Highest Bidder: A Global Snapshot of Antiquities in the Art Market" (Paper presented at Archaeological Institute of America Annual Meeting, Philadephia, 8 January 2009), in *110th Annual Meeting Abstracts* (Boston: Archaeological Institute of America, 2009), at 82.

3   Diagrams in this chapter inspired by Morag M. Kersel, *License to Sell: The Legal Trade of Antiquities in Israel* (Ph.D. Thesis, University of Cambridge Department of Archaeology, 2006) [unpublished].

4   Simon Mackenzie, "Dig a Bit Deeper: Law, Regulation and the Illicit Antiquities Market" 2005 *British Journal of Criminology* 45:249, at 262.

5   Nikos Axarlis, "Corinth Antiquities Returned" *Archaeology*, online feature, 6 February 2001.

6   As quoted in Morag M. Kersel, *supra*, note 3, at 144.

7   Patrick J. Darling, "The Rape of Nok and Kwatakwashi: the Crisis in Nigerian Antiquities" *Culture Without Context* Issue 6 (Spring 2000), online: <http://www.mcdonald.cam.ac.uk/projects/iarc/culturewithoutcontext/issue6/darling.htm>.

8   Patrick J. Darling, *ibid*.

9   Grace Azubuike, "Illicit Trafficking Undermines Nigeria's Tourism: NCMM Boss" *Museum Security Network* (27 January 2010), online: <http://www.museum-security.org/?page_id=2290>.

10 Michael Brent, "Faking African Art" *Archaeology* 54:1 (January/February 2001), online: <http://www.archaeology.org/0101/abstracts/africa.html>.

11 See ICOM Red Lists, Saving Antiquities for Everyone, and US State Department websites for updated information on worldwide looting of antiquities. Other recommended sources include: Peter Watson

and Cecilia Todeschini, *The Medici Conspiracy: The Illicit Journey of Looted Antiquities from Italy's Tomb Raiders to the World's Greatest Museums* (New York: PublicAffairs, 2006); Neil Brodie, Jenny Doole and Peter Watson, *Stealing History: The Illicit Trade in Cultural Material* (Cambridge: The McDonald Institute for Archaeological Research, 2000); Roger Atwood, *Stealing History: Tomb Raiders, Smugglers, and the Looting of the Ancient World* (New York: St. Martin's, 2004); Colin Renfrew, *Loot, Legitimacy, and Ownership: The Ethical Crisis in Archaeology* (London: Duckworth, 2009); Simon Mackenzie, *Going, Going, Gone: Regulating the Market in Illicit Antiquities* (Leicester: Institute of Art and Law, 2005).

12 For recent American examples, see Dennis Wagner, "Looting of Indian Artifacts Targeted; Federal Crackdown Reveals Depth of Criminal Intrigue" *The Arizona Republic* (27 August 2009), online: <http://www.azcentral.com/arizonarepublic/news/articles/2009/08/27/20090827looters.html>; Carson Walker, "5 Indicted in Looting Native American Artifacts" (26 January 2009), online: <http://www.reznetnews.org/article/5-indicted-looting-native-american-artifacts-29100>; US Department of the Interior, "Federal Agents Bust Ring of Antiquity Thieves Looting American Indian Sites for Priceless Treasure" (10 June 2009), online: <http://www.doi.gov/photos/salazar/06102009/index.html>. For a recent Australian example, see Joel Gibson, "Treasures Looted and Sold Online" *Sydney Morning Herald* (2 April 2009), online: <http://www.smh.com.au/news/entertainment/arts/treasures-looted-and-sold-online/2009/04/01/1238261648572.html>. For a recent Canadian example, see Phil Couvrette, "Archaeologist Condemns Historical-Site Looting" (26 August 2009), online: <http://www.canada.com/technology/Archeologist+condemns+historical+site+lootin g/1932323/story.html>.

13 See for example Staffan Lundén, "TV Review: NRK (Norway), Skrift-samleren [The Manuscript Collector]" *Culture Without Context* Issue 16 (Spring 2005), online: <http://www.mcdonald.cam.ac.uk/projects/iarc/culturewithoutcontext/issue16/lunden.htm>.

14 Jane Portal, ed. *The First Emperor: China's Terracotta Army* (London: British Museum Press, 2007).

15 Paul Johnson, Address (Paper presented to the ABA Section of International Law and Practice, Washington, D.C., 7 May 2003) [unpublished].

16 For a detailed description of the statue's journey to California, see Bryan Rostron, "Chasing Getty's 'Youth'" *Spectator* (31 March 2007), online: <http://www.accessmylibrary.com/coms2/summary_0286-30623900_ITM>.

17 The J. Paul Getty Museum, Press Release, "J. Paul Getty Museum to Return 26 Objects to Italy" (21 November 2006), online: <http://www.getty.edu/news/press/center/statement06_getty_italy_meeting111706.html>.

18 See Annex to UNESCO Convention on the Protection of Underwater Cultural Heritage, 2001, rule XI (Appendix A8). Environmental concerns were also raised in the United Nations Law of the Seas Convention in 1972: see <http://www.un.org/Depts/los/convention_agreements/convention_overview_convention.htm>.

19 Charter on the Protection of Underwater Cultural Heritage (1996) ratified by the 11th ICOMOS General Assembly, held in Sofia, Bulgaria, 5-9 October 1996, The Law of the Sea Convention.

20 Paul Johnson, *supra*, note 13.

21 See Appendix A8.

22 Why not the United States and Canada? For debates on the topic, see for example Nancy C. Wilkie, "From the President: Lure of the Deep" *Archaeology* 55:4 (July/August 2002), online: <http://www.archaeology.org/0207/etc/president.html> and editorial response to Wilkie's letter: Mary Beth West, "Flawed Convention" *Archaeology* 56:3 (May/June 2003).

23 For a comprehensive list of UCH laws and treaties, see Sarah Dromgoole, ed. *The Protection of Underwater Cultural Heritage: National Perspectives in Light of the UNESCO Convention 2001*, 2d ed. (Leiden: Martinus Nijhoff, 2006). For documents related to the United Nations Law of the Sea Convention, see <http://www.un.org/

Depts/los/convention_agreements/convention_overview_convention.
htm>.

24 Ricardo Elia, "Titanic in the Courts" *Archaeology* 54:1 (January/February 2001).

25 David Bright, "Law from the Bottom of the Sea: Rights to the Titanic Shipwreck Disputed in US Courts" *Art & Cultural Heritage Law Newsletter* I:V (Spring 2009) 7.

26 Title 16 §450rr, s. 5(a).

27 Patty Gerstenblith, Art, *Cultural Heritage, and the Law: Cases and Materials* 2d ed. (Durham: Carolina Academic Press, 2008), at 821.

28 Sherry Hutt, Caroline Blanco, Walter Stern, and Stan Harris, eds. *Cultural Property Law: A Practitioner's Guide to the Management, Protection and Preservation of Heritage Resources* (Chicago: American Bar Association, 2004).

29 Ricardo Elia, *supra*, note 22. In a later decision, the Court of Appeal confirmed the jurisdiction of American courts to adjudicate *Titanic*-related claims based on Article III of the US Constitution, which gives federal courts power "in all cases of admiralty and maritime Jurisdiction." Based on the longstanding practice of admiralty courts adjudicating claims in the high seas, the Court distinguished the grant of a subject matter jurisdiction over a non-United States shipwreck in international waters from the extraterritorial assertion of sovereignty: see *R.M.S. Titanic Inc. v. Haver*, 171 F.3d 943 (4th Cir. 1999).

30 See *R.M.S. Titanic Inc. v. Wrecked & Abandoned Vessel*, 9 F. Supp. 2d 624 (E.D. Va. 1998), aff'd in part, rev'd in part.

31 *R.M.S. Titanic Inc. v. Haver*, *supra*, note 27.

32 Roberta Garabello and Tullio Scovazzi, eds., *The Protection of Underwater Cultural Heritage Before and After the 2001 UNESCO Convention* (Leiden: Martinus Nijhoff, 2003).

33 *R.M.S. Titanic Inc.v. The Wrecked and Abandoned Vessel believed to be the R.M.S. Titanic*, 2002 U.S. App. LEXIS 6799 (4th Cir., April 12, 2002).

34 *R.M.S. Titanic Inc. v. Wrecked and Abandoned Vessel*, 323 F. Supp 2d 724, 744-45 (E.D. Va. 2004).

35 *R.M.S. Titanic Inc. v. Wrecked and Abandoned Vessel*, 435 F.3d 521, 532-33 (4th Cir. 2006).

36 At time of publication, the decision was still pending.

37 For a more in-depth American perspective, see Chapter 4 in Sherry Hutt, Caroline Blanco, Walter Stern, and Stan Harris, eds. *Cultural Property Law: A Practitioner's Guide to the Management, Protection and Preservation of Heritage Resources* (Chicago: American Bar Association, 2004).

38 43 U.S.C. §§2101-2106.

39 43 U.S.C. §2101(b).

40 *Sea Hunt Inc. v. The Unidentified Shipwrecked Vessel or Vessels*, 221 F.3d 634 (4th Cir. 2000).

41 James Goold, Address (Paper presented to the ABA Section of International Law and Practice, Washington, D.C., 7 May 2003) [unpublished].

42 Tammy L. Shaw, "Up From the Depths: The Changing Face of Maritime Salvage and Shipwreck Law" (Paper presented at the 12th Biennial Coastal Zone Conference held in Cleveland, OH., 15 July 2001), published by Sea Grant.

43 Eric LeGresley, Government of Canada Document BP-322E "The Law of the Sea Convention" (February 1993), online: <http://dsp-psd.tpsgc.gc.ca/Collection-R/LoPBdP/BP/bp322-e.htm#(1)>.

44 Mark Bourrie, "In Court over Ghost Gold: The Atlantic Case" *Canadian Lawyer* (June 2001) 35.

45 Mark Bourrie, *ibid.*, at 35.

46 Mark Bourrie, *ibid.*, at 36.

47 *Ontario v. Mar-Dive Corporation ("The Atlantic")* (1996), 141 D.L.R. (4th) 577, 1997 A.M.C. 1000 (Ont. Gen. Div.).

Chapter 7

1   *Criminal Code*, R.S.C. 1985, c. C-46, s. 366.

2   *Criminal Code, ibid.*, s. 380.

3   Leonard D. Duboff, Christy O. King and Sally Holt Caplan, *The Deskbook of Art Law*, 2d ed. (New York: Oceana Publications, 1999) at K-11.

4   Eric Hebborn, *The Art Forger's Handbook* (Woodstock and New York: The Overlook Press, 1997) at 142, plates 40-42.

5   Leonard D. Duboff, *supra*, note 3 at K-14.

6   See <http://www.rembrandtresearchproject.org/>.

7   Sophie Burnham, "As the Stakes in the Art World Rise, so do Laws and Lawsuits" *New York Times* (15 February 1987) A1.

8   *Hahn v. Duveen* 133 Misc. 871, 234 NYS 185 (Sup. Ct. 1929).

9   As quoted in Andrea Pizzi, *Hahn v. Duveen, New York 1929* (12 December 2007), online: <http://artrule.blogspot.com/2007/12/hahn-v-duveen-new-york-1929.html>.

10   Andrea Pizzi, *ibid.*

11   Matthew Kalman, "The Burial Box of Jesus' Brother: Fraud?" *Time Magazine* (5 September 2009), online: <http://www.time.com/time/world/article/0,8599,1920720,00.html>.

12   See <http://www.irs.gov/individuals/article/0,,id=96804,00.html>.

13   Leonard D. Duboff, *supra*, note 3 at K-20.

14   C. Gavrilov, C. Ibarra-Castanedo, O. Grube, X. Maldague, and R. Maev, "Infrared methods in Noninvasive Inspection of Artwork" (Paper presented to the 9th International Conference on Nondestructive Testing of Art, Jerusalem, Israel, 25-30 May 2008), online: <http://www.ndt.net/article/art2008/papers/040Gavrilov.pdf>.

15   Leonard D. Duboff, *supra*, note 3 at K-44.

16   Jimmy Lee Shreeve, "What Lies Beneath" *The Independent* (3 September 2008), online: <http://www.independent.co.uk/arts-entertainment/art/features/art-forgers-what-lies-beneath-917067.html>.

17   Richard Newman, "Applications of X Rays in Art Authentication: Radiography, X-Ray Diffraction, and X-Ray Fluorescence" (Paper

presented at Conference for Society of Photographic Instrumenta-
tion Engineers, San Jose, California, 29 January 1998), in Walter
McCrone, Duane R. Chartier, and Richard J. Weiss, eds. "Scientific
Detection of Fakery in Art" (Proc. SPIE Vol. 3315) 31.

18 Peter Landesman, "A Crisis of Fakes: The Getty Forgeries" *The New
York Times* (18 March 2001), online: <http://www.law.harvard.edu/
faculty/martin/art-law/crises_of_fakes.htm>.

19 Leonard D. Duboff, *supra*, note 3 at K-36.

20 James Martin, "Testing Objects: Scientific Examination and Materials
Analysis in Authenticity Studies", online: <http://www.orionanalytical.
com/Martin-Testing_Objects-Bruce.pdf>.

21 Richard Newman, *supra*, note 17.

22 Leonard D. Duboff, *supra*, note 3 at K-33.

23 The William R. and Clarice V. Spurlock Museum website, "Careful
Collecting: Fakes and Forgeries", online: <http://www.spurlock.
illinois.edu/explorations/research/collecting.pdf>.

24 See <http://www.orionanalytical.com/Martin-Testing_Objects-Bruce.
pdf>.

25 Peter Klein, "Dendochronological Analyses of Art-Objects" (Paper
presented at Conference for Society of Photographic Instrumenta-
tion Engineers, San Jose, California, 29 January 1998), in Walter
McCrone, Duane R. Chartier, and Richard J. Weiss, eds. "Scientific
Detection of Fakery in Art" (Proc. SPIE Vol. 3315) 21.

26 For more information on Taylor's studies, see <http://www.uoregon.
edu/~msiuo/taylor/art/info.html>.

27 Leonard D. Duboff, *supra*, note 3 at K-3.

28 Leonard D. Duboff, *supra*, note 3 at K-3.

29 Milton Esterow, "The 10 Most Faked Artists" *ARTnews* (June 2000)
103.

30 Abraham Bredius, "A New Vermeer" *Burlington Magazine* (November 1937) 71: 210-211.

31 James Fuentes, "Forgeries Are Real" *The Blow-Up* (19 June 2002),
online: <http://www.theblowup.com/06/Projects/Forgeries_are_Real/
index.html>.

32 "Art: The Price of Forgery." *Time Magazine* (18 November
    1946), online: <http://www.time.com/time/magazine/article/
    0,9171,777318,00.html>. For more on Van Meegeren, see Errol
    Morris's excellent seven-part series: "Bamboozling Ourselves" *New
    York Times* (27 May 2009), online: <http://morris.blogs.nytimes.
    com/2009/05/27/bamboozling-ourselves-part-1/>.

33 As quoted in Ralph Blumenthal, "When a Master Forger Confesses,
    Who Can Tell?" *New York Times* (4 January 1995), online:< http://
    www.nytimes.com/1995/01/04/arts/when-a-forger-confesses-who-
    can-tell.html>.

34 David S. Oderberg, "The Art of the Master Forger" *Quadrant
    Magazine* (1998), online: <http://www.thefreelibrary.com/
    THE+ART+OF+THE+MASTER+FORGER-a053738910>.

35 See Eric Hebborn, *supra*, note 4 at 156.

36 Eric Hebborn, *Drawn to Trouble: Confessions of a Master Forger*
    (New York: Random House, 1991).

37 Denis Dutton, "Death of a Forger" Aesthetics Online (1996), online:
    <http://www.aesthetics-online.org/articles/index.php?articles_id=2>.

38 Andreas Schroeder, *Fakes, Frauds, and Flimflammery* (Toronto:
    McLelland & Stewart, 1999) at 74.

39 Rachel Bell, "Faking It: Elmyr de Hory—The Century's Greatest Art
    Forger" *TruTV Crime Library*, online: <http://www.trutv.com/library/
    crime/criminal_mind/scams/elmyr_de_hory/index.html>.

40 Andreas Schroeder, *supra*, note 38 at 95.

41 Jesse Hamlin, "Master (Con) Artist: Painting Forger Elmyr de Hory's
    Copies are Like the Real Thing" *San Francisco Chronicle* (29 July
    1999), online: <http://www.sfgate.com/cgi-bin/article.cgi?file=/
    chronicle/archive/1999/07/29/DD21995.DTL>.

42 Donald MacGillivray, "When is a Fake not a Fake? When it's a
    Genuine Forgery" *The Guardian* (2 July 2005), online:< http://
    www.guardian.co.uk/money/2005/jul/02/alternativeinvestment.
    jobsandmoney>.

43 David S. Oderberg, *supra*, note 34.

44 "Art: Palming off the Palmers" *Time Magazine* (13 September 1976), online: <http://www.time.com/time/magazine/article/0,9171,914598,00.html>.

45 Donald MacGillivray, *supra*, note 42.

46 Martin Esterow, "Dealer is Indicted In 41 Art Forgeries" (17 May 1967) *New York Times* 1.

47 Leonard D. Duboff, *supra*, note 3 at K-7.

48 64 Misc. 2d 423, 314 N.Y.S.2d 661 (1970).

49 Robert E. Tomasson, "Stein's Right to Sell Forgeries Bearing his Name is Affirmed" *New York Times* (30 September 1970) 36.

50 Martin Esterow, *supra*, note 46.

51 Peter Landesman, "A 20th-Century Master Scam" *The New York Times* (18 July 1999), online: <http://www.nytimes.com/1999/07/18/magazine/a-20th-century-master-scam.html>.

52 Adam Schwartz, Book Review of Provenance: *The Biggest Art Fraud of the Twentieth Century* by Laney Salisbury (12 August 2009), online: <http://indianapublicmedia.org/arts/provenance/>.

53 Clive Thompson, "How to Make a Fake" *New York Magazine*, May 2005.

54 United States Department of Justice, News Release, "Manhattan Art Gallery Owner Sentenced to 41 Months in Federal Prison for Multi-Million Dollar Art Forgery Scheme" (6 July 2005), online: <http://www.usdoj.gov/usao/nys/pressreleases/July05/sakhaisentence.pdf>.

55 Robert Fulford, "Artful Codgers" *The Globe and Mail* (29 January 2008) AL1.

56 Robert Fulford, *ibid*.

57 James Fuentes, *supra*, note 31.

On Becoming an International Art Lawyer

1   Bonnie Czegledi, "Art Galleries and the Spoils of War" *The National Post* (25 April 2000).

2   Bonnie Czegledi, "Legal, Practical, and Business Issues for Exhibitors of Art in Canada" (Paper presented to the International Bar Association, Amsterdam, The Netherlands, 17 September 2000) [unpublished].

3   Bonnie Czegledi, "Fakes and Forgeries: International Art Trade and Stolen Art" (Paper presented to the International Trade Club of Toronto, 28 September 2000) [unpublished].

4   Congressional Record S12102-12104 (6 October 1999).

5   "New Law would Weaken US Ability to Keep out Loot" *The Art Newspaper* 105 (July-August 2000).

6   Bonnie Czegledi, "Who Knew What about Nazi Loot? A public inquiry into art plunder might be in order" *The National Post* (15 December 2000).

7   See Isabel Vincent, "Bad Impressions: Some of the National Gallery's most important impressionistic works were acquired through a shady wartime dealer who sold plundered paintings to Hitler, a discovery that raised serious questions about their Ownership" *The National Post* (21 December 2000) A17, and "Paintings Raise Blunt Questions: How Cold War traitor Anthony Blunt and controversial London art dealer Tomas Harris helped the National Gallery build its collection" *The National Post* (14 December 2000) B10.

8   See Isabel Vincent, "Paintings Raise Blunt Questions: How Cold War traitor Anthony Blunt and controversial London art dealer Tomas Harris helped the National Gallery build its collection" *The National Post* (14 December 2000) B10.

9   See official website of the National Art Gallery of Canada at <www.gallery.ca>.

10 Bonnie Czegledi, "An Overview of the Illicit Market for Canadian Cultural Property and the Means to Control It" (Paper presented to the American Bar Association Section of International Law and Practice, Monterrey, Mexico, 16 October 2001) [unpublished].

11 Bonnie Czegledi, "Import/Export Considerations of the Cultural Property Trade" (Paper presented to the International Bar Association Annual Meeting, Cancun, Mexico, 1 November 2001) [unpublished].

12 Bonnie Czegledi, "Art as the Victim of War: An Historical and Legal Overview of the Problem from a Canadian Perspective" (Canadian Symposium on Holocaust-era Cultural Property, presented by the Canadian Museums Association and the Canadian Jewish Congress, delivered at the National Gallery of Canada, Ottawa, 14-16 November 2001) [unpublished].

13 Bonnie Czegledi, "Part I: Fakes and Forgeries in the International Art World" (Intrigue in the International Art World, delivered at the Royal Ontario Museum, Toronto, Ontario, 18 November 2001) [unpublished]. Synopsis: As much as 40% of the art market involves trade in forgeries. This lecture shed light on current trends, past intrigues, and psychological profiles of the forgers, and their willing and often unwitting accomplices. Bonnie Czegledi, "Part II: Techniques and Authentication Disputes" (Intrigue in the International Art World, delivered at the Royal Ontario Museum, Toronto, Ontario, 25 November 2001) [unpublished]. Synopsis: A discussion of various techniques used to create art forgeries, the methods of detection, and the complications which beset authentication disputes in the international art business. Bonnie Czegledi, "Part III: Pillage and Profit: Legal and Illegal Trade in Indigenous Art" (Intrigue in the International Art World, delivered at the Royal Ontario Museum, Toronto, Ontario, 2 December 2001) [unpublished]. Synopsis: Rising international interest in collecting First Nations art has revealed a number of legal and practical issues relating to the excavation, trade, and export of indigenous art and artifacts. This lecture assisted interested collectors in negotiating their way through the complicated bureaucratic and ethical maze.

14 Letter from Martin Sullivan to President Bush (14 April 2003) in *Washington Report on Middle East Affairs* (June 2003) 15, online: <http://www.wrmea.com/archives/june2003/0306015.html>.

15 Bonnie Czegledi, "Legal, Historical and Ethical Issues Concerning Looted Art from a Canadian Perspective" (Paper presented to the

Hadassah WIZO, Toronto, 9 April 2002) [unpublished]. Bonnie Czegledi, "Holocaust Looted Art" (Paper presented to the American Bar Association, New York, 9 May 2002) [unpublished]. Bonnie Czegledi, "WWII Looted Art: Legal Issues" (Paper presented at Holocaust Education Week, UJA Federation, Toronto, 4 November 2002) [unpublished].

16   At Lyon I gave an intensive course on Law and Taxation in the Art Market from the North American perspective. It was part of a year-long academic program with classes taught by faculty members, art market professionals, and specialized lawyers. It examined issues such as international and domestic laws concerning illegal trafficking of art and antiquities, import/export restrictions, criminal sanctions and leading jurisprudence, due diligence, authentication methods and dispute resolution, provenance research, and restitution issues. The objective of the program was to enable the students to become competent in various art professions, such as auctioneers, specialized lawyers, antique dealers, or gallery owners.

17   Joshua Knelman, "Artful Crimes" *The Walrus* 2:9 (November 2005) 87.

18   Bonnie Czegledi, "From Collector to Criminal: When Collectors Cross the Line" (International Art Law Lecture Series, delivered at the Royal Ontario Museum, Toronto, October 17-November 7). Synopsis: This lecture series looked at hot topics concerning the recovery of stolen art, the black market for archaeological and ethnographic material, fakes and forgeries, money laundering, and the violent crimes related to such activities. It also examined Nazi looted art, pillaging in conflict areas such as Iraq, international treaty law, leading jurisprudence, provenance research, art as an investment, and due diligence for those wishing to make acquisitions.

19   <http://www.fbi.gov/hq/cid/arttheft/artcrimeteam.htm>.

20   "FBI Art Crime Special Unit", International Foundation for Art Research, New York, NY (8-9 June 2005).

21   Christopher Michaud, "Christie's stages record art sale," Reuter's, November 9, 2006.

22 Bonnie Czegledi, "The Restitution of Sacred Items and Human
    Remains to First Nations Peoples from a Canadian Perspective"
    (Paper presented to the Association for the Study of Law, Culture and
    the Humanities, Eighth Annual Conference, Austin, TX,11-12 March
    2005) [unpublished].
23 Bonnie Czegledi, Program Moderator, "The Future of Repatriation"
    (Paper presented to the American Bar Association, Washington,
    D.C.,15 April 2005) [unpublished]. Bonnie Czegledi, "Canadian
    System for the Protection of Cultural Property" (Paper presented to
    the American Bar Association, International Cultural Property Com-
    mittee, Brussels, 28 October 2005) [unpublished].
24 Bonnie Czegledi, "Criminals & the Art Market" (Paper presented
    to the Royal Ontario Museum, Toronto, 27 January 2006) [unpub-
    lished]. Synposis: Trafficking in stolen jewellery and cars, marketing
    illegal drugs, and the sex trade are only part of the underworld of
    criminal activity. Fine art is a target, too. In Europe, Interpol takes
    active steps to stop thieves, but in Canada there is little effective
    action. Why is Toronto a haven for crime? Bonnie Czegledi, "Art
    Crimes" (International Art Law Lecture Series, delivered at the Royal
    Ontario Museum February 20-March 6 2006) [unpublished]. Bonnie
    Czegledi, "Art Crimes" (Paper presented to the Women's Art Asso-
    ciation, Toronto, 12 April 2006) [unpublished]. Bonnie Czegledi,
    "Crimes Against Culture" (Paper presented to the Royal Ontario
    Museum, 20 April 2006) [unpublished]. Synposis: Art theft is not
    a victimless crime. Entire nations suffer when the evidence of their
    histories and identities are sold to the highest bidder. Bonnie Cze-
    gledi, "Criminals & the Art Market" (Paper presented to the Arts and
    Letters Club, Toronto, 8 May 2006) [unpublished].
25 Julius Melnitzer, "The Art of Practicing Art Law," *Law Times* (3 July
    2006). Bonnie Czegledi, "Remember you're a lawyer when buying
    art on your summer holidays," *The Lawyers Weekly* 26:11 (14 July
    2006) 8.
26 Bonnie Czegledi, "Fakes and Forgeries in the Art Market" (Paper
    presented to the American Bar Association, New York, 6 April 2006)
    [unpublished].

27   Bonnie Czegledi, "The Law of Auction in Canada" (Paper presented
     to the International Bar Association, September 2006) [unpub-
     lished]. Bonnie Czegledi, "Legal Issues Concerning Cultural Property
     Removed from the Soil: A Canadian Perspective" (Institute of Art
     and Law Conference, delivered at the University of Pecs, Hungary,
     October 2006) [unpublished]. Bonnie Czegledi, "Art Crimes"
     (International Art Law Lecture Series, delivered at the Royal Ontario
     Museum, 12 November 2006) [unpublished]. Ninja and Special
     K, "Hot Fossils and Rebel Matters 88—Art Theft, Forgery, and the
     Law," Podcast review of the Royal Ontario Museum International
     Art Law Lecture Series (18 February 2007). Bonnie Czegledi, "Col-
     lecting Chinese Artifacts Today" (Paper presented to the Royal
     Ontario Museum, Toronto, 26 November 2006) [unpublished].
     Bonnie Czegledi, "In Search of our Heritage" (Paper presented at the
     International Conference on Strategies for Saving Indoor Metallic
     Collections with a Satellite Meeting on Legal Issues in the Conserva-
     tion of Cultural Heritage, Cairo, 25 February-1 March 2007), pub-
     lished in Vasilike Argyropoulos, Anno Hein, and Mohamed Abdel
     Hareth, eds., *Strategies for Saving our Cultural Heritage* (Athens:
     TEI of Athens, 2008). Bonnie Czegledi, "Hot Trade Heats Up" (Paper
     presented to the American Bar Association, Washington, D.C., 4
     May 2007) [unpublished]. Bonnie Czegledi, "Issues in Owning Art"
     (Paper presented to the International Bar Association, Milan, 31
     May 2007) [unpublished]. Bonnie Czegledi, "Art, Cultural Institu-
     tions and Heritage Law Buying art: can the risks be reduced?" (Paper
     presented to the International Bar Association, Singapore, October
     2007) [unpublished]. Bonnie Czegledi, "International Art Theft"
     (Paper presented to the Arts and Letters Club, Toronto, October
     2007) [unpublished]. Bonnie Czegledi, "Legal Issues of Conserva-
     tion" (Paper presented at the International Council of Museums
     Conference, New Delhi, September 2008) [unpublished].
28   Joshua Knelman, "Art thieves, look out" *The Globe and Mail* (27 Jan
     2007); Philip Alves, "Some of that old black market" *The National
     Post* (27 Jan 2007); Michael Peel, "Art's brush with the lawless,"

Financial Times (12 January 2007); Deena Waisburg, "The Art of the Steal" *Nuvo Magazine* (Autumn 2007) 84.

29 CBC Radio, *Sounds Like Canada* (6 February 2007); CBC Radio, *As It Happens* (August 2007).

APPENDIX A: International Treaties, Conventions, and Agreements

A1. 1970 UNESCO CONVENTION

Convention on the Means of Prohibiting and Preventing the Illicit Import, Export and Transfer of Ownership of Cultural Property

The General Conference of the United Nations Educational, Scientific and Cultural Organization, meeting in Paris from 12 October to 14 November 1970, at its sixteenth session,

RECALLING the importance of the provisions contained in the Declaration of the Principles of International Cultural Co-operation, adopted by the General Conference at its fourteenth session,

CONSIDERING that the interchange of cultural property among nations for scientific, cultural and educational purposes increases the knowledge of the civilization of Man, enriches the cultural life of all peoples and inspires mutual respect and appreciation among nations,

CONSIDERING that cultural property constitutes one of the basic elements of civilization and national culture, and that its true value can be appreciated only in relation to the fullest possible information regarding its origin, history and traditional setting,

CONSIDERING that it is incumbent upon every State to protect the cultural property existing within its territory against the dangers of theft, clandestine excavation, and illicit export,

CONSIDERING that, to avert these dangers, it is essential for every State to become increasingly alive to the moral obligations to respect its own cultural heritage and that of all nations,

CONSIDERING that, as cultural institutions, museums, libraries and archives should ensure that their collections are built up in accordance with universally recognized moral principles, CONSIDERING that the illicit import, export and transfer of ownership of cultural property is an obstacle to that understanding between nations which it is part of Unesco's mission to promote by recommending to interested States, international conventions to this end,

CONSIDERING that the protection of cultural heritage can be effective only if organized both nationally and internationally among States working in close co-operation,

CONSIDERING that the Unesco General Conference adopted a Recommendation to this effect in 1964,

HAVING before it further proposals on the means of prohibiting and preventing the illicit import, export and transfer of ownership of cultural property, a question which is on the agenda for the session as item 19,

HAVING decided, at its fifteenth session, that this question should be made the subject of an international convention,

ADOPT this Convention on the fourteenth day of November 1970.

Article 1

For the purposes of this Convention, the term "cultural property" means property which, on religious or secular grounds, is specifically designated by each State as being of importance for archaeology, prehistory, history, literature, art or science and which belongs to the following categories:

    a.   Rare collections and specimens of fauna, flora, minerals and anatomy, and objects of palaeontological interest;

    b.   property relating to history, including the history of science and technology and military and social history, to the life of national leaders, thinkers, scientists and artists and to events of national importance;

    c.   products of archaeological excavations (including regular and clandestine) or of archaeological discoveries;

    d.   elements of artistic or historical monuments or archaeological sites which have been dismembered;

 e. antiquities more than one hundred years old, such as inscriptions, coins and engraved seals;

 f. objects of ethnological interest;

 g. property of artistic interest, such as:

  i. pictures, paintings and drawings produced entirely by hand on any support and in any material (excluding industrial designs and manufactured articles decorated by hand);

  ii. original works of statuary art and sculpture in any material;

  iii. original engravings, prints and lithographs;

  iv. original artistic assemblages and montages in any material;

 h. rare manuscripts and incunabula, old books, documents and publications of special interest (historical, artistic, scientific, literary, etc.) singly or in collections;

 i. postage, revenue and similar stamps, singly or in collections;

 j. archives, including sound, photographic and cinematographic archives;

 k. articles of furniture more than one hundred years old and old musical instruments.

Article 2

1. The States Parties to this Convention recognize that the illicit import, export and transfer of ownership of cultural property is one of the main causes of the impoverishment of the cultural heritage of the countries of origin of such property and that international co-operation constitutes one of the most efficient means of protecting each country's cultural property against all the dangers resulting therefrom.

2. To this end, the States Parties undertake to oppose such practices with the means at their disposal, and particularly by removing their causes, putting a stop to current practices, and by helping to make the necessary reparations.

Article 3

The import, export or transfer of ownership of cultural property effected contrary to the provisions adopted under this Convention by the States Parties thereto, shall be illicit.

Article 4

The States Parties to this Convention recognize that for the purpose of the Convention property which belongs to the following categories forms part of the cultural heritage of each State:

    a.   Cultural property created by the individual or collective genius of nationals of the State concerned, and cultural property of importance to the State concerned created within the territory of that State by foreign nationals or stateless persons resident within such territory;

    b.   cultural property found within the national territory;

    c.   cultural property acquired by archaeological, ethnological or natural science missions, with the consent of the competent authorities of the country of origin of such property;

    d.   cultural property which has been the subject of a freely agreed exchange;

    e.   cultural property received as a gift or purchased legally with the consent of the competent authorities of the country of origin of such property.

Article 5

To ensure the protection of their cultural property against illicit import, export and transfer of ownership, the States Parties to this Convention undertake, as appropriate for each country, to set up within their territories one or more national services, where such services do not already exist, for the protection of the cultural heritage, with a qualified staff sufficient in number for the effective carrying out of the following functions:

    a.   Contributing to the formation of draft laws and regulations designed to secure the protection of the cultural heritage and particularly prevention of the illicit import, export and transfer of ownership of important cultural property;

b. establishing and keeping up to date, on the basis of a national inventory of protected property, a list of important public and private cultural property whose export would constitute an appreciable impoverishment of the national cultural heritage;

c. promoting the development or the establishment of scientific and technical institutions (museums, libraries, archives, laboratories, workshops...) required to ensure the preservation and presentation of cultural property;

d. organizing the supervision of archaeological excavations, ensuring the preservation "in situ" of certain cultural property, and protecting certain areas reserved for future archaeological research;

e. establishing, for the benefit of those concerned (curators, collectors, antique dealers, etc.) rules in conformity with the ethical principles set forth in this convention; and taking steps to ensure the observance of those rules;

f. taking educational measures to stimulate and develop respect for the cultural heritage of all States, and spreading knowledge of the provisions of this Convention;

g. seeing that appropriate publicity is given to the disappearance of any items of cultural property.

Article 6

The States Parties to this Convention undertake:

a. To introduce an appropriate certificate in which the exporting State would specify that the export of the cultural property in question is authorized. The certificate should accompany all items of cultural property exported in accordance with the regulations;

b. to prohibit the exportation of cultural property from their territory unless accompanied by the above-mentioned export certificate;

c. to publicize this prohibition by appropriate means, particularly among persons likely to export or import cultural property.

Article 7

The States Parties to this Convention undertake:

a. To take the necessary measures, consistent with national legislation, to prevent museums and similar institutions within their territories from acquiring cultural property originating in another State Party which has been illegally exported after entry into force of this Convention, in the States concerned. Whenever possible, to inform a State of origin Party to this Convention of an offer of such cultural property illegally removed from that State after the entry into force of this Convention in both States;

b. i. to prohibit the import of cultural property stolen from a museum or a religious or secular public monument or similar institution in another State Party to this Convention after the entry into force of this Convention for the States concerned, provided that such property is documented as appertaining to the inventory of that institution; ii. at the request of the State Party of origin, to take appropriate steps to recover and return any such cultural property imported after the entry into force of this Convention in both States concerned, provided, however, that the requesting State shall pay just compensation to an innocent purchaser or to a person who has valid title to that property. Requests for recovery and return shall be made through diplomatic offices. The requesting Party shall furnish, at its expense, the documentation and other evidence necessary to establish its claim for recovery and return. The Parties shall impose no customs duties or other charges upon cultural property returned pursuant to this Article. All expenses incident to the return and delivery of the cultural property shall be borne by the requesting Party.

Article 8

The States Parties to this Convention undertake to impose penalties or administrative sanctions on any person responsible for infringing the prohibitions referred to under Articles 6(b) and 7(b) above.

Article 9

Any State Party to this Convention whose cultural patrimony is in jeopardy from pillage of archaeological or ethnological materials may call upon other States Parties who are affected. The States Parties to this Convention undertake, in these circumstances, to participate in a concerted international effort to determine and to carry out the necessary concrete measures, including the control of exports and imports and international commerce in the specific materials concerned. Pending agreement each State concerned shall take provisional measures to the extent feasible to prevent irremediable injury to the cultural heritage of the requesting State.

Article 10

The States Parties to this Convention undertake:

a. To restrict by education, information and vigilance, movement of cultural property illegally removed from any State Party to this Convention and, as appropriate for each country, oblige antique dealers, subject to penal or administrative sanctions, to maintain a register recording the origin of each item of cultural property, names and addresses of the supplier, description and price of each item sold and to inform the purchaser of the cultural property of the export prohibition to which such property may be subject;

b. to endeavour by educational means to create and develop in the public mind a realization of the value of cultural property and the threat to the cultural heritage created by theft, clandestine excavations and illicit exports.

Article 11

The export and transfer of ownership of cultural property under compulsion arising directly or indirectly from the occupation of a country by a foreignpower shall be regarded as illicit.

Article 12

The States Parties to this Convention shall respect the cultural heritage within the territories for the international relations of which they are responsible, and shall take all appropriate measures to prohibit and prevent the illicit import, export and transfer of ownership of cultural property in such territories.

Article 13

The States Parties to this Convention also undertake, consistent with the laws of each State:

a.   To prevent by all appropriate means transfers of ownership of cultural property likely to promote the illicit import or export of such property;

b.   to ensure that their competent services co-operate in facilitating the earliest possible restitution of illicitly exported cultural property to its rightful owner;

c.   to admit actions for recovery of lost or stolen items of cultural property brought by or on behalf of the rightful owners;

d.   to recognize the indefeasible right of each State Party to this Convention to classify and declare certain cultural property as inalienable which should therefore ipso facto not be exported, and to facilitate recovery of such property by the State concerned in cases where it has been exported.

Article 14

In order to prevent illicit export and to meet the obligations arising from the implementation of this Convention, each State Party to the Convention should, as far as it is able, provide the national services responsible for the protection of its cultural heritage with an adequate budget and, if necessary, should set up a fund for this purpose.

Article 15

Nothing in this Convention shall prevent States Parties thereto from concluding special agreements among themselves or from continuing to implement agreements already concluded regarding the restitution of cultural property removed, whatever the reason, from its territory of origin, before the entry into force of this Convention for the States concerned.

Article 16

The States Parties to this Convention shall in their periodic reports submitted to the General Conference of the United Nations Educational, Scientific and Cultural Organization on dates and in a manner to be determined by it, give information on the legislative and administrative provisions which they have adopted and other action which they have taken for the application of this Convention, together with details of the experience acquired in this field.

Article 17

1. The States Parties to this Convention may call on the technical assistance of the United Nations Educational, Scientific and Cultural Organization, particularly as regards:

   a.   Information and education;
   b.   consultation and expert advice;
   c.   co-ordination and good offices.

2. The United Nations Educational, Scientific and Cultural Organization may, on its own initiative conduct research and publish studies on matters relevant to the illicit movement of cultural property.

3. To this end, the United Nations Educational, Scientific and Cultural Organization may also call on the co-operation of any competent non-governmental organization.

4. The United Nations Educational, Scientific and Cultural Organization may, on its own initiative, make proposals to States Parties to this Convention for its implementation.

5. At the request of at least two States Parties to this Convention which are engaged in a dispute over its implementation, UNESCO may extend its good offices to reach a settlement between them.

Article 18

This Convention is drawn up in English, French, Russian and Spanish, the four texts being equally authoritative.

Article 19

1. This Convention shall be subject to ratification or acceptance by States members of the United Nations Educational, Scientific and Cultural Organization in accordance with their respective constitutional procedures.

2. The instruments of ratification or acceptance shall be deposited with the Director-General of the United Nations Educational, Scientific and Cultural Organization.

Article 20

1. This Convention shall be open to accession by all States not members of the United Nations Educational, Scientific and Cultural Organization which are invited to accede to it by the Executive Board of the Organization.

2. Accession shall be effected by the deposit of an instrument of accession with the Director-General of the United Nations Educational, Scientific and Cultural Organization.

Article 21

This Convention shall enter into force three months after the date of the deposit of the third instrument of ratification, acceptance or accession, but only with respect to those States which have deposited their respective instruments on or before that date. It shall enter into force with respect to any other State three months after the deposit of its instrument of ratification, acceptance or accession.

Article 22

The States Parties to this Convention recognize that the Convention is applicable not only to their metropolitan territories but also to all territories for the international relations of which they are responsible; they undertake to consult, if necessary, the governments or other competent authorities of these territories on or before ratification, acceptance or accession with a view to securing the application of the Convention to those territories, and to notify the Director-General of the United Nations Educational, Scientific and Cultural Organization of the territories to which it is applied, the notification to take effect three months after the date of its receipt.

Article 23

1. Each State Party to this Convention may denounce the Convention on its own behalf or on behalf of any territory for whose international relations it is responsible.

2. The denunciation shall be notified by an instrument in writing, deposited with the Director-General of the United Nations Educational, Scientific and Cultural Organization.

3. The denunciation shall take effect twelve months after the receipt of the instrument of denunciation.

Article 24

The Director-General of the United Nations Educational, Scientific and Cultural Organization shall inform the States members of the Organization, the States not members of the Organization which are referred to in Article 20, as well as the United Nations, of the deposit of all the instruments of ratification, acceptance and accession provided for in Articles 19 and 20, and of the notifications and denunciations provided for in Articles 22 and 23 respectively.

Article 25

1. This Convention may be revised by the General Conference of the United Nations Educational, Scientific and Cultural Organization. Any such revision shall, however, bind only the States which shall become Parties to the revising convention.

2. If the General Conference should adopt a new convention revising this Convention in whole or in part, then, unless the new convention otherwise provides, this Convention shall cease to be open to ratification, acceptance or accession, as from the date on which the new revising convention enters into force.

Article 26

In conformity with Article 102 of the Charter of the United Nations, this Convention shall be registered with the Secretariat of the United Nations at the request of the Director-General of the United Nations Educational, Scientific and Cultural Organization.

Done in Paris this seventeenth day of November 1970, in two authentic copies bearing the signature of the President of the sixteenth session of the General Conference and of the Director-General of the United Nations Educational, Scientific and Cultural Organization, which shall be deposited in the archives of the United Nations Educational, Scientific and Cultural Organization, and certified true copies of which shall be delivered to all the States referred to in Articles 19 and 20 as well as to the United Nations.

The foregoing is the authentic text of the Convention duly adopted by the General Conference of the United Nations Educational, Scientific and Cultural Organization during its sixteenth session, which was held in Paris and declared closed the fourteenth day of November 1970.

IN FAITH WHEREOF we have appended our signatures this seventeenth day of November 1970.

A2.   SIGNATORIES TO THE 1970 UNESCO CONVENTION

1	Ecuador	24/03/1971	Acceptance
2	Bulgaria	15/09/1971	Ratification
3	Nigeria	24/01/1972	Ratification
4	Central African Republic	01/02/1972	Ratification
5	Cameroon	24/05/1972	Ratification
6	Kuwait	22/06/1972	Acceptance
7	Cambodia	26/09/1972	Ratification
8	Mexico	04/10/1972	Acceptance
9	Niger	16/10/1972	Ratification
10	Libyan Arab Jamahiriya	09/01/1973	Ratification
11	Argentina	11/01/1973	Ratification
12	Iraq	12/02/1973	Acceptance
13	Brazil	16/02/1973	Ratification
14	Dominican Republic	07/03/1973	Ratification
15	Egypt	05/04/1973	Acceptance
16	Panama	13/08/1973	Acceptance
17	Poland	31/01/1974	Ratification
18	Jordan	15/03/1974	Ratification
19	Algeria	24/06/1974	Ratification
20	Democratic Republic of the Congo	23/09/1974	Ratification
21	Iran (Islamic Republic of)	27/01/1975	Acceptance
22	Syrian Arab Republic	21/02/1975	Acceptance
23	Tunisia	10/03/1975	Acceptance
24	Nepal	23/06/1976	Ratification
25	Saudi Arabia	08/09/1976	Acceptance
26	Bolivia (Plurinational State of)	04/10/1976	Ratification
27	India	24/01/1977	Ratification
28	Nicaragua	19/04/1977	Ratification
29	Qatar	20/04/1977	Acceptance
30	Mauritania	27/04/1977	Ratification
31	United Republic of Tanzania	02/08/1977	Ratification
32	Uruguay	09/08/1977	Ratification
33	El Salvador	20/02/1978	Ratification
34	Mauritius	27/02/1978	Acceptance
35	Canada	28/03/1978	Acceptance
36	Oman	02/06/1978	Acceptance
37	Italy	02/10/1978	Ratification
38	Hungary	23/10/1978	Ratification
39	Guinea	18/03/1979	Ratification
40	Honduras	19/03/1979	Ratification
41	Cyprus	19/10/1979	Ratification
42	Peru	24/10/1979	Acceptance
43	Cuba	30/01/1980	Ratification
44	Sri Lanka	07/04/1981	Acceptance
45	Turkey	21/04/1981	Ratification
46	Pakistan	30/04/1981	Ratification
47	Greece	05/06/1981	Ratification

48	Republic of Korea	14/02/1983	Acceptance
49	Democratic People's Republic of Korea	13/05/1983	Ratification
50	United States of America	02/09/1983	Acceptance
51	Senegal	09/12/1984	Ratification
52	Guatemala	14/01/1985	Ratification
53	Zambia	21/06/1985	Ratification
54	Portugal	09/12/1985	Ratification
55	Spain	10/01/1986	Ratification
56	Mali	06/04/1987	Ratification
57	Burkina Faso	07/04/1987	Ratification
58	Bangladesh	09/12/1987	Ratification
59	Belarus	28/04/1988	Ratification
60	Russian Federation	28/04/1988	Ratification
61	Ukraine	28/04/1988	Ratification
62	Colombia	24/05/1988	Acceptance
63	Madagascar	21/06/1989	Ratification
64	Australia	30/10/1989	Acceptance
65	China	28/11/1989	Acceptance
66	Belize	26/01/1990	Ratification
67	Côte d'Ivoire	30/10/1990	Ratification
68	Mongolia	23/05/1991	Acceptance
69	Angola	07/11/1991	Ratification
70	Croatia	06/07/1992	Notification of succession
71	Lebanon	25/08/1992	Ratification
72	Tajikistan	28/08/1992	Ratification
73	Grenada	10/09/1992	Acceptance
74	Georgia	04/11/1992	Notification of succession
75	Slovenia	05/11/1992	Notification of succession
76	Czech Republic	26/03/1993	Notification of succession
77	Slovakia	31/03/1993	Notification of succession
78	Bosnia and Herzegovina	12/07/1993	Notification of succession
79	Armenia	05/09/1993	Notification of succession
80	Romania	06/12/1993	Acceptance
81	Kyrgyzstan	03/07/1995	Acceptance
82	Estonia	27/10/1995	Ratification
83	Costa Rica	06/03/1996	Ratification
84	Uzbekistan	15/03/1996	Ratification
85	France	07/01/1997	Ratification
86	The former Yugoslav Republic of Macedonia	30/04/1997	Notification of succession
87	Bahamas	09/10/1997	Ratification
88	Lithuania	27/07/1998	Ratification
89	Finland	14/06/1999	Ratification
90	Azerbaijan	25/08/1999	Ratification
91	Serbia	11/09/2001	Notification of succession
92	Rwanda	25/09/2001	Ratification
93	Barbados	10/04/2002	Acceptance
94	Albania	13/06/2002	Acceptance
95	United Kingdom of Great Britain and Northern Ireland	01/08/2002	Acceptance
96	Japan	09/09/2002	Acceptance

97	Bhutan	26/09/2002	Ratification
98	Sweden	13/01/2003	Ratification
99	Morocco	03/02/2003	Ratification
100	Denmark	26/03/2003	Ratification
101	Gabon	29/08/2003	Acceptance
102	Switzerland	03/10/2003	Acceptance
103	South Africa	18/12/2003	Acceptance
104	Seychelles	28/05/2004	Ratification
105	Paraguay	09/11/2004	Ratification
106	Iceland	09/11/2004	Ratification
107	Venezuela (Bolivarian Republic of)	21/03/2005	Acceptance
108	Afghanistan	08/09/2005	Acceptance
109	Viet Nam	20/09/2005	Ratification
110	Zimbabwe	30/05/2006	Acceptance
111	New Zealand	01/02/2007	Acceptance
112	Norway	16/02/2007	Ratification
113	Montenegro	26/04/2007	Notification of succession
114	Republic of Moldova	14/09/2007	Ratification
115	Germany	30/11/2007	Ratification
116	Chad	17/06/2008	Ratification
117	Belgium	31/03/2009	Ratification
118	Netherlands	17/07/2009	Acceptance

¹This Convention entered into force on 24 April 1972. It subsequently entered into force for each State three months after the date of deposit of that State's instrument, except in cases of notifications of succession, where the entry into force occurred on the date on which the State assumed responsibility for conducting its international relations.

A3.   THE HAGUE CONVENTION OF 1954

The High Contracting Parties,

Recognizing that cultural property has suffered grave damage during recent armed conflicts and that, by reason of the developments in the technique of warfare, it is in increasing danger of destruction;

Being convinced that damage to cultural property belonging to any people whatsoever means damage to the cultural heritage of all mankind, since each people makes its contribution to the culture of the world;

Considering that the preservation of the cultural heritage is of great importance for all peoples of the world and that it is important that this heritage should receive international protection;

Guided by the principles concerning the protection of cultural property during armed conflict, as established in the Conventions of The Hague of 1899 and of 1907 and in the Washington Pact of 15 April 1935;

Being of the opinion that such protection cannot be effective unless both national and international measures have been taken to organize it in time of peace;

Being determined to take all possible steps to protect cultural property;

Have agreed upon the following provisions:

CHAPTER I : GENERAL PROVISIONS REGARDING PROTECTION

Definition of Cultural Property

Article 1. For the purposes of the present Convention, the term "cultural property" shall cover, irrespective of origin or ownership:

(a) movable or immovable property of great importance to the cultural heritage of every people, such asmonuments of architecture, art or history, whether religious or secular; archaeological sites; groups of buildings which, as a whole, are of historical or artistic interest; works of art; manuscripts, books and other objects of artistic, historical or archaeological interest; as well as scientific collections and important collections of books or archives or of reproductions of the property defined above;

(b) buildings whose main and effective purpose is to preserve or exhibit the movable cultural property defined in sub-paragraph (a) such as museums, large libraries and depositories of archives, and refuges intended to shelter, in the event of armed conflict, the movable cultural property defined in subparagraph (a);

(c) entres containing a large amount of cultural property as defined in sub-paragraphs (a) and (b), to be known as "centres containing monuments".

Protection of Cultural Property

Art. 2. For the purposes of the present Convention, the protection of cultural property shall comprise the safeguarding of and respect for such property.

Safeguarding of Cultural Property

Art. 3, The High Contracting Parties undertake to prepare in time of peace for the safeguarding of cultural property situated within their own territory against the foreseeable effects of an armed conflict, by taking such measures as they consider appropriate.

Respect for Cultural Property

Art. 4. 1. The High Contracting Parties undertake to respect cultural property situated within their own territory as well as within the territory of other High Contracting Parties by refraining from any use of the property and its immediate surroundings or of the appliances in use for its protection for purposes which are likely to expose it to destruction or damage in the event of armed conflict; and by refraining from any act of hostility directed against such property.

2. The obligations mentioned in paragraph I of the present Article may be waived only in cases where military necessity imperatively requires such a waiver.

3. The High Contracting Parties further undertake to prohibit, prevent and, if necessary, put a stop to any form of theft, pillage or misappropriation of, and any acts of vandalism directed against, cultural property. They shall, refrain from requisitioning movable cultural property situated in the territory of another High Contracting Party.

4. They shall refrain from any act directed by way of reprisals against cultural property.

5. No High Contracting Party may evade the obligations incumbent upon it under the present Article, in respect of another High Contracting Party, by reason of the fact that the latter has not applied the measures of safeguard referred to in Article 3.

Occupation

Art. 5. 1. Any High Contracting Party in occupation of the whole or part of the territory of another High Contracting Party shall as far as possible support the competent national authorities of the occupied country in safeguarding and preserving its cultural property.

2. Should it prove necessary to take measures to preserve cultural property situated in occupied territory and damaged by military operations, and should the competent national authorities be unable to take such measures, the Occupying Power shall, as far as possible, and in close co-operation with such authorities, take the most necessary measures of preservation.

3. Any High Contracting Party whose government is considered their legitimate government by members of a resistance movement, shall, if possible, draw their attention to the obligation to comply with those provisions of the Conventions dealing with respect for cultural property.

Distinctive Marking of Cultural Property

Art. 6. In accordance with the provisions of Article 16, cultural property may bear a distinctive emblem so as to facilitate its recognition.

Military Measures

Art. 7. 1. The High Contracting Parties undertake to introduce in time of peace into their military regulations or instructions such provisions as may ensure observance of the present Convention, and to foster in the members of their armed forces a spirit of respect for the culture and cultural property of all peoples.

2. The High Contracting Parties undertake to plan or establish in peacetime, within their armed forces, services or specialist personnel whose purpose will be to secure respect for cultural property and to co-operate with the civilian authorities responsible for safeguarding it.

CHAPTER II : SPECIAL PROTECTION

Granting of Special Protection

Art. 8. 1. There may be placed under special protection a limited number of refuges intended to shelter movable cultural property in the event of armed conflict, of centres containing monuments and other immovable cultural property of very great importance, provided that they:

(a) are situated at an adequate distance from any large industrial centre or from any important military objective constituting a vulnerable point, such as, for example, an aerodrome, broadcasting station, establishment engaged upon work of national defence, a port or railway station of relative importance or a main line of communication;

(b) are not used for military purposes.

2. A refuge for movable cultural property may also be placed under special protection, whatever its location, if it is so constructed that, in all probability, it will not be damaged by bombs.

3. A centre containing monuments shall be deemed to be used for military purposes whenever it is used for the movement of military personnel or material, even in transit. The same shall apply whenever activities directly connected with military operations, the stationing of military

personnel, or the production of war material are carried on within the centre.

4. The guarding of cultural property mentioned in paragraph 1 above by armed custodians specially empowered to do so, or the presence, in the vicinity of such cultural property, of police forces normally responsible for the maintenance of public order, shall not be deemed to be used for military purposes.

5. If any cultural property mentioned in paragraph 1 of the present Article is situated near an important military objective as defined in the said paragraph, it may nevertheless be placed under special protection if the High Contracting Party asking for that protection undertakes, in the event of armed conflict, to make no use of the objective and particularly, in the case of a port, railway station or aerodrome, to divert all traffic therefrom. In that event, such diversion shall be prepared in time of peace.

6. Special protection is granted to cultural property by its entry in the "International Register of Cultural Property under Special Protection". This entry shall only be made, in accordance with the provisions of the present Convention and under the conditions provided for in the Regulations for the execution of the Convention.

Immunity of Cultural Property under Special Protection

Art. 9. The High Contracting Parties undertake to ensure the immunity of cultural property under special protection by refraining, from the time of entry in the International Register, from any act of hostility directed against such property and, except for the cases provided for in paragraph 5 of Article 8, from any use of such property or its surroundings for military purposes.

Identification and Control

Art. 10. During an armed conflict, cultural property under special protection shall be marked with the distinctive emblem described in Article 16, and shall be open to international control as provided for in the Regulations for the execution of the Convention.

Withdrawal of Immunity

Art. 11. 1. If one of the High Contracting Parties commits, in respect of any item of cultural property under special protection, a violation of the obligations under Article 9, the opposing Party shall, so long as this violation persists, be released from the obligation to ensure the immunity of the property concerned. Nevertheless, whenever possible, the latter Party shall first request the cessation of such violation within a reasonable time.

2. Apart from the case provided for in paragraph I of the present Article, immunity shall be withdrawn from cultural property under special protection only in exceptional cases of unavoidable military necessity, and only for such time as that necessity continues. Such necessity can be established only by the officer commanding a force the equivalent of a division in size or larger. Whenever circumstances permit, the opposing Party shall be notified, a reasonable time in advance, of the decision to withdraw immunity.

3. The Party withdrawing immunity shall, as soon as possible, so inform the Commissioner-General for cultural property provided for in the Regulations for the execution of the Convention, in writing, stating the reasons.

CHAPTER III : TRANSPORT OF CULTURAL PROPERTY

Transport under Special Protection

Art. 12. 1. Transport exclusively engaged in the transfer of cultural property, whether within a territory or to another territory, may, at the request of the High Contracting Party concerned, take place under special protection in accordance with the conditions specified in the Regulations for the execution of the Convention.

2. Transport under special protection shall take place under the international supervision provided for in the aforesaid Regulations and shall display the distinctive emblem described in Article 16.

3. The High Contracting Parties shall refrain from any act of hostility directed against transport under special protection.

Transport in Urgent Cases

Art. 13. 1. If a High Contracting Party considers that the safety of certain cultural property requires its transfer and that the matter is of such urgency that the procedure laid down in Article 12 cannot be followed, especially at the beginning of an armed conflict, the transport may display the distinctive emblem described in Article 16, provided that an application for immunity referred to in Article 12 has not already been made and refused. As far as possible, notification of transfer should be made to the opposing Parties. Nevertheless, transport conveying cultural property to the territory of another country may not display the distinctive emblem unless immunity has been expressly granted to it.

2. The High Contracting Parties shall take, so far as possible, the necessary precautions to avoid acts of hostility directed against the transport described in paragraph 1 of the present Article and displaying the distinctive emblem.

Immunity from Seizure, Capture and Prize

Art. 14. 1. Immunity from seizure, placing in prize, or capture shall be granted to:

(a) cultural property enjoying the protection provided for in Article 12 or that provided for in Article 13;

(b) the means of transport exclusively engaged in the transfer of such cultural property.

2. Nothing in the present Article shall limit the right of visit and search.

CHAPTER IV : PERSONNEL

Personnel

Art. 15. As far as is consistent with the interests of security, personnel engaged in the protection of cultural property shall, in the interests of such property, be respected and, if they fall into the hands of the opposing Party, shall be allowed to continue to carry out duties whenever the cultural property for which they are responsible has also fallen into the hands of the opposing Party.

CHAPTER V : THE DISTINCTIVE EMBLEM

Emblem of the Convention

Art. 16. 1. The distinctive emblem of the Convention shall take the form of a shield, pointed below, per saltire blue and white (a shield consisting of a royal-blue square, one of the angles of which forms the point of the shield, and of a royal-blue triangle above the square, the space on either side being taken up by a white triangle).

2. The emblem shall be used alone, or repeated three times in a triangular formation (one shield below), under the conditions provided for in Article 17.

Use of the Emblem

Art. 17. 1. The distinctive emblem repeated three times may be used only as a means of identification of:

(a) immovable cultural property under special protection;

(b) the transport of cultural property under the conditions provided for in Articles 12 and 13:

(c) improvised refuges, under the conditions provided for in the Regulations for the execution of the Convention.

2. The distinctive emblem may be used alone only as a means of identification of:

(a) cultural property not under special protection;

(b) the persons responsible for the duties of control in accordance with the Regulations for the execution of the Convention;

(c) the personnel engaged in the protection of cultural property;

(d) the identity cards mentioned in the Regulations for the execution of the Convention.

3. During an armed conflict, the use of the distinctive emblem in any other cases than those mentioned in the preceding paragraphs of the present Article, and the use for any purpose whatever of a sign resembling the distinctive emblem, shall be forbidden.

4. The distinctive emblem may not be placed on any immovable cultural property unless at the same time there is displayed an authorization duly dated and signed by the competent authority of the High Contracting Party.

CHAPTER VI : SCOPE OF APPLICATION OF THE CONVENTION

Application of the Convention

Art. 18. 1. Apart from the provisions which shall take effect in time of peace, the present Convention shall apply in the event of declared war or of any other armed conflict which may arise between two or more of the High Contracting Parties, even if the state of war is not recognized by one or more of them.

2. The Convention shall also apply to all cases of partial or total occupation of the territory of a High Contracting Party, even if the said occupation meets with no armed resistance.

3. If one of the Powers in conflict is not a Party to the present Convention, the Powers which are Parties thereto shall nevertheless remain bound by it in their mutual relations. They shall furthermore be bound by the Convention, in relation to the said Power, if the latter has declared that it accepts the provisions thereof and so long as it applies them.

Conflicts Not of an International Character

Art. 19. 1. In the event of an armed conflict not of an international character occurring within the territory of one of the High Contracting Parties, each party to the conflict shall be bound to apply, as a minimum, the provisions of the present Convention which relate to respect for cultural property.

2. The parties to the Conflict shall endeavour to bring into force, by means of special agreements, all or part of the other provisions of the present Convention.

3. The United Nations Educational, Scientific and Cultural Organization may offer its services to the parties to the conflict.

4. The application of the preceding provisions shall not affect the legal status of the parties to the conflict.

CHAPTER VII : EXECUTION OF THE CONVENTION

Regulations for the Execution of the Convention

Art. 20. The procedure by which the present Convention is to be applied is defined in the Regulations for its execution, which constitute an integral part thereof.

Protecting Powers

Art. 21. The present Convention and the Regulations for its execution shall be applied with the co-operation of the Protecting Powers responsible for safeguarding the interests of the Parties to the conflict.

Conciliation Procedure

Art. 22. 1. The Protecting Powers shall lend their good offices in all cases where they may deem it useful in the interests of cultural property, particularly if there is disagreement between the Parties to the conflict as to the application or interpretation of the provisions of the present Convention or the Regulations for its execution.

2. For this purpose, each of the Protecting Powers may, either at the invitation of one Party, of the Director-General of the United Nations Educational, Scientific and Cultural Organization, or on its own initiative, propose to the Parties to the conflict a meeting of their representatives, and in particular of the authorities responsible for the protection of cultural property, if considered appropriate on suitably chosen neutral territory. The Parties to the conflict shall be bound to give effect to the proposals for meeting made to them. The Protecting Powers shall

propose for approval by the Parties to the conflict a person belonging to a neutral Power or a person presented by the Director-General of the United Nations Educational, Scientific and Cultural Organization, which person shall be invited to take part in such a meeting in the capacity of Chairman.

Assistance of UNESCO

Art. 23. 1. The High Contracting Parties may call upon the United Nations Educational, Scientific and Cultural Organization for technical assistance in organizing the protection of their cultural property, or in connexion with any other problem arising out of the application of the present Convention or the Regulations for its execution. The Organization shall accord such assistance within the limits fixed by its programme and by its resources.

2. The Organization is authorized to make, on its own initiative, proposals on this matter to the High Contracting Parties.

Special Agreements

Art. 24. 1. The High Contracting Parties may conclude special agreements for all matters concerning which they deem it suitable to make separate provision.

2. No special agreement may be concluded which would diminish the protection afforded by the present Convention to cultural property and to the personnel engaged in its protection.

Dissemination of the Convention

Art. 25. The High Contracting Parties undertake, in time of peace as in time of armed conflict, to disseminate the text of the present Convention and the Regulations for its execution as widely as possible in their respective countries. They undertake, in particular, to include the study thereof in their programmes of military and, if possible, civilian training, so that its principles are made known to the whole population, especially the armed forces and personnel engaged in the protection of cultural property.

Translations, Reports

Art. 26. 1. The High Contracting Parties shall communicate to one another, through the Director-General of the United Nations Educational, Scientific and Cultural Organization, the official translations of the present Convention and of the Regulations for its execution.

2. Furthermore, at least once every four years, they shall forward to the Director-General a report giving whatever information they think suitable concerning any measures being taken, prepared or contemplated by their respective administrations in fulfilment of the present Convention and of the Regulations for its execution.

Meetings

Art. 27. 1. The Director-General of the United Nations Educational, Scientific and Cultural Organization may, with the approval of the Executive Board, convene meetings of representatives of the High Contracting Parties. He must convene such a meeting if at least one-fifth of the High Contracting Parties so request.

2. Without prejudice to any other functions which have been conferred on it by the present Convention or the Regulations for its execution, the purpose of the meeting will be to study problems concerning the application of the Convention and of the Regulations for its execution, and to formulate recommendations in respect thereof.

3. The meeting may further undertake a revision of the Convention or the Regulations for its execution if the majority of the High Contracting Parties are represented, and in accordance with the provisions of Article 39.

Sanctions

Art. 28. The High Contracting Parties undertake to take, within the framework of their ordinary criminal jurisdiction, all necessary steps to prosecute and impose penal or disciplinary sanctions upon those persons, of whatever nationality, who commit or order to be committed a breach of the present Convention.

FINAL PROVISIONS

Languages

Art. 29. 1. The present Convention is drawn up in English, French, Russian and Spanish, the four texts being equally authoritative.

2. The United Nations Educational, Scientific and Cultural Organization shall arrange for translations of the Convention into the other official languages of its General Conference.

Signature

Art. 30. The present Convention shall bear the date of 14 May 1954 and, until the date of 31 December 1954, shall remain open for signature by all States invited to the Conference which met at The Hague from 21 April 1954 to 14 May 1954.

Ratification

Art. 31. 1. The present Convention shall be subject to ratification by Signatory States in accordance with their respective constitutional procedures.

2. The instruments of ratification shall be deposited with the Director-General of the United Nations Educational, Scientific and Cultural Organization.

Accession

Art. 32. From the date of its entry into force, the present Convention shall be open for accession by all States mentioned in Article 30 which have not signed it, as well as any other State invited to accede by the Executive Board of the United Nations Educational, Scientific and Cultural Organization. Accession shall be effected by the deposit of an instrument of accession with the Director-General of the United Nations Educational, Scientific and Cultural Organization.

Entry into Force

Art. 33. 1. The present Convention shall enter into force three months after five instruments of ratification have been deposited.

2. Thereafter, it shall enter into force, for each High Contracting Party, three months after the deposit of its instrument of ratification or accession.

3. The situations referred to in Articles 18 and 19 shall give immediate effect to ratifications or accessions deposited by the Parties to the conflict either before or after the beginning of hostilities or occupation. In such cases the Director-General of the United Nations Educational, Scientific and Cultural Organization shall transmit the communications referred to in Article 38 by the speediest method.

Effective Application

Art. 34. 1. Each State Party to the Convention on the date of its entry into force shall take all necessary measures to ensure its effective application within a period of six months after such entry into force.

2. This period shall be six months from the date of deposit of the instruments of ratification or accession for any State which deposits its instrument of ratification or accession after the date of the entry into force of the Convention.

Territorial Extension of the Convention

Art. 35. Any High Contracting Party may, at the time of ratification or accession, or at any time thereafter, declare by notification addressed to the Director-General of the United Nations Educational, Scientific and Cultural Organization, that the present Convention shall extend to all or any of the territories for whose international relations it is responsible. The said notification shall take effect three months after the date of its receipt.

Relation to Previous Conventions

Art. 36. 1. In the relations between Powers which are bound by the Conventions of The Hague concerning the Laws and Customs of War on Land (IV) and concerning Naval Bombardment in Time of War (IX), whether those of 29 July 1899 or those of 18 October 1907, and which are Parties to the present Convention, this last Convention shall be supplementary to the aforementioned Convention (IX) and to the Regulations annexed to the aforementioned Convention (IV) and shall substitute for the emblem described in Article 5 of the aforementioned Convention (IX) the emblem described in Article 16 of the Present Convention, in cases in which the present Convention and the Regulations for its execution provide for the use of this distinctive emblem.

2. In the relations between Powers which are bound by the Washington Pact of 15 April 1935 for the Protection of Artistic and Scientific Institutions and of Historic Monuments (Roerich Pact) and which are Parties to the present Convention, the latter Convention shall be supplementary to the Roerich Pact and shall substitute for the distinguishing flag described in Article III of the Pact the emblem defined in Article 16 of the present Convention, in cases in which the present Convention and the Regulations for its execution provide for the use of this distinctive emblem.

Denunciation

Art. 37. 1. Each High Contracting Party may denounce the present Convention, on its own behalf, or on behalf of any territory for whose international relations it is responsible.

2. The denunciation shall be notified by an instrument in writing, deposited with the Director-General of the United Nations Educational, Scientific and Cultural Organization.

3. The denunciation shall take effect one year after the receipt of the instrument of denunciation. However, if, on the expiry of this period, the denouncing Party is involved in an armed conflict, the denunciation

shall not take effect until the end of hostilities, or until the operations of repatriating cultural property are completed, whichever is the later.

Notifications

Art. 38. The Director-General of the United Nations Educational, Scientific and Cultural Organization shall inform the States referred to in Articles 30 and 32, as well as the United Nations, of the deposit of all the instruments of ratification, accession or acceptance provided for in Articles 31, 32 and 39 and of the notifications and denunciations provided for respectively in Articles 35, 37 and 39.

Revision of the Convention and of the Regulations for its Execution

Art. 39. 1. Any High Contracting Party may propose amendments to the present Convention or the Regulations for its execution. The text of any proposed amendment shall be communicated to the Director-General of the United Nations Educational, Scientific and Cultural Organization who shall transmit it to each High Contracting Party with the request that such Party reply within four months stating whether it:

(a) desires that a Conference be convened to consider the proposed amendment;

(b) favours the acceptance of the proposed amendment without a Conference; or

(c) favours the rejection of the proposed amendment without a Conference.

2. The Director-General shall transmit the replies, received under paragraph I of the present Article, to all High Contracting Parties.

3. If all the High Contracting Parties which have, within the prescribed time-limit, stated their views to the Director-General of the United Nations Educational, Scientific and Cultural Organization, pursuant to paragraph 1 (b) of this Article, inform him that they favour acceptance of the amendment without a Conference, notification of their decision shall be made by the Director-General in accordance with Article 38.

The amendment shall become effective for all the High Contracting Parties on the expiry of ninety days from the date of such notification.

4. The Director-General shall convene a Conference of the High Contracting Parties to consider the proposed amendment if requested to do so by more than one-third of the High Contracting Parties.

5. Amendments to the Convention or to the Regulations for its execution, dealt with under the provisions of the preceding paragraph, shall enter into force only after they have been unanimously adopted by the High Contracting Parties represented at the Conference and accepted by each of the High Contracting Parties

6. Acceptance by the High Contracting Parties of amendments to the Convention or to the Regulations for its execution, which have been adopted by the Conference mentioned in paragraphs 4 and 5, shall be effected by the deposit of a formal instrument with the Director-General of the United Nations Educational, Scientific and Cultural Organization.

7. After the entry into force of amendments to the present Convention or to the Regulations for its execution, only the text of the Convention or of the Regulations for its execution thus amended shall remain open for ratification or accession.

Registration

Art. 40. In accordance with Article 102 of the Charter of the United Nations, the present Convention shall be registered with the Secretariat of the United Nations at the request of the Director-General of the United Nations Educational, Scientific and Cultural Organization.

In faith whereof the undersigned, duly authorized, have signed the present Convention.

Done at The Hague, this fourteenth day of May 1954, in a single copy which shall be deposited in the archives of the United Nations Educational, Scientific and Cultural Organization, and certified true copies of which shall be delivered to all the States referred to in Articles 30 and 32 as well as to the United Nations.

A4. FIRST PROTOCOL OF THE HAGUE CONVENTION

I

1. Each High Contracting Party undertakes to prevent the exportation, from a territory occupied by it during an armed conflict, of cultural property as defined in Article 1 of the Convention for the Protection of Cultural Property in the Event of Armed Conflict, signed at The Hague on 14 May, 1954.

2. Each High Contracting Party undertakes to take into its custody cultural property imported into its territory either directly or indirectly from any oc-cupied territory. This shall either be effected automatically upon the importation of the property or, failing this, at the request of the authorities of that territory.

3. Each High Contracting Party undertakes to return, at the close of hostilities, to the competent authorities of the territory previously occupied, cultural property which is in its territory, if such property has been exported in contravention of the principle laid down in the first paragraph. Such property shall never be retained as war reparations.

4. The High Contracting Party whose obligation it was to prevent the exportation of cultural property from the territory occupied by it, shall pay an indemnity to the holders in good faith of any cultural property which has to be returned in accordance with the preceding paragraph.

II

5. Cultural property coming from the territory of a High Contracting Party and deposited by it in the territory of another High Contracting Party for the purpose of protecting such property against the dangers of an armed conflict, shall be returned by the latter, at the end of hostilities, to the competent authorities of the territory from which it came.

III

6. The present Protocol shall bear the date of 14 May, 1954 and, until the date of 31 December, 1954, shall remain open for signature by all States invited to the Conference which met at The Hague from 21 April, 1954 to 14 May, 1954.

7. (a) The present Protocol shall be subject to ratification by signatory States in accordance with their respective constitutional procedures.

    (b) The instruments of ratification shall be deposited with the Director General of the United Nations Educational, Scientific and Cultural Organization.

8. From the date of its entry into force, the present Protocol shall be open for accession by all States mentioned in paragraph 6 which have not signed it as well as any other State invited to accede by the Executive Board of the United Nations Educational, Scientific and Cultural Organization. Accession shall be effected by the deposit of an instrument of accession with the Director-General of the United Nations Educational, Scientific and Cultural Organization.

9. The States referred to in paragraphs 6 and 8 may declare, at the time of signature, ratification or accession, that they will not be bound by the provisions of Section I or by those of Section II of the present Protocol.

10. (a) The present Protocol shall enter into force three months after five instruments of ratification have been deposited.

    (b) Thereafter, it shall enter into force, for each High Contracting Party, three months after the deposit of its instrument of ratification or accession.

    (c) The situations referred to in Articles 18 and 19 of the Convention for the Protection of Cultural Property in the Event of Armed Conflict, signed at The Hague on 14 May, 1954, shall give immediate effect to ratifications and accessions deposited by the Parties to the conflict either before or after the beginning of hostilities or occupation. In such cases, the Director-General of the United Nations Educational, Scientific and Cultural Organization shall transmit the communications' referred to in paragraph 14 by the speediest method.

11. (a) Each State Party to the Protocol on the date of its entry into force shall take all necessary measures to ensure its effective application within a period of six months after such entry into force.

(b) This period shall be six months from the date of deposit of the instruments of ratification or accession for any State which deposits its instrument of ratification or accession after the date of the entry into force of the Protocol.

12. Any High Contracting Party may, at the time of ratification or accession, or at any time thereafter, declare by notification addressed to the Director General of the United Nations Educational, Scientific and Cultural Organization, that the present Protocol shall extend to all or any of the territories for whose international relations it is responsible. The said notification shall take effect three months after the date of its receipt.

13. (a) Each High Contracting Party may denounce the present Protocol, on its own behalf, or on behalf of any territory for whose international relations it is responsible.

(b) The denunciation shall be notified by an instrument in writing, deposited with the Director-General of the United Nations Educational, Scientific and Cultural Organization.

(c) The denunciation shall take effect one year after receipt of the instrument of denunciation. However, if, on the expiry of this period, the denouncing Party is involved in an armed conflict, the denunciation shall not take effect until the end of hostilities, or until the operations of repatriating cultural property are completed, whichever is the later.

14. The Director-General of the United Nations Educational, Scientific and Cultural Organization shall inform the States referred to in paragraphs 6 and 8, as well as the United Nations, of the deposit of all the

instruments of ratification, accession or acceptance provided for in paragraphs 7, 8 and 15 and the notifications and denunciations provided for respectively in paragraphs 12 and 13.

15. (a) The present Protocol may be revised if revision is requested by more than one-third of the High Contracting Parties.

(b) The Director-General of the United Nations Educational, Scientific and Cultural Organization shall convene a Conference for this purpose.

(c) Amendments to the present Protocol shall enter into force only after they have been unanimously adopted by the High Contracting Parties represented at the Conference and accepted by each of the High Contracting Parties.

(d) Acceptance by the High Contracting Parties of amendments to the present Protocol, which have been adopted by the Conference mentioned in sub-paragraphs (b) and (c), shall be effected by the deposit of a formal instrument with the Director-General of the United Nations Educational, Scientific and Cultural Organization.

(e) After the entry into force of amendments to the present Protocol, only the text of the said Protocol thus amended shall remain open for ratification or accession.

In accordance with Article 102 of the Charter of the United Nations, the present Protocol shall be registered with the Secretariat of the United Nations at the request of the Director-General of the United Nations Educational, Scientific and Cultural Organization.

In faith whereof the undersigned, duly authorized, have signed the present Protocol.

Done at The Hague, this fourteenth day of May 1954, in English, French, Russian and Spanish, the four texts being equally authoritative, in a single copy which shall be deposited in the archives of the United Nations Educational, Scientific and Cultural Organization, and certified true copies of which shall be delivered to all the States referred to in paragraphs 6 and 8 as well as to the United Nations.

A5. SECOND PROTOCOL OF THE HAGUE CONVENTION

The Parties,

Conscious of the need to improve the protection of cultural property in the event of armed conflict and to establish an enhanced system of protection for specifically designated cultural property;

Reaffirming the importance of the provisions of the Convention for the Protection of Cultural Property in the Event of Armed Conflict, done at the Hague on 14 May 1954, and emphasizing the necessity to supplement these provisions through measures to reinforce their implementation;

Desiring to provide the High Contracting Parties to the Convention with a means of being more closely involved in the protection of cultural property in the event of armed conflict by establishing appropriate procedures therefor;

Considering that the rules governing the protection of cultural property in the event of armed conflict should reflect developments in international law;

Affirming that the rules of customary international law will continue to govern questions not regulated by the provisions of this Protocol;

Have agreed as follows:

Chapter 1 Introduction

Article 1 Definitions

For the purposes of this Protocol

a. "Party" means a State Party to this Protocol;

b. "cultural property" means cultural property as defined in Article 1 of the Convention;

c. "Convention" means the Convention for the Protection of Cultural Property in the Event of Armed Conflict, done at The Hague on 14 May 1954;

d. "High Contracting Party" means a State Party to the Convention;

e. "enhanced protection" means the system of enhanced protection established by Articles 10 and 11;

f. "military objective" means an object which by its nature, location, purpose, or use makes an effective contribution to military action and whose total or partial destruction, capture or neutralisation, in the circumstances ruling at the time, offers a definite military advantage;

g. "illicit" means under compulsion or otherwise in violation of the applicable rules of the domestic law of the occupied territory or of international law.

h. "List" means the International List of Cultural Property under Enhanced Protection established in accordance with Article 27, sub-paragraph 1(b);

i. "Director-General" means the Director-General of UNESCO;

j. "UNESCO" means the United Nations Educational, Scientific and Cultural Organization;

k. "First Protocol" means the Protocol for the Protection of Cultural Property in the Event of Armed Conflict done at The Hague on 14 May 1954;

Article 2 Relation to the Convention

This Protocol supplements the Convention in relations between the Parties.

Article 3 Scope of application

1. In addition to the provisions which shall apply in time of peace, this Protocol shall apply in situations referred to in Article 18 paragraphs 1 and 2 of the Convention and in Article 22 paragraph 1.

2. When one of the parties to an armed conflict is not bound by this Protocol, the Parties to this Protocol shall remain bound by it in their mutual relations. They shall furthermore be bound by this Protocol in relation to a State party to the conflict which is not bound by it, if the latter accepts the provisions of this Protocol and so long as it applies them.

Article 4 Relationship between Chapter 3 and other provisions of the Convention and this Protocol

The application of the provisions of Chapter 3 of this Protocol is without prejudice to:

a. the application of the provisions of Chapter I of the Convention and of Chapter 2 of this Protocol;

b. the application of the provisions of Chapter 2 of the Convention save that, as between Parties to this Protocol or as between a Party and a State which accepts and applies this Protocol in accordance with Article 3 paragraph 2, where cultural property has been granted both special protection and enhanced protection, only the provisions of enhanced protection shall apply.

Chapter 2 General provisions regarding protection

Article 5 Safeguarding of cultural property

Preparatory measures taken in time of peace for the safeguarding of cultural property against the foreseeable effects of an armed conflict pursuant to Article 3 of the Convention shall include, as appropriate, the preparation of inventories, the planning of emergency measures for protection against fire or structural collapse, the preparation for the removal of movable cultural property or the provision for adequate in situ protection of such property, and the designation of competent authorities responsible for the safeguarding of cultural property.

Article 6 Respect for cultural property

With the goal of ensuring respect for cultural property in accordance with Article 4 of the Convention:

a. a waiver on the basis of imperative military necessity pursuant to Article 4 paragraph 2 of the Convention may only be invoked to direct an act of hostility against cultural property when and for as long as:

    i. that cultural property has, by its function, been made into a military objective; and

    ii. there is no feasible alternative available to obtain a similar military advantage to that offered by directing an act of hostility against that objective;

b. a waiver on the basis of imperative military necessity pursuant to Article 4 paragraph 2 of the Convention may only be invoked to use cultural property for purposes which are likely to expose it to destruction or damage when and for as long as no choice is possible between such use of the cultural property and another feasible method for obtaining a similar military advantage;

c. the decision to invoke imperative military necessity shall only be taken by an officer commanding a force the equivalent of a battalion in size or larger, or a force smaller in size where circumstances do not permit otherwise;

d. in case of an attack based on a decision taken in accordance with sub-paragraph (a), an effective advance warning shall be given whenever circumstances permit.

Article 7 Precautions in attack

Without prejudice to other precautions required by international humanitarian law in the conduct of military operations, each Party to the conflict shall:

a. do everything feasible to verify that the objectives to be attacked are not cultural property protected under Article 4 of the Convention;
b. take all feasible precautions in the choice of means and methods of attack with a view to avoiding, and in any event to minimizing, incidental damage to cultural property protected under Article 4 of the Convention;
c. refrain from deciding to launch any attack which may be expected to cause incidental damage to cultural property protected under Article 4 of the Convention which would be excessive in relation to the concrete and direct military advantage anticipated; and
d. cancel or suspend an attack if it becomes apparent:
  i. that the objective is cultural property protected under Article 4 of the Convention
  ii. that the attack may be expected to cause incidental damage to cultural property protected under Article 4 of the Convention which would be excessive in relation to the concrete and direct military advantage anticipated.

Article 8 Precautions against the effects of hostilities

The Parties to the conflict shall, to the maximum extent feasible:

a. remove movable cultural property from the vicinity of military objectives or provide for adequate in situ protection;
b. avoid locating military objectives near cultural property.

Article 9 Protection of cultural property in occupied territory

1. Without prejudice to the provisions of Articles 4 and 5 of the Convention, a Party in occupation of the whole or part of the territory of another Party shall prohibit and prevent in relation to the occupied territory:
a. any illicit export, other removal or transfer of ownership of cultural property;
b. any archaeological excavation, save where this is strictly required to safeguard, record or preserve cultural property

c. any alteration to, or change of use of, cultural property which is intended to conceal or destroy cultural, historical or scientific evidence.

2. Any archaeological excavation of, alteration to, or change of use of, cultural property in occupied territory shall, unless circumstances do not permit, be carried out in close co-operation with the competent national authorities of the occupied territory.

Chapter 3 Enhanced Protection

Article 10 Enhanced protection

Cultural property may be placed under enhanced protection provided that it meets the following three conditions:

a. it is cultural heritage of the greatest importance for humanity;

b. it is protected by adequate domestic legal and administrative measures recognising its exceptional cultural and historic value and ensuring the highest level of protection;

c. it is not used for military purposes or to shield military sites and a declaration has been made by the Party which has control over the cultural property, confirming that it will not be so used.

Article 11 The granting of enhanced protection

1. Each Party should submit to the Committee a list of cultural property for which it intends to request the granting of enhanced protection.

2. The Party which has jurisdiction or control over the cultural property may request that it be included in the List to be established in accordance with Article 27 sub-paragraph 1(b). This request shall include all necessary information related to the criteria mentioned in Article 10. The Committee may invite a Party to request that cultural property be included in the List.

3. Other Parties, the International Committee of the Blue Shield and other non-governmental organisations with relevant expertise may

recommend specific cultural property to the Committee. In such cases, the Committee may decide to invite a Party to request inclusion of that cultural property in the List.

4. Neither the request for inclusion of cultural property situated in a territory, sovereignty or jurisdiction over which is claimed by more than one State, nor its inclusion, shall in any way prejudice the rights of the parties to the dispute.

5. Upon receipt of a request for inclusion in the List, the Committee shall inform all Parties of the request. Parties may submit representations regarding such a request to the Committee within sixty days. These representations shall be made only on the basis of the criteria mentioned in Article 10. They shall be specific and related to facts. The Committee shall consider the representations, providing the Party requesting inclusion with a reasonable opportunity to respond before taking the decision. When such representations are before the Committee, decisions for inclusion in the List shall be taken, notwithstanding Article 26, by a majority of four-fifths of its members present and voting.

6. In deciding upon a request, the Committee should ask the advice of governmental and non-governmental organisations, as well as of individual experts.

7. A decision to grant or deny enhanced protection may only be made on the basis of the criteria mentioned in Article 10.

8. In exceptional cases, when the Committee has concluded that the Party requesting inclusion of cultural property in the List cannot fulfil the criteria of Article 10 sub-paragraph (b), the Committee may decide to grant enhanced protection, provided that the requesting Party submits a request for international assistance under Article 32.

9. Upon the outbreak of hostilities, a Party to the conflict may request, on an emergency basis, enhanced protection of cultural property under its jurisdiction or control by communicating this request to the Committee. The Committee shall transmit this request immediately to all Parties to the conflict. In such cases the Committee will consider

representations from the Parties concerned on an expedited basis. The decision to grant provisional enhanced protection shall be taken as soon as possible and, notwithstanding Article 26, by a majority of four-fifths of its members present and voting. Provisional enhanced protection may be granted by the Committee pending the outcome of the regular procedure for the granting of enhanced protection, provided that the provisions of Article 10 sub-paragraphs (a) and (c) are met.

10. Enhanced protection shall be granted to cultural property by the Committee from the moment of its entry in the List.

11. The Director-General shall, without delay, send to the Secretary-General of the United Nations and to all Parties notification of any decision of the Committee to include cultural property on the List.

Article 12 Immunity of cultural property under enhanced protection

The Parties to a conflict shall ensure the immunity of cultural property under enhanced protection by refraining from making such property the object of attack from any use of the property or its immediate surroundings in support of military action.

Article 13 Loss of enhanced protection

1. Cultural property under enhanced protection shall only lose such protection:

a. if such protection is suspended or cancelled in accordance with Article 14; or
b. if, and for as long as, the property has, by its use, become a military objective.

2. In the circumstances of sub-paragraph 1(b), such property may only be the object of attack if:

a. the attack is the only feasible means of terminating the use of the property referred to in sub-paragraph 1(b);
b. all feasible precautions are taken in the choice of means and methods of attack, with a view to terminating such use and avoiding, or in any event minimising, damage to the cultural property;

c. unless circumstances do not permit, due to requirements of immediate self-defence:

> i. the attack is ordered at the highest operational level of command;
> ii effective advance warning is issued to the opposing forces requiring the termination of the use referred to in sub-paragraph 1(b); and
> iii. reasonable time is given to the opposing forces to redress the situation.

Article 14 Suspension and cancellation of enhanced protection

1. Where cultural property no longer meets any one of the criteria in Article 10 of this Protocol, the Committee may suspend its enhanced protection status or cancel that status by removing that cultural property from the List.

2. In the case of a serious violation of Article 12 in relation to cultural property under enhanced protection arising from its use in support of military action, the Committee may suspend its enhanced protection status. Where such violations are continuous, the Committee may exceptionally cancel the enhanced protection status by removing the cultural property from the List.

3. The Director-General shall, without delay, send to the Secretary-General of the United Nations and to all Parties to this Protocol notification of any decision of the Committee to suspend or cancel the enhanced protection of cultural property.

4. Before taking such a decision, the Committee shall afford an opportunity to the Parties to make their views known.

Chapter 4 Criminal responsibility and jurisdiction

Article 15 Serious violations of this Protocol

1. Any person commits an offence within the meaning of this Protocol if that person intentionally and in violation of the Convention or this Protocol commits any of the following acts:

a. making cultural property under enhanced protection the object of attack;

b. using cultural property under enhanced protection or its immediate surroundings in support of military action;

c. extensive destruction or appropriation of cultural property protected under the Convention and this Protocol;

d. making cultural property protected under the Convention and this Protocol the object of attack;

e. theft, pillage or misappropriation of, or acts of vandalism directed against cultural property protected under the Convention.

2. Each Party shall adopt such measures as may be necessary to establish as criminal offences under its domestic law the offences set forth in this Article and to make such offences punishable by appropriate penalties. When doing so, Parties shall comply with general principles of law and international law, including the rules extending individual criminal responsibility to persons other than those who directly commit the act.

Article 16 Jurisdiction

1. Without prejudice to paragraph 2, each Party shall take the necessary legislative measures to establish its jurisdiction over offences set forth in Article 15 in the following cases:

a. when such an offence is committed in the territory of that State;

b. when the alleged offender is a national of that State;

c. in the case of offences set forth in Article 15 sub-paragraphs (a) to (c), when the alleged offender is present in its territory.

2. With respect to the exercise of jurisdiction and without prejudice to Article 28 of the Convention:

a. this Protocol does not preclude the incurring of individual criminal responsibility or the exercise of jurisdiction under national and international law that may be applicable, or affect the exercise of jurisdiction under customary international law;

b. Except in so far as a State which is not Party to this Protocol may accept and apply its provisions in accordance with Article 3 paragraph 2, members of the armed forces and nationals of a State which is not Party to this Protocol, except for those nationals serving in the armed forces of a State which is a Party to this Protocol, do not incur individual criminal responsibility by virtue of this Protocol, nor does this Protocol impose an obligation to establish jurisdiction over such persons or to extradite them.

Article 17 Prosecution

1. The Party in whose territory the alleged offender of an offence set forth in Article 15 sub-paragraphs 1 (a) to (c) is found to be present shall, if it does not extradite that person, submit, without exception whatsoever and without undue delay, the case to its competent authorities, for the purpose of prosecution, through proceedings in accordance with its domestic law or with, if applicable, the relevant rules of international law.

2. Without prejudice to, if applicable, the relevant rules of international law, any person regarding whom proceedings are being carried out in connection with the Convention or this Protocol shall be guaranteed fair treatment and a fair trial in accordance with domestic law and international law at all stages of the proceedings, and in no cases shall be provided guarantees less favorable to such person than those provided by international law.

Article 18 Extradition

1. The offences set forth in Article 15 sub-paragraphs 1 (a) to (c) shall be deemed to be included as extraditable offences in any extradition treaty existing between any of the Parties before the entry into force of this Protocol. Parties undertake to include such offences in every extradition treaty to be subsequently concluded between them.

2. When a Party which makes extradition conditional on the existence of a treaty receives a request for extradition from another Party with which it has no extradition treaty, the requested Party may, at its option,

consider the present Protocol as the legal basis for extradition in respect of offences as set forth in Article 15 sub-paragraphs 1 (a) to (c).

3. Parties which do not make extradition conditional on the existence of a treaty shall recognise the offences set forth in Article 15 sub-paragraphs 1 (a) to (c) as extraditable offences between them, subject to the conditions provided by the law of the requested Party.

4. If necessary, offences set forth in Article 15 sub-paragraphs 1 (a) to (c) shall be treated, for the purposes of extradition between Parties, as if they had been committed not only in the place in which they occurred but also in the territory of the Parties that have established jurisdiction in accordance with Article 16 paragraph 1.

Article 19 Mutual legal assistance

1. Parties shall afford one another the greatest measure of assistance in connection with investigations or criminal or extradition proceedings brought in respect of the offences set forth in Article 15, including assistance in obtaining evidence at their disposal necessary for the proceedings.

2. Parties shall carry out their obligations under paragraph 1 in conformity with any treaties or other arrangements on mutual legal assistance that may exist between them. In the absence of such treaties or arrangements, Parties shall afford one another assistance in accordance with their domestic law.

Article 20 Grounds for refusal

1. For the purpose of extradition, offences set forth in Article 15 sub-paragraphs 1 (a) to (c), and for the purpose of mutual legal assistance, offences set forth in Article 15 shall not be regarded as political offences nor as offences connected with political offences nor as offences inspired by political motives. Accordingly, a request for extradition or for mutual legal assistance based on such offences may not be refused on the sole ground that it concerns a political offence or an offence connected with a political offence or an offence inspired by political motives.

2. Nothing in this Protocol shall be interpreted as imposing an obligation to extradite or to afford mutual legal assistance if the requested Party has substantial grounds for believing that the request for extradition for offences set forth in Article 15 sub-paragraphs 1 (a) to (c) or for mutual legal assistance with respect to offences set forth in Article 15 has been made for the purpose of prosecuting or punishing a person on account of that person's race, religion, nationality, ethnic origin or political opinion or that compliance with the request would cause prejudice to that person's position for any of these reasons.

Article 21 Measures regarding other violations

Without prejudice to Article 28 of the Convention, each Party shall adopt such legislative, administrative or disciplinary measures as may be necessary to suppress the following acts when committed intentionally:
a. any use of cultural property in violation of the Convention or this Protocol;

b. any illicit export, other removal or transfer of ownership of cultural property from occupied territory in violation of the Convention or this Protocol.

Chapter 5 The protection of cultural property in armed conflicts not of an international character

Article 22 Armed conflicts not of an international character

1. This Protocol shall apply in the event of an armed conflict not of an international character, occurring within the territory of one of the Parties.

2. This Protocol shall not apply to situations of internal disturbances and tensions, such as riots, isolated and sporadic acts of violence and other acts of a similar nature.

3. Nothing in this Protocol shall be invoked for the purpose of affecting the sovereignty of a State or the responsibility of the government, by all legitimate means, to maintain or re-establish law and order in the State or to defend the national unity and territorial integrity of the State.

4. Nothing in this Protocol shall prejudice the primary jurisdiction of a Party in whose territory an armed conflict not of an international character occurs over the violations set forth in Article 15.

5. Nothing in this Protocol shall be invoked as a justification for intervening, directly or indirectly, for any reason whatever, in the armed conflict or in the internal or external affairs of the Party in the territory of which that conflict occurs.

6. The application of this Protocol to the situation referred to in paragraph 1 shall not affect the legal status of the parties to the conflict.

7. UNESCO may offer its services to the parties to the conflict.

Chapter 6 Institutional Issues

Article 23 Meeting of the Parties

1. The Meeting of the Parties shall be convened at the same time as the General Conference of UNESCO, and in co-ordination with the Meeting of the High Contracting Parties, if such a meeting has been called by the Director-General.

2. The Meeting of the Parties shall adopt its Rules of Procedure.

3. The Meeting of the Parties shall have the following functions:

(a) to elect the Members of the Committee, in accordance with Article 24 paragraph 1;

(b) to endorse the Guidelines developed by the Committee in accordance with Article 27 sub-paragraph 1(a);

(c) to provide guidelines for, and to supervise the use of the Fund by the Committee;

(d) to consider the report submitted by the Committee in accordance with Article 27 sub-paragraph 1(d);

(e) to discuss any problem related to the application of this Protocol, and to make recommendations, as appropriate.

4. At the request of at least one-fifth of the Parties, the Director-General shall convene an Extraordinary Meeting of the Parties.

Article 24 Committee for the protection of cultural property in the event of armed conflict

1. The Committee for the Protection of Cultural Property in the Event of Armed Conflict is hereby established. It shall be composed of twelve Parties which shall be elected by the Meeting of the Parties.

2. The Committee shall meet once a year in ordinary session and in extra-ordinary sessions whenever it deems necessary.

3. In determining membership of the Committee, Parties shall seek to ensure an equitable representation of the different regions and cultures of the world.

4. Parties members of the Committee shall choose as their representatives persons qualified in the fields of cultural heritage, defence or international law, and they shall endeavour, in consultation with one another, to ensure that the Committee as a whole contains adequate expertise in all these fields.

Article 25 Term of office

1. A Party shall be elected to the Committee for four years and shall be eligible for immediate re-election only once.

2. Notwithstanding the provisions of paragraph 1, the term of office of half of the members chosen at the time of the first election shall cease at the end of the first ordinary session of the Meeting of the Parties following that at which they were elected. These members shall be chosen by lot by the President of this Meeting after the first election.

Article 26 Rules of procedure

1. The Committee shall adopt its Rules of Procedure.

2. A majority of the members shall constitute a quorum. Decisions of the Committee shall be taken by a majority of two-thirds of its members voting.

3. Members shall not participate in the voting on any decisions relating to cultural property affected by an armed conflict to which they are parties.

Article 27 Functions

1. The Committee shall have the following functions:

a. to develop Guidelines for the implementation of this Protocol;

b. to grant, suspend or cancel enhanced protection for cultural property and to establish, maintain and promote the List of cultural property under enhanced protection;

c. to monitor and supervise the implementation of this Protocol and promote the identification of cultural property under enhanced protection;

d. to consider and comment on reports of the Parties, to seek clarifications as required, and prepare its own report on the implementation of this Protocol for the Meeting of the Parties;

e. to receive and consider requests for international assistance under Article 32;

f. to determine the use of the Fund

g. to perform any other function which may be assigned to it by the Meeting of the Parties.

2. The functions of the Committee shall be performed in co-operation with the Director-General.

3. The Committee shall co-operate with international and national governmental and non-governmental organizations having objectives similar to those of the Convention, its First Protocol and this Protocol. To assist in the implementation of its functions, the Committee may invite to its meetings, in an advisory capacity, eminent professional organizations such as those which have formal relations with UNESCO, including the International Committee of the Blue Shield (ICBS) and its constituent bodies. Representatives of the International Centre for the

Study of the Preservation and Restoration of Cultural Property (Rome Centre) (ICCROM) and of the International Committee of the Red Cross (ICRC) may also be invited to attend in an advisory capacity.

Article 28 Secretariat

The Committee shall be assisted by the Secretariat of UNESCO which shall prepare the Committee's documentation and the agenda for its meetings and shall have the responsibility for the implementation of its decisions.

Article 29 The Fund for the protection of cultural property in the event of armed conflict

1. A Fund is hereby established for the following purposes:

a. to provide financial or other assistance in support of preparatory or other measures to be taken in peacetime in accordance with, inter alia, Article 5, Article 10 sub-paragraph (b) and Article 30; and

b. to provide financial or other assistance in relation to emergency, provisional or other measures to be taken in order to protect cultural property during periods of armed conflict or of immediate recovery after the end of hostilities in accordance with, inter alia, Article 8 sub-paragraph (a).

2. The Fund shall constitute a trust fund, in conformity with the provisions of the financial regulations of UNESCO.

3. Disbursements from the Fund shall be used only for such purpose as the Committee shall decide in accordance with the guidelines as defined in Article 23 sub-paragraph 3(c). The Committee may accept contributions to be used only for a certain programme or project, provided that the Committe shall have decided on the implementation of such programme or project.

4. The resources of the Fund shall consist of:

a. voluntary contributions made by the Parties;

b. contributions, gifts or bequests made by:

(i) other States;

(ii) UNESCO or other organizations of the United Nations system;

(iii) other intergovernmental or non-governmental organizations; and

(iv) public or private bodies or individuals;

(c) any interest accruing on the Fund;

(d) funds raised by collections and receipts from events organized for the benefit of the Fund; and

(e) all other resources authorized by the guidelines applicable to the Fund.

Chapter 7 Dissemination of Information and International Assistance

Article 30 Dissemination

1. The Parties shall endeavour by appropriate means, and in particular by educational and information programmes, to strengthen appreciation and respect for cultural property by their entire population.

2. The Parties shall disseminate this Protocol as widely as possible, both in time of peace and in time of armed conflict.

3. Any military or civilian authorities who, in time of armed conflict, assume responsibilities with respect to the application of this Protocol, shall be fully acquainted with the text thereof. To this end the Parties shall, as appropriate:

(a) incorporate guidelines and instructions on the protection of cultural property in their military regulations;

(b) develop and implement, in cooperation with UNESCO and relevant governmental and non-governmental organizations, peacetime training and educational programmes;

(c) communicate to one another, through the Director-General, information on the laws, administrative provisions and measures taken under sub-paragraphs (a) and (b);

(d) communicate to one another, as soon as possible, through the Director-General, the laws and administrative provisions which they may adopt to ensure the application of this Protocol.

Article 31 International cooperation

In situations of serious violations of this Protocol, the Parties undertake to act, jointly through the Committee, or individually, in cooperation with UNESCO and the United Nations and in conformity with the Charter of the United Nations.

Article 32 International assistance

1. A Party may request from the Committee international assistance for cultural property under enhanced protection as well as assistance with respect to the preparation, development or implementation of the laws, administrative provisions and measures referred to in Article 10.

2. A party to the conflict, which is not a Party to this Protocol but which accepts and applies provisions in accordance with Article 3, paragraph 2, may request appropriate international assistance from the Committee.

3. The Committee shall adopt rules for the submission of requests for international assistance and shall define the forms the international assistance may take.

4. Parties are encouraged to give technical assistance of all kinds, through the Committee, to those Parties or parties to the conflict who request it.

Article 33 Assistance of UNESCO

1. A Party may call upon UNESCO for technical assistance in organizing the protection of its cultural property, such as preparatory action to safeguard cultural property, preventive and organizational measures for

emergency situations and compilation of national inventories of cultural property, or in connection with any other problem arising out of the application of this Protocol. UNESCO shall accord such assistance within the limits fixed by its programme and by its resources.

2. Parties are encouraged to provide technical assistance at bilateral or multilateral level.

3. UNESCO is authorized to make, on its own initiative, proposals on these matters to the Parties.

Chapter 8 Execution of this Protocol

Article 34 Protecting Powers

This Protocol shall be applied with the co-operation of the Protecting Powers responsible for safeguarding the interests of the Parties to the conflict.

Article 35 Conciliation procedure

1. The Protecting Powers shall lend their good offices in all cases where they may deem it useful in the interests of cultural property, particularly if there is disagreement between the Parties to the conflict as to the application or interpretation of the provisions of this Protocol.

2. For this purpose, each of the Protecting Powers may, either at the invitation of one Party, of the Director-General, or on its own initiative, propose to the parties to the conflict a meeting of their representatives, and in particular of the authorities responsible for the protection of cultural property, if considered appropriate, on the territory of a State not party to the conflict. The parties to the conflict shall be bound to give effect to the proposals for meeting made to them. The Protecting Powers shall propose for approval by the Parties to the conflict a person belonging to a State not party to the conflict or a person presented by the Director-General, which person shall be invited to take part in such a meeting in the capacity of Chairman.

Article 36 Conciliation in absence of Protecting Powers

1. In a conflict where no Protecting Powers are appointed the Director-General may lend good offices or act by any other form of conciliation or mediation, with a view to settling the disagreement.

2. At the invitation of one Party or of the Director-General, the Chairman of the Committee may propose to the Parties to the conflict a meeting of their representatives, and in particular of the authorities responsible for the protection of cultural property, if considered appropriate, on the territory of a State not party to the conflict.

Article 37 Translations and reports

1. The Parties shall translate this Protocol into their official languages and shall communicate these official translations to the Director-General.

2. The Parties shall submit to the Committee, every four years, a report on the implementation of this Protocol.

Article 38 State responsibility

No provision in this Protocol relating to individual criminal responsibility shall affect the responsibility of States under international law, including the duty to provide reparation.

Chapter 9 Final Clauses

Article 39 Languages

This Protocol is drawn up in Arabic, Chinese, English, French, Russian and Spanish, the six texts being equally authentic.

Article 40 Signature

This Protocol shall bear the date of 26 March 1999. It shall be opened for signature by all High Contracting Parties at The Hague from 17 May 1999 until 31 December 1999.

Article 41 Ratification, acceptance or approval

1. This Protocol shall be subject to ratification, acceptance or approval by High Contracting Parties which have signed this Protocol, in accordance with their respective constitutional procedures.

2. The instruments of ratification, acceptance or approval shall be deposited with the Director-General.

Article 42 Accession

1. This Protocol shall be open for accession by other High Contracting Parties from 1 January 2000.

2. Accession shall be effected by the deposit of an instrument of accession with the Director-General.

Article 43 Entry into force

1. This Protocol shall enter into force three months after twenty instruments of ratification, acceptance, approval or accession have been deposited.

2. Thereafter, it shall enter into force, for each Party, three months after the deposit of its instrument of ratification, acceptance, approval or accession.

Article 44 Entry into force in situations of armed conflict

The situations referred to in Articles 18 and 19 of the Convention shall give immediate effect to ratifications, acceptances or approvals of or accessions to this Protocol deposited by the parties to the conflict either before or after the beginning of hostilities or occupation. In such cases the Director-General shall transmit the communications referred to in Article 46 by the speediest method.

Article 45 Denunciation

1. Each Party may denounce this Protocol.

2. The denunciation shall be notified by an instrument in writing, deposited with the Director-General.

3. The denunciation shall take effect one year after the receipt of the instrument of denunciation. However, if, on the expiry of this period, the denouncing Party is involved in an armed conflict, the denunciation shall not take effect until the end of hostilities, or until the operations of repatriating cultural property are completed, whichever is the later.

Article 46 Notifications

The Director-General shall inform all High Contracting Parties as well as the United Nations, of the deposit of all the instruments of ratification, acceptance, approval or accession provided for in Articles 41 and 42 and of denunciations provided for in Article 45.

Article 47 Registration with the United Nations

In conformity with Article 102 of the Charter of the United Nations, this Protocol shall be registered with the Secretariat of the United Nations at the request of the Director-General.

IN FAITH WHEREOF the undersigned, duly authorized, have signed the present Protocol.

DONE at The Hague, this twenty-sixth day of March 1999, in a single copy which shall be deposited in the archives of the UNESCO, and certified true copies of which shall be delivered to all the High Contracting Parties.

A6. AGREEMENT BETWEEN THE GOVERNMENT OF CANADA AND THE UNITED STATES REGARDING THE IMPOSITION OF IMPORT RESTRICTIONS ON CERTAIN CATEGORIES OF ARCHAEOLOGICAL AND ETHNOLOGICAL MATERIAL, E100789—CTS 1997 NO. 8

The Government of Canada and the Government of the United States of America;

Recognizing the rich cultural heritage which both countries share and from which both countries derive national pride;

Acting pursuant to the 1970 UNESCO Convention on the Means of Prohibiting and Preventing the Illicit Import, Export and Transfer of Ownership of Cultural Property, to which both countries are States Party; and

Desiring to reduce the incentive for pillage of certain categories of irreplaceable archaeological and ethnological material;

Have agreed as follows:

ARTICLE I

A.   The Government of the United States of America, in accordance with its legislation entitled the *Convention on Cultural Property Implementation Act*, shall restrict the importation into the United States of, and take appropriate steps to recover within the United States, the archaeological and ethnological material listed in the Appendix to this Agreement (hereafter "Designated List") unless the Government of Canada issues a cultural property export permit or other documentation which certifies that such exportation was not in violation of its laws, as set forth in the *Cultural Property Export and Import Act*, and regulations. The Designated List forms an integral part of this Agreement.

B.   The Government of the United States of America shall offer for return to the Government of Canada any material on the Designated List forfeited to the Government of the United States of America.

C.   Such import restrictions shall take effect on the date the Designated List is published in the U.S. Federal Register, the official United States

Government publication providing fair public notice. The Government of the United States will inform the Government of Canada of the date on which such publication has taken place.

D.   Such import restrictions shall apply to the following in Canada: Inuit (Eskimo) archaeological and ethnological material; Subarctic Indian ethnological material; Northwest Coast Indian archaeological and ethnological material; Plateau Indian archaeological material; Plains Indian ethnological material; and Woodlands Indian archaeological and ethnological material. Such import restrictions shall also apply to underwater archaeological material found at historic shipwrecks and other underwater historic sites in the inland waters of Canada as well as the Canadian territorial waters of the Atlantic, Pacific and Arctic Oceans, and the Great Lakes.

E.   Such import restrictions shall apply only to archaeological and ethnological material subject to control by Canada's *Cultural Property Export and Import Act* and subject to the definitions for such material as set forth in the United States' *Convention on Cultural Property Implementation Act*.

F.   Such import restrictions are not intended by either Government to impede the traditional cross-border movement of cultural objects for the purposes of ongoing communal activities of the Aboriginal or Native groups of both countries.

ARTICLE II

A.   The Government of Canada shall take reasonable steps to prohibit the import into Canada of material originating in the United States consisting of archaeological resources (as defined by the *Archaeological Resources Protection Act* of 1979, as amended (16 U.S.C. 470aa-mm)), cultural items (as defined by the *Native American Graves Protection and Repatriation Act* of 1990 (25 U.S.C. 3001- 3013)), and archaeological items recovered from shipwrecks (as defined by the *Abandoned Shipwreck Act* of 1987 (43 U.S.C. 2101 et seq.)), that have been illegally removed from the United States; and, upon request, shall facilitate recovery by the Government of the United States in the event such archaeological resources and cultural items are found to have illicitly entered Canada.

B.   Nothing in this Agreement shall displace any remedies otherwise available under Canadian law to a claimant to obtain the return of its cultural property.

ARTICLE III

A.   The Government of Canada shall use its best efforts to permit the temporary exchange of the protected archaeological and ethnological materials under circumstances in which such exchange does not jeopardize its cultural patrimony.

B.   Both Governments, through appropriate channels, shall seek to encourage academic institutions, non-governmental institutions and other private organizations to cooperate in the exchange of knowledge and information about the archaeological and ethnological material of both countries and to collaborate, as appropriate, in the preservation and protection of such cultural patrimony.

C.   The Government of the United States and the Government of Canada shall use their best efforts to further the protection and preservation of archaeological and ethnological materials in both countries through other instruments between governmental agencies having appropriate regulatory and enforcement responsibilities.

D.   Representatives of both Governments shall participate in joint efforts to encourage the exchange of knowledge and information about archaeological and ethnological materials through professional exchanges, technical assistance, training and public outreach.

ARTICLE IV

The implementation of this Agreement by both Governments shall be subject to the laws and regulations of each Government, as applicable, including those concerning the availability of funds.

ARTICLE V

A.   This Agreement shall enter into force upon signature. It shall remain in force for five years, unless extended by mutual agreement of both Governments.

B.   This Agreement may be amended by agreement of both Governments through an exchange of diplomatic notes.

C.   Either Government may give written notice to the other of its intention to terminate this Agreement, in which case the Agreement shall terminate six (6) months following the date of such notice.

D.   The implementation of this Agreement and its effectiveness shall be subject to appropriate consultations and continuous review by both Governments.

E.   Each Government shall designate an Executive Agent or Competent Authority for this Agreement, provided that each Government may also communicate through diplomatic channels.

IN WITNESS WHEREOF, the undersigned, being duly authorized by their respective Governments, have signed the present Agreement.

DONE at Washington, this tenth day of April, 1997, in the French and English languages, both texts being equally authentic.

Raymond Chrétien

FOR THE GOVERNMENT OF CANADA

Joseph Duffy

Anthony Wayne

FOR THE GOVERNMENT OF THE UNITED STATES OF AMERICA

APPENDIX

Designated List of Archaeological Artifacts and Ethnographic Material Culture of Canadian Origin Restricted from Importation into the United States of America

For the purposes of this list and in accordance with the United States' *Cultural Property Implementation Act* and *Canada's Cultural Property Export and Import Act*:

Definitions

"archaeological artifact" means an object made or worked by a person or persons and associated with historic or prehistoric cultures that is of cultural significance and at least 250 years old and normally discovered as a result of scientific excavation, clandestine or accidental digging, or exploration on land or under water.

"ethnographic material culture" means an object that was made, reworked or adapted for use by a person who is an Aboriginal person of Canada (e.g. the product of a tribal or non-industrial society), is of ethnological interest and is important to the cultural heritage of a people because of its distinctive characteristics, comparative rarity, or its contribution to the knowledge of the origins, development or history of that people. The terms "ethnographic material culture" and "ethnological material" are used interchangeably.

"Aboriginal Person of Canada" means a person of Indian or Inuit ancestry, including a Métis person, or a person recognized as being a member of an Indian, Inuit or Métis group by the other members of that group, who at any time ordinarily resided in the territory that is now Canada.

General Restrictions

Pursuant to Canada's *Cultural Property Export and Import Act*, certain archaeological artifacts and ethnographic material are subject to export control. Export permits are available at designated offices of Canada Customs. Information about export controls is available from Movable Cultural Property, Department of Canadian Heritage, by telephone at 819-997-7761.

In the absence of export permits where required, United States import restrictions will apply to the following Aboriginal cultural groups in Canada: Inuit (Eskimo) archaeological and ethnological material; Subarctic Indian ethnological material; Northwest Coast Indian archaeological and ethnological material; Plateau Indian archaeological material; Plains Indian ethnological material; and Woodlands Indian archaeological and ethnological material. Such import restrictions will also apply to underwater archaeological material found at historic shipwrecks and other underwater historic sites in the inland waters of Canada as well as the Canadian territorial waters of the Atlantic, Pacific and Arctic Oceans, and the Great Lakes.

Below are representative lists, subject to amendment, of objects covered by these import restrictions.

Ethnographic Material Culture

Below is a representative list, subject to amendment, of objects of ethnographic material culture, organized by primary type of material used to make the object.

In accordance with Canadian law, restrictions only apply to ethnological material listed below which was made, reworked or adapted for use by an Aboriginal person of Canada who is no longer living, which is greater than 50 years old, and which has a fair market value in Canada of more than $3,000 (Canadian).

Ethnographic material from the following Aboriginal cultural groups is included in this list and is subject to United States import restrictions: Inuit (Eskimo); Subarctic Indian; Northwest Coast Indian, Plains Indian; and Woodlands Indian.

Ethnographic material from the following cultural group is excluded from this list and is not subject to United States import restrictions: Plateau Indian.

I.   Animal and Bird Skins (Hide), Fur and Feathers

A.   Hunting and fishing equipment

Quivers (arrow cases)
Rifle scabbards/holsters and bandoliers (ammunition belts)
Kayaks, canoes and other boats made of skin or hide

B.   Horse trappings

Saddle bags and throws, blankets, etc.

C.   Clothing (often decorated with beads, buttons, hair, fur, shells, animal teeth, coloured porcupine quills)

Belts, dresses, jackets, leggings, moccasins, robes, shirts, vests, parkas
Yokes, beaded
Headdresses, decorated with feathers, hair, fur, and/or horn
Ornaments, jewelry and other accessories (including necklaces often with hide-covered stone)

D.   Other sewn objects

Cradle boards and covers
Bags, pouches
Rugs
Tipi covers (with or without paint or other decoration)

E.   Skins with applied writing, drawing, or painted decoration, design or figures

F.   Musical instruments

Drums

G.   Prepared skins of birds and mammals used in sacred bundles or as wrappings

H.   Parfleches (all-purpose hide containers, folded and/or sewn, with or without painted or other applied decoration)

II.   Wood, Bark, Roots, Seeds

A.   Weapons and hunting equipment

Tomahawks
Snowshoes
Clubs
Sheathes for knives
Paddles

Canoes and other boats (carved wood, birchbark)

B.   Containers

Baskets, pouches, bags, mats
Boxes and chests (bark, root, wood), often elaborately carved or painted

C.   Domestic utensils and tools

Bowls
Spoons, ladles
Trays
Spindle whorls (small, usually circular flywheels to regulate textile or other spinning)
Adzes (axe-like tool for trimming and smoothing wood) and other wood-working tools
Bark beaters
Mat creasers

D.   Furniture

Chairs, backrests, settees (seat or small bench with back)
Mats

E.   Carved models

Animal and human figurines
Miniature canoes and totem poles

F.   Toys, dolls and games

G.   Musical instruments

Drums
Whistles, flutes, recorders
Rattles, sometimes elaborately carved in animal or human form and painted or otherwise decorated

H.   Ornaments and accessories

Pendants, chains and other jewelry
Combs

Birchbark belts

I.   Hats (spruce root, wood, bark, woven grass)

J.   Ceremonial objects

Pipes and pipestems
Masks and headdresses (wood or cornhusk, often complexly carved and painted, usually resembling animals, or human faces, sometimes contorted)
Rattles (see description above in G.)
Bowls
Staffs, standards (ceremonial poles, in some cases used to support banners or flags)
Birchbark scrolls with carved pictographic designs or figures

K.   Totem poles, house posts and wall panels (usually carved and/or painted)

III.   Bone, Tooth, Shell, Horn, Ivory, Antler (items made from, or decorated with)

A.   Carved hunting and fishing equipment (such as carved bow handles)

B.   Weapons and tools

Clubs
Needles and sewing kits
Shuttles (small instrument containing a reel or spool or otherwise holding thread or other similar material during weaving or lace-making)

C.   Carved figurines

Representations of people, fish, animals

D.   Ornaments and other accessories

Combs
Beads and pendants
Snow goggles and visors

E. Ceremonial objects

Masks (see description in II J.)
Amulets and charms

F. Miniatures and game pieces (including cribbage boards)

G. Pipes

H. Musical instruments

Whistles

IV. Stone, Argillite Stone, Amber

A. Hunting and fishing equipment

Bola and bola weight (weapon consisting of long cord or thong with stone
balls at the end)
Blubber pounder
Harpoon head
Net weights
Toggles (rod, pin or bolt used with rope to tighten it, to make an attach-
ment or prevent slipping)

B. Tools

Snow knives
Ulus (crescent-shaped knife with small handle on side)

C. Domestic utensils

Plates, platters, bowls
Lamps (bowl or trough-shaped) and wick trimmers
Boxes
Hearthstone

D. Ornaments and other accessories

Especially incised pendants

E. Ceremonial objects

Masks
Seated human and animal figure bowls

F. Pipes

Argillite, catlinite and steatite, often ornately carved with animals and human designs

G. Carved figurines

Especially carved argillite figural groups and miniature totem poles

V. Porcupine Quills (items made from, or ornamented with)

A. Drinking tubes

B. Ornamentation for clothing and other sewn objects, usually coloured

VI. Textiles (cotton, wool, linen, canvas)

A. Decorated cloth panels and ceremonial dance curtains

B. Garments and accessories

Belts, dresses, hats/hoods, jackets, leggings, moccasins, robes, shirts, vests, aprons, tunics
Blankets or capes, often decorated with buttons, quillwork, beads, shells
Pouches and bags

C. Wrappings for ceremonial objects

D. Canvas tipis and tipi models

E. Woven blankets (including Chilkat blankets of woven mountain goat wool and cedar bark, with elaborate coloured designs)

VII. Metals (copper, iron, steel, gold, silver, bronze)

A. Weapons and shields

Daggers

B. Hunting and fishing equipment

Fishing lures

C. Tools

Snow knives
Ulus (see description under IV B.)

D. Clothing and hair ornaments

E. Ceremonial objects

Masks
Rattles, charms
Coppers (large flat copper plates with beaten or incised decoration)

VIII. Clay

A. Figurines (people, fish, animals)

B. Pipes

C. Pottery vessels and containers such as bowls or jars

IX. Beads (glass, clay, shell, bone, brass) (items decorated with)

A. Horse gear (bridles, saddle bags, decorative accessories)

B. Bags, pouches, parfleches (see description in I H.), and knife sheaths (decorative)

C. Clothing: belts, dresses, leggings, moccasins, shirts, vests, jackets, hoods, mantles/robes

D. Musical instruments Drums

E. Ceremonial/sacred amulets and objects

X. Hair (items decorated with, or made from human or animal hair)

Ornamentation used on clothing and other sewn objects, such as pouches, ceremonial objects.

Archaeological Artifacts

Below is a representational list, subject to amendment, of archaeological artifacts recovered from the soil of Canada, the territorial sea of Canada or the inland or other internal waters of Canada.

The Government of Canada, in accordance with Canadian law, will not restrict the export of archaeological artifacts recovered less than 75 years after their loss, concealment or abandonment. United States import restrictions, however, only will apply to archaeological material that is at least 250 years old.

Archaeological artifacts from the following Aboriginal cultural groups are included in this list and are subject to United States import restrictions: Inuit (Eskimo); Northwest Coast Indian; Plateau Indian; and Woodlands Indian. Also included in this list is non-Aboriginal archaeological material from historic shipwrecks and other underwater historic sites.

Archaeological artifacts from the following Aboriginal cultural groups are excluded from this list and are not subject to United States import restrictions: Subarctic Indian, Plains Indian.

I.   Aboriginal Archaeological Artifacts

A.   Animal and bird skins (hide), fur and feathers

Quivers (arrow cases)
Kayaks, canoes and other boats made of skin or hide
Clothing, ornaments and other accessories
Bags, pouches
Drums

B.   Wood, bark, roots, seeds

Snowshoes
Knives sheathes
Canoes and paddles (wood)
Containers (wood baskets, pouches, boxes, chests)
Domestic utensils (wood bowls, spoons, woodworking tools)
Carved models, toys and games

Musical instruments (wood drums, flutes, whistles, rattles)
Ceremonial objects (wood pipes, masks, rattles, bowls)

C.   Bone, tooth. shell, horn, ivory, antler

Carved hunting and fishing equipment
Weapons and tools (clubs, needles, shuttles)
Carved figurines (representations of people, fish, animals)
Ornaments and other accessories (combs, beads and pendants, snow goggles and visors)
Masks and other ceremonial objects
Miniatures and game pieces (including cribbage boards)
Pipes
Whistles

D.   Stone, argillite stone, amber

Hunting and fishing equipment (including harpoon or spear heads, net weights, toggles, bola weights)
Tools (snow knives and ulus - see description in Ethnological Material)
Plates, platters, bowls
Lamps (bowl or trough-shaped)
Boxes
Ornaments and other accessories
Masks
Pipes
Carved figurines

E.   Porcupine quills (items made from or decorated with)

Drinking tubes
Ornamentation for clothing, usually coloured
Pouches, bags
Ceremonial objects

F.   Textiles (wool, cotton, linen, canvas)

Garments (see description under Ethnological Material)
Blankets, often decorated with buttons, quillwork, beads, shells

Pouches, bags
Wrappings for ceremonial objects

G. Metals (copper, iron, steel, gold, silver, bronze)

Weapons and shields
Hunting and fishing equipment, including fishing lures
Tools (including snow knives and ulus - see description under Ethnological Material)
Clothing and hair ornaments
Ceremonial objects, especially coppers (see description under Ethnological Material)

H. Clay

Figurines (people, fish, animals)
Pipes
Pottery vessels and containers such as bowls or jars

I. Beads (glass, clay, shell, bone, brass) (items decorated with)

J. Hair (ornamentation of human or animal hair used on clothing and other sewn objects)

II. Non-Aboriginal Archaeological Artifacts: Historic Shipwrecks

A. General ship's parts (wood and metal)

Anchor
Wheel
Mast
Riggings (block and pulley; deadeye; lanyard)
Bell
Hull and fittings (rudder, keel, keelson, futtock, fasteners, iron supports)
Figurehead and other carved vessel decoration
Windlass and capstan (winches)
Wood of the ship
Furniture
Porthole

Ballast (pig iron) (metal weight carried to stabilize ship)
Pump assembly (plunger, working barrel, piston)
Riggings (cables)
Heating, lighting and plumbing fixtures

B.   Navigational instruments

Compass
Astrolabe or sextant (instruments for calculation of navigation by stars)
Telescope
Nocturnal
Sounding leads
Cross staff or back staff
Dividers
Lanterns
Binnacle (the case enclosing a ship's compass)

C.   Armaments

Cannon, carronade (type of short, light cannon), mortars
Cannonshot (balls, chair and bar)
Arms (guns, knives, pikes, cutlasses, scabbards, swords)
Gun carriage components
Musket shot (metal balls)
Bandoliers (cartridge straps)

D.   Tools and wares

Carpenter's tools
Sail making tools
Rope making tools
Medicinal wares
Galley ware (cooking caldron, crockery, glassware, beverage bottles,
cutlery, treen, stoves)
Caulker tools
Surgeon tools
Chaplain tools
Fishing supplies (lead sinkers, hooks, barrels, try works)

Cooper's tools
Blacksmith's tools

E.   Ship's cargo

Raw metal (iron, copper, bronze, lead)
Wood
Ceramics
Glassware (fine glass decanters)
Trade beads
Containers (casks, baskets)
Stone (for building or ballast)

F.   Personal goods found on ships

Jewelry (gold, silver, stone)
Coins
Gaming pieces (dice)
Buckles and buttons
Chests
Combs
Pipes
Religious items
Timepieces
Bedding, clothing and other textiles
Shoes

A7. EMERGENCY ACTIONS AND BILATERAL AGREEMENTS

CHART OF EMERGENCY ACTIONS & BILATERAL AGREEMENTS

MOU = MEMORANDUM OF UNDERSTANDING OR BILATERAL AGREEMENT

SEE CHART SORTED BY COUNTRY

Country	Year	Event
El Salvador	Sept. 11, '87	Emergency Action on Cara Suda pre-Columbian material.
El Salvador	March 10, '95	MOU on pre-Columbian material. Continues protection for Cara Suda material. (extended March 8, '00, and March 8, '05)
Bolivia	March 14, '89	Emergency Action on certain ethno. textiles. (expired Sept. 11, '96)
Bolivia	Dec. 7, 01	MOU on archaeo. & ethno. material (extended Dec. 4, 06).
Peru	May 7, '90	Emergency Action on pre-Columbian material from Sipán.
Peru	June 11, '97	MOU on pre-Columbian material and Colonial ethnological material. Continues previous protection. (extended June 6, '02, and June 9, 07)
Guatemala	April 15, '91	Emergency Action on pre-Columbian material from Petén.
Guatemala	Oct. 3, '97	MOU on pre-Columbian material. Continues protection for Petén material. (extended Sept. 29, '02); extended & amended Sept. 29, 07.
Mali	Sept. 23, '93	Emergency Action on archaeo. material.
Mali	Sept. 23, '97	MOU on archaeo. material from Niger River Valley & Bandiagara Escarpment. Continues previous protection (extended Sept. 19, '02; extended & amended Sept. 19, 07).
Canada	April 22, '97	MOU on archaeo. and ethno. material. (exp. '02)
Cyprus Ethno	April 12, '99	Emergency Action on ethno. material (extended Aug. 29, '03).
Cyprus Ethno	July 16, '07	Amended Bilateral Agreement on archaeo. & ethno. material is extended.
Cambodia	Dec. 2, '99	Emergency Action archaeo. material.
Cambodia	Sept. 22, '03	MOU on Khmer archaeo. material.
Nicaragua	Oct. 26, '00	MOU on pre-Columbian material (extended 20 Oct '05).
Italy	Jan. 23, '01	MOU on certain archaeological material (extended on 19 January '06).
Cyprus Archaeo	July 19, 2002	MOU on archaeo. material. On Sept. 4, '05, the MOU was amended to include prior protections.
Cyprus Archaeo	July 16, '07	Amended Bilateral Agreement on archaeo. & ethno. material is extended.
Honduras	March 12, '04	MOU on pre-Columbian material.
Colombia	March 15, '06	MOU on archaeo. & ethno. material.

Last updated on September 26, 2007

A8. UNESCO CONVENTION ON THE PROTECTION OF UNDERWATER CULTURAL HERITAGE (2001)

Convention On The Protection Of The Underwater Cultural Heritage

UNESCO

Paris, 2 November 2001

The General Conference of the United Nations Educational, Scientific and Cultural Organization, meeting in Paris from 15 October to 3 November 2001, at its 31st session,

Acknowledging the importance of underwater cultural heritage as an integral part of the cultural heritage of humanity and a particularly important element in the history of peoples, nations, and their relations with each other concerning their common heritage,

Realizing the importance of protecting and preserving the underwater cultural heritage and that responsibility therefor rests with all States,

Noting growing public interest in and public appreciation of underwater cultural heritage,

Convinced of the importance of research, information and education to the protection and preservation of underwater cultural heritage,

Convinced of the public's right to enjoy the educational and recreational benefits of responsible non-intrusive access to *in situ* underwater cultural heritage, and of the value of public education to contribute to awareness, appreciation and protection of that heritage,

Aware of the fact that underwater cultural heritage is threatened by unauthorized activities directed at it, and of the need for stronger measures to prevent such activities,

Conscious of the need to respond appropriately to the possible negative impact on underwater cultural heritage of legitimate activities that may incidentally affect it,

Deeply concerned by the increasing commercial exploitation of underwater cultural heritage, and in particular by certain activities aimed at the sale, acquisition or barter of underwater cultural heritage,

Aware of the availability of advanced technology that enhances discovery of and access to underwater cultural heritage,

Believing that cooperation among States, international organizations, scientific institutions, professional organizations, archaeologists, divers, other interested parties and the public at large is essential for the protection of underwater cultural heritage,

Considering that survey, excavation and protection of underwater cultural heritage necessitate the availability and application of special scientific methods and the use of suitable techniques and equipment as well as a high degree of professional specialization, all of which indicate a need for uniform governing criteria,

Realizing the need to codify and progressively develop rules relating to the protection and preservation of underwater cultural heritage in conformity with international law and practice, including the UNESCO Convention on the Means of Prohibiting and Preventing the Illicit Import, Export and Transfer of Ownership of Cultural Property of 14 November 1970, the UNESCO Convention for the Protection of the World Cultural and Natural Heritage of 16 November 1972 and the United Nations Convention on the Law of the Sea of 10 December 1982,

Committed to improving the effectiveness of measures at international, regional and national levels for the preservation in situ or, if necessary for scientific or protective purposes, the careful recovery of underwater cultural heritage,

Having decided at its twenty-ninth session that this question should be made the subject of an international convention,

Adopts this second day of November 2001 this Convention.

Article 1—Definitions

For the purposes of this Convention:

1. (a) "Underwater cultural heritage" means all traces of human existence having a cultural, historical or archaeological character which have been partially or totally under water, periodically or continuously, for at least 100 years such as:

(i) sites, structures, buildings, artefacts and human remains, together with their archaeological and natural context;

(ii) vessels, aircraft, other vehicles or any part thereof, their cargo or other contents, together with their archaeological and natural context; and

(iii) objects of prehistoric character.

(b) Pipelines and cables placed on the seabed shall not be considered as underwater cultural heritage.

(c) Installations other than pipelines and cables, placed on the seabed and still in use, shall not be considered as underwater cultural heritage.

2. (a) "States Parties" means States which have consented to be bound by this Convention and for which this Convention is in force.

(b) This Convention applies *mutatis mutandis* to those territories referred to in Article 26, paragraph 2(b), which become Parties to this Convention in accordance with the conditions set out in that paragraph, and to that extent "States Parties" refers to those territories.

3. "UNESCO" means the United Nations Educational, Scientific and Cultural Organization.

4. "Director-General" means the Director-General of UNESCO.

5. "Area" means the seabed and ocean floor and subsoil thereof, beyond the limits of national jurisdiction.

6. "Activities directed at underwater cultural heritage" means activities having underwater cultural heritage as their primary object and which may, directly or indirectly, physically disturb or otherwise damage underwater cultural heritage.

7. "Activities incidentally affecting underwater cultural heritage" means activities which, despite not having underwater cultural heritage as their primary object or one of their objects, may physically disturb or otherwise damage underwater cultural heritage.

8. "State vessels and aircraft" means warships, and other vessels or aircraft that were owned or operated by a State and used, at the time of sinking, only for government non-commercial purposes, that are identified as such and that meet the definition of underwater cultural heritage.

9. "Rules" means the Rules concerning activities directed at underwater cultural heritage, as referred to in Article 33 of this Convention.

Article 2—Objectives and general principles

1. This Convention aims to ensure and strengthen the protection of underwater cultural heritage.

2. States Parties shall cooperate in the protection of underwater cultural heritage.

3. States Parties shall preserve underwater cultural heritage for the benefit of humanity in conformity with the provisions of this Convention.

4. States Parties shall, individually or jointly as appropriate, take all appropriate measures in conformity with this Convention and with international law that are necessary to protect underwater cultural heritage, using for this purpose the best practicable means at their disposal and in accordance with their capabilities.

5. The preservation *in situ* of underwater cultural heritage shall be considered as the first option before allowing or engaging in any activities directed at this heritage.

6. Recovered underwater cultural heritage shall be deposited, conserved and managed in a manner that ensures its long-term preservation.

7. Underwater cultural heritage shall not be commercially exploited.

8. Consistent with State practice and international law, including the United Nations Convention on the Law of the Sea, nothing in this Convention

shall be interpreted as modifying the rules of international law and State practice pertaining to sovereign immunities, nor any State's rights with respect to its State vessels and aircraft.

9. States Parties shall ensure that proper respect is given to all human remains located in maritime waters.

10. Responsible non-intrusive access to observe or document *in situ* underwater cultural heritage shall be encouraged to create public awareness, appreciation, and protection of the heritage except where such access is incompatible with its protection and management.

11. No act or activity undertaken on the basis of this Convention shall constitute grounds for claiming, contending or disputing any claim to national sovereignty or jurisdiction.

Article 3—Relationship between this Convention and the United Nations Convention on the Law of the Sea

Nothing in this Convention shall prejudice the rights, jurisdiction and duties of States under international law, including the United Nations Convention on the Law of the Sea. This Convention shall be interpreted and applied in the context of and in a manner consistent with international law, including the United Nations Convention on the Law of the Sea.

Article 4—Relationship to law of salvage and law of finds

Any activity relating to underwater cultural heritage to which this Convention applies shall not be subject to the law of salvage or law of finds, unless it:

(a) is authorized by the competent authorities, and
(b) is in full conformity with this Convention, and
(c) ensures that any recovery of the underwater cultural heritage achieves its maximum protection.

Article 5—Activities incidentally affecting underwater cultural heritage

Each State Party shall use the best practicable means at its disposal to prevent or mitigate any adverse effects that might arise from activities under its jurisdiction incidentally affecting underwater cultural heritage.

Article 6—Bilateral, regional or other multilateral agreements

1. States Parties are encouraged to enter into bilateral, regional or other multilateral agreements or develop existing agreements, for the preservation of underwater cultural heritage. All such agreements shall be in full conformity with the provisions of this Convention and shall not dilute its universal character. States may, in such agreements, adopt rules and regulations which would ensure better protection of underwater cultural heritage than those adopted in this Convention.

2. The Parties to such bilateral, regional or other multilateral agreements may invite States with a verifiable link, especially a cultural, historical or archaeological link, to the underwater cultural heritage concerned to join such agreements.

3. This Convention shall not alter the rights and obligations of States Parties regarding the protection of sunken vessels, arising from other bilateral, regional or other multilateral agreements concluded before its adoption, and, in particular, those that are in conformity with the purposes of this Convention.

Article 7—Underwater cultural heritage in internal waters, archipelagic waters and territorial sea

1. States Parties, in the exercise of their sovereignty, have the exclusive right to regulate and authorize activities directed at underwater cultural heritage in their internal waters, archipelagic waters and territorial sea.

2. Without prejudice to other international agreements and rules of international law regarding the protection of underwater cultural heritage, States Parties shall require that the Rules be applied to activities directed at underwater cultural heritage in their internal waters, archipelagic waters and territorial sea.

3. Within their archipelagic waters and territorial sea, in the exercise of their sovereignty and in recognition of general practice among States, States Parties, with a view to cooperating on the best methods of protecting State vessels and aircraft, should inform the flag State Party to this Convention and, if applicable, other States with a verifiable link, especially

a cultural, historical or archaeological link, with respect to the discovery of such identifiable State vessels and aircraft.

Article 8—Underwater cultural heritage in the contiguous zone

Without prejudice to and in addition to Articles 9 and 10, and in accordance with Article 303, paragraph 2, of the United Nations Convention on the Law of the Sea, States Parties may regulate and authorize activities directed at underwater cultural heritage within their contiguous zone. In so doing, they shall require that the Rules be applied.

Article 9—Reporting and notification in the exclusive economic zone and on the continental shelf

1. All States Parties have a responsibility to protect underwater cultural heritage in the exclusive economic zone and on the continental shelf in conformity with this Convention.

Accordingly:

(a) a State Party shall require that when its national, or a vessel flying its flag, discovers or intends to engage in activities directed at underwater cultural heritage located in its exclusive economic zone or on its continental shelf, the national or the master of the vessel shall report such discovery or activity to it;

(b) in the exclusive economic zone or on the continental shelf of another State Party:

(i) States Parties shall require the national or the master of the vessel to report such discovery or activity to them and to that other State Party;

(ii) alternatively, a State Party shall require the national or master of the vessel to report such discovery or activity to it and shall ensure the rapid and effective transmission of such reports to all other States Parties.

2. On depositing its instrument of ratification, acceptance, approval or accession, a State Party shall declare the manner in which reports will be transmitted under paragraph 1(b) of this Article.

3. A State Party shall notify the Director-General of discoveries or activities reported to it under paragraph 1 of this Article.

4. The Director-General shall promptly make available to all States Parties any information notified to him under paragraph 3 of this Article.

5. Any State Party may declare to the State Party in whose exclusive economic zone or on whose continental shelf the underwater cultural heritage is located its interest in being consulted on how to ensure the effective protection of that underwater cultural heritage. Such declaration shall be based on a verifiable link, especially a cultural, historical or archaeological link, to the underwater cultural heritage concerned.

Article 10—Protection of underwater cultural heritage in the exclusive economic zone and on the continental shelf
1. No authorization shall be granted for an activity directed at underwater cultural heritage located in the exclusive economic zone or on the continental shelf except in conformity with the provisions of this Article.

2. A State Party in whose exclusive economic zone or on whose continental shelf underwater cultural heritage is located has the right to prohibit or authorize any activity directed at such heritage to prevent interference with its sovereign rights or jurisdiction as provided for by international law including the United Nations Convention on the Law of the Sea.

3. Where there is a discovery of underwater cultural heritage or it is intended that activity shall be directed at underwater cultural heritage in a State Party's exclusive economic zone or on its continental shelf, that State Party shall:
(a) consult all other States Parties which have declared an interest under Article 9, paragraph 5, on how best to protect the underwater cultural heritage;
(b) coordinate such consultations as "Coordinating State", unless it expressly declares that it does not wish to do so, in which case the States Parties which have declared an interest under Article 9, paragraph 5, shall appoint a Coordinating State.

4. Without prejudice to the duty of all States Parties to protect underwater cultural heritage by way of all practicable measures taken in accordance with international law to prevent immediate danger to the underwater cultural

heritage, including looting, the Coordinating State may take all practicable measures, and/or issue any necessary authorizations in conformity with this Convention and, if necessary prior to consultations, to prevent any immediate danger to the underwater cultural heritage, whether arising from human activities or any other cause, including looting. In taking such measures assistance may be requested from other States Parties.

5. The Coordinating State:

(a) shall implement measures of protection which have been agreed by the consulting States, which include the Coordinating State, unless the consulting States, which include the Coordinating State, agree that another State Party shall implement those measures;

(b) shall issue all necessary authorizations for such agreed measures in conformity with the Rules, unless the consulting States, which include the Coordinating State, agree that another State Party shall issue those authorizations;

(c) may conduct any necessary preliminary research on the underwater cultural heritage and shall issue all necessary authorizations therefor, and shall promptly inform the Director-General of the results, who in turn will make such information promptly available to other States Parties.

6. In coordinating consultations, taking measures, conducting preliminary research and/or issuing authorizations pursuant to this Article, the Coordinating State shall act on behalf of the States Parties as a whole and not in its own interest. Any such action shall not in itself constitute a basis for the assertion of any preferential or jurisdictional rights not provided for in international law, including the United Nations Convention on the Law of the Sea.

7. Subject to the provisions of paragraphs 2 and 4 of this Article, no activity directed at State vessels and aircraft shall be conducted without the agreement of the flag State and the collaboration of the Coordinating State.

Article 11—Reporting and notification in the Area

1. States Parties have a responsibility to protect underwater cultural heritage in the Area in conformity with this Convention and Article 149 of the United Nations Convention on the Law of the Sea. Accordingly when a

national, or a vessel flying the flag of a State Party, discovers or intends to engage in activities directed at underwater cultural heritage located in the Area, that State Party shall require its national, or the master of the vessel, to report such discovery or activity to it.

2. States Parties shall notify the Director-General and the Secretary-General of the International Seabed Authority of such discoveries or activities reported to them.

3. The Director-General shall promptly make available to all States Parties any such information supplied by States Parties.

4. Any State Party may declare to the Director-General its interest in being consulted on how to ensure the effective protection of that underwater cultural heritage. Such declaration shall be based on a verifiable link to the underwater cultural heritage concerned, particular regard being paid to the preferential rights of States of cultural, historical or archaeological origin.

Article 12—Protection of underwater cultural heritage in the Area
1. No authorization shall be granted for any activity directed at underwater cultural heritage located in the Area except in conformity with the provisions of this Article.

2. The Director-General shall invite all States Parties which have declared an interest under Article 11, paragraph 4, to consult on how best to protect the underwater cultural heritage, and to appoint a State Party to coordinate such consultations as the "Coordinating State". The Director-General shall also invite the International Seabed Authority to participate in such consultations.

3. All States Parties may take all practicable measures in conformity with this Convention, if necessary prior to consultations, to prevent any immediate danger to the underwater cultural heritage, whether arising from human activity or any other cause including looting.

4. The Coordinating State shall:
(a) implement measures of protection which have been agreed by the consulting States, which include the Coordinating State, unless the consulting

States, which include the Coordinating State, agree that another State Party shall implement those measures; and

(b) issue all necessary authorizations for such agreed measures, in conformity with this Convention, unless the consulting States, which include the Coordinating State, agree that another State Party shall issue those authorizations.

5. The Coordinating State may conduct any necessary preliminary research on the underwater cultural heritage and shall issue all necessary authorizations therefor, and shall promptly inform the Director-General of the results, who in turn shall make such information available to other States Parties.

6. In coordinating consultations, taking measures, conducting preliminary research, and/or issuing authorizations pursuant to this Article, the Coordinating State shall act for the benefit of humanity as a whole, on behalf of all States Parties. Particular regard shall be paid to the preferential rights of States of cultural, historical or archaeological origin in respect of the underwater cultural heritage concerned.

7. No State Party shall undertake or authorize activities directed at State vessels and aircraft in the Area without the consent of the flag State.

Article 13—Sovereign immunity
Warships and other government ships or military aircraft with sovereign immunity, operated for non-commercial purposes, undertaking their normal mode of operations, and not engaged in activities directed at underwater cultural heritage, shall not be obliged to report discoveries of underwater cultural heritage under Articles 9, 10, 11 and 12 of this Convention. However States Parties shall ensure, by the adoption of appropriate measures not impairing the operations or operational capabilities of their warships or other government ships or military aircraft with sovereign immunity operated for non-commercial purposes, that they comply, as far as is reasonable and practicable, with Articles 9, 10, 11 and 12 of this Convention.

Article 14—Control of entry into the territory, dealing and possession
States Parties shall take measures to prevent the entry into their territory, the dealing in, or the possession of, underwater cultural heritage illicitly exported and/or recovered, where recovery was contrary to this Convention.

Article 15—Non-use of areas under the jurisdiction of States Parties
States Parties shall take measures to prohibit the use of their territory, including their maritime ports, as well as artificial islands, installations and structures under their exclusive jurisdiction or control, in support of any activity directed at underwater cultural heritage which is not in conformity with this Convention.

Article 16—Measures relating to nationals and vessels
States Parties shall take all practicable measures to ensure that their nationals and vessels flying their flag do not engage in any activity directed at underwater cultural heritage in a manner not in conformity with this Convention.

Article 17—Sanctions
1. Each State Party shall impose sanctions for violations of measures it has taken to implement this Convention.

2. Sanctions applicable in respect of violations shall be adequate in severity to be effective in securing compliance with this Convention and to discourage violations wherever they occur and shall deprive offenders of the benefit deriving from their illegal activities.

3. States Parties shall cooperate to ensure enforcement of sanctions imposed under this Article.

Article 18—Seizure and disposition of underwater cultural heritage
1. Each State Party shall take measures providing for the seizure of underwater cultural heritage in its territory that has been recovered in a manner not in conformity with this Convention.

2. Each State Party shall record, protect and take all reasonable measures to stabilize underwater cultural heritage seized under this Convention.

3. Each State Party shall notify the Director-General and any other State with a verifiable link, especially a cultural, historical or archaeological link, to the underwater cultural heritage concerned of any seizure of underwater cultural heritage that it has made under this Convention.

4. A State Party which has seized underwater cultural heritage shall ensure that its disposition be for the public benefit, taking into account the need for conservation and research; the need for reassembly of a dispersed collection; the need for public access, exhibition and education; and the interests of any State with a verifiable link, especially a cultural, historical or archaeological link, in respect of the underwater cultural heritage concerned.

Article 19—Cooperation and information-sharing
1. States Parties shall cooperate and assist each other in the protection and management of underwater cultural heritage under this Convention, including, where practicable, collaborating in the investigation, excavation, documentation, conservation, study and presentation of such heritage.

2. To the extent compatible with the purposes of this Convention, each State Party undertakes to share information with other States Parties concerning underwater cultural heritage, including discovery of heritage, location of heritage, heritage excavated or recovered contrary to this Convention or otherwise in violation of international law, pertinent scientific methodology and technology, and legal developments relating to such heritage.

3. Information shared between States Parties, or between UNESCO and States Parties, regarding the discovery or location of underwater cultural heritage shall, to the extent compatible with their national legislation, be kept confidential and reserved to competent authorities of States Parties as long as the disclosure of such information might endanger or otherwise put at risk the preservation of such underwater cultural heritage.

4. Each State Party shall take all practicable measures to disseminate information, including where feasible through appropriate international databases, about underwater cultural heritage excavated or recovered contrary to this Convention or otherwise in violation of international law.

Article 20—Public awareness
Each State Party shall take all practicable measures to raise public awareness regarding the value and significance of underwater cultural heritage and the importance of protecting it under this Convention.

Article 21—Training in underwater archaeology
States Parties shall cooperate in the provision of training in underwater archaeology, in techniques for the conservation of underwater cultural heritage and, on agreed terms, in the transfer of technology relating to underwater cultural heritage.

Article 22—Competent authorities
1. In order to ensure the proper implementation of this Convention, States Parties shall establish competent authorities or reinforce the existing ones where appropriate, with the aim of providing for the establishment, maintenance and updating of an inventory of underwater cultural heritage, the effective protection, conservation, presentation and management of underwater cultural heritage, as well as research and education.

2. States Parties shall communicate to the Director-General the names and addresses of their competent authorities relating to underwater cultural heritage.

Article 23—Meetings of States Parties
1. The Director-General shall convene a Meeting of States Parties within one year of the entry into force of this Convention and thereafter at least once every two years. At the request of a majority of States Parties, the Director-General shall convene an Extraordinary Meeting of States Parties.

2. The Meeting of States Parties shall decide on its functions and responsibilities.

3. The Meeting of States Parties shall adopt its own Rules of Procedure.

4. The Meeting of States Parties may establish a Scientific and Technical Advisory Body composed of experts nominated by the States Parties with due regard to the principle of equitable geographical distribution and the desirability of a gender balance.

5. The Scientific and Technical Advisory Body shall appropriately assist the Meeting of States Parties in questions of a scientific or technical nature regarding the implementation of the Rules.

Article 24—Secretariat for this Convention
1. The Director-General shall be responsible for the functions of the Secretariat for this Convention.

2. The duties of the Secretariat shall include:
(a) organizing Meetings of States Parties as provided for in Article 23, paragraph 1; and
(b) assisting States Parties in implementing the decisions of the Meetings of States Parties.

Article 25—Peaceful settlement of disputes
1. Any dispute between two or more States Parties concerning the interpretation or application of this Convention shall be subject to negotiations in good faith or other peaceful means of settlement of their own choice.

2. If those negotiations do not settle the dispute within a reasonable period of time, it may be submitted to UNESCO for mediation, by agreement between the States Parties concerned.

3. If mediation is not undertaken or if there is no settlement by mediation, the provisions relating to the settlement of disputes set out in Part XV of the United Nations Convention on the Law of the Sea apply *mutatis mutandis* to any dispute between States Parties to this Convention concerning the interpretation or application of this Convention, whether or not they are also Parties to the United Nations Convention on the Law of the Sea.

4. Any procedure chosen by a State Party to this Convention and to the United Nations Convention on the Law of the Sea pursuant to Article 287 of the latter shall apply to the settlement of disputes under this Article, unless that State Party, when ratifying, accepting, approving or acceding to this Convention, or at any time thereafter, chooses another procedure pursuant to Article 287 for the purpose of the settlement of disputes arising out of this Convention.

5. A State Party to this Convention which is not a Party to the United Nations Convention on the Law of the Sea, when ratifying, accepting, approving or acceding to this Convention or at any time thereafter shall be free to choose, by means of a written declaration, one or more of the means set out in Article 287, paragraph 1, of the United Nations Convention on the Law of the Sea for the purpose of settlement of disputes under this Article. Article 287 shall apply to such a declaration, as well as to any dispute to which such State is party, which is not covered by a declaration in force. For the purpose of conciliation and arbitration, in accordance with Annexes V and VII of the United Nations Convention on the Law of the Sea, such State shall be entitled to nominate conciliators and arbitrators to be included in the lists referred to in Annex V, Article 2, and Annex VII, Article 2, for the settlement of disputes arising out of this Convention.

Article 26—Ratification, acceptance, approval or accession
1. This Convention shall be subject to ratification, acceptance or approval by Member States of UNESCO.

2. This Convention shall be subject to accession:
(a) by States that are not members of UNESCO but are members of the United Nations or of a specialized agency within the United Nations system or of the International Atomic Energy Agency, as well as by States Parties to the Statute of the International Court of Justice and any other State invited to accede to this Convention by the General Conference of UNESCO;
(b) by territories which enjoy full internal self-government, recognized as such by the United Nations, but have not attained full independence in accordance with General Assembly resolution 1514 (XV) and which have competence over the matters governed by this Convention, including the competence to enter into treaties in respect of those matters.

3. The instruments of ratification, acceptance, approval or accession shall be deposited with the Director-General.

Article 27—Entry into force
This Convention shall enter into force three months after the date of the deposit of the twentieth instrument referred to in Article 26, but solely with respect to the twenty States or territories that have so deposited their

instruments. It shall enter into force for each other State or territory three months after the date on which that State or territory has deposited its instrument.

Article 28—Declaration as to inland waters

When ratifying, accepting, approving or acceding to this Convention or at any time thereafter, any State or territory may declare that the Rules shall apply to inland waters not of a maritime character.

Article 29—Limitations to geographical scope

At the time of ratifying, accepting, approving or acceding to this Convention, a State or territory may make a declaration to the depositary that this Convention shall not be applicable to specific parts of its territory, internal waters, archipelagic waters or territorial sea, and shall identify therein the reasons for such declaration. Such State shall, to the extent practicable and as quickly as possible, promote conditions under which this Convention will apply to the areas specified in its declaration, and to that end shall also withdraw its declaration in whole or in part as soon as that has been achieved.

Article 30—Reservations

With the exception of Article 29, no reservations may be made to this Convention.

Article 31—Amendments

1. A State Party may, by written communication addressed to the Director-General, propose amendments to this Convention. The Director-General shall circulate such communication to all States Parties. If, within six months from the date of the circulation of the communication, not less than one half of the States Parties reply favourably to the request, the Director-General shall present such proposal to the next Meeting of States Parties for discussion and possible adoption.

2. Amendments shall be adopted by a two-thirds majority of States Parties present and voting.

3. Once adopted, amendments to this Convention shall be subject to ratification, acceptance, approval or accession by the States Parties.

4. Amendments shall enter into force, but solely with respect to the States Parties that have ratified, accepted, approved or acceded to them, three months after the deposit of the instruments referred to in paragraph 3 of this Article by two thirds of the States Parties. Thereafter, for each State or territory that ratifies, accepts, approves or accedes to it, the amendment shall enter into force three months after the date of deposit by that Party of its instrument of ratification, acceptance, approval or accession.

5. A State or territory which becomes a Party to this Convention after the entry into force of amendments in conformity with paragraph 4 of this Article shall, failing an expression of different intention by that State or territory, be considered:
(a) as a Party to this Convention as so amended; and
(b) as a Party to the unamended Convention in relation to any State Party not bound by the amendment.

Article 32—Denunciation
1. A State Party may, by written notification addressed to the Director-General, denounce this Convention.

2. The denunciation shall take effect twelve months after the date of receipt of the notification, unless the notification specifies a later date.

3. The denunciation shall not in any way affect the duty of any State Party to fulfil any obligation embodied in this Convention to which it would be subject under international law independently of this Convention.

Article 33—The Rules
The Rules annexed to this Convention form an integral part of it and, unless expressly provided otherwise, a reference to this Convention includes a reference to the Rules.

Article 34—Registration with the United Nations
In conformity with Article 102 of the Charter of the United Nations, this Convention shall be registered with the Secretariat of the United Nations at the request of the Director-General.

Article 35—Authoritative texts

This Convention has been drawn up in Arabic, Chinese, English, French, Russian and Spanish, the six texts being equally authoritative.

Annex
Rules concerning activities directed at underwater cultural heritage

I. General principles

Rule 1. The protection of underwater cultural heritage through *in situ* preservation shall be considered as the first option. Accordingly, activities directed at underwater cultural heritage shall be authorized in a manner consistent with the protection of that heritage, and subject to that requirement may be authorized for the purpose of making a significant contribution to protection or knowledge or enhancement of underwater cultural heritage.

Rule 2. The commercial exploitation of underwater cultural heritage for trade or speculation or its irretrievable dispersal is fundamentally incompatible with the protection and proper management of underwater cultural heritage. Underwater cultural heritage shall not be traded, sold, bought or bartered as commercial goods. This Rule cannot be interpreted as preventing:

(a) the provision of professional archaeological services or necessary services incidental thereto whose nature and purpose are in full conformity with this Convention and are subject to the authorization of the competent authorities;

(b) the deposition of underwater cultural heritage, recovered in the course of a research project in conformity with this Convention, provided such deposition does not prejudice the scientific or cultural interest or integrity of the recovered material or result in its irretrievable dispersal; is in accordance with the provisions of Rules 33 and 34; and is subject to the authorization of the competent authorities.

Rule 3. Activities directed at underwater cultural heritage shall not adversely affect the underwater cultural heritage more than is necessary for the objectives of the project.

Rule 4. Activities directed at underwater cultural heritage must use non-destructive techniques and survey methods in preference to recovery of objects. If excavation or recovery is necessary for the purpose of scientific studies or for the ultimate protection of the underwater cultural heritage, the methods and techniques used must be as non destructive as possible and contribute to the preservation of the remains.

Rule 5. Activities directed at underwater cultural heritage shall avoid the unnecessary disturbance of human remains or venerated sites.

Rule 6. Activities directed at underwater cultural heritage shall be strictly regulated to ensure proper recording of cultural, historical and archaeological information.

Rule 7. Public access to *in situ* underwater cultural heritage shall be promoted, except where such access is incompatible with protection and management.

Rule 8. International cooperation in the conduct of activities directed at underwater cultural heritage shall be encouraged in order to further the effective exchange or use of archaeologists and other relevant professionals.

II. Project design
Rule 9. Prior to any activity directed at underwater cultural heritage, a project design for the activity shall be developed and submitted to the competent authorities for authorization and appropriate peer review.

Rule 10. The project design shall include:
(a) an evaluation of previous or preliminary studies;
(b) the project statement and objectives;
(c) the methodology to be used and the techniques to be employed;
(d) the anticipated funding;
(e) an expected timetable for completion of the project;
(f) the composition of the team and the qualifications, responsibilities and experience of each team member;
(g) plans for post-fieldwork analysis and other activities;

(h) a conservation programme for artefacts and the site in close cooperation with the competent authorities;

(i) a site management and maintenance policy for the whole duration of the project;

(j) a documentation programme;

(k) a safety policy;

(l) an environmental policy;

(m) arrangements for collaboration with museums and other institutions, in particular scientific institutions;

(n) report preparation;

(o) deposition of archives, including underwater cultural heritage removed; and

(p) a programme for publication.

Rule 11. Activities directed at underwater cultural heritage shall be carried out in accordance with the project design approved by the competent authorities.

Rule 12. Where unexpected discoveries are made or circumstances change, the project design shall be reviewed and amended with the approval of the competent authorities.

Rule 13. In cases of urgency or chance discoveries, activities directed at the underwater cultural heritage, including conservation measures or activities for a period of short duration, in particular site stabilization, may be authorized in the absence of a project design in order to protect the underwater cultural heritage.

III. Preliminary work

Rule 14. The preliminary work referred to in Rule 10 (a) shall include an assessment that evaluates the significance and vulnerability of the underwater cultural heritage and the surrounding natural environment to damage by the proposed project, and the potential to obtain data that would meet the project objectives.

Rule 15. The assessment shall also include background studies of available historical and archaeological evidence, the archaeological and environmental characteristics of the site, and the consequences of any potential intrusion for the long-term stability of the underwater cultural heritage affected by the activities.

IV. Project objective, methodology and techniques
Rule 16. The methodology shall comply with the project objectives, and the techniques employed shall be as non-intrusive as possible.

V. Funding
Rule 17. Except in cases of emergency to protect underwater cultural heritage, an adequate funding base shall be assured in advance of any activity, sufficient to complete all stages of the project design, including conservation, documentation and curation of recovered artefacts, and report preparation and dissemination.

Rule 18. The project design shall demonstrate an ability, such as by securing a bond, to fund the project through to completion.

Rule 19. The project design shall include a contingency plan that will ensure conservation of underwater cultural heritage and supporting documentation in the event of any interruption of anticipated funding.

VI. Project duration - timetable
Rule 20. An adequate timetable shall be developed to assure in advance of any activity directed at underwater cultural heritage the completion of all stages of the project design, including conservation, documentation and curation of recovered underwater cultural heritage, as well as report preparation and dissemination.

Rule 21. The project design shall include a contingency plan that will ensure conservation of underwater cultural heritage and supporting documentation in the event of any interruption or termination of the project.

VII. Competence and qualifications
Rule 22. Activities directed at underwater cultural heritage shall only be undertaken under the direction and control of, and in the regular presence of, a qualified underwater archaeologist with scientific competence appropriate to the project.

Rule 23. All persons on the project team shall be qualified and have demonstrated competence appropriate to their roles in the project.

VIII. Conservation and site management

Rule 24. The conservation programme shall provide for the treatment of the archaeological remains during the activities directed at underwater cultural heritage, during transit and in the long term. Conservation shall be carried out in accordance with current professional standards.

Rule 25. The site management programme shall provide for the protection and management *in situ* of underwater cultural heritage, in the course of and upon termination of fieldwork. The programme shall include public information, reasonable provision for site stabilization, monitoring, and protection against interference.

IX. Documentation

Rule 26. The documentation programme shall set out thorough documentation including a progress report of activities directed at underwater cultural heritage, in accordance with current professional standards of archaeological documentation.

Rule 27. Documentation shall include, at a minimum, a comprehensive record of the site, including the provenance of underwater cultural heritage moved or removed in the course of the activities directed at underwater cultural heritage, field notes, plans, drawings, sections, and photographs or recording in other media.

X. Safety

Rule 28. A safety policy shall be prepared that is adequate to ensure the safety and health of the project team and third parties and that is in conformity with any applicable statutory and professional requirements.

XI. Environment

Rule 29. An environmental policy shall be prepared that is adequate to ensure that the seabed and marine life are not unduly disturbed.

XII. Reporting

Rule 30. Interim and final reports shall be made available according to the timetable set out in the project design, and deposited in relevant public records.

Rule 31. Reports shall include:
(a) an account of the objectives;
(b) an account of the methods and techniques employed;
(c) an account of the results achieved;
(d) basic graphic and photographic documentation on all phases of the activity;
(e) recommendations concerning conservation and curation of the site and of any underwater cultural heritage removed; and
(f) recommendations for future activities.

XIII. Curation of project archives

Rule 32. Arrangements for curation of the project archives shall be agreed to before any activity commences, and shall be set out in the project design.

Rule 33. The project archives, including any underwater cultural heritage removed and a copy of all supporting documentation shall, as far as possible, be kept together and intact as a collection in a manner that is available for professional and public access as well as for the curation of the archives. This should be done as rapidly as possible and in any case not later than ten years from the completion of the project, in so far as may be compatible with conservation of the underwater cultural heritage.

Rule 34. The project archives shall be managed according to international professional standards, and subject to the authorization of the competent authorities.

XIV. Dissemination

Rule 35. Projects shall provide for public education and popular presentation of the project results where appropriate.

Rule 36. A final synthesis of a project shall be:
(a) made public as soon as possible, having regard to the complexity of the project and the confidential or sensitive nature of the information; and
(b) deposited in relevant public records.

The foregoing is the authentic text of the Convention duly adopted by the General Conference of the United Nations Educational, Scientific and Cultural Organization during its thirty-first session, which was held in Paris and declared closed the third day of November 2001.

APPENDIX B: LEGISLATION AND RELATED ITEMS

B1. CANADIAN CULTURAL PROPERTY EXPORT AND IMPORT ACT, R.S.C. 1985, C. 51

(excerpt—full text available on CanLII AT <http://www.canlii.org/en/ca/laws/stat/rsc-1985-c-c-51/latest/rsc-1985-c-c-51.html>)

FOREIGN CULTURAL PROPERTY

Definitions
  37. (1) In this section,

"cultural property agreement"
«accord »
"cultural property agreement", in relation to a foreign State, means an agreement between Canada and the foreign State or an international agreement to which Canada and the foreign State are both parties, relating to the prevention of illicit international traffic in cultural property;

"foreign cultural property"
«biens culturels étrangers »
"foreign cultural property" , in relation to a reciprocating State, means any object that is specifically designated by that State as being of importance for archaeology, prehistory, history, literature, art or science;

"reciprocating State"
«État contractant »
"reciprocating State" means a foreign State that is a party to a cultural property agreement.

Illegal imports
(2) From and after the coming into force of a cultural property agreement in Canada and a reciprocating State, it is illegal to import into Canada any foreign cultural property that has been illegally exported from that reciprocating State.

Action for recovery of foreign cultural property
(3) Where the government of a reciprocating State submits a request in writing to the Minister for the recovery and return of any foreign cultural property that has been imported into Canada illegally by virtue of subsection (2) and that is in Canada in the possession of or under the control of any person, institution or public authority, the Attorney General of Canada may institute an action in the Federal Court or in a superior court of a province for the recovery of the property by the reciprocating State.

Notice
(4) Notice of the commencement of an action under this section shall be served by the Attorney General of Canada on such persons and given in such manner as is provided by the rules of the court in which the action is taken, or, where the rules do not so provide, served on such persons and given in such manner as is directed by a judge of the court.

Order for recovery of designated property
(5) A court in which an action has been taken under this section on behalf of a reciprocating State may, after affording all persons that it considers to have an interest in the action a reasonable opportunity to be heard, make an order for the recovery of the property in respect of which the action has been taken or any other order sufficient to ensure the return of the property to the reciprocating State, where the court is satisfied that the property has been illegally imported into Canada by virtue of subsection (2) and that the amount fixed under subsection (6), if any, has been paid to or for the benefit of the person, institution or public authority referred to in that subsection.

Compensation
(6) Where any person, institution or public authority establishes to the satisfaction of the court in which an action under this section is being considered that the person, institution or public authority

(*a*) is a *bona fide* purchaser for value of the property in respect of which the action has been taken and had no knowledge at the time the property was purchased by him or it that the property had been illegally exported from the reciprocating State on whose behalf the action has been taken, or

(b) has a valid title to the property in respect of which the action has been taken and had no knowledge at the time such title was acquired that the property had been illegally exported from the reciprocating State on whose behalf the action has been taken,

the court may fix such amount to be paid as compensation by the reciprocating State to that person, institution or public authority as the court considers just in the circumstances.

Safe-keeping

(7) The court may, at any time in the course of an action under this section, order that the property in respect of which the action has been taken be turned over to the Minister for safe-keeping and conservation pending final disposition of the action.

Permit to export

(8) The Minister shall, on receipt of a copy of an order of a court made under subsection (5), issue a permit authorizing any person authorized by the reciprocating State on behalf of which the action was taken to export the property in respect of which the order was made to that State.

Limitations inapplicable

(9) Section 39 of the *Federal Courts Act* does not apply in respect of any action taken under this section.

R.S., 1985, c. C-51, s. 37; 2002, c. 8, s. 182.

B2. US SENTENCING GUIDELINES: CULTURAL HERITAGE RESOURCE CRIMES, 18 U.S.C. APPX §2B1.5

§2B1.5. Theft of, Damage to, or Destruction of, Cultural Heritage Resources; Unlawful Sale, Purchase, Exchange, Transportation, or Receipt of Cultural Heritage Resources

(a) Base Offense Level: **8**

(b) Specific Offense Characteristics

(1) If the value of the cultural heritage resource (A) exceeded $2,000 but did not exceed $5,000, increase by **1** level; or (B) exceeded $5,000, increase by the number of levels from the table in §2B1.1 (Theft, Property Destruction, and Fraud) corresponding to that amount.

(2) If the offense involved a cultural heritage resource from, or that, prior to the offense, was on, in, or in the custody of (A) the national park system; (B) a National Historic Landmark; (C) a national monument or national memorial; (D) a national marine sanctuary; (E) a national cemetery; (F) a museum; or (G) the World Heritage List, increase by **2** levels.

(3) If the offense involved a cultural heritage resource constituting (A) human remains; (B) a funerary object; (C) cultural patrimony; (D) a sacred object; (E) cultural property; (F) designated archaeological or ethnological material; or (G) a pre-Columbian monumental or architectural sculpture or mural, increase by **2** levels.

(4) If the offense was committed for pecuniary gain or otherwise involved a commercial purpose, increase by **2** levels.

(5) If the defendant engaged in a pattern of misconduct involving cultural heritage resources, increase by **2** levels.

(6) If a dangerous weapon was brandished or its use was threatened, increase by **2** levels. If the resulting offense level is less than level **14**, increase to level **14**.

(c) Cross Reference

(1) If the offense involved arson, or property damage by the use of any explosive, explosive material, or destructive device, apply §2K1.4 (Arson; Property Damage by Use of Explosives), if the resulting offense level is greater than that determined above.

Commentary

Statutory Provisions: 16 U.S.C. §§ 470ee, 668(a), 707(b); 18 U.S.C. §§ 541-546, 641, 661-662, 666, 668, 1152-1153, 1163, 1168, 1170, 1361, 2232, 2314-2315.

Application Notes:

1. "Cultural Heritage Resource" Defined. — For purposes of this guideline, "cultural heritage resource" means any of the following:

(A) A historic property, as defined in 16 U.S.C. § 470w(5) (see also section 16(l) of 36 C.F.R. pt. 800).

(B) A historic resource, as defined in 16 U.S.C. § 470w(5).

(C) An archaeological resource, as defined in 16 U.S.C. § 470bb(1) (see also section 3(a) of 43 C.F.R. pt. 7; 36 C.F.R. pt. 296; 32 C.F.R. pt. 299; 18 C.F.R. pt. 1312).

(D) A cultural item, as defined in section 2(3) of the Native American Graves Protection and Repatriation Act, 25 U.S.C. § 3001(3) (see also 43 C.F.R. § 10.2(d)).

(E) A commemorative work. "Commemorative work" (A) has the meaning given that term in section 2(c) of Public Law 99–652 (40 U.S.C. § 1002(c)); and (B) includes any national monument or national memorial.

(F) An object of cultural heritage, as defined in 18 U.S.C. § 668(a)(2).

(G) Designated ethnological material, as described in 19 U.S.C. §§ 2601(2)(ii), 2601(7), and 2604.

2. Value of the Cultural Heritage Resource Under Subsection (b)(1).— This application note applies to the determination of the value of the cultural heritage resource under subsection (b)(1).

(A) General Rule.—For purposes of subsection (b)(1), the value of the cultural heritage resource shall include, as applicable to the particular resource involved, the following:

(i) The archaeological value. (Archaeological value shall be included in the case of any cultural heritage resource that is an archaeological resource.)

(ii) The commercial value.

*(iii)*The cost of restoration and repair.

(B) Estimation of Value.—For purposes of subsection (b)(1), the court need only make a reasonable estimate of the value of the cultural heritage resource based on available information.

(C) Definitions.—For purposes of this application note:

(i) "Archaeological value" of a cultural heritage resource means the cost of the retrieval of the scientific information which would have been obtainable prior to the offense, including the cost of preparing a research design, conducting field work, conducting laboratory analysis, and preparing reports, as would be necessary to realize the information potential. *(See 43 C.F.R. § 7.14(a); 36 C.F.R. § 296.14(a); 32 C.F.R. § 229.14(a); 18 C.F.R. § 1312.14(a).)*

(ii) "Commercial value" of a cultural heritage resource means the fair market value of the cultural heritage resource at the time of the offense. *(See 43 C.F.R. § 7.14(b); 36 C.F.R. § 296.14(b); 32 C.F.R. § 229.14(b); 18 C.F.R. § 1312.14(b).)*

(iii) "Cost of restoration and repair" includes all actual and projected costs of curation, disposition, and appropriate reburial of, and consultation with respect to, the cultural heritage resource; and any other actual and projected costs to complete restoration and repair of the cultural heritage resource, including (I) its reconstruction and stabilization; (II)

reconstruction and stabilization of ground contour and surface; (III) research necessary to conduct reconstruction and stabilization; (IV) the construction of physical barriers and other protective devices; (V) examination and analysis of the cultural heritage resource as part of efforts to salvage remaining information about the resource; and (VI) preparation of reports. (See 43 C.F.R. § 7.14(c); 36 C.F.R. § 296.14(c); 32 C.F.R. § 229.14(c); 18 C.F.R. § 1312.14(c).)

(D) Determination of Value in Cases Involving a Variety of Cultural Heritage Resources.—In a case involving a variety of cultural heritage resources, the value of the cultural heritage resources is the sum of all calculations made for those resources under this application note.

3. Enhancement in Subsection (b)(2).—For purposes of subsection (b)(2):

(A) "Museum" has the meaning given that term in 18 U.S.C. § 668(a)(1) except that the museum may be situated outside the United States.

(B) "National cemetery" has the meaning given that term in Application Note 1 of the Commentary to §2B1.1 (Theft, Property Destruction, and Fraud).

(C) "National Historic Landmark" means a property designated as such pursuant to 16 U.S.C. § 470a(a)(1)(B).

(D) "National marine sanctuary" means a national marine sanctuary designated as such by the Secretary of Commerce pursuant to 16 U.S.C. § 1433.

(E) "National monument or national memorial" means any national monument or national memorial established as such by Act of Congress or by proclamation pursuant to the Antiquities Act of 1906 (16 U.S.C. § 431).

(F) "National park system" has the meaning given that term in 16 U.S.C. § 1c(a).

(G) "World Heritage List" means the World Heritage List maintained by the World Heritage Committee of the United Nations Educational,

Scientific, and Cultural Organization in accordance with the Convention Concerning the Protection of the World Cultural and Natural Heritage.

4. *Enhancement in Subsection (b)(3).*—For purposes of subsection (b)(3):

(A) "Cultural patrimony" has the meaning given that term in 25 U.S.C. § 3001(3)(D) (see also 43 C.F.R. 10.2(d)(4)).

(B) "Cultural property" has the meaning given that term in 19 U.S.C. § 2601(6).

(C) "Designated archaeological or ethnological material" means archaeological or ethnological material described in 19 U.S.C. § 2601(7) (see also 19 U.S.C. §§ 2601(2) and 2604).

(D) "Funerary object" means an object that, as a part of the death rite or ceremony of a culture, was placed intentionally, at the time of death or later, with or near human remains.

(E) "Human remains" (i) means the physical remains of the body of a human; and (ii) does not include remains that reasonably may be determined to have been freely disposed of or naturally shed by the human from whose body the remains were obtained, such as hair made into ropes or nets.

(F) "Pre-Columbian monumental or architectural sculpture or mural" has the meaning given that term in 19 U.S.C. § 2095(3).

(G) "Sacred object" has the meaning given that term in 25 U.S.C. § 3001(3)(C) (see also 43 C.F.R. § 10.2(d)(3)).

5. *Pecuniary Gain and Commercial Purpose Enhancement Under Subsection (b)(4).*—

(A) "For Pecuniary Gain".—For purposes of subsection (b)(4), "for pecuniary gain" means for receipt of, or in anticipation of receipt of, anything of value, whether monetary or in goods or services. Therefore, offenses committed for pecuniary gain include both monetary and barter transactions, as well as activities designed to increase gross revenue.

(B) Commercial Purpose.—The acquisition of cultural heritage resources for display to the public, whether for a fee or donation and whether by an individual or an organization, including a governmental entity, a private non-profit organization, or a private for-profit organization, shall be considered to involve a "commercial purpose" for purposes of subsection (b)(4).

6. *Pattern of Misconduct Enhancement Under Subsection (b)(5).—*

(A) Definition.—For purposes of subsection (b)(5), "pattern of misconduct involving cultural heritage resources" means two or more separate instances of offense conduct involving a cultural heritage resource that did not occur during the course of the offense (i.e., that did not occur during the course of the instant offense of conviction and all relevant conduct under §1B1.3 (Relevant Conduct)). Offense conduct involving a cultural heritage resource may be considered for purposes of subsection (b)(5) regardless of whether the defendant was convicted of that conduct.

(B) Computation of Criminal History Points.—A conviction taken into account under subsection (b)(5) is not excluded from consideration of whether that conviction receives criminal history points pursuant to Chapter Four, Part A (Criminal History).

7. *Dangerous Weapons Enhancement Under Subsection (b)(6).—For purposes of subsection (b)(6), "brandished" and "dangerous weapon" have the meaning given those terms in Application Note 1 of the Commentary to §1B1.1 (Application Instructions).*

8. *Multiple Counts.—For purposes of Chapter Three, Part D (Multiple Counts), multiple counts involving cultural heritage offenses covered by this guideline are grouped together under subsection (d) of §3D1.2 (Groups of Closely Related Counts). Multiple counts involving cultural heritage offenses covered by this guideline and offenses covered by other guidelines are not to be grouped under §3D1.2(d).*

9. *Upward Departure Provision.—There may be cases in which the offense level determined under this guideline substantially understates the seriousness of the offense. In such cases, an upward departure may*

be warranted. For example, an upward departure may be warranted if (A) in addition to cultural heritage resources, the offense involved theft of, damage to, or destruction of, items that are not cultural heritage resources (such as an offense involving the theft from a national cemetery of lawnmowers and other administrative property in additionto historic gravemarkers or other cultural heritage resources); or (B) the offense involved a cultural heritage resource that has profound significance to cultural identity (e.g., the Statue of Liberty or the Liberty Bell).

B3. LETTER FROM JUDGE DIANA E. MURPHY TO THE HONORABLE PATRICK J. LEAHY AND THE HONORABLE ORRIN G. HATCH (3 APRIL 2002)

(online: United States Sentencing Commission <http://www.ussc.gov/culheritage/leahy_hatch.htm>)

Re: Penalties for Cultural Heritage Resource Crimes

Dear Senators Leahy and Hatch:

On behalf of the Sentencing Commission, and pursuant to the Commission's statutory charge under 28 U.S.C. §§ 994(r) and 995(a)(20), I am writing to recommend that Congress consider enacting legislation to increase the maximum statutory penalties for three federal crimes involving cultural heritage resources. These changes are warranted because the offenses are serious and the proposed increases would correspond to the punishment levels in the Commission's new guideline for cultural heritage resource offenses.

These three statutes—the Archaeological Resources Protection Act (ARPA), 16 U.S.C. § 470ee; the Native American Graves Protection and Repatriation Act (NAGPRA), 18 U.S.C. § 1170; and Theft from Indian Tribal Organizations, 18 U.S.C. § 1163, are basic tools of federal prosecution for offenses involving cultural heritage resources.1 Increased statutory maxima for these offenses will give full effect to the operation of the new sentencing guideline for cultural heritage resource offenses that the Commission will send to Congress on May 1, 2002. We therefore recommend elimination of the 12- and 24-month ceiling for first offenses under NAGPRA and ARPA, respectively, and adoption of a ten year statutory maximum for all three statutes (currently five years).

The Commission recently completed a two year examination of cultural heritage resource crimes and found that existing sentencing guidelines are inadequate for the wide variety of federal crimes involving the theft of, damage to, destruction of, or illicit trafficking in cultural heritage resources. Cultural heritage resources include national memorials, landmarks and parks, together with archaeological and other historic resources specifically dedicated to the preservation of the nation's heritage. Because individuals, communities, and nations identify themselves through intellectual, emotional, and spiritual connections to places and objects, the effect of cultural heritage resource crimes transcends mere monetary considerations. The Commission has determined that a separate guideline is needed that specifically recognizes both the federal government's longstanding obligation and unique role in preserving these resources and the harm caused to the nation and its inhabitants when its history is degraded through the destruction of cultural heritage resources.

As a result, the Commission has approved a separate sentencing guideline which reflects the fact that offenses involving cultural heritage resources are more serious because they involve essentially irreplaceable resources and cause intangible harm to society. The actual and potential cases which the Commission considered in its review range from vandalism and terrorism at historic landmarks and cemeteries to looting and theft of archaeological resources and human remains from federal and Indian lands.

Upon close scrutiny the Commission recognized that treatment of these offenses against unique and irreplaceable resources under traditional property offense guidelines would not be adequate to reflect the significance of the resources and the concomitant harm to the identity of the nation and its communities. Not only are the offenses themselves very serious and deserving of substantially more punishment, but the conduct of many of the offenders, professional looters who are well armed and dangerous to law enforcement and innocent passers-by, requires increased proportional punishment.

For example, currently under the general guideline for theft and property damage at §2B1.1, a sentence for vandalism to the Vietnam Memorial would be determined primarily by the amount of intended or actual pecuniary harm. If a federal administration building sustains the same amount of harm caused by vandals, the same punishment would result under current law. The Commission has determined that the magnitude of the harm caused to a national memorial and landmark is greater precisely because of the symbolic and historic nature of the object of the Senators Leahy and Hatch offense conduct, together with the fact that such resources are unique, nonfungible, and irreplaceable.

Accordingly, the Commission has taken steps to ensure that the punishment for such cultural heritage resource crimes takes such factors into consideration by promulgating a new guideline at §2B1.5 for this unique category of offenses. (See enclosure.) This new guideline will account for the fact that the offense involves items and locations specially designated by Congress over the years for preservation and education about the nation's heritage. The Commission has also been mindful of the potential for terrorist attacks against symbols of our nation and has provided for proportionate increases in punishment in the event that such violence occurs in connection with cultural heritage resources.

Surprisingly, when the Commission scrutinized the panoply of federal statutes that are used to prosecute offenses involving both property and cultural heritage resources, it found three significant disparities among the various statutory maxima for these offenses. These disparities impede Congress's ultimate objectives of proportionality and the elimination of unwarranted disparity, as enunciated in the Sentencing Reform Act of 1984. The examples below illustrate these disparities.

First, two cultural heritage resource statutes subordinate the amount of harm caused by the offender to the number of the offender's convictions under the statute. ARPA has one year and two year statutory maxima (based on a $500 threshold) for the first offense, and NAGPRA has a one year maximum for the first violation, irrespective of the amount of harm caused by the offender's conduct. In contrast, general property crime statutes, such as Theft and Destruction of Government Property at 18 U.S.C. §§ 641 and 1361, do not have a statutory cap based on whether the offense was the defendant's first violation of the particular statute.

The second disparity is that both ARPA and NAGPRA, together with the federal law prohibiting theft from tribal organizations, have five year statutory ceiling, whereas the theft and destruction of government property statutes have ten year limits. The third disparity is that even statutes specifically protecting cultural heritage resources have different statutory maxima. Thus while the ARPA and NAGPRA statutory maxima are both five years, the 1994 federal law proscribing museum theft at 18 U.S.C. § 668 has a ten year statutory maximum, similar to the general property crimes.

The Commission suggests eliminating these caps in ARPA and NAGPRA for first violations and raising the statutory maximum for ARPA, NAGPRA, and Theft from Tribal Organizations to ten years. This change will not only achieve consistency with other federal property crimes but will also eliminate potential obstacles to the proportional punishment of cultural heritage resource crimes and allow for the full implementation of the sentencing guideline structure that the Commission has determined is appropriate for such crimes.

A few illustrations may suffice to underscore the problem. A looter in the Civil War Battlefield at Manassas has violated the Archaeological Resources Protection Act (ARPA) by disturbing human remains while collecting $10,000 worth of buttons, belt buckles, and rifle shells to sell at an antique show, causing $30,000 in damage to the battlefield's terrain. Under the Commission's new guideline, this defendant qualifies for a sentence of between 27 and 33 months (without chapter three adjustments) based on the magnitude of the harm as measured by the aggravating factors that the Commission has delineated. This offender's possible sentence would be twenty-four months under the statutory maximum if it were his first ARPA conviction.

Similarly, a defendant who violates NAGPRA by stealing and attempting to sell Native American ceremonial masks and skulls unearthed from a burial site on tribal lands that have a commercial value on the black market of $150,000, and who threatens the use of a firearm when apprehended by law enforcement agents, qualifies for a sentence under the new guideline of 51 to 63 months. Nonetheless, if it is the defendant's first NAGPRA conviction, his sentence is capped at 12 months. Even if prosecuted and convicted under 18 U.S.C. § 1163 (Theft from Tribal Organizations), its five year statutory maximum comes into play and prevents the sentencing judge both from applying the high end of the guideline range, if appropriate, and from adjusting upwards to account for the defendant's prior criminal history.

In the actual case of a sophisticated and notorious professional looter of ancient Anasazi archaeological sites who operated for over a decade in remote federal lands, both in national parks and national forests, the seventy-eight month sentence calculated in 1997 under §2B1.1 United States v. Shumway, 112 F.3d 1413 (10th Cir. 1997), could double to between 135 and 168 months under the new guideline at §2B1.5. Such a defendant, if convicted only of an ARPA violation, will not serve this appropriately severe penalty reflecting the magnitude of harm because of ARPA's five-year statutory maximum. Such an egregious violator would not even serve his full guideline sentence under the ten year statutory maximum for a single count of damage to government property (18 U.S.C. § 641). Raising ARPA's statutory maximum to correspond to other federal crime statutes would not constrain the operation of the new sentencing guideline which the Commission has promulgated.

The Commission has taken an important step to ensure that damage to our nation's cultural heritage resources is appropriately punished, for example, by requiring that the use of a destructive device to accomplish such a crime receive more severe punishment and providing enhanced punishment for other aggravating factors in the offender's conduct. This goal cannot be completely achieved, however, if the statutory ceiling for these offenses is too low to permit a full application of the guideline criteria for fair and proportionate punishment. For other general property crimes, such as interstate computer or car theft, the statutory maximum does not generally restrict the application of the sentencing guidelines.

I respectfully urge the Congress to consider the changes we have recommended and will be pleased to provide you or your staff with additional information that may assist you in your consideration.

Sincerely,

Judge Diana E. Murphy, Chair

enc.

cc: Commissioners
Timothy McGrath, Staff Director
Kenneth Cohen, Director, Office of Legislative Affairs

B4. NATIVE AMERICAN GRAVES PROTECTION AND REPATRIATION ACT, 1990, PUBLIC LAW 101-601

H.R.5237

One Hundred First Congress of the United States of America
AT THE SECOND SESSION

Begun and held at the City of Washington on Tuesday, the twenty-third day of January, one thousand nine hundred and ninety

An Act

To provide for the protection of Native American graves, and for other purposes.

Be it enacted by the Senate and House of Representatives of the United States of America in Congress assembled,

SECTION 1. SHORT TITLE.

This Act may be cited as the `Native American Graves Protection and Repatriation Act'.

SEC. 2. DEFINITIONS.

For purposes of this Act, the term--

(1) 'burial site' means any natural or prepared physical location, whether originally below, on, or above the surface of the earth, into which as a part of the death rite or ceremony of a culture, individual human remains are deposited.

(2) 'cultural affiliation' means that there is a relationship of shared group identity which can be reasonably traced historically or pre-historically between a present day Indian tribe or Native Hawaiian organization and an identifiable earlier group.

(3) 'cultural items' means human remains and--

(A) 'associated funerary objects' which shall mean objects that, as a part of the death rite or ceremony of a culture, are reasonably believed to have been placed with individual human remains either at the time of death or later, and both the human remains and associated funerary objects are presently in the possession or control of a Federal agency or museum, except that other items exclusively made for burial purposes or to contain human remains shall be considered as associated funerary objects.

(B) 'unassociated funerary objects' which shall mean objects that, as a part of the death rite or ceremony of a culture, are reasonably believed to have been placed with individual human remains either at the time of death or later, where the remains are not in the possession or control of the Federal agency or museum and the objects can be identified by a preponderance of the evidence as related to specific individuals or families or to known human remains or, by a preponderance of the evidence, as having been removed from a specific burial site of an individual culturally affiliated with a particular Indian tribe,

(C) 'sacred objects' which shall mean specific ceremonial objects which are needed by traditional Native American religious leaders for the practice of traditional Native American religions by their present day adherents, and

(D) 'cultural patrimony' which shall mean an object having ongoing historical, traditional, or cultural importance central to the Native American group or culture itself, rather than property owned by an individual Native American, and which, therefore, cannot be alienated, appropriated, or conveyed by any individual regardless of whether or not the individual is a member of the Indian tribe or Native Hawaiian organization and such object shall have been considered inalienable by such Native American group at the time the object was separated from such group.

(4) 'Federal agency' means any department, agency, or instrumentality of the United States. Such term does not include the Smithsonian Institution.

(5) 'Federal lands' means any land other than tribal lands which are controlled or owned by the United States, including lands selected

by but not yet conveyed to Alaska Native Corporations and groups organized pursuant to the Alaska Native Claims Settlement Act of 1971.

(6) 'Hui Malama I Na Kupuna O Hawai'i Nei' means the nonprofit, Native Hawaiian organization incorporated under the laws of the State of Hawaii by that name on April 17, 1989, for the purpose of providing guidance and expertise in decisions dealing with Native Hawaiian cultural issues, particularly burial issues.

(7) 'Indian tribe' means any tribe, band, nation, or other organized group or community of Indians, including any Alaska Native village (as defined in, or established pursuant to, the Alaska Native Claims Settlement Act), which is recognized as eligible for the special programs and services provided by the United States to Indians because of their status as Indians.

(8) 'museum' means any institution or State or local government agency (including any institution of higher learning) that receives Federal funds and has possession of, or control over, Native American cultural items. Such term does not include the Smithsonian Institution or any other Federal agency.

(9) 'Native American' means of, or relating to, a tribe, people, or culture that is indigenous to the United States.

(10) 'Native Hawaiian' means any individual who is a descendant of the aboriginal people who, prior to 1778, occupied and exercised sovereignty in the area that now constitutes the State of Hawaii.

(11) 'Native Hawaiian organization' means any organization which--
    (A) serves and represents the interests of Native Hawaiians,
    (B) has as a primary and stated purpose the provision of services to Native Hawaiians, and
    (C) has expertise in Native Hawaiian Affairs, and
shall include the Office of Hawaiian Affairs and Hui Malama I Na Kupuna O Hawai'i Nei.

(12) 'Office of Hawaiian Affairs' means the Office of Hawaiian Affairs established by the constitution of the State of Hawaii.

(13) 'right of possession' means possession obtained with the voluntary consent of an individual or group that had authority of alienation. The original acquisition of a Native American unassociated funerary object, sacred object or object of cultural patrimony from an Indian tribe or Native Hawaiian organization with the voluntary consent of an individual or group with authority to alienate such object is deemed to give right of possession of that object, unless the phrase so defined would, as applied in section 7(c), result in a Fifth Amendment taking by the United States as determined by the United States Claims Court pursuant to 28 U.S.C. 1491 in which event the 'right of possession' shall be as provided under otherwise applicable property law. The original acquisition of Native American human remains and associated funerary objects which were excavated, exhumed, or otherwise obtained with full knowledge and consent of the next of kin or the official governing body of the appropriate culturally affiliated Indian tribe or Native Hawaiian organization is deemed to give right of possession to those remains.

(14) 'Secretary' means the Secretary of the Interior.

(15) 'tribal land' means--
(A) all lands within the exterior boundaries of any Indian reservation;
(B) all dependent Indian communities;
(C) any lands administered for the benefit of Native Hawaiians pursuant to the Hawaiian Homes Commission Act, 1920, and section 4 of Public Law 86-3.

SEC. 3. OWNERSHIP.
(a) NATIVE AMERICAN HUMAN REMAINS AND OBJECTS- The ownership or control of Native American cultural items which are excavated or discovered on Federal or tribal lands after the date of enactment of this Act shall be (with priority given in the order listed)--

(1) in the case of Native American human remains and associated funerary objects, in the lineal descendants of the Native American; or

(2) in any case in which such lineal descendants cannot be ascertained, and in the case of unassociated funerary objects, sacred objects, and objects of cultural patrimony--

> (A) in the Indian tribe or Native Hawaiian organization on whose tribal land such objects or remains were discovered;
> (B) in the Indian tribe or Native Hawaiian organization which has the closest cultural affiliation with such remains or objects and which, upon notice, states a claim for such remains or objects; or
> (C) if the cultural affiliation of the objects cannot be reasonably ascertained and if the objects were discovered on Federal land that is recognized by a final judgment of the Indian Claims Commission or the United States Court of Claims as the aboriginal land of some Indian tribe-
>> (1) in the Indian tribe that is recognized as aboriginally occupying the area in which the objects were discovered, if upon notice, such tribe states a claim for such remains or objects, or
>> (2) if it can be shown by a preponderance of the evidence that a different tribe has a stronger cultural relationship with the remains or objects than the tribe or organization specified in paragraph (1), in the Indian tribe that has the strongest demonstrated relationship, if upon notice, such tribe states a claim for such remains or objects.

(b) UNCLAIMED NATIVE AMERICAN HUMAN REMAINS AND OBJECTS- Native American cultural items not claimed under subsection (a) shall be disposed of in accordance with regulations promulgated by the Secretary in consultation with the review committee established under section 8, Native American groups, representatives of museums and the scientific community.

(c) INTENTIONAL EXCAVATION AND REMOVAL OF NATIVE AMER-
ICAN HUMAN REMAINS AND OBJECTS- The intentional removal
from or excavation of Native American cultural items from Federal or
tribal lands for purposes of discovery, study, or removal of such items is
permitted only if--

(1) such items are excavated or removed pursuant to a permit issued
under section 4 of the Archaeological Resources Protection Act of
1979 (93 Stat. 721; 16 U.S.C. 470aa et seq.) which shall be consistent with this Act;

(2) such items are excavated or removed after consultation with or,
in the case of tribal lands, consent of the appropriate (if any) Indian
tribe or Native Hawaiian organization;

(3) the ownership and right of control of the disposition of such
items shall be as provided in subsections (a) and (b); and
(4) proof of consultation or consent under paragraph (2) is shown.

(d) INADVERTENT DISCOVERY OF NATIVE AMERICAN REMAINS
AND OBJECTS-
(1) Any person who knows, or has reason to know, that such person
has discovered Native American cultural items on Federal or tribal
lands after the date of enactment of this Act shall notify, in writing, the
Secretary of the Department, or head of any other agency or instrumentality of the United States, having primary management authority
with respect to Federal lands and the appropriate Indian tribe or Native
Hawaiian organization with respect to tribal lands, if known or readily
ascertainable, and, in the case of lands that have been selected by an
Alaska Native Corporation or group organized pursuant to the Alaska
Native Claims Settlement Act of 1971, the appropriate corporation or
group. If the discovery occurred in connection with an activity, including (but not limited to) construction, mining, logging, and agriculture,
the person shall cease the activity in the area of the discovery, make a
reasonable effort to protect the items discovered before resuming such
activity, and provide notice under this subsection. Following the notification under this subsection, and upon certification by the Secretary

of the department or the head of any agency or instrumentality of the United States or the appropriate Indian tribe or Native Hawaiian organization that notification has been received, the activity may resume after 30 days of such certification.

(2) The disposition of and control over any cultural items excavated or removed under this subsection shall be determined as provided for in this section.

(3) If the Secretary of the Interior consents, the responsibilities (in whole or in part) under paragraphs (1) and (2) of the Secretary of any department (other than the Department of the Interior) or the head of any other agency or instrumentality may be delegated to the Secretary with respect to any land managed by such other Secretary or agency head.

(e) RELINQUISHMENT- Nothing in this section shall prevent the governing body of an Indian tribe or Native Hawaiian organization from expressly relinquishing control over any Native American human remains, or title to or control over any funerary object, or sacred object.

SEC. 4. ILLEGAL TRAFFICKING.

(a) ILLEGAL TRAFFICKING- Chapter 53 of title 18, United States Code, is amended by adding at the end thereof the following new section:

Sec. 1170. Illegal Trafficking in Native American Human Remains and Cultural Items

(a) Whoever knowingly sells, purchases, uses for profit, or transports for sale or profit, the human remains of a Native American without the right of possession to those remains as provided in the Native American Graves Protection and Repatriation Act shall be fined in accordance with this title, or imprisoned not more than 12 months, or both, and in the case of a second or subsequent violation, be fined in accordance with this title, or imprisoned not more than 5 years, or both.

(b) Whoever knowingly sells, purchases, uses for profit, or transports for sale or profit any Native American cultural items obtained in violation of the Native American Grave Protection and Repatriation Act shall be fined in accordance with this title, imprisoned not more than one year, or both, and in the case of a second or subsequent violation, be fined in accordance with this title, imprisoned not more than 5 years, or both.'.

(b) TABLE OF CONTENTS- The table of contents for chapter 53 of title 18, United States Code, is amended by adding at the end thereof the following new item:

1170. Illegal Trafficking in Native American Human Remains and Cultural Items.'.

SEC. 5. INVENTORY FOR HUMAN REMAINS AND ASSOCIATED FUNERARY OBJECTS.

(a) IN GENERAL- Each Federal agency and each museum which has possession or control over holdings or collections of Native American human remains and associated funerary objects shall compile an inventory of such items and, to the extent possible based on information possessed by such museum or Federal agency, identify the geographical and cultural affiliation of such item.

(b) REQUIREMENTS- (1) The inventories and identifications required under subsection (a) shall be--

(A) completed in consultation with tribal government and Native Hawaiian organization officials and traditional religious leaders;

(B) completed by not later than the date that is 5 years after the date of enactment of this Act, and

(C) made available both during the time they are being conducted and afterward to a review committee established under section 8.

(2) Upon request by an Indian tribe or Native Hawaiian organization which receives or should have received notice, a museum or Federal agency shall supply additional available documentation to supplement the information required by subsection (a) of this section. The term 'documentation' means a summary of existing museum or Federal agency records, including inventories or catalogues, relevant studies, or other pertinent data for the limited purpose of determining the geographical origin, cultural affiliation, and basic facts surrounding acquisition and

accession of Native American human remains and associated funerary objects subject to this section. Such term does not mean, and this Act shall not be construed to be an authorization for, the initiation of new scientific studies of such remains and associated funerary objects or other means of acquiring or preserving additional scientific information from such remains and objects.

(c) EXTENSION OF TIME FOR INVENTORY- Any museum which has made a good faith effort to carry out an inventory and identification under this section, but which has been unable to complete the process, may appeal to the Secretary for an extension of the time requirements set forth in subsection (b)(1)(B). The Secretary may extend such time requirements for any such museum upon a finding of good faith effort. An indication of good faith shall include the development of a plan to carry out the inventory and identification process.

(d) NOTIFICATION- (1) If the cultural affiliation of any particular Native American human remains or associated funerary objects is determined pursuant to this section, the Federal agency or museum concerned shall, not later than 6 months after the completion of the inventory, notify the affected Indian tribes or Native Hawaiian organizations.

(2) The notice required by paragraph (1) shall include information--
(A) which identifies each Native American human remains or associated funerary objects and the circumstances surrounding its acquisition;
(B) which lists the human remains or associated funerary objects that are clearly identifiable as to tribal origin; and
(C) which lists the Native American human remains and associated funerary objects that are not clearly identifiable as being culturally affiliated with that Indian tribe or Native Hawaiian organization, but which, given the totality of circumstances surrounding acquisition of the remains or objects, are determined by a reasonable belief to be remains or objects culturally affiliated with the Indian tribe or Native Hawaiian organization.

(3) A copy of each notice provided under paragraph (1) shall be sent to the Secretary who shall publish each notice in the Federal Register.

(e) INVENTORY- For the purposes of this section, the term `inventory' means a simple itemized list that summarizes the information called for by this section.

SEC. 6. SUMMARY FOR UNASSOCIATED FUNERARY OBJECTS, SACRED OBJECTS, AND CULTURAL PATRIMONY.

(a) IN GENERAL- Each Federal agency or museum which has possession or control over holdings or collections of Native American unassociated funerary objects, sacred objects, or objects of cultural patrimony shall provide a written summary of such objects based upon available information held by such agency or museum. The summary shall describe the scope of the collection, kinds of objects included, reference to geographical location, means and period of acquisition and cultural affiliation, where readily ascertainable.

(b) REQUIREMENTS- (1) The summary required under subsection (a) shall be--

(A) in lieu of an object-by-object inventory;
(B) followed by consultation with tribal government and Native Hawaiian organization officials and traditional religious leaders; and
(C) completed by not later than the date that is 3 years after the date of enactment of this Act.

(2) Upon request, Indian Tribes and Native Hawaiian organizations shall have access to records, catalogues, relevant studies or other pertinent data for the limited purposes of determining the geographic origin, cultural affiliation, and basic facts surrounding acquisition and accession of Native American objects subject to this section. Such information shall be provided in a reasonable manner to be agreed upon by all parties.

SEC. 7. REPATRIATION.

(a) REPATRIATION OF NATIVE AMERICAN HUMAN REMAINS AND OBJECTS POSSESSED OR CONTROLLED BY FEDERAL AGENCIES

AND MUSEUMS- (1) If, pursuant to section 5, the cultural affiliation of Native American human remains and associated funerary objects with a particular Indian tribe or Native Hawaiian organization is established, then the Federal agency or museum, upon the request of a known lineal descendant of the Native American or of the tribe or organization and pursuant to subsections (b) and (e) of this section, shall expeditiously return such remains and associated funerary objects.

(2) If, pursuant to section 6, the cultural affiliation with a particular Indian tribe or Native Hawaiian organization is shown with respect to unassociated funerary objects, sacred objects or objects of cultural patrimony, then the Federal agency or museum, upon the request of the Indian tribe or Native Hawaiian organization and pursuant to subsections (b), (c) and (e) of this section, shall expeditiously return such objects.

(3) The return of cultural items covered by this Act shall be in consultation with the requesting lineal descendant or tribe or organization to determine the place and manner of delivery of such items.

(4) Where cultural affiliation of Native American human remains and funerary objects has not been established in an inventory prepared pursuant to section 5, or the summary pursuant to section 6, or where Native American human remains and funerary objects are not included upon any such inventory, then, upon request and pursuant to subsections (b) and (e) and, in the case of unassociated funerary objects, subsection (c), such Native American human remains and funerary objects shall be expeditiously returned where the requesting Indian tribe or Native Hawaiian organization can show cultural affiliation by a preponderance of the evidence based upon geographical, kinship, biological, archaeological, anthropological, linguistic, folkloric, oral traditional, historical, or other relevant information or expert opinion.

(5) Upon request and pursuant to subsections (b), (c) and (e), sacred objects and objects of cultural patrimony shall be expeditiously returned where--

(A) the requesting party is the direct lineal descendant of an individual who owned the sacred object;

(B) the requesting Indian tribe or Native Hawaiian organization can show that the object was owned or controlled by the tribe or organization; or

(C) the requesting Indian tribe or Native Hawaiian organization can show that the sacred object was owned or controlled by a member thereof, provided that in the case where a sacred object was owned by a member thereof, there are no identifiable lineal descendants of said member or the lineal descendants, upon notice, have failed to make a claim for the object under this Act.

(b) SCIENTIFIC STUDY- If the lineal descendant, Indian tribe, or Native Hawaiian organization requests the return of culturally affiliated Native American cultural items, the Federal agency or museum shall expeditiously return such items unless such items are indispensable for completion of a specific scientific study, the outcome of which would be of major benefit to the United States. Such items shall be returned by no later than 90 days after the date on which the scientific study is completed.

(c) STANDARD OF REPATRIATION- If a known lineal descendant or an Indian tribe or Native Hawaiian organization requests the return of Native American unassociated funerary objects, sacred objects or objects of cultural patrimony pursuant to this Act and presents evidence which, if standing alone before the introduction of evidence to the contrary, would support a finding that the Federal agency or museum did not have the right of possession, then such agency or museum shall return such objects unless it can overcome such inference and prove that it has a right of possession to the objects.

(d) SHARING OF INFORMATION BY FEDERAL AGENCIES AND MUSEUMS- Any Federal agency or museum shall share what information it does possess regarding the object in question with the known lineal descendant, Indian tribe, or Native Hawaiian organization to assist in making a claim under this section.

(e) COMPETING CLAIMS- Where there are multiple requests for repatriation of any cultural item and, after complying with the requirements of this Act, the Federal agency or museum cannot clearly determine which requesting party is the most appropriate claimant, the agency or museum may retain such item until the requesting parties agree upon its disposition or the dispute is otherwise resolved pursuant to the provisions of this Act or by a court of competent jurisdiction.

(f) MUSEUM OBLIGATION- Any museum which repatriates any item in good faith pursuant to this Act shall not be liable for claims by an aggrieved party or for claims of breach of fiduciary duty, public trust, or violations of state law that are inconsistent with the provisions of this Act.

SEC. 8. REVIEW COMMITTEE.

(a) ESTABLISHMENT- Within 120 days after the date of enactment of this Act, the Secretary shall establish a committee to monitor and review the implementation of the inventory and identification process and repatriation activities required under sections 5, 6 and 7.

(b) MEMBERSHIP- (1) The Committee established under subsection (a) shall be composed of 7 members,

(A) 3 of whom shall be appointed by the Secretary from nominations submitted by Indian tribes, Native Hawaiian organizations, and traditional Native American religious leaders with at least 2 of such persons being traditional Indian religious leaders;

(B) 3 of whom shall be appointed by the Secretary from nominations submitted by national museum organizations and scientific organizations; and

(C) 1 who shall be appointed by the Secretary from a list of persons developed and consented to by all of the members appointed pursuant to subparagraphs (A) and (B).

(2) The Secretary may not appoint Federal officers or employees to the committee.

(3) In the event vacancies shall occur, such vacancies shall be filled by the Secretary in the same manner as the original appointment within 90 days of the occurrence of such vacancy.

(4) Members of the committee established under subsection (a) shall serve without pay, but shall be reimbursed at a rate equal to the daily rate for GS-18 of the General Schedule for each day (including travel time) for which the member is actually engaged in committee business. Each member shall receive travel expenses, including per diem in lieu of subsistence, in accordance with sections 5702 and 5703 of title 5, United States Code.

(c) RESPONSIBILITIES- The committee established under subsection (a) shall be responsible for--

(1) designating one of the members of the committee as chairman;

(2) monitoring the inventory and identification process conducted under sections 5 and 6 to ensure a fair, objective consideration and assessment of all available relevant information and evidence;

(3) upon the request of any affected party, reviewing and making findings related to--
    (A) the identity or cultural affiliation of cultural items, or
    (B) the return of such items;

(4) facilitating the resolution of any disputes among Indian tribes, Native Hawaiian organizations, or lineal descendants and Federal agencies or museums relating to the return of such items including convening the parties to the dispute if deemed desirable;

(5) compiling an inventory of culturally unidentifiable human remains that are in the possession or control of each Federal agency and museum and recommending specific actions for developing a process for disposition of such remains;

(6) consulting with Indian tribes and Native Hawaiian organizations and museums on matters within the scope of the work of the committee affecting such tribes or organizations;

(7) consulting with the Secretary in the development of regulations to carry out this Act;

(8) performing such other related functions as the Secretary may assign to the committee; and

(9) making recommendations, if appropriate, regarding future care of cultural items which are to be repatriated.

(d) Any records and findings made by the review committee pursuant to this Act relating to the identity or cultural affiliation of any cultural items and the return of such items may be admissible in any action brought under section 15 of this Act.

(e) RECOMMENDATIONS AND REPORT- The committee shall make the recommendations under paragraph (c)(5) in consultation with Indian tribes and Native Hawaiian organizations and appropriate scientific and museum groups.

(f) ACCESS- The Secretary shall ensure that the committee established under subsection (a) and the members of the committee have reasonable access to Native American cultural items under review and to associated scientific and historical documents.

(g) DUTIES OF SECRETARY- The Secretary shall--
(1) establish such rules and regulations for the committee as may be necessary, and
(2) provide reasonable administrative and staff support necessary for the deliberations of the committee.

(h) ANNUAL REPORT- The committee established under subsection (a) shall submit an annual report to the Congress on the progress made, and any barriers encountered, in implementing this section during the previous year.

(i) TERMINATION- The committee established under subsection (a) shall terminate at the end of the 120-day period beginning on the day the Secretary certifies, in a report submitted to Congress, that the work of the committee has been completed.

SEC. 9. PENALTY.

(a) PENALTY- Any museum that fails to comply with the requirements of this Act may be assessed a civil penalty by the Secretary of the Interior pursuant to procedures established by the Secretary through regulation. A penalty assessed under this subsection shall be determined on the record after opportunity for an agency hearing. Each violation under this subsection shall be a separate offense.

(b) AMOUNT OF PENALTY- The amount of a penalty assessed under subsection (a) shall be determined under regulations promulgated pursuant to this Act, taking into account, in addition to other factors--
  (1) the archaeological, historical, or commercial value of the item involved;
  (2) the damages suffered, both economic and noneconomic, by an aggrieved party, and
  (3) the number of violations that have occurred.

(c) ACTIONS TO RECOVER PENALTIES- If any museum fails to pay an assessment of a civil penalty pursuant to a final order of the Secretary that has been issued under subsection (a) and not appealed or after a final judgment has been rendered on appeal of such order, the Attorney General may institute a civil action in an appropriate district court of the United States to collect the penalty. In such action, the validity and amount of such penalty shall not be subject to review.

(d) SUBPOENAS- In hearings held pursuant to subsection (a), subpoenas may be issued for the attendance and testimony of witnesses and the production of relevant papers, books, and documents. Witnesses so summoned shall be paid the same fees and mileage that are paid to witnesses in the courts of the United States.

SEC. 10. GRANTS.

(a) INDIAN TRIBES AND NATIVE HAWAIIAN ORGANIZATIONS- The Secretary is authorized to make grants to Indian tribes and Native Hawaiian organizations for the purpose of assisting such tribes and organizations in the repatriation of Native American cultural items.

(b) MUSEUMS- The Secretary is authorized to make grants to museums for the purpose of assisting the museums in conducting the inventories and identification required under sections 5 and 6.

SEC. 11. SAVINGS PROVISIONS.

Nothing in this Act shall be construed to--

(1) limit the authority of any Federal agency or museum to--

(A) return or repatriate Native American cultural items to Indian tribes, Native Hawaiian organizations, or individuals, and

(B) enter into any other agreement with the consent of the culturally affiliated tribe or organization as to the disposition of, or control over, items covered by this Act;

(2) delay actions on repatriation requests that are pending on the date of enactment of this Act;

(3) deny or otherwise affect access to any court;

(4) limit any procedural or substantive right which may otherwise be secured to individuals or Indian tribes or Native Hawaiian organizations; or

(5) limit the application of any State or Federal law pertaining to theft or stolen property.

SEC. 12. SPECIAL RELATIONSHIP BETWEEN FEDERAL GOVERNMENT AND INDIAN TRIBES.

This Act reflects the unique relationship between the Federal Government and Indian tribes and Native Hawaiian organizations and should not be construed to establish a precedent with respect to any other individual, organization or foreign government.

SEC. 13. REGULATIONS.

The Secretary shall promulgate regulations to carry out this Act within 12 months of enactment.

SEC. 14. AUTHORIZATION OF APPROPRIATIONS.

There is authorized to be appropriated such sums as may be necessary to carry out this Act.

SEC. 15. ENFORCEMENT.

The United States district courts shall have jurisdiction over any action brought by any person alleging a violation of this Act and shall have the authority to issue such orders as may be necessary to enforce the provisions of this Act.

Speaker of the House of Representatives.

Vice President of the United States and

President of the Senate.

B5. CONVENTION ON CULTURAL PROPERTY IMPLEMENTATION ACT, 19 U.S.C. §§2601-13 (1983)

Definitions: 19 U.S.C. § 2601

For purposes of this chapter--

(1) The term "agreement" includes any amendment to, or extension of, any agreement under this chapter that enters into force with respect to the United States.

(2) The term "archaeological or ethnological material of the State Party" means--

(A) any object of archaeological interest;

(B) any object of ethnological interest; or

(C) any fragment or part of any object referred to in subparagraph (A) or (B);

which was first discovered within, and is subject to export control by, the State Party. For purposes of this paragraph--

(i) no object may be considered to be an object of archaeological interest unless such object--

(I) is of cultural significance;

(II) is at least two hundred and fifty years old; and

(III) was normally discovered as a result of scientific excavation, clandestine or accidental digging, or exploration on land or under water; and

(ii) no object may be considered to be an object of ethnological interest unless such object is--

(I) the product of a tribal or nonindustrial society, and

(II) important to the cultural heritage of a people because of its distinctive characteristics, comparative rarity, or its contribution to the knowledge of the origins, development, or history of that people.

(3) The term "Committee" means the Cultural Property Advisory Committee established under section 2605 of this title.

(4) The term "consignee" means a consignee as defined in section 1483 of this title.

(5) The term "Convention" means the Convention on the means of prohibiting and preventing the illicit import, export, and transfer of ownership of cultural property adopted by the General Conference of the United Nations Educational, Scientific, and Cultural Organization at its sixteenth session.

(6) The term "cultural property" includes articles described in article 1(a) through (k) of the Convention whether or not any such article is specifically designated as such by any State Party for the purposes of such article.

(7) The term "designated archaeological or ethnological material" means any archaeological or ethnological material of the State Party which--
    (A) is--
        (i) covered by an agreement under this chapter that enters into force with respect to the United States, or
        (ii) subject to emergency action under section 2603 of this title, and
    (B) is listed by regulation under section 2604 of this title.

(8) The term "Secretary" means the Secretary of the Treasury or his delegate.

(9) The term "State Party" means any nation which has ratified, accepted, or acceded to the Convention.

(10) The term "United States" includes the several States, the District of Columbia, and any territory or area the foreign relations for which the United States is responsible.

(11) The term "United States citizen" means--
    (A) any individual who is a citizen or national of the United States;
    (B) any corporation, partnership, association, or other legal entity organized or existing under the laws of the United States or any State; or
    (C) any department, agency, or entity of the Federal Government or of any government of any State.

Agreements to Implement Article 9 of the UNESCO Convention: 19 U.S.C. § 2602

(a) Agreement authority

(1) In general
If the President determines, after request is made to the United States under article 9 of the Convention by any State Party--

> (A) that the cultural patrimony of the State Party is in jeopardy from the pillage of archaeological or ethnological materials of the State Party;
> (B) that the State Party has taken measures consistent with the Convention to protect its cultural patrimony;
> (C) that--
>> (i) the application of the import restrictions set forth in section 2606 of this title with respect to archaeological or ethnological material of the State Party, if applied in concert with similar restrictions implemented, or to be implemented within a reasonable period of time, by those nations (whether or not State Parties) individually having a significant import trade in such material, would be of substantial benefit in deterring a serious situation of pillage, and
>> (ii) remedies less drastic than the application of the restrictions set forth in such section are not available; and
> (D) that the application of the import restrictions set forth in section 2606 of this title in the particular circumstances is consistent with the general interest of the international community in the interchange of cultural property among nations for scientific, cultural, and educational purposes; the President may, subject to the provisions of this chapter, take the actions described in paragraph (2).

(2) Authority of President
For purposes of paragraph (1), the President may enter into--

> (A) a bilateral agreement with the State Party to apply the import restrictions set forth in section 2606 of this title to the archaeological or ethnological material of the State Party the pillage of which is creating the jeopardy to the cultural patrimony of the State Party found to exist under paragraph (1) (A); or

(B) a multilateral agreement with the State Party and with one or more other nations (whether or not a State Party) under which the United States will apply such restrictions, and the other nations will apply similar restrictions, with respect to such material.

(3) Requests

A request made to the United States under article 9 of the Convention by a State Party must be accompanied by a written statement of the facts known to the State Party that relate to those matters with respect to which determinations must be made under subparagraphs (A) through (D) of paragraph (1).

(4) Implementation

In implementing this subsection, the President should endeavor to obtain the commitment of the State Party concerned to permit the exchange of its archaeological and ethnological materials under circumstances in which such exchange does not jeopardize its cultural patrimony.

(b) Effective period

The President may not enter into any agreement under subsection (a) of this section which has an effective period beyond the close of the five-year period beginning on the date on which such agreement enters into force with respect to the United States.

(c) Restrictions on entering into agreements

(1) In general

The President may not enter into a bilateral or multilateral agreement authorized by subsection (a) of this section unless the application of the import restrictions set forth in section 2606 of this title with respect to archaeological or ethnological material of the State Party making a request to the United States under article 9 of the Convention will be applied in concert with similar restrictions implemented, or to be implemented, by those nations (whether or not State Parties) individually having a significant import trade in such material.

(2) Exception to restrictions

Notwithstanding paragraph (1), the President may enter into an agreement if he determines that a nation individually having a significant import trade in such material is not implementing, or is not likely to implement, similar restrictions, but--

(A) such restrictions are not essential to deter a serious situation of pillage, and

(B) the application of the import restrictions set forth in section 2606 of this title in concert with similar restrictions implemented, or to be implemented, by other nations (whether or not State Parties) individually having a significant import trade in such material would be of substantial benefit in deterring a serious situation of pillage.

(d) Suspension of import restrictions under agreements

If, after an agreement enters into force with respect to the United States, the President determines that a number of parties to the agreement (other than parties described in subsection (c) (2) of this section) having significant import trade in the archaeological and ethnological material covered by the agreement--

(1) have not implemented within a reasonable period of time import restrictions that are similar to those set forth in section 2606 of this title, or

(2) are not implementing such restrictions satisfactorily with the result that no substantial benefit in deterring a serious situation of pillage in the State Party concerned is being obtained, the President shall suspend the implementation of the import restrictions under section 2606 of this title until such time as the nations take appropriate corrective action.

(e) Extension of agreements

The President may extend any agreement that enters into force with respect to the United States for additional periods of not more than five years each if the President determines that--

(1) the factors referred to in subsection (a) (1) of this section which justified the entering into of the agreement still pertain, and

(2) no cause for suspension under subsection (d) of this section exists.

(f) Procedures

If any request described in subsection (a) of this section is made by a State Party, or if the President proposes to extend any agreement under subsection (e) of this section, the President shall--

(1) publish notification of the request or proposal in the Federal Register;

(2) submit to the Committee such information regarding the request or proposal (including, if applicable, information from the State Party with respect to the implementation of emergency action under section 2603 of this title) as is appropriate to enable the Committee to carry out its duties under section 2605(f) of this title; and

(3) consider, in taking action on the request or proposal, the views and recommendations contained in any Committee report--
    (A) required under section 2605(f) (1) or (2) of this title, and
    (B) submitted to the President before the close of the one-hundred-and-fifty-day period beginning on the day on which the President submitted information on the request or proposal to the Committee under paragraph (2).

(g) Information on Presidential action

(1) In general

In any case in which the President--
    (A) enters into or extends an agreement pursuant to subsection (a) or (e) of this section, or
    (B) applies import restrictions under section 2603 of this title, the President shall, promptly after taking such action, submit a report to the Congress.

(2) Report

The report under paragraph (1) shall contain--
    (A) a description of such action (including the text of any agreement entered into),
    (B) the differences (if any) between such action and the views and recommendations contained in any Committee report which the President was required to consider, and

(C) the reasons for any such difference.

(3) Information relating to Committee recommendations

If any Committee report required to be considered by the President recommends that an agreement be entered into, but no such agreement is entered into, the President shall submit to the Congress a report which contains the reasons why such agreement was not entered into.

Emergency Implementation of Import Restrictions: 19 U.S.C. § 2603

(a) Emergency condition defined

For purposes of this section, the term "emergency condition" means, with respect to any archaeological or ethnological material of any State Party, that such material is--

(1) a newly discovered type of material which is of importance for the understanding of the history of mankind and is in jeopardy from pillage, dismantling, dispersal, or fragmentation;

(2) identifiable as coming from any site recognized to be of high cultural significance if such site is in jeopardy from pillage, dismantling, dispersal, or fragmentation which is, or threatens to be, of crisis proportions; or

(3) a part of the remains of a particular culture or civilization, the record of which is in jeopardy from pillage, dismantling, dispersal, or fragmentation which is, or threatens to be, of crisis proportions; and application of the import restrictions set forth in section 2606 of this title on a temporary basis would, in whole or in part, reduce the incentive for such pillage, dismantling, dispersal or fragmentation.

(b) Presidential action

Subject to subsection (c) of this section, if the President determines that an emergency condition applies with respect to any archaeological or ethnological material of any State Party, the President may apply the import restrictions set forth in section 2606 of this title with respect to such material.

(c) Limitations

(1) The President may not implement this section with respect to the archaeological or ethnological materials of any State Party unless the State Party has made a request described in section 2602(a) of this title to the United States and has supplied information which supports a determination that an emergency condition exists.

(2) In taking action under subsection (b) of this section with respect to any State Party, the President shall consider the views and recommendations contained in the Committee report required under section 2605(f) (3) of this title if the report is submitted to the President before the close of the ninety-day period beginning on the day on which the President submitted information to the Committee under section 2602(f) (2) of this title on the request of the State Party under section 2602(a) of this title.

(3) No import restrictions set forth in section 2606 of this title may be applied under this section to the archaeological or ethnological materials of any State Party for more than five years after the date on which the request of a State Party under section 2602(a) of this title is made to the United States. This period may be extended by the President for three more years if the President determines that the emergency condition continues to apply with respect to the archaeological or ethnological material. However, before taking such action, the President shall request and consider, if received within ninety days, a report of the Committee setting forth its recommendations, together with the reasons therefor, as to whether such import restrictions shall be extended.

(4) The import restrictions under this section may continue to apply in whole or in part, if before their expiration under paragraph (3), there has entered into force with respect to the archaeological or ethnological materials an agreement under section 2602 of this title or an agreement with a State Party to which the Senate has given its advice and consent to ratification. Such import restrictions may continue to apply for the duration of the agreement.

Designation of Covered Materials: 19 U.S.C. § 2604
After any agreement enters into force under section 2602 of this title, or emergency action is taken under section 2603 of this title, the Secretary,

in consultation with the Secretary of State, shall by regulation promulgate (and when appropriate shall revise) a list of the archaeological or ethnological material of the State Party covered by the agreement or by such action. The Secretary may list such material by type or other appropriate classification, but each listing made under this section shall be sufficiently specific and precise to insure that (1) the import restrictions under section 2606 of this title are applied only to the archeological and ethnological material covered by the agreement or emergency action; and (2) fair notice is given to importers and other persons as to what material is subject to such restrictions.

Cultural Property Advisory Committee: 19 U.S.C. § 2605

(a) Establishment

There is established the Cultural Property Advisory Committee.

(b) Membership

(1) The Committee shall be composed of eleven members appointed by the President as follows:
    (A) Two members representing the interests of museums.
    (B) Three members who shall be experts in the fields of archaeology, anthropology, ethnology, or related areas.
    (C) Three members who shall be experts in the international sale of archaeological, ethnological, and other cultural property.
    (D) Three members who shall represent the interest of the general public.

(2) Appointments made under paragraph (1) shall be made in such a manner so as to insure--
    (A) fair representation of the various interests of the public sectors and the private sectors in the international exchange of archaeological and ethnological materials, and
    (B) that within such sectors, fair representation is accorded to the interests of regional and local institutions and museums.

(3)(A) Members of the Committee shall be appointed for terms of three years and may be reappointed for one or more terms. With respect to the initial appointments, the President shall select, on a representative basis to the maximum extent practicable, four members to serve three-year terms, four members to serve two-year terms, and the remaining members to serve a one-year term. Thereafter each appointment shall be for a three-year term.

(B)(i) A vacancy in the Committee shall be filled in the same manner as the original appointment was made and for the unexpired portion of the term, if the vacancy occurred during a term of office. Any member of the Committee may continue to serve as a member of the Committee after the expiration of his term of office until reappointed or until his successor has been appointed.

(ii) The President shall designate a Chairman of the Committee from the members of the Committee.

(c) Expenses

The members of the Committee shall be reimbursed for actual expenses incurred in the performance of duties for the Committee.

(d) Transaction of business

Six of the members of the Committee shall constitute a quorum. All decisions of the Committee shall be by majority vote of the members present and voting.

(e) Staff and administration

(1) The Director of the United States Information Agency shall make available to the Committee such administrative and technical support services and assistance as it may reasonably require to carry out its activities. Upon the request of the Committee, the head of any other Federal agency may detail to the Committee, on a reimbursable basis, any of the personnel of such agency to assist the Committee in carrying out its functions, and provide such information and assistance as the Committee may reasonably require to carry out its activities.

(2) The Committee shall meet at the call of the Director of the United States Information Agency, or when a majority of its members request a meeting in writing.

(f) Reports by Committee

(1) The Committee shall, with respect to each request of a State Party referred to in section 2602(a) of this title, undertake an investigation and review with respect to matters referred to in section 2602(a) (1) of this title as they relate to the State Party or the request and shall prepare a report setting forth--

(A) the results of such investigation and review;

(B) its findings as to the nations individually having a significant import trade in the relevant material; and

(C) its recommendation, together with the reasons therefor, as to whether an agreement should be entered into under section 2602(a) of this title with respect to the State Party.

(2) The Committee shall, with respect to each agreement proposed to be extended by the President under section 2602(e) of this title, prepare a report setting forth its recommendations together with the reasons therefor, as to whether or not the agreement should be extended.

(3) The Committee shall in each case in which the Committee finds that an emergency condition under section 2603 of this title exists prepare a report setting forth its recommendations, together with the reasons therefor, as to whether emergency action under section 2603 of this title should be implemented. If any State Party indicates in its request under section 2602(a) of this title that an emergency condition exists and the Committee finds that such a condition does not exist, the Committee shall prepare a report setting forth the reasons for such finding.

(4) Any report prepared by the Committee which recommends the entering into or the extension of any agreement under section 2602 of this title or the implementation of emergency action under section 2603 of this title shall set forth--

(A) such terms and conditions which it considers necessary and appropriate to include within such agreement, or apply with respect to such implementation, for purposes of carrying out the intent of the Convention; and

(B) such archaeological or ethnological material of the State Party, specified by type or such other classification as the Committee deems appropriate, which should be covered by such agreement or action.

(5) If any member of the Committee disagrees with respect to any matter in any report prepared under this subsection, such member may prepare a statement setting forth the reasons for such disagreement and such statement shall be appended to, and considered a part of, the report.

(6) The Committee shall submit to the Congress and the President a copy of each report prepared by it under this subsection.

(g) Committee review

(1) In general
The Committee shall undertake a continuing review of the effectiveness of agreements under section 2602 of this title that have entered into force with respect to the United States, and of emergency action implemented under section 2603 of this title.

(2) Action by Committee
If the Committee finds, as a result of such review, that--
    (A) cause exists for suspending, under section 2602(d) of this title, the import restrictions imposed under an agreement;
    (B) any agreement or emergency action is not achieving the purposes for which entered into or implemented; or
    (C) changes are required to this chapter in order to implement fully the obligations of the United States under the Convention; the Committee may submit a report to the Congress and the President setting forth its recommendations for suspending such import restrictions or for improving the effectiveness of any such agreement or emergency action or this chapter.

(h) Federal Advisory Committee Act
The provisions of the Federal Advisory Committee Act (Public Law 92-463; 5 U.S.C.A. Appendix I) shall apply to the Committee except that the requirements of subsections (a) and (b) of section 10 and section 11

of such Act (relating to open meetings, public notice, public participation, and public availability of documents) shall not apply to the Committee, whenever and to the extent it is determined by the President or his designee that the disclosure of matters involved in the Committee's proceedings would compromise the Government's negotiating objectives or bargaining positions on the negotiations of any agreement authorized by this chapter.

(i) Confidential information

(1) In general

Any information (including trade secrets and commercial or financial information which is privileged or confidential) submitted in confidence by the private sector to officers or employees of the United States or to the Committee in connection with the responsibilities of the Committee shall not be disclosed to any person other than to--

> (A) officers and employees of the United States designated by the Director of the United States Information Agency;
>
> (B) members of the Committee on Ways and Means of the House of Representatives and the Committee on Finance of the Senate who are designated by the chairman of either such Committee and members of the staff of either such Committee designated by the chairman for use in connection with negotiation of agreements or other activities authorized by this chapter; and
>
> (C) the Committee established under this chapter.

(2) Governmental information

Information submitted in confidence by officers or employees of the United States to the Committee shall not be disclosed other than in accordance with rules issued by the Director of the United States Information Agency, after consultation with the Committee. Such rules shall define the categories of information which require restricted or confidential handling by such Committee considering the extent to which public disclosure of such information can reasonably be expected to prejudice the interests of the United States.

Such rules shall, to the maximum extent feasible, permit meaningful consultations by Committee members with persons affected by proposed agreements authorized by this chapter.

(j) No authority to negotiate
Nothing contained in this section shall be construed to authorize or to permit any individual (not otherwise authorized or permitted) to participate directly in any negotiation of any agreement authorized by this chapter.

Import Restrictions: 19 U.S.C. § 2606

(a) Documentation of lawful exportation
No designated archaeological or ethnological material that is exported (whether or not such exportation is to the United States) from the State Party after the designation of such material under section 2604 of this title may be imported into the United States unless the State Party issues a certification or other documentation which certifies that such exportation was not in violation of the laws of the State Party.

(b) Customs action in absence of documentation
If the consignee of any designated archaeological or ethnological material is unable to present to the customs officer concerned at the time of making entry of such material--

(1) the certificate or other documentation of the State Party required under subsection (a) of this section; or

(2) satisfactory evidence that such material was exported from the State Party--
    (A) not less than ten years before the date of such entry and that neither the person for whose account the material is imported (or any related person) contracted for or acquired an interest, directly or indirectly, in such material more than one year before that date of entry, or
    (B) on or before the date on which such material was designated under section 2604 of this title,
the customs officer concerned shall refuse to release the material from customs custody and send it to a bonded warehouse or store to be held

at the risk and expense of the consignee, notwithstanding any other provision of law, until such documentation or evidence is filed with such officer. If such documentation or evidence is not presented within ninety days after the date on which such material is refused release from customs custody, or such longer period as may be allowed by the Secretary for good cause shown, the material shall be subject to seizure and forfeiture. The presentation of such documentation or evidence shall not bar subsequent action under section 2609 of this title.

(c) "Satisfactory evidence" defined
The term "satisfactory evidence" means--

(1) for purposes of subsection (b) (2) (A) of this section--
(A) one or more declarations under oath by the importer, or the person for whose account the material is imported, stating that, to the best of his knowledge--
(i) the material was exported from the State Party not less than ten years before the date of entry into the United States, and
(ii) neither such importer or person (or any related person) contracted for or acquired an interest, directly or indirectly, in such material more than one year before the date of entry of the material; and
(B) a statement provided by the consignor, or person who sold the material to the importer, which states the date, or, if not known, his belief, that the material was exported from the State Party not less than ten years before the date of entry into the United States, and the reasons on which the statement is based; and

(2) for purposes of subsection (b) (2) (B) of this section--
(A) one or more declarations under oath by the importer or the person for whose account the material is to be imported, stating that, to the best of his knowledge, the material was exported from the State Party on or before the date such material was designated under section 2604 of this title, and

(B) a statement by the consignor or person who sold the material to the importer which states the date, or if not known, his belief, that the material was exported from the State Party on or before the date such material was designated under section 2604 of this title, and the reasons on which the statement is based.

(d) Related persons

For purposes of subsections (b) and (c) of this section, a person shall be treated as a related person to an importer, or to a person for whose account material is imported, if such person--

(1) is a member of the same family as the importer or person of account, including, but not limited to, membership as a brother or sister (whether by whole or half blood), spouse, ancestor, or lineal descendant;

(2) is a partner or associate with the importer or person of account in any partnership, association, or other venture; or

(3) is a corporation or other legal entity in which the importer or person of account directly or indirectly owns, controls, or holds power to vote 20 percent or more of the outstanding voting stock or shares in the entity.

Stolen Cultural Property: 19 U.S.C. § 2607

No article of cultural property documented as appertaining to the inventory of a museum or religious or secular public monument or similar institution in any State Party which is stolen from such institution after the effective date of this chapter, or after the date of entry into force of the Convention for the State Party, whichever date is later, may be imported into the United States.

Temporary Disposition of Materials and Articles: 19 U.S.C. § 2608

Pending a final determination as to whether any archaeological or ethnological material, or any article of cultural property, has been imported into the United States in violation of section 2606 of this title or section 2607 of this title, the Secretary shall, upon application by any museum or other cultural or scientific institution in the United States which is open to the public, permit such material or article to be retained at such institution if he finds that--

(1) sufficient safeguards will be taken by the institution for the protection of such material or article; and

(2) sufficient bond is posted by the institution to ensure its return to the Secretary.

Seizure and Forfeiture: 19 U.S.C. § 2609
a) In general
Any designated archaeological or ethnological material or article of cultural property, as the case may be, which is imported into the United States in violation of section 2606 of this title or section 2607 of this title shall be subject to seizure and forfeiture. All provisions of law relating to seizure, forfeiture, and condemnation for violation of the customs laws shall apply to seizures and forfeitures incurred, or alleged to have been incurred, under this chapter, insofar as such provisions of law are applicable to, and not inconsistent with, the provisions of this chapter.

(b) Archaeological and ethnological material
Any designated archaeological or ethnological material which is imported into the United States in violation of section 2606 of this title and which is forfeited to the United States under this chapter shall--

(1) first be offered for return to the State Party;

(2) if not returned to the State Party, be returned to a claimant with respect to whom the material was forfeited if that claimant establishes--
   (A) valid title to the material,
   (B) that the claimant is a bona fide purchaser for value of the material; or

(3) if not returned to the State Party under paragraph (1) or to a claimant under paragraph (2), be disposed of in the manner prescribed by law for articles forfeited for violation of the customs laws.
No return of material may be made under paragraph (1) or (2) unless the State Party or claimant, as the case may be, bears the expenses incurred incident to the return and delivery, and complies with such other requirements relating to the return as the Secretary shall prescribe.

(c) Articles of cultural property

(1) In any action for forfeiture under this section regarding an article of cultural property imported into the United States in violation of section 2607 of this title, if the claimant establishes valid title to the article, under applicable law, as against the institution from which the article was stolen, forfeiture shall not be decreed unless the State Party to which the article is to be returned pays the claimant just compensation for the article. In any action for forfeiture under this section where the claimant does not establish such title but establishes that it purchased the article for value without knowledge or reason to believe it was stolen, forfeiture shall not be decreed unless--

(A) the State Party to which the article is to be returned pays the claimant an amount equal to the amount which the claimant paid for the article, or

(B) the United States establishes that such State Party, as a matter of law or reciprocity, would in similar circumstances recover and return an article stolen from an institution in the United States without requiring the payment of compensation.

(2) Any article of cultural property which is imported into the United States in violation of section 2607 of this title and which is forfeited to the United States under this chapter shall--

(A) first be offered for return to the State Party in whose territory is situated the institution referred to in section 2607 of this title and shall be returned if that State Party bears the expenses incident to such return and delivery and complies with such other requirements relating to the return as the Secretary prescribes; or

(B) if not returned to such State Party, be disposed of in the manner prescribed by law for articles forfeited for violation of the customs laws.

Evidentiary Requirements: 19 U.S.C. § 2610
Notwithstanding the provisions of section 1615 of this title [burden of proof in forfeiture proceedings], in any forfeiture proceeding brought

under this chapter in which the material or article, as the case may be, is claimed by any person, the United States shall establish--

(1) in the case of any material subject to the provisions of section 2606 of this title, that the material has been listed by the Secretary in accordance with section 2604 of this title; and

(2) in the case of any article subject to section 2607 of this title, that the article--

(A) is documented as appertaining to the inventory of a museum or religious or secular public monument or similar institution in a State Party, and

(B) was stolen from such institution after the effective date of this chapter, or after the date of entry into force of the Convention for the State Party concerned, whichever date is later.

Exempted Materials and Articles: 19 U.S.C. § 2611
The provisions of this chapter shall not apply to--

(1) any archaeological or ethnological material or any article of cultural property which is imported into the United States for temporary exhibition or display if such material or article is immune from seizure under judicial process pursuant to section 2459 of Title 22; or

(2) any designated archaeological or ethnological material or any article of cultural property imported into the United States if such material or article--

(A) has been held in the United States for a period of not less than three consecutive years by a recognized museum or religious or secular monument or similar institution, and was purchased by that institution for value, in good faith, and without notice that such material or article was imported in violation of this chapter, but only if--

(i) the acquisition of such material or article has been reported in a publication of such institution, any regularly published newspaper or periodical with a circulation of at least fifty thousand, or a periodical or exhibition catalog which is concerned with the type of article or materials sought to be exempted from this chapter,

(ii) such material or article has been exhibited to the public for a period or periods aggregating at least one year during such three-year period, or

(iii) such article or material has been cataloged and the catalog material made available upon request to the public for at least two years during such three-year period;

(B) if subparagraph (A) does not apply, has been within the United States for a period of not less than ten consecutive years and has been exhibited for not less than five years during such period in a recognized museum or religious or secular monument or similar institution in the Unites [United] States open to the public; or

(C) if subparagraphs (A) and (B) do not apply, has been within the United States for a period of not less than ten consecutive years and the State Party concerned has received or should have received during such period fair notice (through such adequate and accessible publication, or other means, as the Secretary shall by regulation prescribe) of its location within the United States; and

(D) if none of the preceding subparagraphs apply, has been within the United States for a period of not less than twenty consecutive years and the claimant establishes that it purchased the material or article for value without knowledge or reason to believe that it was imported in violation of law.

Regulations: 19 U.S.C. § 2612
The Secretary shall prescribe such rules and regulations as are necessary and appropriate to carry out the provisions of this chapter.

Convention on Cultural Property Implementation Act, Enforcement: 19 U.S.C. § 2613
In the customs territory of the United States, and in the Virgin Islands, the provisions of this chapter shall be enforced by appropriate customs officers. In any other territory or area within the United States, but not within such customs territory or the Virgin Islands, such provisions shall be enforced by such persons as may be designated by the President.

B6. CONVENTION ON INTERNATIONAL TRADE IN ENDANGERED SPECIES OF WILD FLORA AND FAUNA (CITES)

Convention on International Trade in Endangered Species of Wild Fauna and Flora

Signed at Washington, D.C., on 3 March 1973

Amended at Bonn, on 22 June 1979

The Contracting States,

Recognizing that wild fauna and flora in their many beautiful and varied forms are an irreplaceable part of the natural systems of the earth which must be protected for this and the generations to come;

Conscious of the ever-growing value of wild fauna and flora from aesthetic, scientific, cultural, recreational and economic points of view;

Recognizing that peoples and States are and should be the best protectors of their own wild fauna and flora;

Recognizing, in addition, that international co-operation is essential for the protection of certain species of wild fauna and flora against over-exploitation through international trade;

Convinced of the urgency of taking appropriate measures to this end; *Have agreed* as follows:

Article I
Definitions

For the purpose of the present Convention, unless the context otherwise requires:

(a) "Species" means any species, subspecies, or geographically separate population thereof;

(b) "Specimen" means:

(i) any animal or plant, whether alive or dead;

(ii) in the case of an animal: for species included in Appendices I and II, any readily recognizable part or derivative thereof; and for species included in Appendix III, any readily recognizable part or derivative thereof specified in Appendix III in relation to the species; and

(iii) in the case of a plant: for species included in Appendix I, any readily recognizable part or derivative thereof; and for species included in Appendices II and III, any readily recognizable part or derivative thereof specified in Appendices II and III in relation to the species;

(c) "Trade" means export, re-export, import and introduction from the sea;

(d) "Re-export" means export of any specimen that has previously been imported;

(e) "Introduction from the sea" means transportation into a State of specimens of any species which were taken in the marine environment not under the jurisdiction of any State;

(f) "Scientific Authority" means a national scientific authority designated in accordance with Article IX;

(g) "Management Authority" means a national management authority designated in accordance with Article IX;

(h) "Party" means a State for which the present Convention has entered into force.

Article II
Fundamental Principles

1. Appendix I shall include all species threatened with extinction which are or may be affected by trade. Trade in specimens of these species must be subject to particularly strict regulation in order not to endanger further their survival and must only be authorized in exceptional circumstances.

2. Appendix II shall include:

(a) all species which although not necessarily now threatened with extinction may become so unless trade in specimens of such species is subject to strict regulation in order to avoid utilization incompatible with their survival; and

(b) other species which must be subject to regulation in order that trade in specimens of certain species referred to in sub-paragraph (a) of this paragraph may be brought under effective control.

3. Appendix III shall include all species which any Party identifies as being subject to regulation within its jurisdiction for the purpose of preventing or restricting exploitation, and as needing the co-operation of other Parties in the control of trade.

4. The Parties shall not allow trade in specimens of species included in Appendices I, II and III except in accordance with the provisions of the present Convention.

Article III
Regulation of Trade in Specimens of Species Included in Appendix I

1. All trade in specimens of species included in Appendix I shall be in accordance with the provisions of this Article.

2. The export of any specimen of a species included in Appendix I shall require the prior grant and presentation of an export permit. An export permit shall only be granted when the following conditions have been met:

(a) a Scientific Authority of the State of export has advised that such export will not be detrimental to the survival of that species;

(b) a Management Authority of the State of export is satisfied that the specimen was not obtained in contravention of the laws of that State for the protection of fauna and flora;

(c) a Management Authority of the State of export is satisfied that any living specimen will be so prepared and shipped as to minimize the risk of injury, damage to health or cruel treatment; and

(d) a Management Authority of the State of export is satisfied that an import permit has been granted for the specimen.

3. The import of any specimen of a species included in Appendix I shall require the prior grant and presentation of an import permit and either an export permit or a re-export certificate. An import permit shall only be granted when the following conditions have been met:

(a) a Scientific Authority of the State of import has advised that the import will be for purposes which are not detrimental to the survival of the species involved;

(b) a Scientific Authority of the State of import is satisfied that the proposed recipient of a living specimen is suitably equipped to house and care for it; and

(c) a Management Authority of the State of import is satisfied that the specimen is not to be used for primarily commercial purposes.

4. The re-export of any specimen of a species included in Appendix I shall require the prior grant and presentation of a re-export certificate. A re-export certificate shall only be granted when the following conditions have been met:

(a) a Management Authority of the State of re-export is satisfied that the specimen was imported into that State in accordance with the provisions of the present Convention;

(b) a Management Authority of the State of re-export is satisfied that any living specimen will be so prepared and shipped as to minimize the risk of injury, damage to health or cruel treatment; and

(c) a Management Authority of the State of re-export is satisfied that an import permit has been granted for any living specimen.

5. The introduction from the sea of any specimen of a species included in Appendix I shall require the prior grant of a certificate from a Management Authority of the State of introduction. A certificate shall only be granted when the following conditions have been met:

(a) a Scientific Authority of the State of introduction advises that the introduction will not be detrimental to the survival of the species involved;

(b) a Management Authority of the State of introduction is satisfied that the proposed recipient of a living specimen is suitably equipped to house and care for it; and

(c) a Management Authority of the State of introduction is satisfied that the specimen is not to be used for primarily commercial purposes.

Article IV
Regulation of Trade in Specimens of Species Included in Appendix II

1. All trade in specimens of species included in Appendix II shall be in accordance with the provisions of this Article.

2. The export of any specimen of a species included in Appendix II shall require the prior grant and presentation of an export permit. An export permit shall only be granted when the following conditions have been met:

(a) a Scientific Authority of the State of export has advised that such export will not be detrimental to the survival of that species;

(b) a Management Authority of the State of export is satisfied that the specimen was not obtained in contravention of the laws of that State for the protection of fauna and flora; and

(c) a Management Authority of the State of export is satisfied that any living specimen will be so prepared and shipped as to minimize the risk of injury, damage to health or cruel treatment.

3. A Scientific Authority in each Party shall monitor both the export permits granted by that State for specimens of species included in Appendix II and the actual exports of such specimens. Whenever a Scientific Authority determines that the export of specimens of any such species should be limited in order to maintain that species throughout its range at a level consistent with its role in the ecosystems in which it occurs and well above the level at which that species might become eligible for inclusion in Appendix I, the Scientific Authority shall advise the appropriate Management Authority of suitable measures to be taken to limit the grant of export permits for specimens of that species.

4. The import of any specimen of a species included in Appendix II shall require the prior presentation of either an export permit or a re-export certificate.

5. The re-export of any specimen of a species included in Appendix II shall require the prior grant and presentation of a re-export certificate. A re-export certificate shall only be granted when the following conditions have been met:

(a) a Management Authority of the State of re-export is satisfied that the specimen was imported into that State in accordance with the provisions of the present Convention; and

(b) a Management Authority of the State of re-export is satisfied that any living specimen will be so prepared and shipped as to minimize the risk of injury, damage to health or cruel treatment.

6. The introduction from the sea of any specimen of a species included in Appendix II shall require the prior grant of a certificate from a Management Authority of the State of introduction. A certificate shall only be granted when the following conditions have been met:

(a) a Scientific Authority of the State of introduction advises that the introduction will not be detrimental to the survival of the species involved; and

(b) a Management Authority of the State of introduction is satisfied that any living specimen will be so handled as to minimize the risk of injury, damage to health or cruel treatment.

7. Certificates referred to in paragraph 6 of this Article may be granted on the advice of a Scientific Authority, in consultation with other national scientific authorities or, when appropriate, international scientific authorities, in respect of periods not exceeding one year for total numbers of specimens to be introduced in such periods.

Article V
Regulation of Trade in Specimens of Species Included in Appendix III

1. All trade in specimens of species included in Appendix III shall be in accordance with the provisions of this Article.

2. The export of any specimen of a species included in Appendix III from any State which has included that species in Appendix III shall require the prior grant and presentation of an export permit. An export permit shall only be granted when the following conditions have been met:

(a) a Management Authority of the State of export is satisfied that the specimen was not obtained in contravention of the laws of that State for the protection of fauna and flora; and

(b) a Management Authority of the State of export is satisfied that any living specimen will be so prepared and shipped as to minimize the risk of injury, damage to health or cruel treatment.

3. The import of any specimen of a species included in Appendix III shall require, except in circumstances to which paragraph 4 of this Article applies, the prior presentation of a certificate of origin and, where the import is from a State which has included that species in Appendix III, an export permit.

4. In the case of re-export, a certificate granted by the Management Authority of the State of re-export that the specimen was processed in that State or is being re-exported shall be accepted by the State of import as evidence that the provisions of the present Convention have been complied with in respect of the specimen concerned.

Article VI
Permits and Certificates

1. Permits and certificates granted under the provisions of Articles III, IV, and V shall be in accordance with the provisions of this Article.

2. An export permit shall contain the information specified in the model set forth in Appendix IV, and may only be used for export within a period of six months from the date on which it was granted.

3. Each permit or certificate shall contain the title of the present Convention, the name and any identifying stamp of the Management Authority granting it and a control number assigned by the Management Authority.

4. Any copies of a permit or certificate issued by a Management Authority shall be clearly marked as copies only and no such copy may be used in place of the original, except to the extent endorsed thereon.

5. A separate permit or certificate shall be required for each consignment of specimens.

6. A Management Authority of the State of import of any specimen shall cancel and retain the export permit or re-export certificate and any corresponding import permit presented in respect of the import of that specimen.

7. Where appropriate and feasible a Management Authority may affix a mark upon any specimen to assist in identifying the specimen. For these purposes "mark" means any indelible imprint, lead seal or other suitable means of identifying a specimen, designed in such a way as to render its imitation by unauthorized persons as difficult as possible.

Article VII
Exemptions and Other Special Provisions Relating to Trade

1. The provisions of Articles III, IV and V shall not apply to the transit or transhipment of specimens through or in the territory of a Party while the specimens remain in Customs control.

2. Where a Management Authority of the State of export or re-export is satisfied that a specimen was acquired before the provisions of the present Convention applied to that specimen, the provisions of Articles III, IV and V shall not apply to that specimen where the Management Authority issues a certificate to that effect.

3. The provisions of Articles III, IV and V shall not apply to specimens that are personal or household effects. This exemption shall not apply where:

(a) in the case of specimens of a species included in Appendix I, they were acquired by the owner outside his State of usual residence, and are being imported into that State; or

(b) in the case of specimens of species included in Appendix II:

(i) they were acquired by the owner outside his State of usual residence and in a State where removal from the wild occurred;

(ii) they are being imported into the owner's State of usual residence; and

(iii) the State where removal from the wild occurred requires the prior grant of export permits before any export of such specimens; unless a Management Authority is satisfied that the specimens were acquired before the provisions of the present Convention applied to such specimens.

4. Specimens of an animal species included in Appendix I bred in captivity for commercial purposes, or of a plant species included in Appendix I artificially propagated for commercial purposes, shall be deemed to be specimens of species included in Appendix II.

5. Where a Management Authority of the State of export is satisfied that any specimen of an animal species was bred in captivity or any specimen of a plant species was artificially propagated, or is a part of such an animal or plant or was derived therefrom, a certificate by that Management Authority to that effect shall be accepted in lieu of any of the permits or certificates required under the provisions of Article III, IV or V.

6. The provisions of Articles III, IV and V shall not apply to the non-commercial loan, donation or exchange between scientists or scientific institutions registered by a Management Authority of their State, of herbarium specimens, other preserved, dried or embedded museum specimens, and live plant material which carry a label issued or approved by a Management Authority.

7. A Management Authority of any State may waive the requirements of Articles III, IV and V and allow the movement without permits or certificates

of specimens which form part of a travelling zoo, circus, menagerie, plant exhibition or other travelling exhibition provided that:

(a) the exporter or importer registers full details of such specimens with that Management Authority;

(b) the specimens are in either of the categories specified in paragraph 2 or 5 of this Article; and

(c) the Management Authority is satisfied that any living specimen will be so transported and cared for as to minimize the risk of injury, damage to health or cruel treatment.

Article VIII
Measures to Be Taken by the Parties

1. The Parties shall take appropriate measures to enforce the provisions of the present Convention and to prohibit trade in specimens in violation thereof. These shall include measures:

(a) to penalize trade in, or possession of, such specimens, or both; and

(b) to provide for the confiscation or return to the State of export of such specimens.

2. In addition to the measures taken under paragraph 1 of this Article, a Party may, when it deems it necessary, provide for any method of internal reimbursement for expenses incurred as a result of the confiscation of a specimen traded in violation of the measures taken in the application of the provisions of the present Convention.

3. As far as possible, the Parties shall ensure that specimens shall pass through any formalities required for trade with a minimum of delay. To facilitate such passage, a Party may designate ports of exit and ports of entry at which specimens must be presented for clearance. The Parties shall ensure further that all living specimens, during any period of transit, holding or shipment, are properly cared for so as to minimize the risk of injury, damage to health or cruel treatment.

4. Where a living specimen is confiscated as a result of measures referred to in paragraph 1 of this Article:

(a) the specimen shall be entrusted to a Management Authority of the State of confiscation;

(b) the Management Authority shall, after consultation with the State of export, return the specimen to that State at the expense of that State, or to a rescue centre or such other place as the Management Authority deems appropriate and consistent with the purposes of the present Convention; and

(c) the Management Authority may obtain the advice of a Scientific Authority, or may, whenever it considers it desirable, consult the Secretariat in order to facilitate the decision under sub-paragraph (b) of this paragraph, including the choice of a rescue centre or other place.

5. A rescue centre as referred to in paragraph 4 of this Article means an institution designated by a Management Authority to look after the welfare of living specimens, particularly those that have been confiscated.

6. Each Party shall maintain records of trade in specimens of species included in Appendices I, II and III which shall cover:

(a) the names and addresses of exporters and importers; and

(b) the number and type of permits and certificates granted; the States with which such trade occurred; the numbers or quantities and types of specimens, names of species as included in Appendices I, II and III and, where applicable, the size and sex of the specimens in question.

7. Each Party shall prepare periodic reports on its implementation of the present Convention and shall transmit to the Secretariat:

(a) an annual report containing a summary of the information specified in sub-paragraph (b) of paragraph 6 of this Article; and

(b) a biennial report on legislative, regulatory and administrative measures taken to enforce the provisions of the present Convention.

8. The information referred to in paragraph 7 of this Article shall be available to the public where this is not inconsistent with the law of the Party concerned.

Article IX
Management and Scientific Authorities

1. Each Party shall designate for the purposes of the present Convention:

(a) one or more Management Authorities competent to grant permits or certificates on behalf of that Party; and

(b) one or more Scientific Authorities.

2. A State depositing an instrument of ratification, acceptance, approval or accession shall at that time inform the Depositary Government of the name and address of the Management Authority authorized to communicate with other Parties and with the Secretariat.

3. Any changes in the designations or authorizations under the provisions of this Article shall be communicated by the Party concerned to the Secretariat for transmission to all other Parties.

4. Any Management Authority referred to in paragraph 2 of this Article shall, if so requested by the Secretariat or the Management Authority of another Party, communicate to it impression of stamps, seals or other devices used to authenticate permits or certificates.

Article X
Trade with States not Party to the Convention

Where export or re-export is to, or import is from, a State not a Party to the present Convention, comparable documentation issued by the competent authorities in that State which substantially conforms with the requirements of the present Convention for permits and certificates may be accepted in lieu thereof by any Party.

Article XI
Conference of the Parties

1. The Secretariat shall call a meeting of the Conference of the Parties not later than two years after the entry into force of the present Convention.

2. Thereafter the Secretariat shall convene regular meetings at least once every two years, unless the Conference decides otherwise, and extraordi-

nary meetings at any time on the written request of at least one-third of the Parties.

3. At meetings, whether regular or extraordinary, the Parties shall review the implementation of the present Convention and may:

(a) make such provision as may be necessary to enable the Secretariat to carry out its duties, and adopt financial provisions;

(b) consider and adopt amendments to Appendices I and II in accordance with Article XV;

(c) review the progress made towards the restoration and conservation of the species included in Appendices I, II and III;

(d) receive and consider any reports presented by the Secretariat or by any Party; and

(e) where appropriate, make recommendations for improving the effectiveness of the present Convention.

4. At each regular meeting, the Parties may determine the time and venue of the next regular meeting to be held in accordance with the provisions of paragraph 2 of this Article.

5. At any meeting, the Parties may determine and adopt rules of procedure for the meeting.

6. The United Nations, its Specialized Agencies and the International Atomic Energy Agency, as well as any State not a Party to the present Convention, may be represented at meetings of the Conference by observers, who shall have the right to participate but not to vote.

7. Any body or agency technically qualified in protection, conservation or management of wild fauna and flora, in the following categories, which has informed the Secretariat of its desire to be represented at meetings of the Conference by observers, shall be admitted unless at least one-third of the Parties present object:

(a) international agencies or bodies, either governmental or non-governmental, and national governmental agencies and bodies; and

(b) national non-governmental agencies or bodies which have been approved for this purpose by the State in which they are located. Once admitted, these observers shall have the right to participate but not to vote.

Article XII
The Secretariat

1. Upon entry into force of the present Convention, a Secretariat shall be provided by the Executive Director of the United Nations Environment Programme. To the extent and in the manner he considers appropriate, he may be assisted by suitable inter-governmental or non-governmental international or national agencies and bodies technically qualified in protection, conservation and management of wild fauna and flora.

2. The functions of the Secretariat shall be:

(a) to arrange for and service meetings of the Parties;

(b) to perform the functions entrusted to it under the provisions of Articles XV and XVI of the present Convention;

(c) to undertake scientific and technical studies in accordance with programmes authorized by the Conference of the Parties as will contribute to the implementation of the present Convention, including studies concerning standards for appropriate preparation and shipment of living specimens and the means of identifying specimens;

(d) to study the reports of Parties and to request from Parties such further information with respect thereto as it deems necessary to ensure implementation of the present Convention;

(e) to invite the attention of the Parties to any matter pertaining to the aims of the present Convention;

(f) to publish periodically and distribute to the Parties current editions of Appendices I, II and III together with any information which will facilitate identification of specimens of species included in those Appendices;

(g) to prepare annual reports to the Parties on its work and on the implementation of the present Convention and such other reports as meetings of the Parties may request;

(h) to make recommendations for the implementation of the aims and provisions of the present Convention, including the exchange of information of a scientific or technical nature;

(i) to perform any other function as may be entrusted to it by the Parties.

Article XIII
International Measures

1. When the Secretariat in the light of information received is satisfied that any species included in Appendix I or II is being affected adversely by trade in specimens of that species or that the provisions of the present Convention are not being effectively implemented, it shall communicate such information to the authorized Management Authority of the Party or Parties concerned.

2. When any Party receives a communication as indicated in paragraph 1 of this Article, it shall, as soon as possible, inform the Secretariat of any relevant facts insofar as its laws permit and, where appropriate, propose remedial action. Where the Party considers that an inquiry is desirable, such inquiry may be carried out by one or more persons expressly authorized by the Party.

3. The information provided by the Party or resulting from any inquiry as specified in paragraph 2 of this Article shall be reviewed by the next Conference of the Parties which may make whatever recommendations it deems appropriate.

Article XIV
Effect on Domestic Legislation and International Conventions

1. The provisions of the present Convention shall in no way affect the right of Parties to adopt:

(a) stricter domestic measures regarding the conditions for trade, taking, possession or transport of specimens of species included in Appendices I, II and III, or the complete prohibition thereof; or

(b) domestic measures restricting or prohibiting trade, taking, possession or transport of species not included in Appendix I, II or III.

2. The provisions of the present Convention shall in no way affect the provisions of any domestic measures or the obligations of Parties deriving from any treaty, convention, or international agreement relating to other aspects of trade, taking, possession or transport of specimens which is in force or subsequently may enter into force for any Party including any measure pertaining to the Customs, public health, veterinary or plant quarantine fields.

3. The provisions of the present Convention shall in no way affect the provisions of, or the obligations deriving from, any treaty, convention or international agreement concluded or which may be concluded between States creating a union or regional trade agreement establishing or maintaining a common external Customs control and removing Customs control between the parties thereto insofar as they relate to trade among the States members of that union or agreement.

4. A State party to the present Convention, which is also a party to any other treaty, convention or international agreement which is in force at the time of the coming into force of the present Convention and under the provisions of which protection is afforded to marine species included in Appendix II, shall be relieved of the obligations imposed on it under the provisions of the present Convention with respect to trade in specimens of species included in Appendix II that are taken by ships registered in that State and in accordance with the provisions of such other treaty, convention or international agreement.

5. Notwithstanding the provisions of Articles III, IV and V, any export of a specimen taken in accordance with paragraph 4 of this Article shall only require a certificate from a Management Authority of the State of introduction to the effect that the specimen was taken in accordance with the provisions of the other treaty, convention or international agreement in question.

6. Nothing in the present Convention shall prejudice the codification and development of the law of the sea by the United Nations Conference on the Law of the Sea convened pursuant to Resolution 2750 C (XXV) of the General Assembly of the United Nations nor the present or future claims and legal views of any State concerning the law of the sea and the nature and extent of coastal and flag State jurisdiction.

Article XV
Amendments to Appendices I and II

1. The following provisions shall apply in relation to amendments to Appendices I and II at meetings of the Conference of the Parties:

(a) Any Party may propose an amendment to Appendix I or II for consideration at the next meeting. The text of the proposed amendment shall be communicated to the Secretariat at least 150 days before the meeting. The Secretariat shall consult the other Parties and interested bodies on the amendment in accordance with the provisions of sub-paragraphs (b) and (c) of paragraph 2 of this Article and shall communicate the response to all Parties not later than 30 days before the meeting.

(b) Amendments shall be adopted by a two-thirds majority of Parties present and voting. For these purposes "Parties present and voting" means Parties present and casting an affirmative or negative vote. Parties abstaining from voting shall not be counted among the two-thirds required for adopting an amendment.

(c) Amendments adopted at a meeting shall enter into force 90 days after that meeting for all Parties except those which make a reservation in accordance with paragraph 3 of this Article.

2. The following provisions shall apply in relation to amendments to Appendices I and II between meetings of the Conference of the Parties:

(a) Any Party may propose an amendment to Appendix I or II for consideration between meetings by the postal procedures set forth in this paragraph.

(b) For marine species, the Secretariat shall, upon receiving the text of the proposed amendment, immediately communicate it to the Parties. It shall also consult inter-governmental bodies having a function in relation to those species especially with a view to obtaining scientific data these bodies may be able to provide and to ensuring co-ordination with any conservation measures enforced by such bodies. The Secretariat shall communicate the views expressed and data provided by these bodies and its own findings and recommendations to the Parties as soon as possible.

(c) For species other than marine species, the Secretariat shall, upon receiving the text of the proposed amendment, immediately communicate it to the Parties, and, as soon as possible thereafter, its own recommendations.

(d) Any Party may, within 60 days of the date on which the Secretariat communicated its recommendations to the Parties under sub-paragraph (b) or (c) of this paragraph, transmit to the Secretariat any comments on the proposed amendment together with any relevant scientific data and information.

(e) The Secretariat shall communicate the replies received together with its own recommendations to the Parties as soon as possible.

(f) If no objection to the proposed amendment is received by the Secretariat within 30 days of the date the replies and recommendations were communicated under the provisions of sub-paragraph (e) of this paragraph, the amendment shall enter into force 90 days later for all Parties except those which make a reservation in accordance with paragraph 3 of this Article.

(g) If an objection by any Party is received by the Secretariat, the proposed amendment shall be submitted to a postal vote in accordance with the provisions of sub-paragraphs (h) , (i) and (j) of this paragraph.

(h) The Secretariat shall notify the Parties that notification of objection has been received.

(i) Unless the Secretariat receives the votes for, against or in abstention from at least one-half of the Parties within 60 days of the date of notification under sub-paragraph (h) of this paragraph, the proposed amendment shall be referred to the next meeting of the Conference for further consideration.

(j) Provided that votes are received from one-half of the Parties, the amendment shall be adopted by a two-thirds majority of Parties casting an affirmative or negative vote.

(k) The Secretariat shall notify all Parties of the result of the vote.

(l) If the proposed amendment is adopted it shall enter into force 90 days after the date of the notification by the Secretariat of its acceptance for all Parties except those which make a reservation in accordance with paragraph 3 of this Article.

3. During the period of 90 days provided for by sub-paragraph (c) of paragraph 1 or sub-paragraph (l) of paragraph 2 of this Article any Party may by notification in writing to the Depositary Government make a reservation with respect to the amendment. Until such reservation is withdrawn the Party shall be treated as a State not a Party to the present Convention with respect to trade in the species concerned.

Article XVI
Appendix III and Amendments thereto

1. Any Party may at any time submit to the Secretariat a list of species which it identifies as being subject to regulation within its jurisdiction for the purpose mentioned in paragraph 3 of Article II. Appendix III shall include the names of the Parties submitting the species for inclusion therein, the scientific names of the species so submitted, and any parts or derivatives of the animals or plants concerned that are specified in relation to the species for the purposes of sub-paragraph (b) of Article I.

2. Each list submitted under the provisions of paragraph 1 of this Article shall be communicated to the Parties by the Secretariat as soon as possible after receiving it. The list shall take effect as part of Appendix III 90 days after the date of such communication. At any time after the communication of such list, any Party may by notification in writing to the Depositary Government enter a reservation with respect to any species or any parts or derivatives, and until such reservation is withdrawn, the State shall be treated as a State not a Party to the present Convention with respect to trade in the species or part or derivative concerned.

3. A Party which has submitted a species for inclusion in Appendix III may withdraw it at any time by notification to the Secretariat which shall communicate the withdrawal to all Parties. The withdrawal shall take effect 30 days after the date of such communication.

4. Any Party submitting a list under the provisions of paragraph 1 of this Article shall submit to the Secretariat a copy of all domestic laws and regulations applicable to the protection of such species, together with any interpretations which the Party may deem appropriate or the Secretariat may request. The Party shall, for as long as the species in question is included in Appendix III, submit any amendments of such laws and regulations or any interpretations as they are adopted.

Article XVII
Amendment of the Convention

1. An extraordinary meeting of the Conference of the Parties shall be convened by the Secretariat on the written request of at least one-third of the Parties to consider and adopt amendments to the present Convention. Such amendments shall be adopted by a two-thirds majority of Parties present and voting. For these purposes "Parties present and voting" means Parties present and casting an affirmative or negative vote. Parties abstaining from voting shall not be counted among the two-thirds required for adopting an amendment.

2. The text of any proposed amendment shall be communicated by the Secretariat to all Parties at least 90 days before the meeting.

3. An amendment shall enter into force for the Parties which have accepted it 60 days after two-thirds of the Parties have deposited an instrument of acceptance of the amendment with the Depositary Government. Thereafter, the amendment shall enter into force for any other Party 60 days after that Party deposits its instrument of acceptance of the amendment.

Article XVIII
Resolution of Disputes

1. Any dispute which may arise between two or more Parties with respect to the interpretation or application of the provisions of the present

Convention shall be subject to negotiation between the Parties involved in the dispute.

2. If the dispute can not be resolved in accordance with paragraph 1 of this Article, the Parties may, by mutual consent, submit the dispute to arbitration, in particular that of the Permanent Court of Arbitration at The Hague, and the Parties submitting the dispute shall be bound by the arbitral decision.

Article XIX
Signature
The present Convention shall be open for signature at Washington until 30th April 1973 and thereafter at Berne until 31st December 1974.

Article XX
Ratification, Acceptance, Approval
The present Convention shall be subject to ratification, acceptance or approval. Instruments of ratification, acceptance or approval shall be deposited with the Government of the Swiss Confederation which shall be the Depositary Government.

Article XXI
Accession
The present Convention shall be open indefinitely for accession. Instruments of accession shall be deposited with the Depositary Government.

Article XXII
Entry into Force
1. The present Convention shall enter into force 90 days after the date of deposit of the tenth instrument of ratification, acceptance, approval or accession, with the Depositary Government.

2. For each State which ratifies, accepts or approves the present Convention or accedes thereto after the deposit of the tenth instrument of ratification, acceptance, approval or accession, the present Convention shall enter into force 90 days after the deposit by such State of its instrument of ratification, acceptance, approval or accession.

Article XXIII
Reservations

1. The provisions of the present Convention shall not be subject to general reservations. Specific reservations may be entered in accordance with the provisions of this Article and Articles XV and XVI.

2. Any State may, on depositing its instrument of ratification, acceptance, approval or accession, enter a specific reservation with regard to:

(a) any species included in Appendix I, II or III; or

(b) any parts or derivatives specified in relation to a species included in Appendix III.

3. Until a Party withdraws its reservation entered under the provisions of this Article, it shall be treated as a State not a Party to the present Convention with respect to trade in the particular species or parts or derivatives specified in such reservation.

Article XXIV
Denunciation

Any Party may denounce the present Convention by written notification to the Depositary Government at any time. The denunciation shall take effect twelve months after the Depositary Government has received the notification.

Article XXV
Depositary

1. The original of the present Convention, in the Chinese, English, French, Russian and Spanish languages, each version being equally authentic, shall be deposited with the Depositary Government, which shall transmit certified copies thereof to all States that have signed it or deposited instruments of accession to it.

2. The Depositary Government shall inform all signatory and acceding States and the Secretariat of signatures, deposit of instruments of ratification, acceptance, approval or accession, entry into force of the present

Convention, amendments thereto, entry and withdrawal of reservations and notifications of denunciation.

3. As soon as the present Convention enters into force, a certified copy thereof shall be transmitted by the Depositary Government to the Secretariat of the United Nations for registration and publication in accordance with Article 102 of the Charter of the United Nations.

In witness whereof the undersigned Plenipotentiaries, being duly authorized to that effect, have signed the present Convention.

Done at Washington this third day of March, One Thousand Nine Hundred and Seventy-three.

B7. AMERICAN ENDANGERED SPECIES LEGISLATION

Selected Excerpts

Migratory Bird Treaty Act 16 U.S.C. §704-712

§708 It shall be unlawful to ship, transport, or carry, by any means whatever, from one State, Territory, or district to or through another State, Territory, or district, or to or through a foreign country, any bird, or any part, nest, or egg thereof, captured, killed, taken, shipped, transported, or carried at any time contrary to the laws of the State, Territory, or district in which it was captured, killed, or taken, or from which it was shipped, transported, or carried. It shall be unlawful to import any bird, or any part, nest, or egg thereof, captured, killed, taken, shipped, transported, or carried contrary to the laws of any Province of the Dominion of Canada in which the same was captured, killed, or taken, or from which it was shipped, transported, or carried.

Endangered Species Act 7 U.S.C. §136, 16 U.S.C. §1531

SEC. 9. Title 16 U.S.C. 1538

(a) GENERAL.—(1) Except as provided in sections 6(g)(2) and 10 of this Act, with respect to any endangered species of fish or wildlife listed pursuant to section 4 of this Act it is unlawful for any person subject to the jurisdiction of the United States to—

(A) import any such species into, or export any such species from the United States;

(B) take any such species within the United States or the territorial sea of the United States;

(C) take any such species upon the high seas;

(D) possess, sell, deliver, carry, transport, or ship, by any means whatsoever, any such species taken in violation of subparagraphs (B) and (C);

(E) deliver, receive, carry, transport, or ship in interstate or foreign commerce, by any means whatsoever and in the course of a commercial activity, any such species;

(F) sell or offer for sale in interstate or foreign commerce any such species; or

(G) violate any regulation pertaining to such species or to any threatened species of fish or wildlife listed pursuant to section 4 of this Act and promulgated by the Secretary pursuant to authority provided by this Act.

(2) Except as provided in sections 6(g)(2) and 10 of this Act, with respect to any endangered species of plants listed pursuant to section 4 of this Act, it is unlawful for any person subject to the jurisdiction of the United States to—

(A) import any such species into, or export any such species from, the United States;

(B) remove and reduce to possession any such species from areas under Federal jurisdiction; maliciously damage or destroy any such species on any such area; or remove cut, dig up, or damage or destroy any such species on any other area in knowing violation of any law or regulation of any state or in the course of any violation of a state criminal trespass law;

(C) deliver, receive, carry, transport, or ship in interstate or foreign commerce, by any means whatsoever and in the course of a commercial activity, any such species;

(D) sell or offer for sale in interstate or foreign commerce any such species; or

(E) violate any regulation pertaining to such species or to any threatened species of plants listed pursuant to section 4 of this Act and promulgated by the Secretary pursuant to authority provided by this Act.

(b)(1) SPECIES HELD IN CAPTIVITY OR CONTROLLED ENVIRONMENT.—
The provisions of subsections (a)(1)(A) and (a)(1)(G) of this section shall not apply to any fish or wildlife which was held in captivity or in a

controlled environment on (A) December 28, 1973, or (B) the date of the publication in the Federal Register of a final regulation adding such fish or wildlife species to any list published pursuant to subsection (c) of section 4 of this Act: *Provided,* That such holding and any subsequent holding or use of the fish or wildlife as not in the course of a commercial activity. With respect to any act prohibited by subsections (a)(1)(A) and (a)(1)(G) of this section which occurs after a period of 180 days from (i) December 28, 1973, or (ii) the date of publication in the Federal Register of a final regulation adding such fish or wildlife species to any list published pursuant to subsection (c) of section 4 of this Act, there shall be a rebuttable presumption that the fish or wildlife involved in such act is not entitled to the exemption contained in this subsection.

(2)(A) The provisions of subsections (a)(1) shall not apply to—
(i) any raptor legally held in captivity or in a controlled environment on the effective date of the Endangered Species Act Amendments of 1978; or
(ii) any progeny of any raptor described in clause (i); until such time as any such raptor or progeny is intentionally returned to a wild state.

(B) Any person holding any raptor or progeny described in subparagraph (A) must be able to demonstrate that the raptor or progenydoes, in fact, qualify under the provisions of this paragraph, and shall maintain and submit to the Secretary, on request, such inventories, documentation, and records as the Secretary may by regulation require as being reasonably appropriate to carry out the purposes of this paragraph. Such requirements shall not unnecessarily duplicate the requirements of other rules and regulations promulgated by the Secretary.

(c) VIOLATION OF CONVENTION.—(1) It is unlawful for any person subject to the jurisdiction of the United States to engage in any trade in any specimens contrary to the provisions of the Convention, or to possess any specimens traded contrary to the provisions of the Convention, including the definitions of terms in article I thereof.

(2) Any importation into the United States of fish or wildlife shall, if—

(A) such fish or wildlife is not an endangered species listed pursuant to section 4 of this Act but is listed in Appendix II of the Convention;

(B) the taking and exportation of such fish or wildlife is not contrary to the provisions of the Convention and all other applicable requirements of the Convention have been satisfied;

(C) the applicable requirements of subsection (d), (e), and (f) of this section have been satisfied; and

(D) such importation is not made in the course of a commercial activity; be presumed to be an important not in violation of any provision of this Act or any regulation issued pursuant to this Act.

(d) IMPORTS AND EXPORTS. —
(1) IN GENERAL. — It is unlawful for any person, without first having obtained permission from the Secretary, to engage in business —

(A) as an importer or exporter of fish or wildlife (other than shellfish and fishery products which (i) are not listed pursuant to section 4 of this Act as endangered species or threatened species, and (ii) are imported for purposes of human or animal consumption or taken in waters under the jurisdiction of the United States or on the high seas for recreational purposes) or plants; or

(B) as an importer or exporter of any amount of raw or worked African elephant ivory.
(2) REQUIREMENTS.— Any person required to obtain permission under paragraph (1) of this subsection shall —

(A) keep such records as will fully and correctly disclose each importation or exportation of fish, wildlife, plants, or African elephant ivory made by him and the subsequent disposition, made by him with respect to such fish, wildlife, plants, or ivory;

(B) at all reasonable times upon notice by a duly authorized representative of the Secretary, afford such representative access to his place of business, an opportunity to examine his inventory of imported fish, wildlife, plants, or African elephant ivory and the records required to be kept under subparagraph (A) of this paragraph, and to copy such records; and

(C) file such reports as the Secretary may require.

(3) REGULATIONS.—The Secretary shall prescribe such regulations as are necessary and appropriate to carry out the purposes of this subsection.

(4) RESTRICTION ON CONSIDERATION OF VALUE OF AMOUNT OF AFRICAN ELEPHANT IVORY IMPORTED OR EXPORTED.—In granting permission under this subsection for importation or exportation of African elephant ivory, the Secretary shall not vary the requirements for obtaining such permission on the basis of the value or amount of ivory imported or exported under such permission.

(e) REPORTS. — It is unlawful for any person importing or exporting fish or wildlife (other than shellfish and fishery products which (1) are not listed pursuant to section 4 of this Act as endangered or threatened species, and (2) are imported for purposes of human or animal consumption or taken in waters under the jurisdiction of the United States or on the high seas for recreational purposes) or plants to fail to file any declaration or report as the Secretary deems necessary to facilitate enforcement of this Act or to meet the obligations of the Convention.

(f) DESIGNATION OF PORTS.—(1) It is unlawful for any person subject to the jurisdiction of the United States to import into or export from the United States any fish or wildlife (other than shellfish and fishery products which

(A) are not listed pursuant to section 4 of this Act as endangered species or threatened species, and

(B) are imported for purposes of human or animal consumption or taken in waters under the jurisdiction of the United States or on the high seas for recreational purposes) or plants, except at a port of ports designated by the Secretary of the Interior. For the purposes of facilitating enforcement of this Act and reducing the costs thereof, the Secretary of the Interior, with approval of the Secretary of the Treasury and after notice and opportunity for public hearing, may, by regulation, designate ports and change such designations. The Secretary of the Interior, under such terms and conditions as he may prescribe, may permit the importation or exportation at nondesignated ports in the interest of the health or safety of the fish or wildlife or plants, or for other reasons if, in his discretion, he deems it appropriate and consistent with the purpose of this subsection.

(2) Any port designated by the Secretary of the Interior under the authority of section 4(d) of the Act of December 5, 1969 (16 U.S.C. 666cc–4(d), shall, if such designation is in effect on the day before the date of the enactment of this Act, be deemed to be a port designated by the Secretary under paragraph (1) of this subsection until such time as the Secretary otherwise provides.

(g) VIOLATIONS.—It is unlawful for any person subject to the jurisdiction of the United States to attempt to commit, solicit another to commit, or cause to be committed, any offense defined in this section.

B8. CANADIAN ENDANGERED SPECIES LEGISLATION

Selected Excerpts

Species at Risk Act (SARA), S.C. 2002, c. 29

GENERAL PROHIBITIONS

32. (1) No person shall kill, harm, harass, capture or take an individual of a wildlife species that is listed as an extirpated species, an endangered species or a threatened species.
Possession, collection, etc.

(2) No person shall possess, collect, buy, sell or trade an individual of a wildlife species that is listed as an extirpated species, an endangered species or a threatened species, or any part or derivative of such an individual.

[...]

OFFENCES AND PUNISHMENT

Contraventions

97. (1) Every person who contravenes subsection 32(1) or (2), section 33, subsection 36(1), 58(1), 60(1) or 61(1) or section 91 or 92 or any prescribed provision of a regulation or an emergency order, or who fails to comply with an alternative measures agreement the person has entered into under this Act,

   (*a*) is guilty of an offence punishable on summary conviction and is liable

   (i) in the case of a corporation, other than a non-profit corporation, to a fine of not more than $300,000,

   (ii) in the case of a non-profit corporation, to a fine of not more than $50,000, and

   (iii) in the case of any other person, to a fine of not more than $50,000 or to imprisonment for a term of not more than one year, or to both; or

   (*b*) is guilty of an indictable offence and is liable

   (i) in the case of a corporation, other than a non-profit corporation, to a fine of not more than $1,000,000,

(ii) in the case of a non-profit corporation, to a fine of not more than $250,000, and

(iii) in the case of any other person, to a fine of not more than $250,000 or to imprisonment for a term of not more than five years, or to both.

Prescription of provisions

(2) A regulation or emergency order may prescribe which of its provisions may give rise to an offence.

Subsequent offence

(3) If a person is convicted of an offence a subsequent time, the amount of the fine for the subsequent offence may, despite subsection (1), be double the amount set out in that subsection.

Continuing offence

(4) A person who commits or continues an offence on more than one day is liable to be convicted for a separate offence for each day on which the offence is committed or continued.

Fines cumulative

(5) A fine imposed for an offence involving more than one animal, plant or other organism may be calculated in respect of each one as though it had been the subject of a separate information and the fine then imposed is the total of that calculation.

Additional fine

(6) If a person is convicted of an offence and the court is satisfied that monetary benefits accrued to the person as a result of the commission of the offence, the court may order the person to pay an additional fine in an amount equal to the court's estimation of the amount of the monetary benefits, which additional fine may exceed the maximum amount of any fine that may otherwise be imposed under this Act.

Migratory Birds Convention Act, S.C. 1994, c. 22

Prohibition

5. Except as authorized by the regulations, no person shall, without lawful excuse,

(a) be in possession of a migratory bird or nest; or

(b) buy, sell, exchange or give a migratory bird or nest or make it the subject of a commercial transaction.

[...]

Contravention of Act or regulations

13. (1) A person or vessel commits an offence if the person or vessel contravenes

(*a*) a provision of this Act or the regulations;

(*b*) an obligation or prohibition arising from this Act or the regulations;

(*c*) an order or direction made under this Act; or

(*d*) an order, direction or decision of a court made under this Act.

Penalties

(1.1) Every person or vessel that commits an offence is liable

(*a*) on conviction on indictment, to a fine of not more than $1,000,000 or to imprisonment for a term of not more than three years, or to both; and

(*b*) on summary conviction, to a fine of not more than $300,000 or to imprisonment for a term of not more than six months, or to both.

Wild Animal and Plant Protection and Regulation of International and Interprovincial Trade Act (WAPPRIITA), S.C. 1992, c. 52

Importation

6. (1) No person shall import into Canada any animal or plant that was taken, or any animal or plant, or any part or derivative of an animal or plant, that was possessed, distributed or transported in contravention of any law of any foreign state.

Importation and exportation

(2) Subject to the regulations, no person shall, except under and in accordance with a permit issued pursuant to subsection 10(1), import into Canada or export from Canada any animal or plant, or any part or derivative of an animal or plant.

[...]

Possession

8. Subject to the regulations, no person shall knowingly possess an animal or plant, or any part or derivative of an animal or plant,

(*a*) that has been imported or transported in contravention of this Act;

(*b*) for the purpose of transporting it from one province to another province in contravention of this Act or exporting it from Canada in contravention of this Act; or

(*c*) for the purpose of distributing or offering to distribute it if the animal or plant, or the animal or plant from which the part or derivative comes, is listed in Appendix 1 to the Convention.

[...]

Offence and punishment

22. (1) Every person who contravenes a provision of this Act or the regulations

(*a*) is guilty of an offence punishable on summary conviction and is liable

(i) in the case of a person that is a corporation, to a fine not exceeding fifty thousand dollars, and

(ii) in the case of a person other than a person referred to in subparagraph (i), to a fine not exceeding twenty-five thousand dollars or to imprisonment for a term not exceeding six months, or to both; or

(*b*) is guilty of an indictable offence and is liable

(i) in the case of a person that is a corporation, to a fine not exceeding three hundred thousand dollars, and

(ii) in the case of a person other than a person referred to in subparagraph (i), to a fine not exceeding one hundred and fifty thousand dollars or to imprisonment for a term not exceeding five years, or to both.

B9. FOREIGN CULTURAL OBJECTS IMMUNITY FROM SEIZURE ACT, R.S.O. 1990, C. F.23

Immunity of certain foreign cultural objects from seizure while in Ontario

1. (1) When any work of art or other object of cultural significance from a foreign country is brought into Ontario pursuant to an agreement between the foreign owner or custodian thereof and the Government of Ontario or any cultural or educational institution in Ontario providing for the temporary exhibition or display thereof in Ontario administered, operated or sponsored by the Government of Ontario or any such cultural or educational institution, no proceeding shall be taken in any court and no judgment, decree or order shall be enforced in Ontario for the purpose or having the effect of depriving the Government of Ontario or such institution, or any carrier engaged in transporting such work or object within Ontario, of custody or control of such work or object if, before such work or object is brought into Ontario, the Minister determines that such work or object is of cultural significance and that the temporary exhibition or display thereof in Ontario is in the interest of the people of Ontario and notice of the Minister's determination is published in *The Ontario Gazette*. R.S.O. 1990, c. F.23, s. 1 (1); 2002, c. 18, Sched. F, s. 1 (1).

Subs. (1) not to preclude enforcement of agreements, etc.

(2) Subsection (1) does not preclude any judicial action for or in aid of the enforcement of the terms of any such agreement or the enforcement of the obligation of any carrier under any contract for the transportation of any such work or object or the fulfilment of any obligation assumed by the Government of Ontario or such institution pursuant to any such agreement. R.S.O. 1990, c. F.23, s. 1 (2).

Definition of Minister

(3) In this Act,

"Minister" means the Minister of Culture or such other member of the Executive Council to whom the administration of this Act may be assigned under the *Executive Council Act*. 2002, c. 18, Sched. F, s. 1 (2).

APPENDIX C: Museum and Gallery Policies and Codes of Ethics

C1. UK DUE DILIGENCE GUIDELINES FOR MUSEUMS, LIBRARIES AND ARCHIVES ON COLLECTING AND BORROWING CULTURAL MATERIAL

Department for Culture, Media and Sport
Cultural Property Unit

Combating Illicit Trade:

Due diligence guidelines for museums, libraries and
archives on collecting and borrowing cultural material

October 2005

Combating Illicit Trade

Contents

1	Introduction	2
2	Scope of guidelines	3
3	Basic Principles	4
4	What to do when considering the acquisition or loan of an item	5
5	What to do if there are problems establishing the provenance:	7
6	Due diligence – What should it involve	8
7	The results of due diligence	10
8	Specific permission from the country of origin, courts, etc	12
9	Due diligence when acquiring collections	13
10	Archaeological material from the UK	14
11	Museums of last resort for items originating in the UK	17
12	Museum policies, procedures and expertise	18
13	Inward Loans	20
	Appendices	
Appendix 1		23
Appendix 2		27
Appendix 3		37
Appendix 4		39

1.   Introduction

There is general agreement within museums, libraries and archives that the illicit trade in cultural material must be resisted, that they should set high ethical standards for acquisitions and that they should avoid giving tacit support to the market in unprovenanced material through their acquisition activities. There is, however, much ethically acceptable material on the market, and for many reasons it is vitally important that museums, libraries and archives continue to be able to develop their collections.

New acquisitions inform, entertain and inspire visitors, encourage new audiences and raise the profile of the institution (and of all of those bodies involved in the acquisition). They provide an impetus for research and can play a vital role in education, outreach and training. The process of acquisition in itself can be an important stimulus and catalyst for other processes within and between institutions.

Museums, libraries and archives must take precautions to ensure that they acquire, or borrow, only ethically acceptable items and reject items that might have been looted or illegally exported. To ensure they do this, they need to exercise due diligence. The following guidelines explain what that entails.

These guidelines have been produced by a sector-wide working group established under the auspices of the Department for Culture, Media and Sport's Illicit Trade Advisory Panel.

The sector-wide working group was made up of representatives from the following organisations:

The Department for Culture, Media and Sport, the Museums, Libraries and Archives Council, the Museums Association, the National Art Collections Fund, the British Museum, the V&A, the Ashmolean Museum, the Fitzwilliam Museum, the Society of Antiquaries of London, York Museums Trust, the Manchester Museum, the British Library and the National Archives.

These guidelines have been endorsed by The Museums Association, The National Art Collections Fund, The Museums, Libraries and Archives Council (including the MLA/V&A Purchase Fund), The Society of Archivists, Chartered Institute of Library and Information Professionals, The National Fund for Acquisitions (Scotland), Society of Museum Archaeologists. The funding bodies expect museums to adhere to these guidelines when applying for funding for acquisitions.

2.   Scope of guidelines

These guidelines aim to assist museums, libraries and archives when considering the acquisition by purchase, gift or bequest of items of cultural property originating outside the UK. The guidelines apply to museums, libraries and archives, but it is anticipated that museums will need to refer to them more often. For the sake of brevity, the term 'museum' is used throughout but should be taken to include libraries, archives and galleries.

They also apply to inward loans. They apply equally to contemporary material from those countries that restrict its trade or export. They apply to items of UK origin that may have been illicitly excavated or illicitly removed from a building, monument, site or wreck. They do not, however, cover the specific factors relevant to natural science material or any other material covered by CITES[1].

The guidelines aim to help museums to ensure that they reject illicit material. They do not cover other aspects of the acquisition process, such as checking whether the item falls within the institution's acquisition policy or that it has not been stolen. They should be used in conjunction with documents such as Spectrum (the Museum Documentation standard), the Museums Association Ethical Guidelines on Acquisition and the National Museum Directors' Conference Spoliation Guidelines.

The details of these guidelines apply to museums in England and Wales, and the general principles apply to museums elsewhere.

The guidelines are provided as an information guide only. They are not a full and authoritative statement of the law and do not constitute professional or legal advice.

No responsibility is accepted by the working group, the Illicit Trade Advisory Panel, or the Department for Culture, Media and Sport for any errors, omissions or misleading statements in these guidelines. In particular it must be noted that although the working group, the panel and the DCMS have made every effort to ensure that the information set out in this document is correct at October 2005, changes in the law may mean that the guidance given in these guidelines becomes gradually less accurate. While every effort has been made to ensure the accuracy of statements found in these guidelines responsibility is not accepted where information is inaccurate.

---

1   Accredited museums that acquire natural science material will need to take account of this as part of their acquisition policy; see paragraph 8d of the specimen acquisition and disposal policy in MLA accreditation guidelines.

3.   Basic Principles

Museums should acquire and borrow items only if they are legally and ethically sound. They should reject an item if there is any suspicion about it, or about the circumstances surrounding it, after undertaking due diligence. Documentary evidence, or if that is unavailable an affidavit, is necessary to prove the ethical status of a major item. Museums should acquire or borrow items only if they are certain they have not been illegally excavated or illegally exported since 1970.

The 1970 threshold

The 1970 threshold is a clear, pragmatic and practicable watershed that is already widely understood and supported. However, museums also need to be fully aware of the implications of any legislation, in the UK or the country of origin or an intermediate country, that might apply to the period before 1970

1970 is generally accepted as the key point for an ethical approach to museum acquisitions in this area because:

- in 1970 UNESCO adopted the *Convention on the Means of Prohibiting and Preventing the Illicit Import, Export and Transfer of Cultural Property.* The 1970 Convention transformed the ethical landscape of the museum world.
- in 1998 the British Museum published its statement on the acquisition of antiquities in which it stated its commitment to avoid acquisition of unprovenanced antiquities appearing on the market after 1970. This was reinforced in the same year by a similar resolution by the Council of the British Academy.
- in 2000 the UK government stated its support for the 1970 threshold. In a response to the House of Commons Culture, Media and Sport Committee it stated 'The Government endorses the broad principle that museums should avoid acquiring any item that has no secure ownership history, unless there is reliable documentation to show that it was exported from its country of origin before 1970, or the museum is able to obtain permission for the acquisition from the relevant authorities in the country of origin.'
- the Museums Association Code of Ethics, published in 2002, also includes the 1970 threshold.

---

4.   What to do when considering the acquisition or loan of an item

The first step is to ensure that checks on provenance are carried out as soon as a potential acquisition is identified. Museums must be able to establish where an item came from, and when and how it left its country of origin and any intermediate country.

At the outset of any negotiations it is important to inform the vendor, donor, or lender that museums are unable to acquire or borrow items unless due diligence has been satisfactorily undertaken.

For an item originating outside the UK

The museum must either:

* be certain and have evidence that the item was in the UK before 1970 and have no reason to suspect it was illegally exported from its country of origin

or

* be certain that the item was out of the country of origin (but not in the UK) before 1970 and have evidence that its subsequent export to the UK was in line with the regulations of the country from which it was exported to the UK

or

* be certain that the item was in its country of origin after 1970 and have evidence that it was legally exported in line with the regulations of the country of origin

In order to do this, the museum should ask the vendor or donor to provide documentary evidence verifying the presence of the item in the UK prior to 1970, or confirming the legitimate export of the item to the UK after 1970. In the case of an auction sale, if the sale catalogue does not confirm that the item was legally exported or entered the UK before 1970 then the museum should ask for necessary documentary proof of provenance before the sale.

The museum needs to be fully aware of the implications of any legislation, in the UK or the country of origin or an intermediate country, that might apply to the period before 1970 and make every reasonable effort to ascertain that its export was not in violation of that legislation.

What constitutes acceptable evidence:

- Export licence from country of origin

- Publication in a reputable source prior to 1970, or at a date that proves its legitimate subsequent permanent export from country of origin

The following types of documents might also provide acceptable evidence that the item was legally exported, removed or excavated, or that prior to 1970 it was already in the UK:

- Will/inventory

- Photographic evidence

- Family correspondence

- Auction catalogue

- Excavation field notes

Beware fake documentation. If there is any doubt about the authenticity of a document, then consult with colleagues in the UK and, if possible, representatives of the country of origin. Do not accept a document if there are any suspicions about it.

For an item originating in the UK

See separate guidance below (section 10)

5.   What to do if there are problems establishing the provenance:

If the vendor cannot provide acceptable documentary evidence of the item's provenance then it is the museum's duty to undertake due diligence. That is, to make every endeavour to establish the facts of the case before deciding its course of action.

At any stage of the due diligence process outlined below the museum may decide that there are doubts about the item's ethical status and it therefore cannot proceed with the acquisition or loan.

6.   Due diligence – What it should involve

a) Initial examination of item:

Although it is not always possible, it is best practice to examine the item at first hand to determine, as the case may be, whether it:

- shows signs of certain types of ingrained dust, dirt or other accretions, or has annotations. If so it may have been displayed, used or stored for some years – so could be from an older collection.

- has a distinctive type of mount, mounting or binding that is likely to be from a particular period.

- has been mended, partially restored or otherwise interfered with. If so, it may be possible to decide whether the methods used are old or new and estimate when work was done.

- carries old labels, inscriptions, or other marks. These could offer clues about presence and/or use in former collections – but they might be forged, or if genuine, transferred from other items.

- in the case of archaeological material, still retains patches of fairly fresh-looking soil or encrustations, and may thus be recently excavated and so more likely to be illicit.

b) Consider the type of item and likely place of origin

If there is nothing obviously suspicious about the physical appearance of the item, then consider carefully the following factors:

- there are certain 'hot' areas from which items come on to the market illegally, i.e. areas where extensive looting is happening now or in the recent past; at the time of publication examples include Afghanistan, SE Asia and Iraq.

- there are some recognised classes of 'red list' item (cultural objects defined as 'at risk' by ICOM – see Appendix 1) that are extremely likely to be illicit; eg certain sorts of African, Latin American and Iraqi artefacts.

There is no single source of guidance on 'hot' areas and types of item but sources of information are suggested in Appendix 1. If there is any suspicion at all that the object under consideration might fall into a 'red list' category, then extreme diligence and caution are required. It is important to bear in mind that certain categories of item have almost certainly been illicitly traded and that it is likely that these items cannot be legitimately acquired.

c) Take expert advice

In problematic cases, or in areas outside the museum's field of expertise, it is important to seek assistance and advice from specialists in appropriate national museums or museums with designated collections, or local experts – for example in the British or foreign schools of archaeology and in museums in the country of origin. Advice may be available from cultural attaches in embassies and high commissions or Unesco. Such experts can advise both about geographical areas, particular types of item and possible sources of evidence of provenance. Colleagues might also be able to provide informed opinion about the reputation of the owner of the object. However, expert advisers cannot be held responsible for the purchase itself or any consequences of it, and this responsibility remains with the purchasing institution.

d) Determine whether the item was lawfully exported to the United Kingdom

Check whether the export of the item was in line with the regulations of the country of origin, and other cultural property legislation applicable at the time the item was exported. If necessary seek legal advice and advice from the country of origin about whether the export of the item complied with legislation.

e) Evaluate the account given by the vendor or donor

In all cases, the account of the provenance (including export) of the item provided by the owner (whether private individual or dealer) is vital, and should be supported by documentation or other acceptable evidence, or failing that, a sworn statement (affidavit).

- The museum must decide whether the vendor/donor's story, supposing he/she claims to know its history, is convincing. The problem is often one of objective history blending with family folklore 'I think it belonged to my great aunt who was in Italy before the war.' The vague generic descriptions seen in sales catalogues like 'Property of a gentleman' or 'from a European private collection' are not acceptable proof of provenance.

- It is important to try to ascertain whether the owner's word can be accepted. If a member of the trade, is he/she a member of an appropriate and recognised trade association with a reliable Code of Practice? If the source or contact is not personally known to the museum, it might be advisable to consult a colleague who has had dealings with them before.

7.   The results of due diligence

The due diligence process outlined above may raise doubts about the item's ethical status, in which case it cannot be acquired or borrowed. **In all cases if there is any suspicion whatsoever about the item, then you should not proceed with the acquisition.**

However, as a result of the due diligence process the museum may conclude that the item's ethical status is acceptable. In this case one of the following will apply:

a)   The vendor/donor gave a plausible account of the item's history and provided documentary or other acceptable evidence to support the provenance, proving that it was not illegally exported or excavated after 1970.

b)   The museum is clear that the item entered the UK prior to 1970, or was legally exported from the country of origin (and any intermediate country) to the UK after 1970, but there is no documentary evidence of provenance.

In situation b) the museum should ask for a sworn statement (affidavit), prepared by a lawyer, from the vendor or donor, or their agent, to confirm their account of the item's provenance.

In the case of major items the absence of documentary evidence, or an affidavit from the owner, donor or their agent, confirming their account of the item's provenance means that there must be doubts about the item's status, so it cannot be acquired or borrowed.

In the case of a minor item[2] instead of requiring an affidavit it is acceptable to record in writing the vendor/donor's account and ask him/her to sign it as a true account. Note that under the Data Protection Act the vendor/donor has the right to inspect records concerning them.

---

2 Minor items

Many minor items appear on the market or are offered to museums with no acquisition history. This may be because they are illicit but it may equally be because none of their previous owners has ever thought it worthwhile to catalogue or record them, or to provide or keep receipts of purchase. There is also the possibility that documentary evidence of a legitimate provenance has been lost. The only satisfactory way to decide whether in individual cases it is ethically admissible to attempt to acquire such items is through the exercise of due diligence.

'Minor items' are not easy to define comprehensively, since most categories of material, from manuscripts and coins to porcelain and Greek vases, necessarily include both minor and major items. Nor is it appropriate to use financial value as the main criterion, since items which are very cheap and which may seem insignificant can have major archaeological and cultural significance. However, they share the following characteristics:

- may be of common types, or may be items of which multiple examples were made and have survived
- are usually made of relatively cheap or plentifully available materials
- are often (but not always) small in physical size
- may lack conventional beauty or other appeal
- tend to be (but are not always) of relatively low monetary value

If a museum is unsure whether an item falls into the category of 'minor items' they should consult with colleagues from other institutions (see Appendix 1). They should ensure that the decision to treat an item as minor is fully recorded.

c) If the item is minor and the owner cannot provide a plausible account of its provenance and if it does not fall into any of the categories outlined above (e.g. freshly excavated, from a 'hot' area, or a 'hot' category of item), then the decision to accept or purchase the item is a matter for the judgement of the individual museum, having considered all the relevant points mentioned above. If the museum does embark on the purchase, it is the museum's responsibility to act openly and transparently and record the ways in which due diligence has been exercised. This is important not only in cases where funds are being sought for a purchase, but also to avoid potential future difficulties for the acquiring institution.

In all cases if there is any suspicion whatsoever about the item, then you should not proceed with the acquisition. If, after all necessary checks have been made, it is felt to be inappropriate to pursue the acquisition further, then the process should be closed formally, with all relevant documentation put on file. Note that under freedom of information requirements, the file may be open to future examination.

If a museum believes that a criminal offence has taken place they should report it to the police.

8.   Specific permission from the country of origin, courts, etc

Under some government policies, laws or conventions there may be procedures that can give consent to museums to acquire an item that would otherwise be unacceptable under the law or convention, or retrospectively approve an export. In such cases it is vital that the museum obtains such consent in writing before acquiring the item.

9.   Due diligence when acquiring collections

All items considered for acquisition or loan should necessarily be subject to the measures
of due diligence outlined above. However, when assessing the suitability for acquisition of
large collections of items particular issues arise. If a discrete collection is accompanied by
documentation or acceptable evidence verifying its provenance, then acquisition of the collection
is not a problem.

In the cases where there is no documentation for the entire collection, or where it relates only to
some objects, or seems suspect, then each individual item in the collection should be subjected to
exactly the same due diligence processes as any other individual item and acquired, or rejected
accordingly. This is a delicate area and it is possible that, for example, a collector might decide
not to bequeath his/her collection to a particular institution were he/she to believe that parts
of it might be rejected. However, this does not lessen the need to follow the procedures set out
above. If the donor were to go ahead and make the bequest regardless of the museum's expressed
concerns, then the museum could not accept the suspect items.

When an unacceptable item is offered as a gift, the museum might, with the donor's agreement,
arrange to accept it temporarily with the intention of returning it to the country of origin. In this
case the museum must not accession the item, nor retain it longer than strictly necessary.

10.   Archaeological material from the UK

This section includes advice specifically for archaeological items originating in the UK. Sections (a) to (c) apply to terrestrial finds; for objects from wrecks from any part of the UK see section (d).[3]

a)   Material originating in England and Wales

The acquisition by museums of items from England and Wales that are treasure under the Treasure Act 1996[4] should present no difficulties as these are Crown property and any issues regarding their discovery will have been considered either at the coroner's inquest or by the Treasure Valuation Committee. If museums are acquiring treasure finds that the vendor says have been disclaimed they should make sure that the vendor has documentary evidence to prove this.

There are particular issues that museums need to consider before acquiring gold and silver objects and hoards of coins that were found before the commencement of the Treasure Act on 24 September 1997. Under the old common law of treasure trove which the Treasure Act replaced all gold and silver objects were required to be reported to the coroner but only those objects that had been buried with the intention of recovery could qualify as treasure trove. As a result many precious-metal finds were not reported, particularly if they were single coins or other small items which would have been unlikely to qualify.

Under the Treasure Act 1996, objects found before the commencement of the Act qualify as treasure only if they would have passed the old treasure trove test. If gold or silver objects or coin hoards said to have been found before 24 September 1997 are offered to a museum, it would be advisable to report them to the coroner so that they can determine whether they should be considered as treasure, as this is the only way that the museum can be assured that they will acquire title to the find. The Treasure/Portable Antiquities section at the British Museum is able to advise on such cases.

---

3 It is also important to avoid acquiring or borrowing items illegally removed from listed buildings.
Museums should be aware that under the Planning (Listed Building and Conservation Areas) Act 1990, it is illegal to demolish, alter or extend a listed building in a way that affects its character as a building of special architectural or historic interest, without suitable listed building consent from the local planning authority. Before acquiring material, which has been removed from a listed building, the museum should satisfy itself that the object was removed as part of authorised alterations. Dealing in objects whose removal was not authorised is an offence under the Dealing in Cultural Objects (Offences) Act 2003.

4 That is: objects, other than coins, with at least 10% of gold and silver that are at least 300 years old and coins from the same find that are at least 300 years old, found after 24 September 1997. From 1 January 2003 the Treasure Act was extended to include deposits of prehistoric base-metal objects. The Act applies in England, Wales and Northern Ireland.
For full details see: www.finds.org.uk/background/treasure_summary.asp

So far as non-treasure objects are concerned, museums need to be aware that title normally rests with the landowner rather than the finder. When acquiring newly-discovered objects from either the finder or a dealer the curator should attempt to establish the exact location of the findspot and the identity of the landowner and to satisfy him/herself that the landowner has given his/her consent that the object should be offered to the museum (whether by purchase or by gift). It is also good practice to ensure that such objects have been recorded with the Portable Antiquities Scheme. In the case of archaeological objects from England and Wales which do not appear to be recent discoveries, then the curator should ask the vendor to sign a statement verifying their account of the item's provenance.

b) Material originating in Scotland

In order to legally acquire Scottish archaeological material it is necessary to ensure items have been reported through the Treasure Trove/bona vacantia system and disclaimed. All items which are claimed under TreasureTrove/bona vacantia are allocated specifically to museums within Scotland; material which is disclaimed may be acquired by any museum (by donation, purchase, etc) after confirming its status (by seeing the appropriate disclaim certificate). Any Scottish material found after the 1st January 2004 implementation of the Dealing in Cultural Objects (Offences) Act is tainted elsewhere in the UK unless previously disclaimed as Treasure Trove/bona vacantia. The status of Scottish material newly available from old collections will be judged on a case-by-case basis by the Treasure Trove Advisory Panel, to which all such matters should be referred.

c) Material originating in Northern Ireland

In the case of finds from Northern Ireland, museums need to be aware that there has been a legal obligation to report all archaeological finds since 1926. This was most recently restated in the Historic Monuments and Archaeological Objects (Northern Ireland) Order 1995 which includes a statutory requirement under Article 42 for the finder of any archaeological object to report the circumstances of its finding and the nature of the object within 14 days.

The Treasure Act applies in Northern Ireland, which has its own Code of Practice reflecting the different statutory position there. Before 24 September 1997, therefore, the common law of treasure trove also applied to Northern Ireland. In consequence the comments above about finds of potential treasure from England and Wales that are said to have been made before 24 September 1997 will also apply in Northern Ireland, with the additional proviso that museums need to be aware of the requirement that all archaeological objects should be reported. Museums should consult the Environment & Heritage Service for advice.

d) Material from wreck

Any wreck material found in UK territorial waters (to 12 mile limit), or outside the UK and brought within UK territorial waters must by law be reported to the Receiver of Wreck (under *s. 236 of the Merchant Shipping Act 1995*). All wreck material discovered must be reported, however small or seemingly insignificant. Museums should be aware that in the past many items from wrecks were not reported.

The Receiver of Wreck deals with wreck which comes from tidal waters. Material from non-tidal waters are treated as if they were found on land, and come under other legislation (eg Treasure Act 1996, Ancient Monuments and Archaeological Areas Act 1979).

11.   Museums of last resort for items originating in the UK

See Appendix 3 for examples

Museums occasionally act as repositories of last resort for antiquities originating within their local areas of responsibility, and they will on occasion approve the acquisition of antiquities without documented provenance where it can reliably be inferred that they originated within their collecting area within the United Kingdom, and where such payment as may be made is not likely to encourage illicit excavation. This does not apply to items originating outside the UK.

In such cases the following principles should apply:

● The museum should not make a decision to acquire such an item on its own, but should seek external advice and approval from appropriate experts (See Appendix 1)

● The museum should pursue the acquisition in as open a way as possible, including, for example, publishing a note of it in Museums Journal, the museum's annual report, or other appropriate publication

● Museums should report items known, or strongly suspected, to have been stolen or illegally removed to the police

● Record details of all actions and discussions concerning the item

It is not possible to foresee any circumstances under which museums should purchase items known to have been stolen or illegally removed. If museums do acquire such items, they would normally come via law enforcement agencies.

It is also crucial to ensure that any such acquisitions are lawful under, for example, the Dealing in Cultural Objects (Offences) Act 2003 and other legislation.

12.   Museum policies, procedures and expertise

Any museum that collects cultural property from overseas, or cultural property that may have been illicitly excavated or illicitly removed in the UK, should agree and publish a policy consistent with these guidelines. See Appendix 2 for the acquisitions policy of the Trustees of the British Museum which may provide a model. The museum's governing body should consider giving their audit committee, or a specially appointed committee, or an external panel, responsibility for checking compliance with acquisition procedures.

The museum must also have access to adequate expertise. Normally the museum should employ staff with the necessary expertise and experience, and ensure that their expertise is kept up to date. The museum should also take specialist advice from external sources, such as other museums, whenever necessary. Guidance on organisations, individuals and publications that can provide specialist advice can be found in Appendix 1.

There must be a clear line of responsibility for approving acquisitions. Ensuring the ethical acceptability of acquisitions is ultimately the responsibility of the governing body.

It is essential that the acquisition, whether by purchase or gift, is registered through a standard, recognised form (an example of the British Museum's form can be found in Appendix 3). Proper records must be kept on a file of due diligence enquiries. As appropriate record the following:

- conclusions drawn from a physical examination of the item

- information about factors specific to the type of item or place of origin

- expert advice requested and any assessment made of advice received

- checks made into the item's provenance

- documentary proof of provenance, or any sworn statements confirming provenance

- checks made to ensure the item falls within relevant legislation of the country of origin, or any intermediate country

- advice received about the item or the vendor

In cases where documentary evidence or an affidavit is not available it is essential to record the reasons why the acquisition was nevertheless made. This will be for one of the reasons specified above. There should be a statement, signed by the staff member responsible, noting the deficiencies in documentation and setting out the case for the exception. In the case of minor items an explanation must be given for the definition of the item as minor and confirming that there is no suspicion about the item's ethical status.

Relationships with dealers should be well documented with formal contracts. If buying at auction take careful account of the auction house's standard conditions of sale. Making enquiries about the provenance of an item offered for sale at auction is more important than concealing the museum's interest in bidding for the item (which can be done anonymously, through an agent).

An effective means of securing compliance with necessary legal, ethical and professional standards may be to require that a party supplying an object to a museum (whether by sale, loan or otherwise) give a binding contractual promise that its own acquisition was accompanied by equivalent standards. By embedding the necessary principles into the transacting structure and demanding a commitment to comparable standards from its contractual neighbours, a museum not only safeguards its own legal and ethical integrity but tests the integrity of its suppliers and sources, in a manner underpinned by strong civil law sanctions. Museums could usefully consider devising a standard contractual term to that effect. Such contractual obligations should of course be kept under review in the light of legal developments.

13   Inward Loans

The same standards should be applied to inward loans as to acquisitions, with the exception of taking short-term custody of an item for purposes of undertaking due diligence or assisting law enforcement authorities or others aiming to curb the illicit trade. In these cases the item is more likely to be entered in a day book than accepted under a loan agreement.

Summary flowchart (1): archaeological items from England and Wales

(Note: for items from Scotland consult the Treasure Trove Secretariat; for items from Northern Ireland, the Environment and Heritage Service, Northern Ireland)

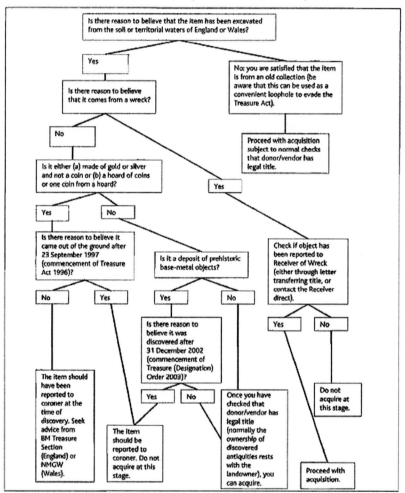

Summary Flowchart (2) for objects from outside the UK

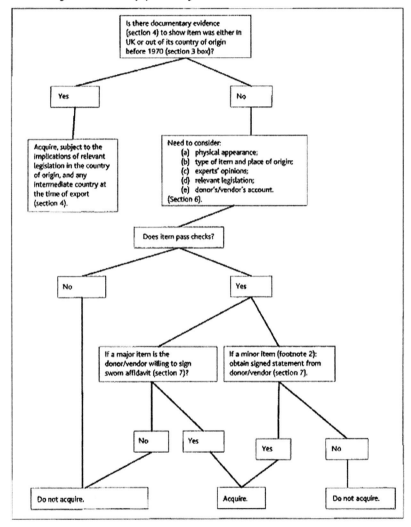

*note: appendices from UK Due Diligence Guidelines omitted. For complete document, see Department for Culture, Media and Sport online: <http://www.culture.gov.uk/reference_library/publications/3697.aspx/>.

C2. REPORT OF THE AAMD TASK FORCE ON THE ACQUISITION OF ARCHAEOLOGICAL MATERIALS AND ANCIENT ART (REVISED 2008)

Preamble

The AAMD recognizes that the acquisition of archaeological materials and ancient art has in recent years become an increasingly complex task that requires the careful consideration of a number of different and, at times, seemingly contradictory goals. This report is intended to help its members understand the issues they will face when evaluating the purchase or acceptance of a gift of archaeological materials and ancient art and provides a framework for responsible decision-making in the development of their collections. Acknowledging that these subjects are interrelated, it also reaffirms the importance and the possibility of protecting archaeological sites as well as collecting archaeological materials and ancient art. This dual objective can only be accomplished through enhanced cooperation between source countries (i.e., countries of modern discovery of archaeological materials and ancient art) and museums that collect such works as well as the development of a mutual understanding and respect for the rights of these countries to protect their cultural property and those of museums whose work is to enhance—through collecting, research, and exhibition—knowledge and appreciation of the artistic achievements of the past.

I. Statement of Principles

A. AAMD is committed to the responsible acquisition, whether by purchase, gift, bequest or exchange, of archaeological materials and ancient art. AAMD believes that the artistic achievements of all civilizations should be represented in art museums, which, uniquely, offer the public the opportunity to encounter works of art directly, in the context of their own and other cultures, and where these works may educate, inspire and be enjoyed by all. The interests of the public are served by art museums around the world working to preserve, study and interpret our shared cultural heritage.

B. AAMD deplores the illicit and unscientific excavation of archaeological materials and ancient art from archaeological sites, the destruction or defacing of ancient monuments, and the theft of works of art from individuals, museums, or other repositories.

C. AAMD is committed to the principle that acquisitions be made according to the highest standards of ethical and professional practice and in accordance with applicable law and in such a way that they do not provide a direct and material incentive to looting.

D. AAMD is committed to the exercise of due diligence in the acquisition process, in particular in the research of proposed acquisitions, transparency in the policy applicable to acquisitions generally, and full and prompt disclosure following acquisition.

E. The November 1970 UNESCO Convention on the Means of Prohibiting and Preventing the Illicit Import and Export and Transfer of Ownership of Cultural Property (the "UNESCO Convention") began a new dialogue about the best ways to protect and preserve archaeological materials and ancient art, although regrettably the looting of sites, destruction of monuments and theft of objects continue to this day. The AAMD, along with others in the international community, including source countries, recognizes the date of the Convention, November 17, 1970 ("1970"), as providing the most pertinent threshold for the application of more rigorous standards to the acquisition of archaeological materials and ancient art as well as for the development of a unified set of expectations for museums, sellers and donors.

F. Recognizing that a complete recent ownership history may not be obtainable for all archaeological material and every work of ancient art, the AAMD believes that its member museums should have the right to exercise their institutional responsibility to make informed and defensible judgments about the appropriateness of acquiring such an object if, in their opinion, doing so would satisfy the requirements set forth in the Guidelines below and meet the highest standards of due diligence and transparency as articulated in this Statement of Principles.

G. AAMD reaffirms the value of licit markets for the legal sale and export of works of art as an effective means of deterring the illicit excavation and trafficking of archaeological materials and ancient art

H. AAMD encourages the creation of licit markets and strongly urges all nations to provide a legal method for the sale and export of art, thereby furthering the goal of deterring the illicit excavation and trafficking of archaeological materials and ancient art.

II. Guidelines

Since its founding in 1916, AAMD has regularly published professional guidelines. Given the increasingly complex set of ethical questions and rapidly evolving legal issues that need to be considered in the acquisition process, AAMD has developed the following guidelines to assist members in revising their acquisition policies. These guidelines apply to acquisitions of archaeological materials and ancient art by purchase, gift, bequest, or exchange.

A. Member museums should thoroughly research the ownership history of archaeological materials or works of ancient art (individually a "work") prior to their acquisition, including making a rigorous effort to obtain accurate written documentation with respect to their history, including import and export documents.

B. When the work is being imported into the U.S. in connection with its acquisition by the member museum, import documentation should be obtained and compliance with the export laws of the country of immediate past export to the U.S. should be confirmed.

C. Member museums should require sellers, donors, and their representatives to provide all information of which they have knowledge, and documentation that they possess, related to the work being offered to the museum, as well as appropriate warranties.

D. Member museums must comply with all applicable local, state, and federal U.S. laws,* most notably those governing ownership and title, import, and other issues pertinent to acquisition decisions.

E. Member museums normally should not acquire a work unless provenance research substantiates that the work was outside its country of probable modern discovery before 1970 or was legally exported from its probable country of modern discovery after 1970. The museum should promptly publish acquisitions of archaeological materials and ancient art, in print or electronic form, including in these publications an image of the work (or representative images in the case of groups of objects) and its provenance, thus making this information readily available to all interested parties.

F. The AAMD recognizes that even after the most extensive research, many works will lack a complete documented ownership history. In some instances, an informed judgment can indicate that the work was outside its probable country of modern discovery before 1970 or legally exported from its probable country of modern discovery after 1970, and therefore can be acquired. In other instances, the cumulative facts and circumstances resulting from provenance research, including, but not limited to, the independent exhibition and publication of the work, the length of time it has been on public display and its recent ownership history, allow a museum to make an informed judgment to acquire the work, consistent with the Statement of Principles above.

In both instances, the museum must carefully balance the possible financial and reputational harm of taking such a step against the benefit of collecting, presenting, and preserving the work in trust for the educational benefit of present and future generations.

The museum must prominently post on the AAMD website, to be established, an image and the information about the work as described in Section E above, and all facts relevant to the decision to acquire it, including its known provenance.

G. If a member museum, as a result of its continuing research, gains information that establishes another party's right to ownership of a work, the museum should bring this information to the attention of the party, and if the case warrants, initiate the return of the work to that party, as has been done in the past. In the event that a third party brings to the attention of a member museum information supporting the party's claim to a work, the museum should respond promptly and responsibly and take whatever steps are necessary to address this claim, including, if warranted, returning the work, as has been done in the past.

C3. J. PAUL GETTY MUSEUM POLICY STATEMENT

POLICY STATEMENT

Acquisitions by the J. Paul Getty Museum

(Adopted by the Board of Trustees of the J. Paul Getty Trust on October 23, 2006)

General

The Getty Museum seeks to foster in a broad audience a greater appreciation and understanding of art by collecting and preserving, exhibiting, and interpreting works of art. Our collection is the principal means by which the Museum's mission is fulfilled, and the Museum is therefore committed to further developing the collection according to the highest ethical standards and in compliance with all applicable laws.

The Getty Museum's collection originated in the restricted interests of J. Paul Getty. Despite having been broadened, strengthened, and enlarged in the years since his death, the collection remains strongly focused in its scope. At present the collection encompasses art of the ancient Greek, Roman, and Etruscan world; European paintings, sculpture, drawings, illuminated manuscripts, and decorative arts created before 1900; photography from the inception of that medium to the present day; and a select group of modern and contemporary works of art, mainly European and American outdoor sculpture. It is a collection formed primarily for exhibition, although not all objects can be exhibited at all times.

This policy governs the acquisition of works of art for the Museum's collection no matter how they are made, whether by purchase, gift, bequest, exchange, or any other method.

Criteria for acquisitions

A potential acquisition should be of excellent quality (involving a variable combination of visual power, inventiveness, strong content, and art-historical importance); fall within our existing collecting areas as stated above; advance the Getty's educational mission; and have survived in a good state of preservation (unless, in special circumstances, its importance outweighs condition concerns or its restoration is deemed to be feasible by the relevant Museum conservation department).

Conditions of acquisition
1. No object will be acquired without assurance that valid and legal title can be transferred.
2. The Museum will undertake due diligence to establish the legal status of an object under consideration for acquisition, making every reasonable effort to investigate, substantiate, or clarify the provenance of the object.
3. No object will be acquired that, to the knowledge of the Museum, has been stolen, removed in contravention of treaties and international conventions of which the United States is a signatory, illegally exported from its country of origin or the country where it was last legally owned, or illegally imported into the United States.
4. In addition, for the acquisition of any ancient work of art or archaeological material, the Museum will require:
a.) Documentation or substantial evidence that the item was in the United States by November 17, 1970 (the date of the UNESCO Convention on the Means of Prohibiting and Preventing the Illicit Import, Export and Transfer of Ownership of Cultural Property) and that there is no reason to suspect it was illegally exported from its country of origin, OR
b.) Documentation or substantial evidence that the item was out of its country of origin before November 17, 1970 and that it has been or will be legally imported into the United States, OR
c.) Documentation or substantial evidence that the item was legally exported from its country of origin after November 17, 1970 and that it has been or will be legally imported into the United States.
c.) Documentation or substantial evidence that the item was legally exported from its country of origin after November 17, 1970 and that it has been or will be legally imported into the United States.
5. Warranties of good title and legal export shall be required as a condition of each acquisition or donation, except for objects purchased at public auction.
6. All information obtained about the provenance of an acquisition must be preserved, and (unless, in the opinion of the Museum Director and

the Getty Trust's Office of General Counsel, specific circumstances dictate otherwise) all such information shall be made available to the public upon written request. This policy shall not be interpreted so as to impose upon the Museum a duty to locate and provide detailed information not readily available through its collection management system, other current records, or the resources readily available onsite at the Getty.

7. The Museum will not buy works of art from any person or entity barred from transacting with the Museum by applicable law, nor from its staff, Trustees, or business entities in which these individuals or their spouses hold any beneficial interest.

8. The Museum will not buy, or accept the gift, bequest, or exchange of, works of art that bear restrictions on their display, publication, or other uses (unless, in the opinion of the Museum Director and the Getty Trust's Board of Trustees, the proposed restrictions are not deemed onerous or inappropriate and the Museum's best interest is served by accepting them). In addition, the Museum reserves the right to decline a gift or bequest if the costs of its transportation, installation, storage, or conservation are prohibitive.

Accessioning, exhibition and publication

Once acquired, a work of art will be promptly accessioned and catalogued in accordance with the Museum's standard procedures. If appropriate for display, it will be placed on exhibition as soon as it can be suitably installed; in any case, it will be published no later than in the annual report for the year in which it was acquired.

Claims

Should the Museum find itself in possession of an object which can be shown, by clear and convincing evidence, to have been acquired, excavated, or exported in violation of Paragraph III.3 or III.4 above, the Museum shall proceed in good faith to determine what steps might be taken to preserve the interests of all concerned parties. These steps may, in the appropriate circumstances, include a return of the object to its country of origin or restitution of an object to an earlier owner, provided such a return or restitution is consistent with the Trustees' legal and fiduciary duties as stewards of a charitable trust.

C4. AMERICAN ASSOCIATION OF MUSEUMS, "CODE OF ETHICS FOR MUSEUMS" (2000)

Online: AAM <http://www.aam-us.org/museumresources/ethics/coe.cfm>

Code of Ethics for Museums

Introduction

Ethical codes evolve in response to changing conditions, values, and ideas. A professional code of ethics must, therefore, be periodically updated. It must also rest upon widely shared values. Although the operating environment of museums grows more complex each year, the root value for museums, the tie that connects all of us together despite our diversity, is the commitment to serving people, both present and future generations. This value guided the creation of and remains the most fundamental principle in the following *Code of Ethics for Museums*.

Code of Ethics for Museums

Museums make their unique contribution to the public by collecting, preserving, and interpreting the things of this world. Historically, they have owned and used natural objects, living and nonliving, and all manner of human artifacts to advance knowledge and nourish the human spirit. Today, the range of their special interests reflects the scope of human vision. Their missions include collecting and preserving, as well as exhibiting and educating with materials not only owned but also borrowed and fabricated for these ends. Their numbers include both governmental and private museums of anthropology, art history and natural history, aquariums, arboreta, art centers, botanical gardens, children's museums, historic sites, nature centers, planetariums, science and technology centers, and zoos. The museum universe in the United States includes both collecting and noncollecting institutions. Although diverse in their missions, they have in common their nonprofit form of organization and a commitment of service to the public. Their collections and/or the objects they borrow or fabricate are the basis for research, exhibits, and programs that invite public participation.

Taken as a whole, museum collections and exhibition materials represent the world's natural and cultural common wealth. As stewards of that wealth, museums are compelled to advance an understanding of all natural forms and of the human experience. It is incumbent on museums to be resources for humankind and in all their activities to foster an informed appreciation of the rich and diverse world we have inherited. It is also incumbent upon them to preserve that inheritance for posterity.

Museums in the United States are grounded in the tradition of public service. They are organized as public trusts, holding their collections and information as a benefit for those they were established to serve. Members of their governing authority, employees, and volunteers are committed to the interests of these beneficiaries. The law provides the basic framework for museum operations. As nonprofit institutions, museums comply with applicable local, state, and federal laws and international conventions, as well as with the specific legal standards governing trust responsibilities. This *Code of Ethics for Museums* takes that compliance as given. But legal standards are a minimum. Museums and those responsible for them must do more than avoid legal liability, they must take affirmative steps to maintain their integrity so as to warrant public confidence. They must act not only legally but also ethically. This *Code of Ethics for Museums*, therefore, outlines ethical standards that frequently exceed legal minimums.

Loyalty to the mission of the museum and to the public it serves is the essence of museum work, whether volunteer or paid. Where conflicts of interest arise—actual, potential, or perceived—the duty of loyalty must never be compromised. No individual may use his or her position in a museum for personal gain or to benefit another at the expense of the museum, its mission, its reputation, and the society it serves.

For museums, public service is paramount. To affirm that ethic and to elaborate its application to their governance, collections, and programs, the American Association of Museums promulgates this *Code of Ethics for Museums*. In subscribing to this code, museums assume responsibility for the actions of members of their governing authority, employees, and volunteers in the performance of museum-related duties. Museums, thereby, affirm their chartered purpose, ensure the prudent application of their resources, enhance their effectiveness, and maintain public confidence. This collective endeavor strengthens museum work and the contributions of museums to society—present and future.

Governance

Museum governance in its various forms is a public trust responsible for the institution's service to society. The governing authority protects and enhances the museum's collections and programs and its physical, human, and financial resources. It ensures that all these resources support the museum's mission, respond to the pluralism of society, and respect the diversity of the natural and cultural common wealth.

Thus, the governing authority ensures that:

- all those who work for or on behalf of a museum understand and support its mission and public trust responsibilities
- its members understand and fulfill their trusteeship and act corporately, not as individuals
- the museum's collections and programs and its physical, human, and financial resources are protected, maintained, and developed in support of the museum's mission
- it is responsive to and represents the interests of society
- it maintains the relationship with staff in which shared roles are recognized and separate responsibilities respected
- working relationships among trustees, employees, and volunteers are based on equity and mutual respect
- professional standards and practices inform and guide museum operations
- policies are articulated and prudent oversight is practiced
- governance promotes the public good rather than individual financial gain.

Collections

The distinctive character of museum ethics derives from the ownership, care, and use of objects, specimens, and living collections representing the world's natural and cultural common wealth. This stewardship of collections entails the highest public trust and carries with it the presumption of rightful ownership, permanence, care, documentation, accessibility, and responsible disposal.

Thus, the museum ensures that:

- collections in its custody support its mission and public trust responsibilities

- collections in its custody are lawfully held, protected, secure, unencumbered, cared for, and preserved

- collections in its custody are accounted for and documented

- access to the collections and related information is permitted and regulated

- acquisition, disposal, and loan activities are conducted in a manner that respects the protection and preservation of natural and cultural resources and discourages illicit trade in such materials

- acquisition, disposal, and loan activities conform to its mission and public trust responsibilities

- disposal of collections through sale, trade, or research activities is solely for the advancement of the museum's mission. Proceeds from the sale of nonliving collections are to be used consistent with the established standards of the museum's discipline, but in no event shall they be used for anything other than acquisition or direct care of collections.

- the unique and special nature of human remains and funerary and sacred objects is recognized as the basis of all decisions concerning such collections

- collections-related activities promote the public good rather than individual financial gain

- competing claims of ownership that may be asserted in connection with objects in its custody should be handled openly, seriously, responsively and with respect for the dignity of all parties involved.

Programs

Museums serve society by advancing an understanding and appreciation of the natural and cultural common wealth through exhibitions, research, scholarship, publications, and educational activities. These programs further the museum's mission and are responsive to the concerns, interests, and needs of society.

Thus, the museum ensures that:

- programs support its mission and public trust responsibilities

- programs are founded on scholarship and marked by intellectual integrity

- programs are accessible and encourage participation of the widest possible audience consistent with its mission and resources

- programs respect pluralistic values, traditions, and concerns

- revenue-producing activities and activities that involve relationships with external entities are compatible with the museum's mission and support its public trust responsibilities

- programs promote the public good rather than individual financial gain.

Promulgation

This *Code of Ethics for Museums* was adopted by the Board of Directors of the American Association of Museums on November 12, 1993. The AAM Board of Directors recommends that each nonprofit museum member of the American Association of Museums adopt and promulgate its separate code of ethics, applying the *Code of Ethics for Museums* to its own institutional setting.

A Committee on Ethics, nominated by the president of the AAM and confirmed by the Board of Directors, will be charged with two responsibilities:

- establishing programs of information, education, and assistance to guide museums in developing their own codes of ethics

- reviewing the *Code of Ethics for Museums* and periodically recommending refinements and revisions to the Board of Directors.

Afterword

In 1987 the Council of the American Association of Museums determined to revise the association's 1978 statement on ethics. The impetus for revision was recognition throughout the American museum community that the statement needed to be refined and strengthened in light of the expanded role of museums in society and a heightened awareness that the collection, preservation, and interpretation of natural and cultural heritages involve issues of significant concern to the American people.

Following a series of group discussions and commentary by members of the AAM Council, the Accreditation Commission, and museum leaders throughout the country, the president of AAM appointed an Ethics Task Force to prepare a code of ethics. In its work, the Ethics Task Force was committed to codifying the common understanding of ethics in the museum profession and to establishing a framework within which each institution could develop its own code. For guidance, the task force looked to the tradition of museum ethics and drew inspiration from AAM's first code of ethics, published in 1925 as Code of Ethics for Museum Workers, which states in its preface:

Museums, in the broadest sense, are institutions which hold their possessions in trust for mankind and for the future welfare of the [human] race. Their value is in direct proportion to the service they render the emotional and intellectual life of the people. The life of a museum worker is essentially one of service.

This commitment to service derived from nineteenth-century notions of the advancement and dissemination of knowledge that informed the founding documents of America's museums. George Brown Goode, a noted zoologist and first head of the United States National Museum, declared in 1889:

The museums of the future in this democratic land should be adapted to the needs of the mechanic, the factory operator, the day laborer, the salesman, and the clerk, as much as to those of the professional man and the man of leisure. . . . In short, the public museum is, first of all, for the benefit of the public.

John Cotton Dana, an early twentieth-century museum leader and director of the Newark Museum, promoted the concept of museum work as public service in essays with titles such as "Increasing the Usefulness of Museums" and "A Museum of Service." Dana believed that museums did not exist solely to gather and preserve collections. For him, they were important centers of enlightenment.

By the 1940s, Theodore Low, a strong proponent of museum education, detected a new concentration in the museum profession on scholarship and methodology. These concerns are reflected in Museum Ethics, published by AAM in 1978, which elaborated on relationships among staff, management, and governing authority.

During the 1980s, Americans grew increasingly sensitive to the nation's cultural pluralism, concerned about the global environment, and vigilant regarding the public institutions. Rapid technological change, new public policies relating to nonprofit corporations, a troubled educational system, shifting patterns of private and public wealth, and increased financial pressures all called for a sharper delineation of museums' ethical responsibilities. In 1984 AAM's Commission on Museums for a New Century placed renewed emphasis on public service and education, and in 1986 the code of ethics adopted by the International Council of Museums (ICOM) put service to society at the center of museum responsibilities. ICOM defines museums as institutions "in the service of society and of its development" and holds that "employment by a museum, whether publicly or privately supported, is a public trust involving great responsibility."

Building upon this history, the Ethics Task Force produced several drafts of a Code of Ethics for Museums. These drafts were shared with the AAM Executive Committee and Board of Directors, and twice referred to the field for comment. Hundreds of individuals and representatives of professional organizations and museums of all types and sizes submitted thoughtful critiques. These critiques were instrumental in shaping the document submitted to the AAM Board of Directors, which adopted the code on May 18, 1991. However, despite the review process, when the adopted code was circulated, it soon became clear that the diversity of the museum field prevented immediate consensus on every point.

Therefore, at its November 1991 meeting, the AAM Board of Directors voted to postpone implementation of the Code of Ethics for at least one year. At the same meeting an Ethics Commission nominated by the AAM president was confirmed. The newly appointed commission—in addition to its other charges of establishing educational programs to guide museums in developing their own code of ethics and establishing procedures for addressing alleged violations of the code—was asked to review the code and recommend to the Board changes in either the code or its implementation.

The new Ethics Commission spent its first year reviewing the code and the hundreds of communications it had generated, and initiating additional dialogue. AAM institutional members were invited to comment further on the issues that were most divisive—the mode of implementation and the restrictions placed on funds from deaccessioned objects. Ethics Commission members also met in person with their colleagues at the annual and regional meetings, and an ad hoc meeting of museum directors was convened by the board president to examine the code's language regarding deaccessioning.

This process of review produced two alternatives for the board to consider at its May meeting: (1) to accept a new code developed by the Ethics Commission, or (2) to rewrite the sections of the 1991 code relating to use of funds from deaccessioning and mode of implementation. Following a very lively and involved discussion, the motion to reinstate the 1991 code with modified language was passed and a small committee met separately to make the necessary changes.

In addition, it was voted that the Ethics Commission be renamed the Committee on Ethics with responsibilities for establishing information and educational programs and reviewing the Code of Ethics for Museums and making periodic recommendations for revisions to the board. These final changes were approved by the board in November 1993 and are incorporated into this document, which is the AAM *Code of Ethics for Museums*.

Each nonprofit museum member of the American Association of Museums should subscribe to the AAM *Code of Ethics for Museums*. Subsequently, these museums should set about framing their own institutional codes of ethics, which should be in conformance with the AAM code and should expand on it through the elaboration of specific practices. This recommendation is made to these member institutions in the belief that engaging the governing authority, staff, and volunteers in applying the AAM code to institutional settings will stimulate the development and maintenance of sound policies and procedures necessary to understanding and ensuring ethical behavior by institutions and by all who work for them or on their behalf.

With these steps, the American museum community expands its continuing effort to advance museum work through self-regulation. The *Code of Ethics for Museums* serves the interests of museums, their constituencies, and society. The primary goal of AAM is to encourage institutions to regulate the ethical behavior of members of their governing authority, employees, and volunteers. Formal adoption of an institutional code promotes higher and more consistent ethical standards. To this end, the Committee on Ethics will develop workshops, model codes, and publications. These and other forms of technical assistance will stimulate a dialogue about ethics throughout the museum community and provide guidance to museums in developing their institutional codes.

2000

C5. ARCHAEOLOGICAL INSTITUTE OF AMERICA CODE OF ETHICS

Archaeological Institute of America
Located at Boston University
656 Beacon Street
Boston, Massachusetts 02215
Tel 617.353.9361 · Fax 6550
www.archaeolgogical.org

AIA Code of Ethics

The following Code of Ethics was approved by the Council at its December 28, 1990 meeting, and amended at its December 29, 1997 meeting.

The Archaeological Institute of America is dedicated to the greater understanding of archaeology, to the protection and preservation of the world's archaeological resources and the information they contain, and to the encouragement and support of archaeological research and publication.

In accordance with these principles, members of the AIA should:

1. Seek to ensure that the exploration of the archaeological sites be conducted according to the highest standards under the direct supervision of qualified personnel, and that the results of such research be made public;

2. Refuse to participate in the trade in undocumented antiquities and refrain from activities that enhance the commercial value of such objects. Undocumented antiquities are those which are not documented as belonging to a public or private collection before December 30, 1970, when the AIA Council endorsed the UNESCO Convention on Cultural Property, or which have not been excavated and exported from the country of origin in accordance with the laws of that country;

3. Inform appropriate authorities of threats to, or plunder of archaeological sites, and illegal import or export of archaeological material.

D1. FABIANI AFFAIR—ARCHIVAL MATERIALS

The following is a partial list of the paintings aboard the *SS Excalibur*. The first page is an image from the National Archives. The other three pages have been transcribed for legibility.

ANNEX "D"

PICTURES IN S.S. "EXCALIBUR"

PAINTING — RENOIR	PAINTING — RENOIR
Marine	Catalan
Portrait	Etudes
Portrait de femme	Etudes
Marine	La lecture
Marine	Paysage
Paysage	Paysage
Paysage	Fruits (etudes)
Portrait	Poissons
Paysage	Dans le parc
Jeune fille au ruban	Poissons
Etude de nu	Baigneuse
Baigneuse	Roses
Paysage (arbres)	Faisans
Portrait d'enfant	Pot
Interieur	Blond avec rose [illegible]
Portrait de jeune fille assise	La lecture
Portrait	[illegible]
Etude (buste de femme et fleurs)	Foret
Paysage	Paysage du Midi Cagnes
Paysage	Portrait d'une jeune femme
Paysage (des vaches)	Jeune femme a l'ours
La rose	Bretagne
A la campagne	Sous bois
Des laveuses	Paysages avec laveuses
Buste nu et etudes	Paysage de Bretagne
Nature morte (huitres)	Paysage
A la plage	Paysage du Midi
A la campagne	Etudes de Nu
La femme à la cloche blanche	Paysage du Midi
Nature morte (fruits)	Paysage du Midi
"Coco" a table	Chien
Vollard	Pot
Jeune fille aux meches blondes	Reverie
Sur la meuse	Nu assis
Portrait blonde	La campagnarde
Portrait (corsage rouge)	Opulente
Buste de femme nu	Enfant au mouchoir rouge
Reverie	La lecture
Le nu debout	Paysage
Enfant blond (etudes)	Roses
Vase bleu	Fraises et tasses
Portrait de femme	Somnolente
Portrait de femme	Jeune au [illegible]
Compotier	Meches blondes (etude)
Fraises	Portrait de [illegible]
Interieur	La glaneuse
Nu (etudes)	Pot
Buste de femme [illegible]	Les meches de [illegible]
Paysage	Femme nu [illegible]
Paysage	La menagere
Etudes	Nature morte (fruits)
Nu couche	Femme a la veste de toreador (etude)
Nu debout	

ANNEX "B"

PICTURES EX S.S. "EXCALIBUR"

PAINTING   RENOIR
Marine
Portrait
Portrait de femme
Marine
Marine
Paysage
Paysage
Portrait
Paysage
Jeune fille au ruban
Etude de nu
Baigneuse
Paysage (arbres)
Portrait d'enfant
Interieur
Portrait de jeune fille russe
Portrait
Etude (buste de femme et fleurs)
Paysage
Paysage
Paysage (des vaches)
Nu rose
A la campagne
Buste nu et etudes
Nature morte (huitres)
A la plage
A la campagne
La femme et la cloche blanche
Nature morte (fruits)
"Coco" a table
Vollard
Jeune fille aux meches blondes
Sur la scene
L'enfant blonde
Portrait (corsage rouge)
Buste de femme nue
Reverie
Le nu debout
Enfant blond (etudes)
Vase bleu
Portrait de femme
Portrait de femm
Compotier
Fraises
Interieur
Nu (etudes)
Buste de femme (sein nu)
Paysage
Paysage
Etudes
Nu couche
Nu debout

PAINTING   RENOIR
Catalan
Etudes
Etudes
La lecture
Paysage
Paysage
Fruits (etudes)
Poissons
Dans le parc
Poissons
Paysages
Roses
Faience
Pot
Blond avec roses dans les cheveux
Jeune pensive
La lecture
Lecture dans le parc
Foret
Paysage du Midi Gagnes
Portrait d'une jeune femme
Jeune femme a l'ours
Bretagne
Sous bois
Paysages avec laveuses
Paysages de Bretagne
Paysage
Paysage du Midi
Etudes de Nus
Paysage du Midi
Paysage du Midi
Chien
Pot
Reverie
Nu assis
La campagnarde
Opulence
Enfant au mouchoir rouge
La lecture
Paysage
Roses
Fraises et tasses
Somnolente
Jeune au corsage bleu (liseuse)
Meches blondes (etude)
Portrait de Pierre Renoir
La glaneuse
Pot
Les meûles de foin
Femme ans a la compagne
Le menagere
Nature morte (fruits)
Femme a la veste de toreador (etude)

PAINTING   RENOIR
Le nu drape
Nature morte (pommes)
Paysage de Bretagne
Paysage de Bretagne
Nature morte (Reine Claude
Planche au assis et naute morte
Planche Deux nus et fruits
La promenade
Portrait de Wagner
Les jumelles
Paysage
La Campagne
Nu debout
Ovale (la lecture)
La Bonne
Pot et soupiere
Paysage
Etude rose vase vert
Le menagere
La corsage mauve
Nature morte (pommes)
Nature morte (poires)
Fleurs et nu
Planche etudes
Jeune fille a la cloche blanche
Paysage Bretagne
Planche portrait femme et enfant
Portrait de Coco
Fleurs
Fleurs
Paysage
Poissons
Planche Portrait et etudes
Roses et arbres
Roses
Roses
Planche Paysage
Paysage
Paysage
Pot
Fleurs et fruits
Planche nu jaune
Portrait d'une femme bleu
Paysage
Paysage
Paysage
Paysage
Paysage
Dans le paro
Nature morte fruits
Roses
Les laveuses
Nature morte pommes
Paysage
Planche Deux paysages
La couseuse
Paysages
Planche Tete et fruits
Planches Tete et fruits
Paysage
Paysage
Paysage du Midi
Pensive
Paysage
Dans la campagne

PAINTING   RENOIR
Planche tetes etudes
Planche deux paysages
Femme assise
La toilette
Pot
Paysage
Nu a la toilette
En robe rose
Fleurs
Fleurs
Paysage
Femme assise
Nature morts fraises
Tasse
Paysage
Theatre
Planche Nus
Theatre
Planche Femme assise et paysage
Planche Paysages
Nature morte pommes
Paysage
Paysage
Isabey
Le toréador
L'homme barba
Paysage
La fillette blonde
Fleurs
Poissons
Poissons
Portrait etude
Enfants etudes
Planche un fruit tete
Nu allonge
Paysage
Planche paysage nu allonge
Poissons
Roses
Nu assis
Paysage
Roses
Roses
Bretagne
Paysage
Bretagne
Fruits
Fruits
Fruits
Nu de dos
La bonne
Poissons
Portrait
Coco
Compotier et oranges
Planche corsage rose et vert
Planche enfant tete et cuisse
La bergere
La lecture
Planche jeune fille
Paysage
Paysage
Paysage
Paysage
Paysage
Paysage

PAINTING   RENOIR
Jeune fille sous l'arbre
Portrait
Le dècollete
Paysage
Paysage
Planche nu tete fleurs
A la campagne
La theiere
Coco et rose
Paysage
Le carafon
Planche theatre
La route tournante
Paysage
Paysage
Fuits les pommes
Theiere verre citron
Le carafon
Paysage
Paysage
Paysage
Grenade et pommes
Planche au assis tete maison
Brune a la cocarde
Anemone
Planche tete fleurs
Paysage
Planche fleurs paysage
Paysage
Nu se chaussant
Planche paysage tete
Planche tete fleurs
Paysage

CEZANNE
Portrait de Paul
Tete d'enfant
Arbre
Paysage
Paysannerie
Le ponte noire
Paysage
Baigneurs AQUARELLE
Fauns AQUARELLE
Montagnes St. Victoire AQARELLE
Foret AQARELLE
St. Victoire AQARELLE
St. Victoire AQARELLE
Baigneuses
Paysages
Paysage
Paysage
Paysage
Paysage
Paysage
Paysage
Crane
Portrait (esquiese)
Paysage
Nu etudes
Fruits AQUARELLE

            GAUGUIN
Musicien sur la arène
Tahitienne
Fleurs
Fleurs

PAINTING   GAUGUIN
Fleurs
Paysage
Paysage Bretagne
Nature morte
Nature morte Tahiti
            DELACROIX
Nu allonge
            FANTIN-LATOUR
Portrait de Emile Barnard
            BONNARD
Paysage
La beignade
Place Clichy
Femme au salon
Portrait de Vollard
Paysage
Portrait de Vollard avec
Portrait de femme
Femme assise
Au jardin
Fleurs
Nu
            ROUAULE
WATER
COLOURS Ubu colon
Pierrot
Theatre
Pierrot
Passion
Arlequin
Le baie des trepasser
Nocturie
Christ
Pierrot
Automobilistes
Pierrot
Personnage
Pere boeuf
Juge et pierrot
Passion paysage
Passion
Passion
Procession
Colombine-Pierrot
Baby Campagnarde
Automne
Clown
Vieil arabe
Clowns
Suaire
Paysage double face
Christ et docteur
Passion
Christ
            DOMIER
DRAWING D. Quichotte et Banche
            VUILLARD
DRAWING Interieur
            M. UTRILLO
Montmartre (Bought from M. Bignou
            Art Dealer, Paris)

Telegram from the French Government

Enclosure 3

C
O
P
Y

NO DISTRIBUTION   CONFIDENTIAL

9B-135341

URGENT

AMEMBASSY,

    OTTAWA.

The French Govt has requested the assistance of this Govt in
locating certain paintings belonging to the Vollard estate recently
reported to have been shipped from Canada to United States, as there
was an arbitrary division of the estate which took place illegally
with respect to registration and prejudiced the interest of the State
and of certain heirs, of which the City of Paris is one.

Approximately 560 paintings belonging to estate of Ambroise
Vollard who died in 1939 were assigned to the United States during
occupation of France, seized by British authorities in Bermuda as
a war prize and sent to Ottawa. They were removed from seizure by
decision of the Prize-Court in London dated April 29, 1949, and turned
over to Messrs. Jonas and Fabiani, who are said to have taken possession
of paintings on May 30, 1949, and to have sent them to the United States.

The Department requests number of and information from the consular
invoice of the shipment to the United States if it can be located.

Also

CONFIDENTIAL

– 2 –

CONFIDENTIAL

Also request full name of Jonas. For info on Martin Fabiani, see

Art Looting Investigation Unit Final Report. Reply at once.

NONE

OEX: ILI: ARHall:mms   7/13/49   EUR   WE

Art Looting Investigation Report on Fabiani and his Collaborators

Enclosure 4

confidential

Memoranda on Fabiani, Jonas, and Bignou

MARTIN FABIANI

Corsican adventurer, gigolo, and race track tout, who married the daughter of a wealthy banker. Became a friend and protegé of Ambrose VOLLARD, who named him an executor of the estate, a large part of which he still owns. With DEQUOY, the arch-collaborationist of the Paris dealer milieu. Received looted objects from the ERR by undetermined means. Has personally returned 34 pictures to Paul ROSENBERG, from whose collection they were looted by the ERR. When last interviewed, stated that his relationship with ROSENBERG was now (January 1946) on a "new basis," because they had come to an agreement which concerned FABIANI's property in the U.S.A. See CIRs #2, #4, DIRs #1, #6, #13.

> Art Looting Investigation Unit,
> Final Report, War Department,
> p. 101.

Paris 26, Avenue Matignon. (Tel. Bat. 05-32). A Corsican age about 45. Before 1939 was known to be the homme d'affaires of LUCIEN VOLLARD, brother of Ambrose. After Ambrose Vollard's death in July, 1939, the remains of the collection were divided between LUCIEN and MADAME DE GALEA, the former mistress of AMBROSE VOLLARD. The liquidation by sale was entrusted by LUCIEN VOLLARD to FABIANI. In April, 1940, some 500 pictures were sold on a profit-sharing basis to ETIENNE BIGNOUS (qv) and MESSRS. REID & LEFEVRE of London and BIGNOU Gallery of New York (32 E. 57th Street). These pictures were shipped by FABIANI (with German connivance) from Paris via Spain and Lisbon to New York in September, 1940, but were seized by the British customs at Bermuda.

> A List of French Art Dealers,
> 16th July 1945, Commission
> for the Protection and Resti-
> tution of Cultural Material

confidential

D2. SAMPLE DEEDS OF GIFT

Sample Deed of Gift (developed by an Art Museum)

XYZ MUSEUM DEED OF GIFT

Please complete this deed of gift and return this form to _____
_____ . Upon acceptance of your gift by the Trustees, a copy certifying the
fact will be returned to you.

I/We, _____ hereby give to the Trustees of
the XYZ Museum absolute and unconditional ownership of the following, together with all
copyright (in all media by any means or method now known or hereafter invented) and
associated rights which I/we have:

(ARTIST)   (WORK)   (MEDIUM)

I/We wish that the gift be identified to the public and in the records of the Museum as:

Gift of _____

To the best of my/our belief, the subject of this gift is free and clear of all encumbrances
and restrictions and since _____ has not been
imported or exported into or from any country contrary to its laws.

Date: _____   Signature of Donor: _____

Date: _____   Signature of Donor: _____

Address of Donor: _____

_____

Telephone No.: _____

.   .   .   .

Delivery: Works of Art offered to the Trustees should be physically present in the Museum for consideration at
their next meeting. Please write or call _____ to obtain
information on the dates of scheduled meetings of the Trustees and to make arrangements for transportation
and insurance of your gift.

Provenance: For many reasons it is important that the Museum have as complete as possible a history of the
subject of a gift. To that end, it will be helpful if you will forward any information or documentation which you
may have with respect to your ownership, display and restoration, and all prior ownership, display and
restoration, of the subject of your gift.

Valuation: The Museum may accept your valuation of your gift for insurance purposes but may not determine
value for any purpose.

I certify that a deed of gift and the subject thereof were physically present in the XYZ Museum prior to the
meeting of the Trustees of the Museum on _____ at which meeting
the Trustees accepted the gift as described above.

_____

(signed by the director of the museum)

Sample Deed of Gift (developed by a History Museum)

DEED OF GIFT TO THE _____ MUSEUM

By these presents I(we) irrevocably and unconditionally give, transfer, and assign to the _____ Museum by way of gift, all right, title, and interests (including all copyright, trademark, related interests* in all media by any means or method now known or hereafter invented), in, to, and associated with the object(s) described below. I(we) affirm that I(we) own said object(s) and that to the best of my(our) knowledge I(we) have good and complete right, title, and interests (including all transferred copyright, trademark and related interests) to give.

1. Dated _____   _____
   (month)(day)(year)   (signature of donor)

2. Dated _____   _____
   (month)(day)(year)   (signature of donor)

The _____ Museum hereby acknowledges receipt of the above Deed of Gift.

Dated _____   _____
   (month)(day)(year)   (signature of curator)

Source: Marie C. Malaro, *A Legal Primer on Managing Museum Collections*, 2nd ed. (Washington and London: Smithsonian Institution Press, 1998), at 209-211.

D3. SAMPLE LOAN AGREEMENTS

Agreement for Incoming Loan (developed by an Art Museum)

NAME OF MUSEUM (hereafter "Museum")
ADDRESS OF MUSEUM
TELEPHONE NUMBER OF MUSEUM
FAX NUMBER OF MUSEUM

LOAN AGREEMENT

Return this agreement to: _____

Exhibition Title: _____

Venues (Borrowers) and Dates: _____

Lender: _____

Address: _____

Telephone: _____ Fax: _____

Name, Address, and Telephone (if different from above) for collection & return: _____

Exact form of Lender's Name or Credit Line for exhibition label, catalogue, and other publications: _____

Artist Name or Attribution: _____

Title of Work: _____

Medium or Materials: _____

Support: _____

Date of Work: _____ Inventory Number: _____

Signature, Other Inscriptions, and Their Location on Work: _____

CIRCLE ONE:
Dimensions   Height: _____   Width: _____
(Without Mat, Frame, or Base)   Depth: _____   Weight: _____

Continued on next page

Dimensions   Height: _____   Width: _____
(With Mat, Frame, or Base)   Depth: _____   Weight: _____

(Loan Agreement Continued on Reverse Side)

.   .   .   .

INSURANCE

The Borrowers will exercise the same care with respect to the Work as they do in the safekeeping of their own works. The [NAME OF MUSEUM] will arrange for the insurance of the Work on a nail-to-nail basis for the value stipulated below, using standard fine arts commercial insurance and/or United States Government indemnity.

Insurance Value of the Work (U.S. Dollars):

$_____

The Lender agrees that in the event that the Work is lost or damaged, recovery, if any, will be limited to such amount as may be paid by the insurer plus any deductible, hereby releasing the Borrowers from any further liability for claims arising out of such loss or damage. If the Lender elects to maintain his own insurance, the Borrowers must be supplied with a certificate of insurance naming the Borrowers as additional insureds under the Lender's policy or waiving subrogation against the Borrowers. If the Lender elects to maintain his own insurance, this shall constitute a release of the Borrowers from any liability in connection with the Work. The Borrowers will accept no responsibility for any error or deficiency in information furnished to the Lender's insurers or for lapses in coverage.

PHOTOGRAPHY AND REPRODUCTION

Unless permission to do so has been specifically denied in writing by the Lender at or prior to the time this agreement is executed, the Lender authorizes the Borrowers to photograph, reproduce, and publish the Work in any medium for archival, educational, and publicity purposes.

Please send one black-and-white photograph of the work. If a photograph is not available, where can the Borrowers obtain one?

_____

_____

SHIPPING

Date Work due at first venue:

_____

(Month / Day / Year)

The [NAME OF MUSEUM] assumes all costs of packing and transportation of the work, and will contact the Lender approximately three months before the opening of the exhibition to make necessary shipping arrangements.

SIGNATURES

The Lender declares that he has full authority to make this loan, that the information listed above is correct, and that he has read and accepts the conditions of this agreement.

SIGNED: _____   Date: _____
Name: _____   Title: _____
(Lender or Authorized Agent)

SIGNED: _____   Date: _____
Name: _____   Title: _____
(For the [NAME OF MUSEUM] and other Borrowers*)

*Reference to "other Borrowers" is used when the exhibition will travel to other venues.

Sample Loan Agreement (developed by a History Museum)

Museum Control No. _____

NAME OF MUSEUM (hereafter "Museum")
ADDRESS OF MUSEUM
TELEPHONE NUMBER OF MUSEUM
FAX NUMBER OF MUSEUM

AGREEMENT FOR INCOMING LOAN   Date: _____

From: _____   **Telephone:** _____
             (name of lender)   **Fax:** _____

Address: _____
_____

In accordance with the conditions printed on the reverse, the objects listed below are borrowed for the following purpose(s): (give name of exhibition when applicable)
_____
_____

for the period* _____ to _____
(*from estimated time objects leave lender's custody until their return and receipt by lender; see "Shipping" below.)

Objects   Description   Insurance Value
                       (Please include size, weight,   (please itemize)
                       and brief report of condition;
                       and attach a recent photo if
                       possible.)

Initiated by
_____

      (museum curator)   (museum department)

INSURANCE: (see conditions on reverse)

[ ] to be carried by Museum
[ ] to be carried by Lender: estimated premium charge
$ _____

[ ] insurance waived

PACKING and SHIPPING: The following packing and shipping arrangements are proposed subject to review and approval by the Museum's Registrar's Office in consultation with the Lender.

Objects to be packed by: _____ Lender _____ Museum
Other: _____

To be shipped from (address and contact):
_____
_____

To arrive no later than (date): _____
Via: _____

To be returned to above address (unless otherwise notified)
Via: _____

COSTS: Borrower will pay all costs of packing, shipping, insurance, unless otherwise noted here: _____
_____

CREDIT LINE (for exhibition label and catalog):
_____
_____

SPECIAL REQUIREMENTS for handling, installation, etc. (attach continuation sheet if necessary): _____
_____
_____

(Loan Agreement continued on reverse side.)

· · · · · · · · · · · · · · · · · · · ·

CONDITIONS GOVERNING LOANS

Care, Preservation & Exhibition
1. The Museum will give to objects borrowed the same care as it does comparable property of its own. Precautions will be taken to protect objects from fire, theft, mishandling, dirt and insects, and extremes of light,

temperature and humidity while in the Museum's custody. It is understood by the Lender and the Museum that all tangible objects are subject to gradual inherent deterioration for which neither party is responsible.

2. Evidence of damage at the time of receipt or while in the Museum's custody will be reported immediately to the Lender. It is understood that objects, which in the opinion of the Museum show evidence of infestation, may be fumigated at the discretion of the Museum.

3. The Lender will be requested to provide written authorization for any alteration, restoration or repair. The Museum may examine objects by all modern scientific methods.

4. The Museum retains the right to determine when, if and for how long objects borrowed will be exhibited. The Museum retains the right to cancel the loan upon reasonable notice to the Lender.

Transportation and Packing

1. The Lender certifies that the objects lent are in such condition as to withstand ordinary strains of packing and transportation and handling. A written report of condition of objects prior to shipment must be sent by the Lender to the Museum. Otherwise, it will be assumed that objects are received in the same condition as when leaving the Lender's possession. Condition records which may include photographs will be made at the Museum on arrival and departure.

2. Costs of transportation and packing will be borne by the Museum unless the loan is at the Lender's request. The method of shipment must be agreed upon by both parties.

3. Government regulations will be adhered to in international shipments. As a rule, the Lender is responsible for adhering to its country's import/export requirements and the borrower is responsible for adhering to its country's import/export requirements.

4. The Lender will assure that said objects are adequately and securely packed for the type of shipment agreed upon, including any special instructions for unpacking and repacking. Objects will be returned packed in the same or similar materials as received unless otherwise authorized by the Lender.

Insurance

1. Objects will be insured for the amount specified herein by the Museum under its "all risk" wall-to-wall policy subject to the following standard exclusions: wear and tear, gradual deterioration, insects, vermin or inherent vice; repairing, restoration or retouching process; hostile or warlike action, insurrection, rebellion, etc.; nuclear reaction, nuclear radiation or radioactive contamination. Insurance will be placed in the amount specified by the Lender herein which must reflect fair market value. If the Lender fails to indicate an amount, the Museum, with the implied concurrence of the Lender, will set a value only for purposes of insurance for the period of the loan. Said value is not to be considered an appraisal.

2. If the Lender elects to maintain his own insurance coverage, then prior to shipping the Museum must be supplied with a certificate of insurance naming the Museum as an additional insured or waiving rights of subrogation. If the Lender fails to provide said certificate, this failure shall constitute a waiver of insurance by the Lender (see No. 4 below). The Museum shall not be responsible for any error or deficiency in information furnished by the Lender to the insurer or for any lapses in such coverage.

3. In the case of long-term loans, it is the responsibility of the Lender to notify the Museum of updated insurance valuations.

4. If insurance is waived by the Lender, this waiver shall constitute the agreement of the Lender to release and hold harmless the Museum from any liability for damages to or loss of the loan property.

5. The amount payable by insurance secured in accordance with this loan agreement is the sole recovery available to the Lender from the Museum in the event of loss or damage. Any recovery for depreciation or loss of value shall be calculated as a percentage of the insured value specified by the Lender in the agreement.

Reproduction and Credit

Unless otherwise notified in writing by the Lender, the Museum may photograph or reproduce the objects lent for educational, catalog and publicity purposes. It is understood that objects on exhibit may be photographed by the general public. Unless otherwise instructed in writing, the Museum will give credit to the Lender as specified on the face of this agreement in any publications. Whether individual labels are provided for objects on display is at the discretion of the Museum.

Continued on next page

Change in Ownership and/or Address

It is the responsibility of the Lender or his agent to notify the Museum promptly in writing if there is any change in ownership of the objects (whether through *inter vivos* transfer or death) or if there is a change in the identity or address of the Lender. The Museum assumes no responsibility to search for a Lender (or owner) who cannot be reached at the address of record.

Return of Loans

1. Unless otherwise agreed in writing, a loan terminates on the date specified on the face of this agreement. If no date is specified, the loan shall be for a reasonable period of time, but in no event to exceed three years. Upon termination of a loan, the Lender is on notice that a return or renewal must be effected, or else an unrestricted gift of the objects will be inferred.

2. Objects will be returned only to the Lender of record or to a location mutually agreed upon in writing by the Museum and the Lender of record. In case of uncertainty, the Museum reserves the right to require a Lender/claimant to establish title by proof satisfactory to the Museum.

3. When the loan is returned, the Museum will send the Lender a receipt form. If this form is not signed and returned within thirty days after mailing, the Museum will not be responsible for any damage or loss.

4. If the Museum's efforts to return objects within a reasonable period following the termination of the loan are unsuccessful, then the objects will be maintained at the Lender's risk and expense for a maximum of _____ years. If after _____ years the objects have not been claimed, then and in consideration for maintenance and safeguarding, the Lender/Owner shall be deemed to have made the objects an unrestricted gift to the Museum.

Applicable Law

This agreement shall be construed in accordance with the law of the _____ (name of the applicable jurisdiction).

I have read and agree to the above conditions and certify that I have full authority to enter into this agreement.

Signed: _____ Date: _____
         (Lender*)

Title: _____

*If Lender is not the owner, complete the following two lines:
Name of owner: _____
Address of owner: _____

APPROVED FOR MUSEUM:

Signed: _____ Date: _____
Title: _____

(Please sign and return both copies.)

Source: Marie C. Malaro, *A Legal Primer on Managing Museum Collections*, 2nd ed. (Washington and London: Smithsonian Institution Press, 1998), at 253-259..

D4. FILMS ABOUT ART AND LAW

The Architecture of Doom: A Film by Peter Cohen. *119 minutes, colour/b&w, 1991.*
The film argues that a tremendously powerful motivation behind Nazism has long been overlooked. This force was an extreme aesthetic aspiring to return beauty to the world, to counteract the miscegenation and degeneration that had defiled it, through sheer violence. The result is to consider the Nazis' atrocities as a wholly rational extension of a fundamental tenet to beautify the world.

The Art of the Steal. *101 minutes, colour, 2009, dir. Don Argott.*
Documentary that follows the struggle for control of Dr. Albert C. Barnes' 25 billion dollar collection of modern and post-impressionist art. His vast collection included 181 Renoirs, 69 Cezannes, 59 Matisses, 46 Picassos, 21 Soutines, 18 Rousseaus, 16 Modiglianis, 11 Degas, 7 Van Goghs, 6 Seurats, 4 Manets and 4 Monets.

Art City: Making It in Manhattan. *58 minutes, colour, 1996.*
Interviewing critics, collectors, and artists—among them Louis Bourgeois, Chuck Close, Elizabeth Murray, and Gary Simmons—director Chris Maybach looks at the contemporary art scene of the 1990s. Covering collectors, studio visits, the 1980s, finances, daily routines, and success, the film is dynamic, interspersing images of the work with the creators themselves, and avoiding talking heads. For a broad view of a seemingly cloistered artistic community, *Art City* provides insight into and explanation of the fascinating and varied lives of artists

Concert of Wills—Making the Getty Center. *100 minutes, colour, 1997.*
Written and directed by Susan Froemke, Bob Eisenhardt, and Albert Maysles, this acclaimed video traces the building of the Getty Center, one of the most ambitious cultural undertakings of the twentieth century. Spanning fourteen years, from the early blueprints, to the groundbreaking, to the public opening of the Center in December 1997, the film takes viewers from California to a rock quarry in Italy where the Center's signature travertine originated. The gathering of creative personalities needed

to complete this monumental complex gave rise to conflict as well as con-sensus, to tension as well as resolution. *Concert of Wills* looks behind the scenes and chronicles intimate moments of success as well as frustration and heated debates. Featured at work during the creation of the Getty Center are architects Richard Meier and Michael Palladino; artist Robert Irwin who designed the Central Garden; Museum Director emeritus John Walsh; former Getty Trust president and CEO Harold M. Williams; and others.

Degenerate Art. *56 minutes, colour, 1993, dir. David Grubin.*
This is an award-winning, one-hour documentary about the most widely-seen art exhibition ever assembled: *Entartete Kunst* (Degenerate Art), com-missioned by Hitler as an attack on modern art and artists. Based on the Los Angeles County Museum of Art exhibition where the Nazi show was recreated by Frank Gehry in 1990-91, the film, which premiered on PBS nationally in April 1993, incorporates footage of the original exhibition, reminiscences by visitors to *Entartete Kunst*, and commentary by critics and historians.

Dirty Pictures. *104 minutes, colour, 2000.*
Directed by Frank Pierson and starring James Woods, the film depicts the trial of Dennis Barrie, curator of the Cincinnati Arts Center, for obscenity by exhibiting the show, *The Perfect Moment*, by late photographer Robert Mapplethorpe. Much to the credit of the filmmakers, all 175 photos from the original Mapplethorpe exhibit, including those named in the indict-ment, are shown in the course of this film. Another plus is the inclusion of series of short interviews on the subject of censorship from William F. Buckley, Jr., Rep. Barney Frank, Fran Lebowitz, Salman Rushdie, Susan Sarandon, and Nadine Strossen. These thoughtful, well-selected exchanges underscore the issues and are artfully interspersed with events. Thanks to that kind of cleverness in the structure, as well as a satisfying performance by James Woods in the leading role as Barrie, this superior made-for-TV movie won the Golden Globe award for "Best Mini-Series or Motion Picture Made for TV."

Entrapment. *113 minutes, colour, 1999, dir. Jon Amiel.*
Catherine Zeta-Jones works for an insurance agency that sends her to track down and help capture an art thief, played by Sean Connery.

F is for Fake. *85 minutes, colour, 1973.*
Orson Welles' free-form documentary about fakery focuses on the notorious art forger Elmyr de Hory and Elmyr's biographer, Clifford Irving, who also wrote the celebrated fraudulent Howard Hughes autobiography, then touches on the reclusive Hughes and Welles' own career (which started with a faked resume and a phony Martian invasion).

Graffiti Verité (*Read the Writing on the Wall*). *45 minutes, colour, 1995.*
Bob Bryan's *Graffiti Verité* makes a very good attempt at documenting the Los Angeles graffiti culture, placing graffiti in its own context, away from its hip-hop brethren in breaking and rap.

The Maiden Heist. *90 minutes, colour, 2009.*
Roger (Christopher Walken), Charles (Morgan Freeman), and George (William H. Macy) are security guards at the Maiden Museum. When a new curator comes to town and the guards learn that their favourite pieces are going to be sold, they plan a heist from the inside. Their plan is to replace each of their favourites with a forgery between the time they're packed and the time they're loaded onto the plane. Can these three bumbling criminals pull off the heist?

Maya Lin: A Strong Clear Vision. *105 minutes, colour, 1994.*
An Oscar-winning feature documentary film by Freida Lee Mock, produced by Freida Lee Mock and Terry Sanders, of sculptor/architect Maya Lin who designed the Vietnam Veterans Memorial in Washington, D.C., and the Civil Rights Memorial in Montgomery, Alabama.

Masterpiece or Forgery: the Story of Elmyr de Hory. *52 minutes, colour, 1997.*
Elmyr de Hory was called "The Myth of the Century" when the world found out that he had forged over 1,000 paintings, estimated to be worth over 100 million dollars, many of which are probably still in museums around the world.

Me, My Brother and My Father's Van Gogh. *60 minutes, colour, 2001, dir. Elise Swerhone.*
Monica and Michael de Jong have inherited a painting from their father. The painting, known as *F614*, has been considered throughout the century as either an authentic van Gogh or a clever forgery. Are they the owners of a painting worth millions? In the film, they try to answer this question.

Network. *80 minutes, colour, 2005.*
A documentary from Andreas Apostolidis about the illicit trade of Greek antiquities and how it mirrors the deeper crisis facing our shared global cultural heritage. Important cases are presented such as the Corinth Museum theft, the Euphronios krater controversy, Marion True's alleged involvement in the smuggled bronze statue (the Saarbrucken Affair), and the Robin Symes and Giacomo Medici prosecutions.

Plunder! *60 minutes, colour, 1990.*
Frontline correspondent Carl Nagin investigates the looting of pre-Columbian tombs in Latin America and the trafficking of stolen artifacts, exposing a trail that leads to auction houses, galleries, museums, and private collections in the United States.

Robbing the Cradle of Civilization. *42 minutes, colour, 2004, dir. Robin Benger.*
This film about the looting of the Baghdad Museum documents the US government's inadequate reaction to the loss of cultural heritage. It reminds us of the 7000-year-old history of Mesopotamia and its rich culture.

Sinking City of Venice. *60 minutes, colour, 2002.*
In a follow-up to its 1989 production, Nova covers the battle to keep the world's most unusual city from drowning beneath the rising tides of the Adriatic Sea. The lessons we learn about how to stop rising sea levels will prove essential for other coastal cities around the world, from New York to Shanghai.

Stolen. *85 minutes, colour, 2006, dir. Rebecca Dreyfus.*
In 1990, the Isabella Stewart Gardner Museum in Boston suffered the largest art heist in American history, resulting in the loss of 13 of the world's most famous

artworks, worth $300 million, including pieces from Degas, Rembrandt, and Vermeer's masterpiece "The Concert." Not a single work has been recovered. With an eccentric cast of characters, including a reformed fence nicknamed Turbo, cunning art detective Harold Smith, and Isabella Stewart Gardner herself, we journey into the mysterious world of stolen art where conspiracies abound, rumors are left unhinged, and a painting can change your life forever.

The Thomas Crown Affair. *113 minutes, colour, 1999, dir. John McTiernan.*
In a remake of the 1968 thriller, Pierce Brosnan plays Crown, a bored multi-millionaire who arranges a heist of a Monet painting. This sets a sexy insurance investigator after him, but unexpectedly the two fall in love. Does she keep her ethics and pin him for the crime she knows he committed or does she follow her heart?

The Train. *133 minutes, colour, 1964, dir. John Frankenheimer.*
Oberst von Waldheim wants to bring modern paintings, the ones the Nazis called "degenerated", out of Paris before the Allied Forces liberate Paris. He is able to persuade his bosses to give him the train. Labiche (Burt Lancaster), a French railway official is asked by the museum to stop this train, but he is not willing to risk the life of his people for art. But when his old friend Boule is shot by the Germans accusing him of sabotaging the engine, he starts to work against the Germans, and tries to delay the departure of the train until the Allies arrive.

Treasure: In Search of Nazi Plunder. *48 minutes, colour/b&w, 1998.*
By the end of WWII, the Nazis had assembled the greatest collection of gold, precious artifacts and artwork in history. More than 50 years later, the work of returning it to its rightful owners remains incomplete. This A&E production reveals how the Nazis' acquisition of these treasures was organized in as much detail as any military campaign. Public and private collections were confiscated, and many of the artworks, along with millions of dollars in gold and other valuables, remain missing or unclaimed.

Trial of Tilted Arc. *52 minutes, b&w, 1985, dir. Shu Lea Cheang.*
This low-budget documentary discusses three issues surrounding the 1985 trial for the removal of Richard Serra's public sculpture, "Tilted Arc", from the Federal Plaza in NYC.

The Vanishing Rembrandts. *52 minutes, colour, 1994, BBC Television.*
A controversial process of attribution that began in the 1960s when the Dutch government began the Rembrandt Research Project has reduced the number of paintings attributed to Rembrandt from 1,000 to 300. X-rays and laboratory examinations are bringing new evidence to the formerly subjective tradition of connoisseurship. By and large, what is revealed is not that there were conscious fakes or copies, but that many worthy and remarkable paintings were made by students of the master and misattributed in the eighteenth century. Inevitably, the findings of the project are controversial, especially when the objects disputed are valued at millions of dollars and form part of a nation's cultural heritage and wealth.

Will Venice Survive Its Rescue? *60 minutes, colour, 1989.*
Venice floods so regularly that it now goes unnoticed. After all, the city is built on canals. But, since 1966, when the main square sank under four feet of water, the government has been trying to stop the submergence. Nova goes to Italy to document the search for a solution.

INDEX

ARCHEOLOGICAL SITE LOOTING
Organized crime business model, 139
  • ethically collecting antiquities, 145
  • Nigeria: anatomy of looting, 143
Underwater cultural heritage,
protecting, 146
American legal framework, 152
Canadian legal framework, 155
International legal framework, 148
UNESCO Convention, App A8: 307

ART HEISTS, CONTEMPORARY
Art-knappings in France: 1960-1961, 16
Art thefts rock France: 2009-2010, 55
Ashmolean: 1999-2000, 40
Beatty: 2007, 51
Buhrle: 2008, 52
Bumbling Thief who left Calling Card:
2005, 48
Caravaggio: 1969, 17
Cavalier: 2007, 51
Cellini Salt Cellar: 2003, 47
Colnaghi Heist: 1988, 24
Duke of Wellington: 1961, 15
Fabiani Affair: 1949, 14
  • archival materials, App D1: 463
Gainsborough and Bellotto: 2001, 43
Gardner Heist: 1990, 25
Goya Stolen in Transit: 2006, 49
Gulf War: 1991, 33
Italian Heist: 1975, 20
Juan B. Castagnino Museum of Fine Art:
1987, 23
Kuwait: 1990, 33
Lucian Freud Cold Case: 1988, 24
Madonna of the Yarwinder: 2003, 47
Manchester Heist: 2003, 47

Marmatton Museum: 1985, 22
Mexican Museum of Anthropology:
1985, 22
Mona Lisa: 1911, 13
Monet's Beach at Pourville: 2000, 42
Montreal Museum of Fine Arts: 1972, 18
Netherlands:1991, 33
O'Keefe: 1946, 14
Paraguay Museum of Fine Arts: 2002, 46
Picasso on the Yacht: 1999, 39
Picasso's Sketchbook: 2009, 54
Rio de Janeiro Heist: 2006, 49
Scream, The: 1994 and 2004, 35
Sevso Treasure: 1978, 20
Stephen Blumberg,
the "Bibliokleptomaniac": 1990, 34
Stradivarius, The: 1995, 38
Swedish Heist: 2000, 41
Systematic Looting in Cyprus: 1974, 19
Theft at the Fair: 2000, 41
Van Gogh Cold Case: 2002, 44
Van Gogh Heists: 1988, 23

CRIMINAL SANCTIONS
Canada, criminal sanctions
  • *Cultural Property Export Import
    Act*, 89, App B1: 333
  • willful blindness, 93
Dealing with theft, 74
  • BATA shoe museum heist
    example, 75
Iraqi cultural property: US sanctions,
107
Motives for art theft, 71
United States, criminal sanctions, 76
  • Archeological Resources Protection
    Act, 78

CRIMINAL SANCTIONS—continued
- Cultural Property Implementation Act, 80
- Federal Anti-Smuggling Statute, 79
  - • Immigration and Customs Enforcement, 81
  - • Importation of Pre-Columbian Monumental or Architectural Sculpture or Murals Act, 81
  - • National Stolen Property Act, 77, 83
  - • Native American Grave Protection Repatriation Act, 80, App B4: 349
  - • Racketeer Influenced Corrupt Organization Act, 82
  - • state laws for recovery of stolen property, 79

CULTURAL HERITAGE LAW
Emergence of field, 5

CULTURAL PROPERTY
Historical overview, 5
- theft and pillage, 8

DATABASES OF INTERNATIONAL STOLEN ART
American Association of Museums Nazi Era Provenance Trace, 101
Bruno Kreisky Archives Foundation, 103
Central Registry of Information on Looted Property 1933-1945, 103
Czech Republic Restitution, 104
Enemy Property, UK, 103
FBI: National Stolen Art File, 100
Find Stolen Art, 107
ICOM Red List, 96
IFAR—Stolen Art Alert, 107
Interpol Stolen Works of Art, 99

Holocaust Assets: US State Department, 102
Holocaust-Era Assets, 102
Hungarian National Gallery of Budapest, 105
Italian Carabinieri—Culture Police, 107
Italian Government, 105
London Stolen Arts Database, 96
Looted Art, 105
Lost Art Database, 101
Musées Nationaux Récupération, 104
Museum Provenance List Cleveland Museum of Art, 104
Nazi-Era Provenance Internet Portal, 106
Origins Unknown, 104
Presidential Commission on Holocaust Assets in the US, 102
Project for the Documentation of Wartime Cultural Losses, 102
RCMP: Sûreté du Québec Art Crime Unit, 95
Sazanoff's SAZTV.com, 95
Schloss Collection, works looted 1943-1998, 102
UK Museums' Provenance Research, 106
US State Department, 99
Wartime Losses: Polish Paintings, 105

DUE DILIGENCE
Art as investment, 118
Checklist for art purchasers, 109
Commentary, 112
Donations and loans, 113
- law of gifts, 115
- loans and law of bailment, 116
Purchasing on the Internet, 112
UK Due Diligence Guidelines for Museums, Libraries and Archives on Collecting and Borrowing Cultural Material, App C1: 421

FAKES AND FORGERIES
Cases of international intrigue, 172
- David Stein, 179
- Elmyr de Hory, 177
- Ely Sakhai, 181
- Eric Hebborn, 174
- Greenhalgh Family, 183
- Han van Meegeren, 173
- John Drewe & John Myatt, 180
- Tom Keating, 17 8

Generally, 159
Importance of authenticity, 184
Methods of detecting, 161
- expert witness, 161
- scientific testing, 164
  - AAS and ICP-MS, 169
  - auto-radiography, 168
  - CAT scans, 169
  - chemical analysis, 166
  - computer-based authentication, 171
  - dendrochronology, 170
  - fission tracks, 170
  - infrared imaging, 167
  - microscopic techniques, 166
  - obsidian hydration, 169
  - radiocarbon dating, 165
  - reconstructing manufacturing techniques, 167
  - stable isotope analysis, 170
  - thermoluminescent analysis, 165
  - ultraviolent imaging, 167
  - x-ray, conventional, 167
  - x-ray diffraction, 168
  - x-ray fluorescence, 168

Types of, 160

FILMS
About art and law, App D4: 478

GIFTS
Sample deeds of gift, App D2: 470
- developed by art museum, 470
- developed by history museum, 471

HAGUE CONVENTION, 1954, App A3: 244
First protocol, 69, App A4: 262
Generally, 66
Second protocol, 70, App A5: 266

INTERNATIONAL TREATIES, CONVENTIONS AND ENABLING DOMESTIC LAWS
Agreement between Canada & United States regarding imposition of import restrictions on certain categories of archaeological and ethnological material, App A6: 289
Emergency actions and bilateral agreements, App A7: 306
Generally, 59
Hague Convention, 1954, 66, App A3: 244
UNESCO convention, 1970, 59, App A1: 229
- Canadian experience with US implementation, 61
- Canadian implementation, 63
- *Cultural Property Export and Import Act*, reforming, 64
- implementing, US approach, 61
- signatories to, App A2: 241

UNESCO Convention on the Protection of Underwater Cultural Heritage (2001), App A8: 307

LAWYER, INTERNATIONAL ART
Becoming, 185

LEGISLATION & RELATED ITEMS
American Endangered Species Legislation, App B7: 410
 • Endangered Species Act, 410
 • Migratory Bird Treaty Act, 410
Canadian Endangered Species Legislation, App B8: 416
 • *Migratory Birds Convention Act*, 418
 • *Species at Risk Act*, 416
 • *Wild Animal and Plant Protection and Regulation of International and Interprovincial Trade Act*, 418
Convention on Cultural Property Implementation Act, App B5: 367
Convention on International Trade in Endangered Species of Wild Flora and Fauna, App B6: 387
Cultural Property Export and Import Act, App B1: 333
Foreign Cultural Objects Immunity from Seizure Act, App B9: 420
Letter from Judge Diana E. Murphy to the Honorable Patrick J. Leahy and Honorable Orrin G. Hatch, App B3: 343
Native American Graves Protection and Repatriation Act, App B4: 349
US sentencing guidelines: cultural heritage resource crimes, App B2: 336

LOANS
Sample loan agreements, App D3: 472
 • agreement for incoming loan, developed by art museum, 472
 • developed by history museum, 474

POLICIES & CODES OF ETHICS, MUSEUMS & GALLERIES
American Association of Museums, Code of Ethics for Museums, App C4: 452
Archaeological Institute of America Code of Ethics, App C5: 461
J. Paul Getty Museum Policy Statement, App C3: 449
Report of the AAMD Task Force on the Acquisition of Archaeological Materials and Ancient Art, App C2: 444
UK Due Diligence Guidelines for Museums, Libraries and Archives on Collecting and Borrowing Cultural Material, App C1: 421

UNESCO CONVENTION, App A1
Canadian experience with US implementation, 61
Canadian implementation, 63
Cultural Property Export and Import Act, reforming, 64
Implementing, US, 61
Signatories to, App A2: 241

WAR AND ART
Holocaust-era looted art, 121
 • Canadian perspective,129
 • International Legal Commitments
   • • Bretton Woods Conference, 123
   • • London Declaration, 123
   • • Terezin Declaration, 125
   • • Washington Principles, 123
 • Restitution and the Adversarial System, 125
Iraq, 131
Lessons learned, 137
War—opportunity for cultural heritage destruction, 134